D1500649

CHASING

❖ ❖

VILLA

THE LAST CAMPAIGN OF

THE U.S. CAVALRY

By Colonel Frank Tompkins

Originally published by the Military Service Publishing Company,
Harrisburg, Pennsylvania, 1934

ISBN: 0-944383-39-4

This edition 1996 by
High-Lonesome Books
Silver City, New Mexico

VILLA RIDES!

PREFACE

by

Louis R. Sadler

In the pre-dawn hours of March 9, 1916, the infamous Mexican revolutionary Pancho Villa and some 484 men crossed the United States/Mexico Border and carried out a stunning surprise attack on the unsuspecting New Mexico border village of Columbus.

During the raid the *Villistas* killed 18 Americans (including ten 13th Cavalry troopers) and another eight were wounded. In addition, Villa's men looted the town, burned a number of buildings (including the hotel and local bank) and to add insult to injury rode off with an estimated 100 U.S. Army horses.

Following initial disarray, the Army garrison fought back and after some two hours of street fighting succeeded in driving Villa's troops from the village. In the process, the 13th Cavalry with rifle and machine gun fire killed an estimated 62 Mexican attackers and wounded another 25 or so.

In Washington, a stunned Wilson administration ordered a so-called "Punitive Expedition" to invade Mexico, disperse Villa's guerrilla band and, hopefully, capture or kill Villa. Brigadier General John J. "Black Jack" Pershing was given command of the pursuit and a mere six days after Villa's raid led his troops across the border in northwestern Chihuahua. During the following thirteen weeks U.S. Army Cavalry penetrated more than 400 miles into Mexico, engaging in two fire fights and several smaller skirmishes with *Villista* contingents, and two major clashes with hundreds of troops of the Mexican government of Venustiano Carranza.

As a result, by late June, 1916, the United States and Mexico were within hours of a declared war. But cooler heads prevailed, war was avoided, and the Punitive Expedition was left in northwestern Chihuahua until the Wilson administration finally ordered the troops home in late January, 1917. On the afternoon of February 5, 1917, the last cavalryman crossed the border at Columbus and the Punitive Expedition, after ten and one-half months in Mexico, was finally home.

In the eight decades since the Columbus Raid, historians, documentary film producers, folklorists, and scribblers have continued to be fascinated by the raid and the Punitive Expedition.

For example, on November, 3, 1993, PBS debuted "The Hunt for Pancho Villa," a one hour documentary in the American Experience series, produced and directed to excellent reviews by Hector Galán and Paul Espinosa. The documentary portrayed the raid at Columbus and the pursuit of Villa utilizing both Mexican and United States newsreel footage. In October, 1995, "The Rivals," a new series on the Discovery Channel, had as one of its opening one hour episodes, "Villa V. Pershing," focusing on the raid and the Punitive Expedition.

More than films, for historians of the U.S./Mexico border region, as well as students of military history, Old West adventure, and the history of the U.S. Cavalry, the Columbus Raid has yielded a seemingly never-ending stream of articles in professional journals, masters theses, popular accounts in magazines, pot-boilers and historical monographs. For example, *The American Historical Review*, the journal of the American Historical Association, had as its lead article in a 1978 issue, an examination of Villa's motives for the raid, utilizing recently uncovered documents from the U.S. Department of State.

The most recent monograph which deals with the raid and pursuit was a chapter entitled "Termination with Extreme Prejudice: The United States Versus Pancho Villa," first published in 1988 (and reprinted in 1990 by High-Lonesome Books) in a volume entitled *The Border and the Revolution*, co-authored by Charles H. Harris and this writer. The chapter dealt with an effort by officers of the Punitive Expedition to make use of a team of Japanese agents to assassinate Villa by poisoning his coffee. The plot failed and the U.S. Army covered up the attempt and Pershing's apparent sponsorship of the conspiracy.

Two of the better known studies of the raid and the Punitive Expedition are Clarence Clendenon's *Blood On The Border*, which has several chapters on the subject and was published in 1969; and, Herbert Malloy Mason's excellent *The Great Pursuit* (1970) which comprehensively covered both the raid and the expedition.

Studies published in Mexico by Mexican writers include Alberto Salinas Carranza's *La Expedición Punitiva*, the first edition of which appeared in 1935; and, Alberto Calzadiaz Barrera's *Porque Villa Atacó Columbus* which came out in 1972.

In addition, during the 1950s and 60s University of Texas at El Paso folklorist Haldeen Brady authored several volumes on Villa, including: *Cock of the Walk - The Legend of Pancho Villa, Pershing's Mission in Mexico, and Pancho Villa at Columbus: The*

Raid of 1916. A lively and generally accurate account is *Pancho Villa and the Columbus Raid* by Larry Harris, first published in 1949 and reprinted in 1988 as *Pancho Villa - Strong Man of the Revolution* by High-Lonesome Books.

Despite the plethora of volumes on the raid and the Punitive Expedition, pride of place and authenticity unquestionably goes to a monograph authored by U.S. Army Colonel Frank Tompkins, who was there for the entirety of the raid and subsequent expedition. *Chasing Villa* was first published six decades ago (1934 by Military Service Publishing Company).

First, if anyone can truly be said to be the American hero of the raid and the Punitive Expedition, it is of course Tompkins. It was after all Tompkins who organized and led the pursuit of Villa in violation of the U.S. Army's rules of engagement. For more than six hours Tompkins' outnumbered troopers galloped fifteen miles into Mexico and killed dozens of *Villistas* before finally returning to Columbus when they ran low on ammunition. Weeks later, still pressing Villa and hoping for cooperation from Carranza troops, Tompkins led a picked detachment of cavalry into Parral, Chihuahua on April 12, 1916. When the much larger force of Carranza cavalry turned on him, Tompkins succeeded in extracting his men from the town, although two American cavalrymen were killed and half a dozen wounded, including Tompkins. Carranza cavalry who clashed with Tompkins' troopers lost substantially higher casualties. A lesser commander than Tompkins could well have lost his entire command.

Having stated the above, there are several disclaimers that should be noted about *Chasing Villa*. First, regarding Tompkins: reading between the lines of correspondence of Tompkins' superior, one has the impression that although he was a superb combat commander, Tompkins apparently was something of a "hot dog." To use the example of another member of the Punitive Expedition, he and George S. Patton Jr., (who was a lieutenant during the expedition) were kindred souls.

Tompkins' literary method was to splice his own narrative with numerous official reports and letters by other officers and soldiers. While the result is thorough and authentic, there is an uneven flow to the narrative. At the same time it should be noted that Tompkins managed to lay his hands on a substantial quantity of documents and primary material which even now are difficult to find in the National Archives.

The appendices are fascinating, dealing with the arcane but interesting details of motor transport in Mexico, the expedition Aero

Squadron, the signal corps, the huge National Guard call-up, and finally the author's practical recommendations for changes in cavalry gear.

This writer must disagree with the author with regards to the number of *Villistas* who attacked Columbus. Tompkins, who should have known better, apparently went along with Maude Wright, who had been captured by Villa and released outside Columbus, and who testified that Villa had several thousand men. *Villista* documents, since recovered, indicate he had precisely 484 men; and, other indications to the contrary, it would appear the "larger the number the greater the victory" school of military history prevailed.

That aside, Tompkins' book is generally reliable and is the best account by a participant of the last great cavalry campaign of the U.S. Army. In particular, his description of the non-stop hunt for Villa between March 15 and April 12, 1916, while occasionally confusing (it was of course a confusing chase) provides the best description we have of this gut-wrenching campaign. Tompkins paints a vivid picture of the cavalry horses his men rode, the tactics of the pursuit, and the privations of the chase.

Indeed, to live off the land for months in hostile territory, where every hand is against you—with weather conditions varying from snow and sleet to heat and blowing dust—makes for compelling military history. At the fight at Guerrero, Chihuahua, one column of the expedition was within a whisker of intercepting the elusive Villa. Thus the portrayal of the Punitive Expedition in some of the literature as the cavalry chasing it's own tail is quite simply inaccurate. Whatever else Tompkins and his fellow officers and enlisted men were, they were indeed the "old breed" of soldier; tough, implacable, and it should be noted obedient.

After all, because Pershing and his men obeyed orders, the commander of the Punitive Expedition became the commander of the American Expeditionary Force which went to France in the summer of 1917. And it was Pershing who became Chief of Staff of the United States Army after World War I.

It all began with Villa's attack on Columbus and the United States Army *Chasing Villa.*

Louis R. Sadler is with the Department of History at New Mexico State University, Las Cruces, and the co-author, with Charles H. Harris, of *The Border and the Revolution: Clandestine Activities of the Mexican Revolution, 1910 - 1920.*

U.S. Army supply wagon

Mounted Army trooper in the Chihuahuan Desert

American Cavalrymen with dead Villista

Pack Mules were used extensively during the Punitive Expedition

General Pershing lead the "flying column" from the Culberson Ranch
Courtesy New Mexico State Parks

After the raid

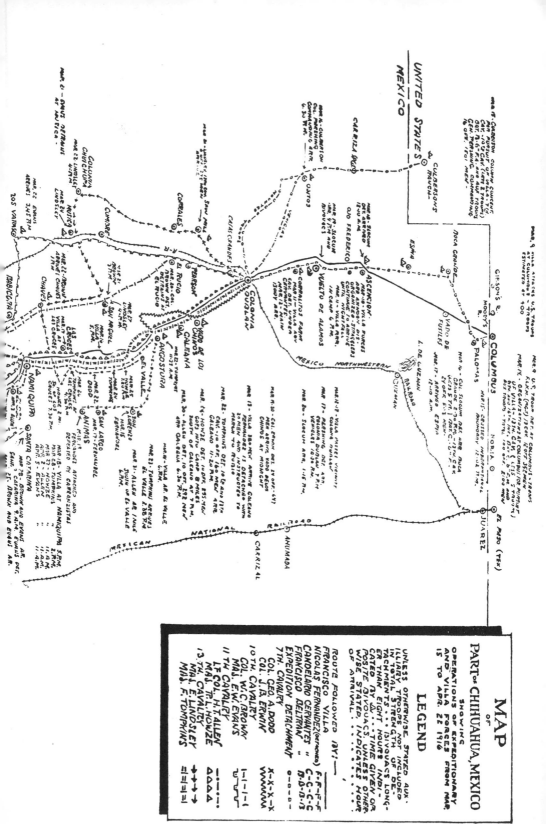

MAP of PART of CHIHUAHUA, MEXICO

SHOWING OPERATIONS OF EXPEDITIONARY AND VILLA FORCES FROM MAR. 15 to APR. 22 1916

LEGEND

UNLESS OTHERWISE STATED AUXILIARY "STRENGTH" OF DETACHMENTS. (BIVOUACS LONGER THAN EIGHT HOURS INDICATED BY...). TIME GIVEN OPPOSITE BIVOUACS, UNLESS OTHERWISE STATED, INDICATES HOUR OF ARRIVAL.

ROUTE FOLLOWED BY:—

FRANCISCO VILLA	F-F-F-F
COL. GEO. A. DODD	X-X-X-X
COL. J. B. ERWIN	WWWW
10TH. CAVALRY	
COL. W.C. BROWN	C-C-C-C
11 TH CAVALRY	B-B-B-B
LT.COL. H.T. ALLEN	o-o-o-o
MAJ. TR. L. HOWZE	Δ Δ Δ Δ
13 TH. CAVALRY	
MAJ. E. LINDSLEY	→→→→
MAJ. F. TOMPKINS	═║═║═║

NICOLAS FERNANDEZ (detached)
CANDELARIO CERVANTES
FRANCISCO BELTRAN
EXPEDITION DETACHMENT
7TH. CAVALRY
MAJ. E.W. EVANS

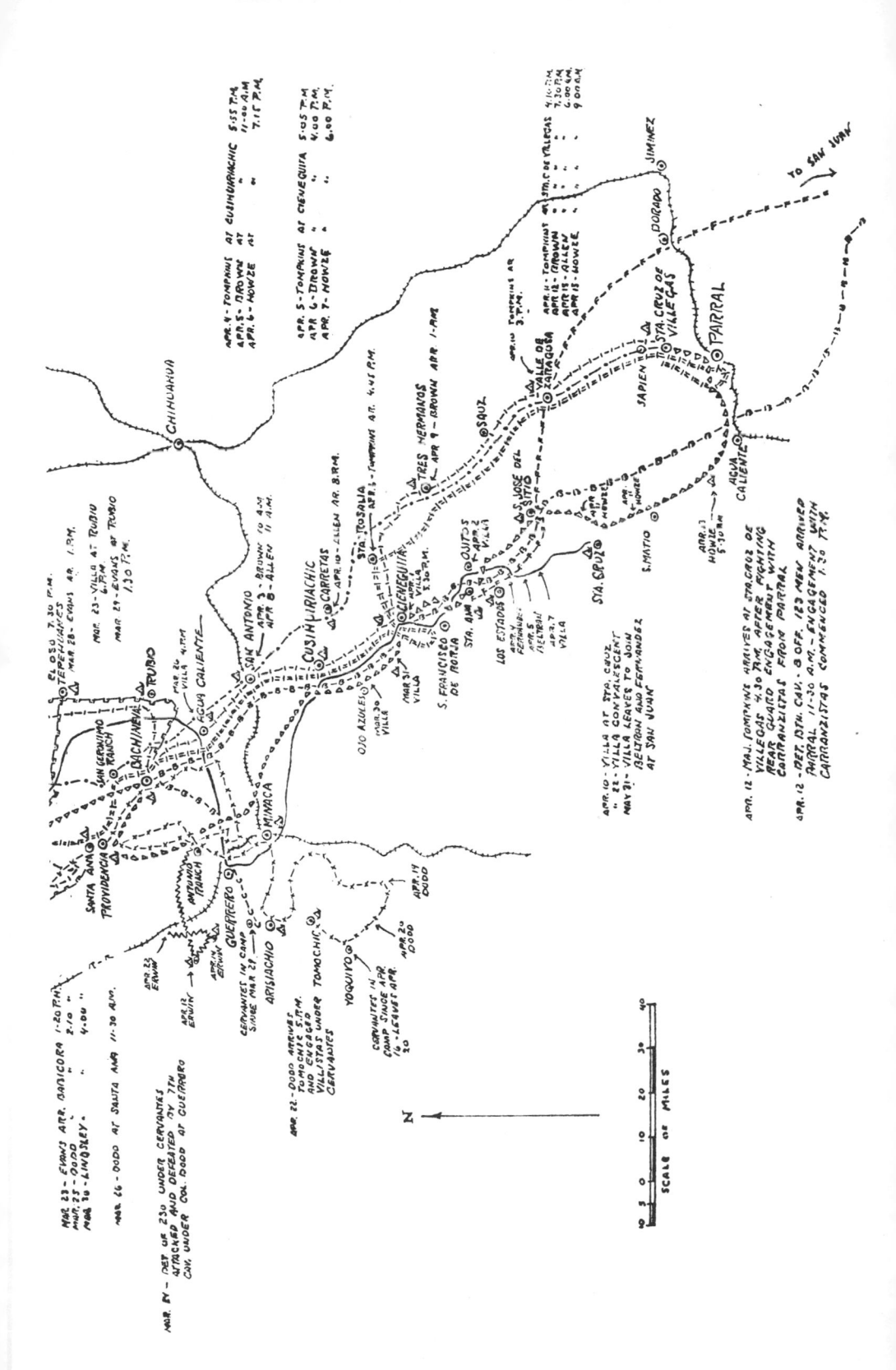

COLONEL FRANK TOMPKINS, U . S . A.

CHASING VILLA

The Story Behind the Story of

PERSHING'S EXPEDITION INTO MEXICO

By

Col. Frank Tompkins

THE MILITARY SERVICE PUBLISHING COMPANY

1934

DEDICATION

This book is dedicated to the officers and men of the Old Army whose gallant services, whether in the deserts of Arizona, the snows of the far north, the jungles of Cuba, the rice swamps of the Philippines, or the plateaus and mountains of Mexico, have added many a brilliant page to our National history.

THE AUTHOR

❖   ❖   ❖   ❖   ❖

My dear Colonel Tompkins:

I thank you very much for allowing me to read your manuscript. It is intensely interesting because it covers a period of activity in which our Cavalry was engaged on foreign soil, and its record of adverse conditions of lack of forage, food and water, among an unfriendly people, will always excite the pride and emulation of American Cavalrymen.

JOHN J. PERSHING,
General of the Armies

❖   ❖   ❖   ❖   ❖

PUBLISHER'S NOTE

Within the historical records contained in this book is the occasional use of racial slurs by American soldiers. While the publisher condemns such usage, it would be a perversion of the historical record to alter such language or leave it out. And lest we forget, the Mexicans had their own choice epithets for the Anglo-Americans who invaded their country in 1916

HIGH-LONESOME BOOKS

THE AUTHOR

The dashing raid of a squadron of the 13th United States Cavalry under command of Major Frank Tompkins, across the international border from Columbus, N. M., into Mexico, in pursuit of Francisco Villa, a Mexican bandit, in March, 1916 was an event of national importance. Major Tompkins' small force of 29 United States Cavalrymen pursued 2500 Mexicans under the leadership of the famous bandit, for 15 miles south of the Border, killed 75 of the bandits and captured many horses and supplies without losing a single American soldier. It was one of the most romantic and satisfying raids in the history of American Cavalry.

The author, Colonel Frank Tompkins, U. S. Army, Retired, a veteran of many campaigns, comes of a military family. Born in Washington, D. C., September 28, 1868, a son of General Charles H. Tompkins, U.S.A., he attended private schools in St. Paul, Minnesota and Chicago, Illinois, the Shattuck Military Academy in Minnesota, and Braden's West Point Preparatory School. Although his father and grandfather were West Point graduates, Tompkins declined an appointment to West Point and entered the Army direct from civil life, thus gaining two years in promotion. His son graduated from West Point in June, 1918, just 99 years from the time his great-grandfather graduated.

Entering the Army as a Second Lieutenant on August 1, 1891, Tompkins was promoted to First Lieutenant and assigned to the Second Cavalry July 13, 1898. His Captaincy came in February, 1901, with assignment to the 11th Cavalry. He is a graduate of the Infantry and Cavalry School at Fort Leavenworth (1897). (The Infantry and Cavalry School at Fort Leavenworth, founded in 1881, was the forerunner of the Service Schools of today at the same post.)

As a First Lieutenant he is credited with having broken all records in Cavalry marching, when he led Troop G, 11th U. S. Cavalry 127 miles through the tropics in less than 30 hours. This was in April, 1908. He served with distinction in the Philippines under the command of General J. F. Bell and was mentioned in orders for efficient service, especially for his work in commanding an expedition that forced its way into the crater at Mt. Banahao and captured the Catalorum stronghold there.

Having served during the hostilities in Cuba with distinction, in June, 1910, he was detailed as Professor of Military Science and Tactics at Norwich University, Vermont.

As a Major of Cavalry, Tompkins was stationed at Columbus, New Mexico, at the time of the Villa raid. For his raid into Mexico he was given a citation by the President of the United States and was recommended for the Medal of Honor, but received instead the Distinguished Service Cross. He was cited several times by General John J. Pershing, for services in the Punitive Expedition into Mexico in 1916.

When the United States entered the World War, Colonel Tompkins was assigned to command the 376th Infantry, 76th Division, at Camp Devens, Massachusetts, sailing overseas with this organization on July 6, 1918. At his own request, Colonel Tompkins was transferred to a combat Division, the 28th, and was placed in command of the 110th Infantry, with which he saw severe fighting in the Oise-Aisne Offensive until he was wounded. Returning to the United States in December, 1918, Colonel Tompkins was retired, after 30 years service, "for injuries received in battle with an enemy of the United States," and again detailed to Norwich University, where he is still in active service.

In 1925 and 1926 Colonel Tompkins served as representative from Northfield in the Vermont Legislature.

During his years of service as Professor of Military Science and Tactics and Commandant at Norwich University, Vermont, he has improved the military training of the University, developed the morale of the Cadets to a high standing, built two large buildings, and through his personal efforts has increased the endowment fund of the institution to the extent of a half million dollars.

FOREWORD

By Major General J. G. Harbord

In mid-November Colonel Frank Tompkins, U. S. Army, Retired, sent me a letter asking me to write a foreword for his book on the Pershing Expedition into Mexico after Villa in 1916. He said his publisher wanted it before Christmas and that there was not time to send me the manuscript. In his Cavalry innocence as he sits up there in the hills of Vermont enduring the twinges of old wounds, he does not realize that it is about as safe to write a foreword for a book which you have never read as it is to sign a blank check or marry a divorced lady without reference from her previous place. So I declined, but he came back. He does not easily give up. He thought I might object to writing the foreword because the book carried a criticism of President Wilson's Mexican policy. Though nothing now can hurt him, I should be reluctant to endorse a criticism of President Wilson for his Mexican policy, though in twenty years I have never heard anyone praise it, because of the splendid way in which he sustained his Commanders in the field during the World War. Nothing could have been finer.

When I joined Troop B of the 5th Cavalry in the Indian Territory, in 1891, its best tradition was that in 1861 it made a cavalry charge at Fairfax Court House, Virginia, led by its only officer, Lieutenant Charles H. Tompkins, father of this Colonel Tompkins.

Colonel Tompkins probably remembers a few things which I have forgotten of our many years of acquaintance and I may remember some that have passed from his memory. He probably recalls that he entered the Cavalry as a Second Lieutenant one day later than I did in 1891, making him forever my junior. We reached the grade of First Lieutenant within a week of each other; were Captains the same day; and became Lieutenant Colonels on the same day in 1917. We were rival Captains in the 11th Cavalry as to which should have the better troop, he having perhaps a shade the better of it. But he has probably forgotten that, in that hot summer of 1916, while he was gallantly leading a squadron of the 13th Cavalry following Pershing through the plains and mountains of Chihuahua, I was riding the line from Nogales, Arizona, to the New Mexican border, thinking of his opportunity with great envy. He has also probably forgotten that one day in the late summer of 1902 a dirty little coastwise vessel, rolling in the trough of the southwest Monsoon, arrived at the port of San Fernando from the mouth of the Laoag River, a night's run farther north. There was on that old ship my wife, desperately ill from malaria and being sent to Manila because of the epidemic of Asiatic cholera. At San Fernando, Captain Tompkins, with his attractive young wife, were members of the 11th Cavalry garrison. Word came to them from the ship that my lady's condition was such that she could travel no farther, and they had her brought off the little coaster and, though neither of them had ever seen her before, they nursed her back to comparative health. Such things were done in the old Army. He has also probably forgotten that twenty years ago last summer, when I was stationed in the Imperial Valley, he sent me, at the instance of the late Colonel Spencer Borden, of Fall River, Massachusetts, "Halim," the most beautiful and lovely thoroughbred Arab horse that ever brought delight to the heart of a cavalryman.

With all this balance of accounts between us extending over a period of forty-three years, I will take a chance on submitting this as a foreword to Tompkins' book whether I ever read it or not.

The Cavalry seems on its way out. They have mechanized its historic First regiment, and its ideal is now General Motors instead of General Sheridan. So far is it to differ from the old Cavalry that Colonel Tompkins and I knew and loved, that the mechanized regiment has been stationed by itself in Kentucky, very far removed from the opportunity to be coordinated with such as are left of the old Cavalry principles of warfare taught at the United States Cavalry School at Fort Riley. Colonel Tompkins' book can hardly fail to be a stirring account of the last time that our Cavalry guidons will ever flutter in a foreign land.

ILLUSTRATIONS

TABLE OF CONTENTS*

* For statements contained in this volume, see FOREIGN RELATIONS OF THE UNITED STATES, 1916.

Railroad accident near Cumbre—Major Evans detrains at Musica (Cumbre) and marches to Las Vegas—He is ordered to Babicora—Great loss of time due to treachery and inefficiency of railroad officials—Joins Col. Brown at El Toro —March to Namiquipa—Further treachery of Col. Cano— Camp in Oso Canyon—Advance on Sta. Catalina—Prairie fire—Evans marches alone to Tepehuanes—Use of telephone lines—March to Rubio and San Diego del Monte—The united squadrons remain in camp, awaiting orders—Reports concerning Villa.

quipa—Fired on by snipers—When the Columbus raid was organized—On to San Geronimo—March to San Antonio—Dealing with snipers—Visit of Gen. Pershing—Chasing Pablo Lopez—Camp at Carretas—March to Satevo—Long march to Sta. Cruz by Lieut. Eby—March to Sta. Cruz de Valerio—Attitude of the inhabitants—Long march to Sta. Cruz de Villegas to reinforce Tompkins—Mutual support by the various forces—Assembly at Sta. Cruz de Villegas—Activity of Gen. Pershing.

Defense—Conferences between Gens. Scott and Obregon—
Danger of Gen. Pershing's position—Gen. Funston recom-
mends mobilization of the guard—The Secretary of War
issues the call—Tentative organization by divisions—Divisional organization not accomplished—Lack of strategic railways—Strategic advantages of the Mexican railroads—Difficulties of transporting the troops—Total of troops in Federal service—Lack of reserves—Recruiting for the National
Guard—General officers of the Guard—Conditions of service on the Border—Events of special interest—Need for a
larger Regular Army and for selective service—Advantages
from the experiences of the mobilization—The Guard is
ordered home.

INTRODUCTION

After waiting nearly two decades, hoping that some other member of the Mexican Punitive Expedition wielding a more facile pen than my own would write a history of that memorable campaign, the author, at the request of numerous members of that expedition, has reluctantly undertaken the task.

I do not expect to write anything of especial literary merit, but do hope to produce a brief history to be placed on library shelves for those who come after us; one which will be accurate as to facts, dates, and such like matters, in order that future readers may obtain a fairly accurate conception of the military operations in Mexico in 1916 and of the political events leading up to that unique campaign.

Perhaps I have made a mistake in referring to this work as a "History." Students of history are well aware that authors, both of ancient and of modern history have falsified their writings in the interest of patriotism. There are educators who plead for the abandonment of the teaching of history from such records, which they criticise as nationalistic and bellicose, and the substitution of a method which would show more clearly the operation of international agencies in the development of civilization. They claim that history as taught today deals too much with wars. Children are impressed with the idea that the chief contact of their own country with foreigners has been conflict, and that in such conflict their own nation has generally been both right and victorious. History texts differ widely in their accounts of the same war. English text books do not go into great detail about Joan of Arc, who drove the English out of France, but devote considerable space to Napoleon who was wicked enough to wish to invade England; and in our own country over 80 American school histories on file in the Congressional Library Bureau of Education, have serious errors of commission and omission. Some of these school histories are ridiculous, absurd and stupid.

Occasional advocates of this system have attempted to tell the stories of nations dealing with other things than activities of national heroes on the field of battle. Macaulay was successful, and yet he wrote a good deal about the wars in Ireland and the Low Countries. Green and Lecky have made some noble contributions to the study of peoples apart from courts and camps, and here in America we have McMaster's monumental work, besides the histories of Fiske, Rhodes, Channing, Morison and many others.

It is contended that history, while dealing lightly with the military heroes, should be a record, not only of one's own country, but of the progress of the world as a whole, a history which would show how each element, race or nation, contributed its share to the work of advancement; how one did most, we will say, for government, another for science, another for literature and art, and so on. It is a noble conception. The majestic work of the immortal Gibbon might perhaps serve as a model did it not deal overmuch with wars. It was Gibbon himself who said that history was indeed little more than a register of the crimes, follies, and misfortunes of mankind.

Others have spoken disparagingly of history. Pascal called it a perpetual conspiracy against truth. Voltaire said it was little less than a picture of human crimes and misfortunes. Bolingbroke spoke of the "dignity of history." When Frederick the Great would have his secretary read history to him he would say: "Bring me my liar." Napoleon asked the famous question: "What is history but a fable agreed upon?" Sir Robert Walpole was more direct: "All history is a lie."

Journalists are sometimes spoken of as contemporary historians. Both journalists and historians write with a like aim, to instruct and to interest—above all to interest, for it is useless to deal with happenings and movements which people will refuse to read about. If histories and newspapers devote much attention to wars it does not mean that the writers are lovers of war. For four years the front page of every paper in this peace loving country bore the latest news of the struggle in Europe. It was no pleasure to record those daily slaughters, but it was a duty, for it was the most important news of the day.

By war Greece fell; by wars Rome rose, the British empire thrived, the United States came into existence and preserved the Union. How could a conscientious historian fail to emphasize such things?

In this history I shall endeavor to present a truthful picture, though it may contain unpleasant revelations of our political relations with Mexico from the fall of Porfirio Diaz in May, 1911, to the Columbus Raid in March, 1916; the Columbus Raid; and the Mexican Punitive Expedition under the command of General John J. Pershing.

It is necessary that the reader have an understanding of the weak and vacillating Mexican policy of the United States during the period from the abdication of Diaz in May, 1911, to the Columbus Raid by Pancho Villa in March, 1916, in order to have a clear picture of the causes which finally led up to and culminated in the unprovoked attack on Columbus, New Mexico. This crime against the sovereignty of the United States made itself evident that a stronger policy towards Mexico was necessary than "Watchful waiting," so the Punitive Expedition was organized and started in pursuit of Villa and his band.

The reader must not confuse anything recorded in this book with Mexico of the present day. This narrative deals with Mexico of 1916 and before. During the last decade Mexico has developed into a country vastly different from the Mexico of the time of which I write.

FRANK TOMPKINS

Northfield, Vermont
  Dec. 1, 1934.

The San Joaquin Canyon

CHAPTER I

Trouble Brews on the Border

In stepping across the southern border of the United States into Mexico we pass from a land of prosperity, a land of splendid industry, wealth and culture, a land of political and religious freedom, a land where the standards of living for all of our people are high, a land where a free education is provided for all regardless of race or color, a land of opportunity where there is no limit to the rise of the ambitious and the industrious; into a land of poverty and ignorance, a land of hungry and undisciplined armies followed by bedraggled women and children, a land of insecurity for life, property and religion, a land whose population is two-thirds illiterate and largely Indian, a land where the people, from the highest to the lowest, believe the "Colossus of the North" is really imperialistic as regards Mexico. All Mexicans, whether or not they can read or write, are fully aware that the United States now possesses a vast domain that a short century ago was Mexico's. The blood of the humblest peon grows hot when he wonders if the names Sonora, Chihuahua, Coahuila, Nueva Leon may not also cease to be Mexican and become American.

This suspicion on the part of ninety per cent of the Mexican people is fertile soil in which the jingo politician may plant his propaganda. Under Porfirio Diaz American capital, energy and brains went into Mexico. Relations were friendly, industry thrived, and the twenty-six years of his rule were the period of the country's greatest prosperity. Diaz overcame all opposition until his enemies fostered a feeling among the people that Diaz was friendly with American Capitalists who were exploiting Mexican resources to Mexico's disadvantage. Then Diaz fell, and ever since Mexico has been torn by civil strife, and the United States has, because of its weak-kneed policy, been the victim of the Mexican family quarrel.

During the Diaz rule the people were governed with an iron hand, but though his rule of twenty-six years was despotic it was a benevolent despotism and marked the period of the country's greatest prosperity. Relations between the United States and Mexico were friendly, and, except for the border troubles of 1877 and 1878, American soil was not violated as it was during the years 1912-16. This immunity from border warfare being due largely to the agreement between the two governments which provided that armed forces of either country might freely cross into the territory of the other to pursue and chastise marauders regardless of their nationality.

After Diaz this agreement lapsed, armed Mexican factions were quick to avail themselves of the immunity from pursuit and our border was

1

ravished by lawless bands. And in addition the territory adjacent to our border towns soon became a favorite battle ground for the Mexican revolutionists, as both sides knew we would not actively resent any damage to life and property which might result, and did result, from the wild firing of the battling forces. And they also knew that if defeated they need but step across the boundary line into the United States to be safe from capture.

Six months before the abdication of Diaz advices had been received by our State Department indicating serious unrest and intrigue on both sides of the Mexican border. Information having been received from the Mexican Government through its Ambassador in Washington that bands of revolutionists were assembling at various places along the frontier of Texas, directions were issued on November 19, 1910, to the commanding generals of the Departments of Texas and Colorado to investigate the situation along the frontier and to advise the War Department as to what precautionary measures were deemed practicable and necessary. As a result of the reports received, the commanding general, Department of Texas, was authorized, under date of November 21, 1910, whenever in his judgment such action became necessary, to send troops to aid the civil authorities in enforcing the neutrality laws, and under date of November 22, 1910, he reported to the War Department that, in pursuance of these instructions, he had sent one troop of cavalry to Del Rio, and another troop to Eagle Pass, Texas.

The internal situation in Mexico having become more acute, and reports received from the State Department and the Department of Justice, as well as from officers of the army on duty on the Mexican border, having indicated that serious disturbances were imminent, additional troops were sent to various places on the border. Finally the entire line from the mouth of the Rio Grande to San Diego, California, was patrolled by United States troops in order to secure the strict enforcement of the rules of international law and the statutes of our Federal government as to neutrality. To this end the proper officers were directed to use diligence to see that such rules and laws were observed.

The Mexican border is a long and irregular line, passing in places through cities and towns, but for great stretches running through sparsely settled regions and a wild and difficult country. The forces at the disposal of the commander of the Southern Department for the protection of this border had been strengthened from time to time by transfer to that department of a very large part of the Regular Army within the limits of the continental United States. This force included some detachments of Coast Artillery, withdrawn from their coast defense stations. But the known presence of large numbers of bandits and irregular military organizations, hostile alike to the de facto Government of Mexico and to the Government and people of the United States, made it apparent that even as thus strengthened the forces on the border were inadequate to patrol this long and difficult line and to assure safety to the life and property of American citizens against raids and depredations under the conditions imposed upon our military forces by our spineless Mexican policy.

Conditions grew steadily worse until finally the President called out the militia and the national guard for service with the Border Patrol. In August, 1916, the troops in the Southern Department consisted of 2,160 officers and 45,873 enlisted men of the Regular Army, and 5,446 officers and 105,080 enlisted men of the National Guard; a total of 7,606 officers and 150,953 enlisted men in that department. Earlier in this year we were dangerously close to war with Mexico but the mere presence of this enlarged force on the border served to preserve peace and to protect life and property. Disturbances by outlaws and bandits in northern Mexico continued, and roving bands of greater or less strength moved through the territory, harassing Mexican forces and raiding Mexican communities, but they had not ventured an attack upon the people of the United States. Had our Mexican policy been positive and firm from the first the necessity for calling out our citizen soldiers would not have arisen and our border would not have been harried as it was during the four years of President Wilson's first administration.

CHAPTER II

Madero and Huerta

The reader may wonder why the Mexican people as a whole, both those within the law and those without, those of the *de facto* Government and those of the opposition, should entertain a hatred towards the United States and her people—a hatred so strong and vindictive that it led them to burn, plunder and sack American property, and murder American citizens both in Mexico and in the United States. And the reader may wonder still more why the United States, the richest and mightiest country in the world should tolerate, over a period of years, the inhuman and cruel treatment of her nationals both at home and in Mexico by her neighbor to the south. The answer to the first of these questions at least, is easy. The Mexicans hated us because they resented our meddling with their internal affairs and because we had already seized, and they were convinced we were scheming to seize even more Mexican territory. They showed their resentment by acts of violence against our people and their property because they knew our Mexican policy consisted of protests and not punishment.

After Diaz came Franciso I. Madero. The people of the United States, through the medium of the press, were led to believe that the Government of Madero was a pure democracy of pure ideals, devoted to the uplifting of the masses and the betterment of their condition. Nothing could be further from the truth.

It is true that Madero came into power with an altruistic program and apparently with many high ideals, but his character and that of his administration departed each day of its incumbency further from its supposed benign character, degenerating rapidly into a despotism of the worst sort, accompanied by the most positive evidences of corruption, incompetency, impotency, inefficiency and nepotism.

During the last months of its existence a virtual reign of terror existed, supported by espionage, the reckless squandering of public money, illegal and unwarranted seizures of the press, the deception of the public at home and abroad by paid native and foreign agents, bribery of congress and the army. There was a complete misconception and disregard of international obligations, and the Republic was actually governed by one family, unfitted by training for public affairs and devoid of those virtues of patriotism, prudence, and policy which were imperatively necessary in view of the abnormal and chaotic condition of the country.

The government was active in small things and evasive, sluggish, and neglectful in greater things. Madero came into power as an apostle of liberty, but he was simply a man of disordered intellect who happened

4

to be in the public eye at the psychological moment. The responsibilities of office and the disappointments growing out of rivalries
and intrigues shattered his reason completely, and in the last days of
his government, during the bombardment of the city, his mental qualities, always abnormal, developed all of the characteristics of that
dangerous form of lunacy of which the best example in ancient times
is a Nero and in modern times a Castro.

Remote from the high position where his misguided ambition and
force of circumstances carried him, he doubtless would have remained
a quiet and simple country gentleman of benevolent ideals and blame-
less life. Clothed with the chief power of the nation, dormant evil
qualities in the blood or in the race came to the surface and wrought
ruin to him and to thousands upon thousands of the Mexican people.

Such a disordered rule bred rebellious elements, different political
factions and revolutionists in arms against the Madero Government, including a movement initiated by the northern border states to form an
independent republic, of which Carranza, governor of Coahuila, was
the originator and prime mover.

This political unrest was not confined to the northern states of Mexico
alone, but permeated the entire country, until in February, 1913, a
part of the garrison of the City of Mexico revolted. The chief of the
movement was General Bernardo Reyes. The rebels, with Reyes at
their head, tried unsuccessfully to occupy the National Palace. General Reyes perished in the attempt, and the rebels who, from that
moment, were under the orders of Felix Diaz (nephew of former President Porfirio Diaz), marched to the arsenal or citadel, which they
occupied after a brief combat. There they shut themselves in and
fortified the place.

The Government immediately determined to attack the Citadel and
suppress the uprising. Troops were brought from different parts of
the Republic, and the command of these, as well as the direction of
the operations, was entrusted to General Victoriano Huerta.

After ten days of fighting, with grave damage to the buildings of
the city and considerable loss of life among the inhabitants, the situation suddenly changed. General Huerta, secretly placing himself in
accord with the rebels, took possession of the persons of President
Madero and Vice President Pino Suarez. The attacks against the
Citadel ceased and peace again reigned in the city. This happened on
the 18th day of February, 1913.

A few hours after the President and Vice-President were arrested
General Huerta and General Felix Diaz held a conference in which it
was agreed and declared that the Government of Mr. Madero had ceased,
that Huerta would exercise the executive power and that Diaz would
reserve to himself the right of presenting himself as candidate in the
presidential election which would have to be convoked. This famous
(or infamous) conference took place in the *Embassy of the United
States!!*

The principal aim of Huerta consisted in having his authority recognized throughout the Republic. He could count upon the inertia of
the people, but it was impossible that his spurious government would

be accepted by the various military chiefs and by the governors of the twenty-seven states. The situation, however, was cleared within twenty-four hours by the attitude of President Madero and Vice President Pino Suarez, who consented to resign their offices. The following plan was contrived for the purpose, to which Mr. Madero agreed: Upon the acceptance by the Chamber of Deputies, which according to the Mexican Constitution is competent for the case, of the resignation of the President and Vice President, the Minister of Foreign Relations, Lascurain, would be converted automatically into provisional president, Lascurain would appoint Huerta to the first position in the Cabinet and thereupon he would resign the presidency in order that Huerta, at the same time, might remain, also automatically, as provisional president. This plan was executed to the very letter.

The complaisant attitude of Madero and the action of the Chamber of Deputies were the salvation of Huerta. The latter was immediately recognized as president by the entire army and by the governors of twenty-five of the twenty-seven states into which the Republic is divided. The government was organized without delay, and all the nations of the world, with the exception of five, recognized it as the legitimate government of Mexico. One of the five was the United States, who in addition succeeded by direct requests in influencing the governments of Brazil, Chile, Argentina and Cuba to withhold recognition.

The attitude of the United States towards the Huerta Government seems inconsistent when we recall that within a few days of this time a military chief in Peru headed an uprising of his soldiers, took possession of the person of President Billinghurst and imprisoned him in the penitentiary. The new Peruvian Government, born in this manner out of betrayal and military revolt, was recognized by all, including the United States.

From the moment in which the resignations of Madero and Suarez were accepted by the Chamber of Deputies they were converted into simple private citizens. Three days afterwards these ex-officials, who had been detained in the National Palace, were conducted toward the Penitentiary and were assassinated on the road. Mr. Madero was assassinated on the 22nd of February, 1913, at midnight. Huerta had taken the oath of office as provisional President of the Republic before the Congress on the 19th of February, 1913, three days earlier. This order of events is of considerable political importance as the Wilson administration, through Mr. Lane, Secretary of the Interior, stated that Madero and Suarez were assassinated *while in office.*

A few days after Huerta became President of Mexico, Mr. Wilson became President of the United States. During the next four years the "Mexican Policy" of the United States presented a confusion of ideas.

Mr. Henry Lane Wilson, our Ambassador to Mexico and dean of the diplomatic corps in the City of Mexico, kept our State Department informed at all times of the sequence of events as they occurred. As early as February 21, 1913, he wrote:

In the absence of instructions and in view of the extreme urgency, I assembled the Diplomatic Corps last night relative to the recognition of the new Government. This step was necessary in view of the fact that we are invited to meet the President at noon today, when an exchange of brief addresses is expected. My colleagues, all of whom are without instructions, agreed that recognition of the new Government was imperative, to enable it to impose its authority and reestablish order. I shall accordingly unite with my colleagues, believing that I am interpreting the desires of the Department and assisting in the tranquilization.

Under date of February 24, 1913, he sent the following telegram:

I think we are on the eve of the procurement of peace, except perhaps in the districts immediately south of Mexico City, where the Government informed me they do not intend to negotiate but to suppress all disorders with a firm hand, sparing no violators of the law, and furnishing an immediate proof to the World of the stability and vigor of the present administration. I urge the Department to inform the American public of the friendly disposition of this Government toward the United States and of the activity it is displaying in restoring order; also of the fact that one of the last acts of Madero was to send out telegrams to all of the governors which amounted to an incitement against American residents in Mexico. The Secretary of the British legation believes his Government will not recognize the Provisional Government on account of the murder of Madero. This would be a great error, endangering the present Government, upon which the safety of all foreigners depends. Mr. de la Barra informed me today that at a meeting which occurred at the Palace immediately after the death of Madero he stated to the President that unless he were convinced that Madero had not been murdered with the connivance of the Government he would immediately resign with two of his colleagues. He added that he was convinced and that he had therefore given out the statement published by the Associated Press. I am disposed to accept the Government's version of the affair and consider it a closed incident, in spite of all current rumors. The cooperation of the Department in this direction will be of infinite value.

On March 4, 1913 President Wilson was inaugurated and fell heir to the Mexican problem. Mr. Bryan was made Secretary of State. On March 12th Ambassador Wilson wrote to Mr. Bryan in part as follows:

Concerning the facts of the deplorable death of the ex-President and ex-Vice President it is not possible for this Embassy to furnish the Department with a reliable account beyond the official version, which, in the absence of any other, I felt obliged to accept. A dozen different accounts by "eye-witnesses", all differing absolutely in details, have been offered to the Embassy, but all are lacking in the elements of probability, and none convincing or positive.

My own opinion is that the Government was not privy to the killing of these men, but that either their deaths resulted as related in the official version or that they resulted from a subordinate military conspiracy actuated by sentiments of revenge for the murder of General Ruiz in the National Palace, the probable murder of General Reyes, and the shooting to death by the ex-President of Colonels Riverol and Izquierdo at the time he was made prisoner.

History will undoubtedly straighten out this tangle, and while the crime was revolting to all people of humane and civilized sentiments it is not evident to me that, politically speaking, the death of these two Mexicans, relegated to private life by their resignations, should arouse greater expressions of popular disapproval in the United States than the murders, unrequited by justice, of some 75 or 80 Americans in Mexico during the last two years.

I believe that in announcing publicly my acceptance of the official version of the death of these two men—and indeed I could not, in consideration of the gravity of the situation, take any other course—I adopted the surest method of arresting hasty judgment and of allaying that singular and perverse sentimentality which frequently leads to the commission of greater crimes as punishment for the lesser ones.

As the Department is aware, an official investigation, apparently impartial, is being made of all the circumstances connected with the death of Madero, and in due time its conclusions will be published and transmitted by this Embassy.

There can be no doubt as to the legal constitution of the present Provisional Government in conformity with precedents and the Mexican Constitution. The incumbency of Huerta is as legal as was the incumbency of de la Barra after the resignation of Diaz. From this it would appear that if the Provisional Government of de la Barra, which was recognized without any question by the Government of the United States and by all other Governments as constitutionally inducted into office, the Provisional Government of Huerta is entitled to the same acceptance.

The second consideration for recognizing this Government lies in the imperative need for sustaining and strengthening it. Without our recognition, upon which the recognition of many other Governments depends, it will be constantly exposed to attacks from its enemies; and our attitude will take on a color of at least constructive sympathy with the elements conspiring against the reestablishment of order and peace in a neighboring and friendly Republic.

The financial situation, too, which at the present moment is pressing and urgent, cannot be solved by the procurement of the necessary loans while the question of the legitimacy and constitutionality of this Government is in doubt. By hesitating too long, therefore, we might contribute to the weakening and possible demolition of the present Government and reinvoke the movements of disorder and anarchy which so recently brought us to the verge of an intervention in the affairs of this Republic, fraught with great dangers to its future integrity and placing burdens of responsibility upon us the gravity of which cannot be accurately estimated but which may easily be imagined.

The present Provisional Government has shown remarkable activity and energy in restoring order, in subduing rebellious elements, and in consolidating different political factions and revolutionists in arms against the Government of Madero. In the brief period of two weeks the whole of the Republic to the south and west of the Federal District has, either by force or persuasion, been brought into a state of comparative peace.

The Sonora situation presents some aspects of gravity which should have the attention of the Department. It is not a Maderista movement, but the remains of the movement which was initiated by the border governors to form an independent republic, in which Carranza, then Governor of Coahuila and now a fugitive from justice, was the originator and prime mover.

It must be understood by the Department that the people of Sonora and of a large part of the State of Sinaloa have never been closely identified with this Republic. Most of the people in these states are of Texan origin, of mixed American and Spanish blood, and, as a matter of fact, they would prefer unity with the United States rather than with Mexico. There is evident, notwithstanding the reassuring advices sent hither by the Department, a movement there to declare an independent republic comprising the States of Sonora and Sinaloa and the Territory of Lower California; and while I have no positive proofs of intrigues by American interests in that direction it is believed here that they exist. The situation, therefore, at this point should be carefully watched by the Department in order that we may not be involved in a movement aimed to disintegrate this Republic.

General Huerta is preeminently a soldier, a man of iron mold, of absolute courage, who knows what he wants and how to get it, and is not, I believe, over particular as to methods. He is a firm believer in the policy of General Porfirio Diaz and believes in the cultivation of the closest and most friendly relations with the United States. I believe him to be a sincere patriot, and so far as my observation goes at the present moment he will cheerfully relinquish the responsibilities of office as soon as peace is restored in the country and financial stability reestablished. I may possibly err in my estimate of his character, but I am supported in it by the opinion of Captain Burnside who spent a month with him in the campaign in the State of Chihuahua.

Present indications point to the reestablishment of peace and order throughout the Republic within a fairly reasonable space of time, when due allowances are made for the enormous extent of territory which must be covered.

The new administration is not popular, but it is respected, and it, in its existence, has given birth not only in the minds of Mexicans but in the minds of foreigners, to a new feeling of confidence and belief in conditions which will permit the resumption of peaceful occupations in the cities and throughout the agricultural districts.

In all probability Mexico will become and afterwards remain quiet for some time, but ultimately, unless the same type of government as was implanted here by General Porfirio Diaz is again established, new revolutionary movements will break forth and general unrest will be renewed.

With eighty percent of its population unable to read and write permanent democratic government cannot be established in Mexico. But if we desire to contribute to the continued existence of democratic government and institutions under healthy conditions we should direct our efforts towards inducing this government to adopt and encourage a plan for universal education, assisting in the meantime in the maintenance of such a government as may guarantee protection to life and property and peace and progress, without being especially particular as to whether its character is in accordance with our ideas of general democratic institutions.

The result of the investigation into the death of Madero must have been satisfactory to the British Government for Great Britain recognized the Huerta Government as the de facto Government of Mexico on March 31, 1913.

On April 9, 1913 Ambassador Wilson sent the following message to Mr. Bryan:

Without being advised of the policy of our government but from considerations relating to the peace and good will of this continent, I deem it my duty to say to the Department that upon the high grounds of international polity, American interests and procurement of peace and order in Mexico, this Government should have the earnest moral support and assistance of ours, for if it does not succeed in sustaining itself absolute chaos will come and intervention will be inevitable. This is said with due regard for our proposals for an international claims commission which is vastly important but not so vital, responsibility having been accepted in principle, as the restoration of peace and order in this unfortunate country.

The days lengthened into weeks and the weeks into months and the Provisional Government of Mexico remained unrecognized by the United States although by the first of June, 1913 all Governments accredited to Mexico, but two South American Republics, had accorded official recognition. While the Huerta Government displayed in the earlier stages of its incumbency marked activity, great sagacity, and a broad and conciliatory spirit, as time went on it did not entirely fulfill the hopes of all those who anxiously desired the restoration of peace and order throughout Mexico. In no inconsiderable measure the failures of the provisional administration to secure better results was due to the lamentable condition in which the finances of the country were left by the Madero administration and the unfriendly policy of the United States. The public credit had been greatly injured and the national prestige greatly lowered by the peculiar methods of the administration and its inability or disinclination promptly to fulfill its

internal obligations. In addition to this the public treasury had undoubtedly been looted by the vast horde of greedy adventurers who
surrounded Madero, controlled his councils, and led him into the commission not only of financial blunders but of serious attacks on the
constitutional rights of the people. Thus, the new administration was
confronted at the time of taking office with a grave economic situation,
with a disordered administrative system, with a hostile legislative
majority, and with an army which had been reduced to diminutive
proportions and demoralized in discipline and morale. Moreover, the
vast extent of territory over which the government must assert its
authority, against the violent and destructive spirits which were loosed
by the Madero administration and which continued to be encouraged
by secret agents in the United States and in every part of Mexico to
revolt, made the task of restoring peace enormously difficult and
caused both natives and foreigners to despair of the restoration of
normal conditions by any government.

At this time, May, June and July, 1913, the phase of the entire situation in Mexico which caused the most comment by foreign and native
opinion and which was a matter of lively concern to the Huerta Government, was that resulting from an apparent collusion between a more
or less clearly defined interventionist organization in the United States
and the State authorities on the American side of the border. This
organization, according to reports received at the American Embassy,
was contributing moral and material support to the revolutionary cause
and was conducting a campaign in conjunction with the aid of representatives of the Madero political party refugees in the United States
with the primary object of forming an independent Republic from
Mexican territory contiguous to the border and reaching as far south
as the 26th parallel. This would embrace Lower California, the States
of Sonora, Chihuahua, Coahuila, and parts of the States of Nuevo Leon,
Durango, and Sinaloa. The program of the organization was first, to
secede from Mexico and then following the Texas precedent, to apply
for admission into the American Union.

The existence of this organization and its power were not in the least
doubted by the Mexican Government and its people, and the opinion
was general that it was influencing the attitude of the United States
toward Mexico. To this large section of public opinion the failure of
our government officially and formally to recognize the Huerta Government was unhesitatingly accepted as evidence that it was secretly in
sympathy with the plotters against the integrity of the Mexican Republic and was conniving at the overthrow of the authority of a neighboring and friendly State. Mexico actively propagated this idea not
only at home but abroad, and it found lodgment in the opinion of the
Diplomatic Corps in the City of Mexico.

The resentment against our policy was profound, and found expression in excited discussions in the press in open attacks on our government and its embassy (which was supposed to be making representations against recognition) and by what appeared to be an organized
boycott of American commodities of all kinds, which would have been

most effective if any great amount of American products had been going into the country.

Our Government's attitude toward Mexico in her hour of distress was most disastrous. It not only created and revived a new and intense anti-American spirit which made itself felt in all the channels of trade and the daily relations of life, but gave ground for a false interpretation by the rebels that our attitude was a sign of friendliness toward them. The other foreign interests seized the opportunity to take open advantage of our unpopularity, and, through their diplomatic representatives and in other ways took from American trade and privileges that which under normal conditions belonged to us. A semi-official statement in the Mexican press emanated from the president to the effect that his Government intended in all ways to show a preference for the nationals of those Governments which had recognized Mexico over those which had failed to do so.

The economic situation of the country was desperate. Exchange on Europe and the United States during the time of which I write rose as high as 2.40. These rates were of course practically prohibitive except for small transactions, causing an abnormal situation of foreign trade relations without parallel for half a century. The destruction of railways and lines of communication, extensively carried on by the revolutionists, resulted in the annihalation of over sixty percent of the railway systems of Mexico, adding much to the general economic distress. The coffee, sugar, rubber, and fruits of the south either went to waste on account of a diminished labor market or because the products if harvested could not be transported to market. The closing of silver and gold mines and the suspension of the smelting and iron mills of the country, which are the principal sources for foreign exchange, enormously increased the difficulties of a situation already strained almost to the breaking point. This situation bid fair to receive relief by the dissemination through all the channels of trade of a loan of $150,000,000 secured through a Belgian-English-French syndicate, but this remedy to the situation was nullified by the American Government, which influenced the French Government to interpose its veto to prevent certain French bankers from completing the loan which they had contracted with Huerta, and of which he had received only one third part.

On July 9, 1913, Ambassador Wilson sent another of his many appeals to Washington:

On account of our great trade and commercial interests with this country, which have been practically wiped out, of those harmonious relations which should exist between contiguous and friendly nations, of the 30,000 suffering Americans who are still left in Mexico, the objects of public hatred and without any guaranties of protection for their lives and property, of the more than 100,000 Mexicans whose lives have now been sacrificed in the struggle to restore order and peace in Mexico, I am obliged again to urge upon the President the pressing necessity for some action of a drastic and convincing kind that will convince the Government and this people that our nationals must be protected in life and property, and that the barbarous and inhuman warfare which has now been waged for three years shall cease.

The transaction of business of any kind by the American Embassy with the Huerta Government had by now become practically impossible, as no attention was paid to representations concerning protection to either property or life, even when repeatedly made. Americans were told by subordinate officials that they had instructions to discriminate against, delay and ignore all American interests. A practical boycott was directed by the Mexican Government against not only our official representatives, but also individual Americans all over the Republic who required protection or who had matters pending with the Government. The Ambassador could not obtain protection for our people because of the deliberate policy of the Mexican Government not to accord it, and because of the further fact that the whole course of events during the preceding three months, including the presence in Mexico of persons claiming to be representatives of President Wilson, lowered the dignity of the Embassy and detracted from the respect and deference which the Mexican people had been taught to regard it. This was accompanied by a rising tide of bitter resentment which found unlicensed expression in the press, which excited the mob and furnished almost the sole topic of conversation. Ambassador Henry Lane Wilson, convinced that he was helpless in the face of President Wilson's peculiar Mexican Policy, resigned his post and on July 17, 1913 left for the United States. The Embassy was taken over by Nelson O'Shaughnessy, the American Charge d'Affaires to the Secretary of State.

CHAPTER III

Wilson and Huerta

Early in August, 1913, Mr. John Lind, ex-Governor of Minnesota, was sent to Mexico as the personal representative of President Wilson, to act as adviser of the Embassy. Mr. Lind knew as little of the Mexican character as did President Wilson and Secretary Bryan. His mission to Mexico was explained by President Wilson in his message to Congress late in August, 1913, as follows:

Accordingly, I took the liberty of sending the Honorable John Lind, former Governor of Minnesota, as my personal spokesman and representative to the City of Mexico, with the following instructions:

"Press very earnestly upon the attention of those who are now exercising authority or wielding influence in Mexico the following considerations and advice:

"The Government of the United States does not feel at liberty any longer to stand inactively by while it becomes daily more and more evident that no real progress is being made towards the establishment of a Government at the City of Mexico which the country will obey and respect.

"The Government of the United States does not stand in the same case with the other great Governments of the world in respect to what is happening or what is likely to happen in Mexico. We offer our good offices, not only because of our genuine desire to play the part of a friend, but also because we are expected by the powers of the world to act as Mexico's nearest friend.

"We wish to act in these circumstances in the spirit of the most earnest and disinterested friendship. It is our purpose in whatever we do or propose in this perplexing and distressing situation not only to pay the most scrupulous regard to the sovereignty and independence of Mexico—that we take as a matter of course to which we are bound by every obligation of right and honor—but also to give every possible evidence that we act in the interest of Mexico alone, and not in the interest of any person or body of persons who may have personal or property claims in Mexico which they may feel that they have a right to press. We are seeking to counsel Mexico for her own good and in the interest of her own peace, and for not any other purpose whatever. The Government of the United States would deem itself discredited if it had any selfish or ulterior purpose in transactions where the peace, happiness and prosperity of a whole people are involved. It is acting as its friendship for Mexico, not as any selfish interest, dictates.

"The present situation in Mexico is incompatable with the fulfillment of international obligations on the part of Mexico, with the civilian development of Mexico herself, and with the maintenance of tolerable political and economic conditions in Central America. It is upon no common occasion, therefore, that the United States offers her counsel and assistance. All America calls out for a settlement.

"A satisfactory settlement seems to us to be conditioned on—

"(a) An immediate cessation of fighting throughout Mexico, a definite armistice solemnly entered into and scrupulously observed;

"(b) Security given for an early and free election in which all will agree to take part;

13

"(c) The consent of General Huerta to bind himself not to be a candidate for election as President of the Republic at this election; and

"(d) The agreement of all parties to abide by the results of the election and cooperate in the most loyal way in organizing and supporting the new administration.

"The Government of the United States will be glad to play any part in this settlement or in its carrying out which it can play honorably and consistently with international right. It pledges itself to recognize and in every way possible and proper to assist the administration chosen and set up in Mexico in the way and on the conditions suggested.

"Taking all the existing conditions into consideration, the Government of the United States can conceive of no reasons sufficient to justify those who are now attempting to shape the policy or exercise the authority of Mexico in declining these offers of friendship. Can Mexico give the civilized world a reason for rejecting our good offices? If Mexico can suggest any better way in which to show our friendship, serve the people of Mexico, and meet our international obligations, we are more than willing to consider the suggestion."

This remarkable document was presented to the Mexican Department of Foreign Affairs upon the assurance of the Charge d'Affaires ad interim of the United States, that Mr. Lind was in fact the Confidential Agent of the President of the United States. Mr. Lind's first request for an audience was unfortunate in that it was lacking in that courtesy which is insisted upon in all diplomatic intercourse. Senor Gamboa, Secretary of Foreign Affairs, made very clear to Mr. Lind the unhappy impression made by Mr. Wilson's note when he said in part:

The Confidential Agent may believe that solely because of the sincere esteem in which the people and the Government of the United States of America are held by the people and Government of Mexico, and because of the consideration it has for all friendly nations (and especially in this case for those which have offered their good offices), my Government consented to take into consideration, and to answer as briefly as the matter permits, the representations of which you are the bearer. Otherwise, it would have rejected them immediately because of their humiliating and unusual character, hardly admissible even in a treaty of peace after a victory, inasmuch as in a like case any nation which in the least respects itself would do likewise.

The Wilsonian appeal was denied in a lengthy document which is entirely too long to quote in full. I shall quote those parts which deal directly with the conditions of President Wilson's plan for a settlement, viz:

The imputation contained in the first paragraph of your instructions—that no progress has been made toward establishing in the capital of Mexico a government enjoying the respect and obedience of the Mexican people—is unfounded. In contradiction of that gross imputation, which is not supported by any proofs, principally because there are none, it affords me pleasure to refer, Mr. Confidential Agent, to the following facts which abound in evidence and which to a certain extent must be known to you by direct observation. The Mexican Republic, Mr. Confidential Agent, is formed of 27 States, 3 Territories, and one Federal District in which the supreme power of the Republic has its seat. Of these 27 States, 18 of them, the three Territories and the Federal District (making a total of 22 political entities) are under the absolute control of the present Government, which, aside from the above, exercises its authority over almost every part of the Republic and consequently over the customhouses therein established. Its southern frontier is open and at peace. Moreover my Government has an army of 80,000 men in the field with no other purpose than to insure complete peace in the Republic, the only national aspiration and solemn promise of the present provisional President. The above is sufficient to exclude any doubt that my Government is worthy of the respect and obedience of the Mexican people; because the latter consideration has been gained at the cost of the greatest sacrifice and in spite of the most evil influences.

My Government fails to understand what the Government of the United States means by saying that it does not find itself in the same case with reference to other nations of the earth concerning what is happening and is likely to happen in Mexico. The conditions in Mexico at the present time are unfortunately neither doubtful nor secret; it is inflicted with an internal strife which has been raging almost three years, and which I can only classify in these lines as a fundamental mistake. With reference to what might happen in Mexico neither you, Mr. Confidential Agent, nor any one else can prognosticate, because no assertion is possible on incidents which have not occured. On the other hand, my Government greatly appreciates the good offices tendered to it by the Government of the United States of America in the present circumstances; it recognizes that they are inspired by the noble desire to act as a friend as well as by the wishes of all the other Governments which expect the United States to act as Mexico's nearest friend. But if such good offices are to be of the character of those now tendered to us we should have to decline them in the most categorical and definite manner.

Inasmuch as the Government of the United States is willing to act in the most disinterested friendship, it will be difficult for it to find a more propitious opportunity than the following: If it would only watch that no material and monetary assistance is given to the Rebels who find refuge, conspire, and provide themselves with arms and food on the other side of the border; if it would demand from its minor and local authorities the strictest observance of its neutrality laws, I assure you, Mr. Confidential Agent, that the complete pacification of this Republic would be accomplished within a relatively short time.

I intentionally refrain from replying to the allusion that it is the purpose of the United States of America to show the greatest respect for the sovereignty and independence of Mexico, because, Mr. Confidential Agent, there are matters which not even from the standpoint of the idea itself could be given an answer in writing.

His Excellency, Mr. Wilson, is laboring under a serious delusion when he declares that the present situation of Mexico is incompatible with the compliance with her international obligations, with the development of her civilization, and with the required maintenance of certain political and economic conditions tolerable in Central America. Strongly backing that there is a mistake, because to this date no charge has been made by any foreign government accusing us of the above lack of compliance, we are punctually meeting all of our credits, we are still maintaining diplomatic missions cordially accepted in almost all the countries of the world, and we continue to be invited to all kinds of international congresses and conferences. With regard to our interior development, the following proof is sufficient, to wit, a contract has just been signed with Belgian capitalists which means to Mexico the construction of something like 5000 kilometers of railway. In conclusion, we fail to see the evil results, which are prejudicial only to ourselves, felt in Central America by our present domestic war. In one thing I do agree with you, Mr. Confidential Agent, and it is that the whole of America is clamoring for a prompt solution of our disturbances, this being a very natural sentiment if it is borne in mind that a country which was prosperous only yesterday has been suddenly caused to suffer a great internal misfortune.

Consequently, Mexico cannot for one moment take into consideration the four conditions which his Excellency Mr. Wilson has been pleased to propose through your worthy and honorable channel. I must give you the reasons for it: An immediate suspension of the struggle in Mexico, a definite armistice "Solemnly entered into and scrupulously observed," is not possible, as to do this it would be necessary that there should be some one capable of proposing it without causing a profound offense to civilization, to the many bandits, who, under this or that pretext, are marauding toward the south and committing the most outrageous depredations; and I know of no country in the world, the United States included, which has ever dared to enter into agreement or to propose an armistice to individuals who, perhaps on account of a physiological accident, can be found all over the world beyond the pale of the divine and human laws. Bandits, Mr. Confidential Agent, are not admitted to armistice, the first action against them is one of correction, and when this unfortunately fails, their lives must be severed for the sake of the biological and fundamental principle; then the useful sprouts should grow and fructify.

With reference to the rebels who style themselves "Constitutionalists," one of the representatives of whom has been given an ear by members of the United States Senate, what could there be more gratifying to us than if, convinced of the precipice to which we are being dragged by the resentment of their defeat, in a moment of reaction they were to put aside their rancor and add their strength to ours, so that all together we would undertake the great and urgent task of national reconstruction? Unfortunately they do not avail themselves of the amnesty law enacted by the Provisional Government immediately after its inauguration, but, on the contrary, well known rebels holding elective positions in the capital of the Republic or profitable employments left the country without molestation, notwithstanding the information which the Government had that they were going to foreign lands to work against its interests, many of whom have taken upon themselves the unfortunate task of exposing the miseries and infirmities from which we are suffering, the same as any other human aggregation.

Were we to agree with them to the armistice suggested this would, ipso facto, recognize their belligerency, and this is something which cannot be done for many reasons which cannot escape the perspicacity of the Government of the United States of America, which to this day, and publicly, has at least classed them as rebels just the same as we have. And it is an accepted doctrine that no armistice can be concerted with rebels.

The assurance asked of my Government that it will promptly call free elections is the most evident proof and the most unequivocal consession that the Government of the United States considers it legally and solidly constituted and that it is exercising, like all those of its class, acts of such importance as to indicate the perfect civil operation of a sovereign nation. Inasmuch as our laws already provide such assurance, there is no fear that the latter will not be observed during the coming elections; and as the present Government is of a provisional character it will cede its place to the definite Government which may be selected by the people.

The request that General Victoriano Huerta should agree not to appear as a candidate for the Presidency of the Republic in the coming elections cannot be taken into consideration, because, aside from its strange and unwarranted character, there is a risk that the same might be interpreted as a matter of personal dislike. This point can be decided only by Mexican public opinion expressed at the polls.

The pledge that all parties should agree beforehand to the results of the election and to cooperate in the most loyal manner to support and organize the new administration is something to be tacitly supposed and desired; the experience of which this internal strife means to us in loss of life and the destruction of property will cause all contending political factions to abide by the results; but it would be untimely to make any assertion in this respect, even by the countries most experienced in civil matters, as no one can forecast or foresee the errors and excesses which men are likely to commit, especially under the influence of political passion.

We hasten to signify to the United States of America our appreciation of their agreement to recognize henceforth and aid the future Government which we, the Mexican people, may elect to rule our destinies. On the other hand, we greatly deplore the present tension in our relations with your country, a tension which has been produced without Mexico having afforded the slightest cause therefor. The legality of the Government of

GEN. PERSHING IN 1916
He was at this time about 55 years of age

General Huerta cannot be disputed. The point of issue is exclusively one of constitutional law in which no foreign nation, no matter how powerful and respectable it may be, should mediate in the least. Moreover, my Government considers that at the present time the recognition of the Government of General Huerta by that of the United States of America is not concerned, inasmuch as facts which exist on their own account are not and cannot be susceptible of recognition. The only thing which is being discussed is a suspension of relations as abnormal and without reason: abnormal because the Ambassador of the United States of America, in his high diplomatice investiture and appearing as Dean of the Diplomatic Corps accredited to the Government of the Republic, congratulated General Huerta upon his elevation to the Presidency, continued to correspond with this Department by means of diplomatic notes, and on his departure left the First Secretary of the Embassy of the United States of America as Charge d'affaires ad interim, and the latter continues here in the free exercise of his functions; and without reason, because, I repeat, we have not given the slightest pretext.

With reference to the final part of the instructions of President Wilson, which I beg to include herewith and which say, "If Mexico can suggest any better way in which to show our friendship, serve the people of Mexico, and meet our international obligations, we are more than willing to consider the suggestion," that final part causes me to propose the following decorous arrangement. One, that our Ambassador be received in Washington; two, that the United States of America send us a new Ambassador without previous conditions. And all this threatening and distressing situation will have reached a happy conclusion; mention will not be made of the causes which might carry us, if the tension persists, to no one knows what incalculable extremities for two peoples who have the unavoidable obligation to continue mutual respect, which is indispensable between two soverign entities wholly equal before the law and justice.

The above reply to President Wilson's note was delivered to Mr. Lind on August 16, 1913. On August 25th Mr. Lind submitted another note which in addition to the conditions and suggestions of the first note suggested that the Mexican Election scheduled for October be held in accordance with the Constitutional laws of Mexico, that Huerta be not a candidate and that should the Mexican Government act immediately and favorably on these suggestions the American Government would use its influence with American bankers to make possible an immediate loan sufficient in amount to meet the temporary requirements of the present Mexican administration. This last, of course, was a bribe and nothing else. As this second note showed no intention on the part of President Wilson to remove himself an iota from the position originally assumed by him, Mr. Gamboa said in part:

It would have been sufficient to answer this note in its totality by reproducing the whole of my note of the 16th instant as negative as it is categorical.

Then Mr. Gamboa answered the note, giving it the same keen analysis as the previous note, which must have made Mr. Lind squirm and hate his job. In his lengthy reply Mr. Gamboa said in part:

If your original proposals were not to be admitted, they are now, in the "more restricted" form in which they are produced, even more inadmissible, and one's attention is called to the fact that they are insisted upon, if it be noticed that the first proposal had already been declined. Precisely because we comprehend the immense value of the principle of sovereignty which the Government of the United States so opportunely invokes in the question of our recognition or non-recognition—precisely for this reason we believe that it would never be proposed to us that we should forget our own sovereignty by permitting that a foreign government should modify the line of conduct which we have followed in our public and independent life. If even once we were to admit the counsels and advice (let us call them thus) of the United States of America. not only would we, as I say above, forego our sovereignty, but we would as well compromise for an indefinite future our destinies as a soverign entity and all the future elections for president would be submitted to the veto of any President of the United States of America. And such an enormity, Mr. Confidential Agent, no Government will even attempt to perpetrate, and this I am sure of. unless some monstrous and almost impossible cataclysm should occur in the conscience of the Mexican people.

Then Mr. Gamboa expresses surprise to Mr. Lind that considering the disproportionate interest President Wilson had shown concerning the internal affairs of Mexico he would not know perfectly well the provisions of the Mexican constitution in the matter of elections which state "The Secretary of State in charge of the Executive power shall not be eligible to the office of either President or vice-President when the elections shall take place." This would prevent Huerta from becoming a candidate at the forthcoming elections. Then Mr. Gamboa went on to say:

I beg to inform you, Mr. Confidential Agent, that up to the present time, at least, only the President of the United States has spoken of the candidacy of the constitutional ad interim President at the forthcoming elections. Neither the solemn declarations of this high functionary nor the most insignificant of his acts—all of which have been done with a view of obtaining a complete pacification of the country, which is the supreme national aim and which he has decided to bring about in spite of everything—have authorized any one even to suspect that such are his ultimate intentions. It is perfectly well known that there does not exist in the whole country a single newspaper, a single club, a single corporation or group of individuals who have launched his candidacy or even discussed it.

Touching upon the bribe feature of the Wilson note Mr. Gamboa stated:

Permit me, Mr. Confidential Agent, not to reply for the time being to the significant offer in which the Government of the United States of America insinuated that it will recommend to American Bankers the immediate extension of a loan which will permit us, among other things. to cover the innumerable urgent expenses required by the progressive pacification of the country, for in the terms in which it is couched it appears more to be an attractive antecedent proposal to the end that. moved by petty interests. we should renounce a right which incontrovertibly upholds us. When the dignity of the nation is at stake, I believe that there are not loans enough to induce those charged by the law to maintain it to permit it to be lessened.

President Wilson stated that Mr. Lind executed his mission with tact, firmness and good judgment, but the proposals were rejected because the Mexicans failed to recognize the spirit of the American people in this matter, their earnest friendliness and yet sober determination that some just solution be found for the Mexican difficulties; and they did not believe that the administration spoke, through Mr. Lind, for the people of the United States. He then advised patience on the part of the friends of Mexico, stating that the situation must be given a little more time to work itself out, and that in the meantime it would become our duty to show what true neutrality would do to enable the people of Mexico to set their affairs in order; and to let every one who assumes to exercise any authority in any part of Mexico know in the most unequivocal way that we shall vigilantly watch the fortunes of those Americans who cannot get away, and shall hold those responsible for their sufferings and losses to a definite reckoning.

In the furtherance of his policy of strict neutrality Mr. Wilson stated to Congress shortly following the failure of the Lind mission:

I deem it my duty to exercise the authority confered upon me by the law of March 4, 1912, to see to it that neither side to the struggle now going on in Mexico receive any assistance from this side of the border. I shall follow the best practice of nations in the matter of neutrality by forbidding the exportation of arms or munitions of war of any kind from the United States to any part of the Republic of Mexico—a policy suggested by several interesting precedents and certainly dictated by many manifest considerations of practical expediency. We cannot in the circumstances be the partisans of either party to the contest that now distracts Mexico, or constitute ourselves the virtual umpire between them.

This attitude of impartiality and neutrality lasted less than three months, for on November 24, 1913, Secretary of State Bryan sent the following note to Charge O'Shaughnessy:

The present policy of the Government of the United States is to isolate General Huerta entirely; to cut him off from foreign sympathy and aid and from domestic credit, whether moral or material, and to force him out.

The embassies and European legations were notified in detail of this policy.

Great Britain suggested that the British Government and other European Governments might be willing to request Huerta to resign on two conditions: First, if such a request would be agreeable to President Wilson; and second, if President Wilson would present a definite plan whereby after Huerta's resignation the pacification of Mexico might be expected. But the United States refused to assume any responsibility for any government which might take the place of the one the United States was trying to destroy. The Russian reaction to our policy was clearly expressed by her Minister for Foreign Affairs in these words:

I consider the Mexican question as concerning only the United States. In my opinion the only satisfactory solution is annexation, and this action Russia would see with approval.

From the first Woodrow Wilson claimed that the Huerta Government was unconstitutional and that he would not recognize an unconstitutional government. The fact that all the other great nations of the world had acknowledged the constitutionality of the Huerta Government, thus leaving Mr. Wilson isolated in his stand on recognition, did not move him in the least; the consequences to American lives and property in Mexico and along our southern border as a corollary to his stubborn stand were explained by the slogan: "We are too proud to fight." And during all of the bickering Wilson maintained in Mexico an Ambassador for a year and a half and afterwards a Charge d'Affaires, and Huerta appointed a Charge d'Affaires in Washington who was for more than a year recognized as such. The Department of State in Washington published constantly in its monthly bulletin the name of this Charge d'Affaires as the "Representative of Mexico." Lastly, the official relations between the governments were expressly and solemnly interrupted by the delivery of their respective passports to the Charges d'Affaires when the forces of the United States occupied Vera Cruz in April, 1914, fourteen months after Huerta took possession of the Government. The express recognition has little to do with the case if both governments treat each other reciprocally as such governments. It was fully within the constitutional rights of the United States to deny recognition to the Huerta Government, but to destroy Huerta, to throw him from power was an act contrary to the law of nations.

The reaction of the Mexican people to Wilson's war on Huerta was to strengthen him. It offered to Huerta the occasion of exhibiting himself as champion of the national dignity, as the defender of the sovereignty of Mexico against the intrusion of a foreign government. The European press so considered it. The people of various South American cities acclaimed Huerta as a hero, the paladin of the honor of the Latin race. The special embassy which Huerta sent to Japan was received with public enthusiasm and with great acclamations to the Mexican President.

The first step of President Wilson in the execution of his policy (of destroying Huerta) was that of stationing powerful naval squadrons in Vera Cruz and other Mexican ports. The Government of Huerta informed that of the United States that the Mexican constitution fixed a limit of one month for the stay of foreign vessels of war in the waters of the Republic, but the notice was disregarded and the ships remained in the ports. The stay of the war vessels in Mexican waters in defiance of the laws of the country irritated the public sentiment and served as a sad prologue to the second step of intervention which was the sending of Mr. John Lind to Mexico to invite Huerta to abandon his office. When this step, which was taken as the purpose of the United States to dictate to Mexico the class of government which it must have, became known to the public, a sentiment of indignation was manifest everywhere. Up to the arrival of Mr. Lind, Huerta's power was gradually slipping, but the Lind mission changed this. "Huerta, right or wrong," said everybody, "rather than accept a foreign imposition."

The Lind mission having failed Mr. Wilson launched a new attack against Huerta through the medium of the rebels who were operating in Northern Mexico close to the protection of the American border. This "revolution"—to which was given the name of "Constitutionalist" because its alleged object was the re-establishment of the Constitution— was increasing in the north of the Republic, thanks to the impetuous military action of "General" Francisco Villa. This counter-revolution furnished President Wilson with his new line of attack, namely strengthening the "Constitutionalists." For this purpose the prohibition against exporting arms and ammunition from the United States to Mexico, called the "embargo," was raised early in February, 1914, less than six months from the date when President Wilson told Congress: "It is now our duty to show what true neutrality will do to enable the people of Mexico to set their affairs in order again and wait for a further opportunity to offer our friendly counsels;" and "I shall follow the best practice of nations in the matter of neutrality by *forbidding* the exportation of arms or munitions of war of any kind from the United States to any part of the Republic of Mexico." * * * "We cannot in the circumstances be the partisans of either party to the contest that now distracts Mexico, or constitute ourselves the virtual umpire between them."

With this aid Villa was able to organize and arm a powerful force and the strength of the revolutionary movement against Huerta became formidable. But because not even with this aid did the power of Huerta disappear, the American Government influenced the French Government to interpose its veto to prevent certain French bankers from completing the loan which they had contracted with Huerta and of which he had received but one-third.

The embargo on all implements of warfare was raised February 3, 1914. Three days previously Secretary of State Bryan sent a note to all diplomatic missions of the United States in which he said in part:

There are no influences at Mexico City that can be counted on to do anything more than to try to perpetuate and strengthen the selfish oligarchical and military interests which it is clear the rest of the country can be made to endure only by constant warfare and a pitiless harrying of the north. The President is so fully convinced of this, after months of most careful study at close range, that he no longer feels justified in maintaining an irregular position as regards the contending parties in the matter of neutrality. He intends, therefore, almost immediately, to remove the inhibition on the exportation of arms and ammunition from the United States into Mexico. Settlement by civil war carried to its bitter conclusion is a terrible thing, but it must come now whether we wish it or not, unless some outside power is to sweep Mexico with its armed forces from end to end; which would be the beginning of a more difficult problem.

The day will come when the universal conscience will consider civil wars equally as abominable as international wars. Those who admit, aid and abet the warfare of classes and factions, with their result in wholesale murders, stupidly affect to blame nations that seek to impose some form of respect for law on barbarous peoples. It is only by an absurd kind of pharisaism that any one could pretend to oppose the intervention and occupation of Mexico by the United States at this time, as it was perfectly evident to the nations of the world that the Mexicans were incapable of maintaining any sort of political or moral order among themselves. So strong was this opinion that the United States realized, as expressed in its note lifting the embargo on arms, that unless a decided change for the better came soon, some outside power would sweep Mexico with its armed forces from end to end. Our Mexican policy, unaccompanied by intervention and occupation, resulted merely in permitting the collective accomplishment of crimes that are severely punished when committed by individuals.

CHAPTER IV

The Tampico Affair, the Occupation of Vera Cruz and the Overthrow of Huerta

President Wilson's efforts to destroy the Huerta Government finally met with success. Mention has been made of the protest by the Huerta Government as to American war vessels in Mexican waters. The city of Tampico, an important Mexican port, was, in April, 1914, practically besieged on land by the Carranza forces. The city was under martial law. Under these conditions, on the 9th of April, a paymaster of the United States Ship *Dolphin* landed at the Iturbide Bridge with a whale boat and crew to take off certain supplies needed by his ship, and while engaged in loading the boat was arrested by an officer and squad of men of the army of General Huerta. Neither the paymaster nor any one of the boat's crew was armed. Two of the men were in the boat when the arrest took place and were obliged to leave it and to submit to be taken into custody, notwithstanding the fact that the boat carried, both at her bow and at her stern, the flag of the United States. The officer who made the arrest was proceeding up one of the streets of the town with his prisoners when met by an officer of higher authority, who ordered him to return to the landing and await orders; and within an hour and a half from the time of the arrest orders were received from the commander of the Huertista forces at Tampico for the release of the paymaster and his men. The release was followed by apologies from the commander and later by an expression of regret from General Huerta himself. General Huerta urged that martial law obtained at the time, that orders had been issued that no one should be allowed to land at the Iturbide Bridge, and that our sailors had no right to land there. Our naval commanders at the port had not been notified of any such prohibition; and, even if they had been, the only justifiable course open to the local authorities would have been to request the paymaster and his crew to withdraw, and to lodge a protest with the commanding officer of the fleet. Admiral Mayo regarded the arrest as so serious an affront that he was not satisfied with the apologies offered, but demanded that the flag of the United States be saluted with special ceremony by the military commander of the port.

This incident was especially annoying as two of the men arrested were taken from the boat itself—that is to say, from the territory of the United States. But the reader must remember that for the past year, due to Wilson's war on him, General Huerta and his officials had retaliated by going out of their way to show disregard for the dignity and rights of the United States, and felt perfectly safe in doing what they pleased, making free to show in many ways their irritation and contempt. President Wilson saw his opportunity and seized it. He demanded that the apologies of Huerta and his representatives go much further, that they should be such as to attract the attention of the whole population to their significance, and such as to impress upon General Huerta himself the necessity of seeing to it that no further occasion for explanations and professed regrets should arise. Wilson therefore sustained Admiral Mayo in the whole of his demand that the flag of the United States should be saluted in such a way as to indicate a new spirit and attitude on the part of the Huertistas. In other words the conditions were of such a humiliating nature to Mexico that Huerta refused to comply. So President Wilson went before Congress and said:

I, therefore, come to ask your approval that I should use the armed forces of the United States in such ways and to such an extent as may be necessary to obtain from General Huerta and his adherents the fullest recognition of the rights and dignity of the United States, even amidst the distressing conditions now unhappily obtaining in Mexico.

In the discussion that followed, Mr. Underwood, the distinguished democratic leader, pronounced these unequivocal words: "*The flag has been dishonored* in a foreign land, on foreign soil. The President of the United States comes here today and though he has not asked you to declare war, asks you to sustain him in using the military forces of our Government to require *a decent respect for that flag* and an honorable consideration of your Government."

This appeal to Congress was made on April 20, 1914, and that very night, in obedience to the orders of the President of the United States, Admiral Fletcher, commanding the naval forces then stationed off Vera Cruz, Mexico, was directed to seize and hold the custom house at Vera Cruz and not to permit war supplies to be delivered to the Huerta Government or to any other party. In accordance with these orders the custom house was taken by a landing force on April 21, 1914, and by April 24th, the entire city was in the hands of the United States Navy.

General Funston was immediately dispatched to the "front" with a large force of regular troops of the United States Army, and on May 4th announced himself as Military Governor of Vera Cruz, and the adjacent territory under control of the armed forces of the United States. This territory was held until November 23, 1914, when the military forces of the United States evacuated Vera Cruz.

The repercussions of this occupation, as might have been expected, were manifold. Of course Americans resident and having business in Mexico suffered in their persons and property. A single illustration is enough and is covered in a telegram from the American Consul at Tampico to the Secretary of State under date of April 26, a few days following the taking of Vera Cruz:

Practically all Americans have been brought out of this Consular district. Two thousand have been sent to Galveston. Vast oil properties and interests have been totally abandoned, wells are left running wild, millions of barrels of oil in storage completely at mercy of natives. Other foreign interests safe. Interests abandoned by Americans have valuation of not less than two hundred million dollars.

But these casualties of American lives and property did not influence

President Wilson to deviate a hair's breadth from his determination to crush Huerta. This seizure of the important coastal city of Vera Cruz, cutting off from the Huertista Government about one-fourth of their total imports, amounting to approximately one million pesos a month, caused Huerta to resign the Presidency of Mexico July 15, 1914.

So Wilson won his war on Huerta, but in order to win he (the United States) had to do to Vera Cruz what Japan has done to Shanghai. Vera Cruz was taken and in the process some American marines were killed, some Mexican soldiers were killed, and some Mexican civilians (men, women and children), were also killed. A few weeks later President Wilson, in an oration at the funeral of these dead marines, said: "We have gone down to Mexico to serve mankind * * * We want to serve the Mexicans * * * a war of service is a thing in which it is a proud thing to die."

The Congress of the United States authorized the President to use the armed forces of the United States to exact from the Government of Mexico a suitable redress for an outrage to the flag and the dignity of the United States. In the funeral oration above no mention was made of our outraged flag. It seems that the object of occupying Vera Cruz was to "serve mankind"; but there are many who are convinced that the occupation of Vera Cruz was neither to avenge an insult to our flag nor to serve mankind, but was launched solely to destroy the Huerta Government.

In this connection it is interesting to note another insult to the flag, another outrage to the dignity of the United States which occurred two years later when Carranza was President of Mexico and so recognized by President Wilson. On the 17th of June, 1916, a proclamation was issued by Governor Flores of the State of Sinaloa, under orders from the central Carranza Government, stating that war would be declared on the United States of America. This proclamation was taken in Mazatlan as an actual declaration of war, so on June 18th the Mazatlan authorities published an order prohibiting any communication with the shore by any American man-of-war. The consul living in Mazatlan had no knowledge of this prohibition so that he could notify the United States Naval authorities in the harbor. A little after nine on the morning of the 18th the commander of the U.S.S. *Annapolis* sent in a boat with two officers; this boat was turned back with the advice that no communication was allowed with the shore. The boat took back a copy of the proclamation to the commander, and the commander immediately sent another boat in with the request that the authorities advise the Vice Consul and all Americans who wished to avail themselves of the opportunity, to come aboard the *Annapolis* for refuge. The officers had orders not to land, but upon nearing the wharf were invited to come up on the wharf and talk the matter over. Upon accepting this invitation they were immediately arrested and attacked by an infuriated mob of soldiers and civilians. They were protected by a few of the better class of Mexican officers from this mob, and were escorted under guard to the commandancia militar under arrest.

When these American Naval officers were seized by the Mexican officers, one of whom had invited them to come up on the wharf, the three seamen accompanying the boat from the *Annapolis* were ordered to get out of the boat. This they refused to do; the boat pushed off from the wharf, and almost immediately was fired upon by a squad of Mexican soldiers under the same captain who had invited the officers to come up on the wharf. One seaman was wounded in the beginning of the fight; the seamen returned the fire, wounding three Mexicans, one of whom died next day. The wounded American sailor also died.

The American Vice Consul pleaded with the local Mexican commander, General Mezta, for the release of these Naval Officers who had been captured through treachery. The Mexican General rudely declined. After considerable talk it was agreed to get the statement of the commander of the *Annapolis*. For this purpose the Consul was escorted to the wharf under armed guard where he took a launch and obtained from Commander Kavanaugh of the *Annapolis* a very concise, direct and diplomatic statement of his side of the affair. General Mezta also treated this letter with indifference and refused to release the officers, saying the matter had been referred to General Carranza, General Obregon and General Flores, and that they would have to reply to his telegram before he would release them. The Consul continued to plead for about an hour for he knew that if the officers were detained over night their lives would be in danger from the angry mob of soldiers and civilians who had been armed by the authorities. Finally the Consul told the General that if these officers were detained over night the affair would assume an international significance, which both he and his country would regret; moreover that should war be declared on account of this outrage, that not only would it be bad for his country but that he personally would suffer from angry Americans. This outburst was effective, for a few moments later General Mezta signed the release of the officers and they returned to their ship.

Admiral Winslow reporting this incident to the Secretary of the Navy stated:

The evidence is conclusive that uniformed officers of the Mexican Army and Mexican soldiers, without the slightest provocation, opened fire on USS *Annapolis* boat. I approve action of boat in returning fire. Commander Kavanaugh's action withholding fire from the ship's battery because of the certainty of killing noncombatants, and possibly Americans and foreigners, was good judgment. The prisoners would undoubtedly have been murdered had he bombarded. The outrage was wholly unprovoked, and I believe it to be a far more serious affront than the Tampico affair. The self-control and temperate action of Commander Kavanaugh prevented a situation which might have been the cause of immediate war.

Under date of July 13th, our State Department sent to Special Representative Rodgers in Mexico City the report of the Vice Consul and the message of Admiral Winslow and stated:

You are instructed to bring the foregoing to the attention of the de facto Government of Mexico, and to request that a full and searching investigation be made of this brutal attack upon American naval forces. You will also request that the Mexican officers and soldiers responsible for this serious affront be adequately dealt with by the proper authorities, pointing out that leniency in this case may lead to other unprovoked attacks upon American Naval forces that may hereafter visit Mazatlan.

You are directed to make known to the de facto Government that the Government of the United States must insist on adequate action being taken in this matter and that it desires to be informed of the steps the Mexican authorities propose to take in connection with this regrettable affair.

So far as the author can learn this matter died a natural death through neglect. This was in 1916, and for three years the Mexican Government had been receiving Wilsonian notes differing from an ultimatum only in that they contained no prescribed limitation of time for the performance of the demands made. We clearly and fully recited our grievances and demanded specific performance. Having assumed this position and having stated clearly to the Mexican Government that unless compliance with the demands made therein were forthcoming we should feel compelled to take such steps for the protection of our rights as might seem proper to us, we could not, with due regard to our dignity, prestige and consistency, retrace our steps, ignore the formal diplomatic exchanges, and reappear before the Mexican Government in the light of an humble supplicant. But this was exactly our position after three years of President Wilson's Mexican policy. Our Government had sent to the Mexican Government note after note which the Mexican Government could interpret only in one of two ways, viz: either the Mexican Government must yield, repair the damages it had done to us, and give clear guaranties for the future, or we would take some vigorous and drastic action with the purpose of securing redress for our wrongs, an abatement of the situation, and perhaps, incidentally, the downfall of a Government which had given us innumerable evidences of its bad faith, hostility and insincerity. As for three years the United States had failed to make good its threats, the Mexicans looked upon these notes as just pure bluff and treated them with the indifference and disrespect such a policy invited. President Wilson was ignorant of the Latin-American character. Those citizens of the United States who had been given the opportunity to study Latin-America and Latin-American conditions became more and more impressed with the circumstance that the government of these countries, alien in speech, customs and race, was, under our form of government a most difficult enterprise, and that each new burden which we assumed and each new adventure which we essayed would lead to the creation of additional burdens and the invitation to more perilous adventures. But President Wilson, submerged in his ignorance and blind to all worthwhile advice, continued to insist on the kind of government Mexico should have; his methods and policy being the opposite of what experience had taught, that these Latin-American countries should be dealt with justly and calmly but severely and undeviatingly. He failed to see that any other course was sure to bring disaster and forfeit to us, in the estimation of the Mexican people, the respect and awe with which they had been taught to regard us and would sacrifice the genuine benefits which spring from a consistent, firm, and well understood attitude in all international affairs. The unprovoked and brutal treatment of our naval officers and the murder of an American seaman in Mazatlan by Carranza soldiers is a point in fact.

Compare this incident, in which two American Naval officers were subjected to indignities and a marine who wore the uniform of the United States Navy was murdered while in a United States boat—that is to say, while on the territory of the United States—with the occurrence at Tampico. The Mazatlan incident was not made the motive of any intemperate discussion nor was any salute to the flag exacted nor any especial apology demanded. It was not Huerta who was involved but Carranza, favored and protected by the United States, and, therefore the offended flag remained offended, the insulted officials remained with their insults, and the dead sailor remained dead.

If, in the Tampico incident, where a naval officer was arrested but immediately released with apologies from the military commander and even from the defacto President of Mexico, President Wilson "regarded the arrest as so serious an affront that he was not satisfied with the apologies, but demanded that the flag of the United States be saluted with special ceremony by the military commander of the port," why was he, President Wilson, not equally insistent on proper redress for the Mazatlan outrage where *two* naval officers were arrested through treachery and then assaulted by a mob of civilians and soldiers and even had their lives threatened? If, in the Tampico affair, President Wilson considered it necessary that the apologies of General Huerta and his representatives should go much further, that they should be such as to attract the attention of the whole population to their significance, and such as to impress upon General Huerta himself the necessity of seeing to it that no further occasion for explanation and professed regrets should arise because the exterritoriality of the United States was violated when two seamen were forcibly arrested from a ship of war's small boat, why did he, President Wilson, not become equally solicitous over the Mazatlan case when a boat's crew was fired on by Carranza soldiers and an American sailor killed? If, in the Tampico affront, President Wilson considered the insult to the flag and the affront to the dignity to the United States so serious that he called upon Congress for authority to use the army and navy to exact more impressive apologies than had been offered, why did he fail to exact from Carranza full and complete disavowal of any intentional affront to the United States, and satisfactory punishment of Carranza's generals responsible for the treacherous, brutal and unprovoked assault upon our naval officers and the deliberate murder of the American sailor at Mazatlan, offenses similar to but vastly more serious than those of Tampico which resulted in such positive and drastic reprisals?

The answer is that the Tampico incident in April, 1914, was caused by Huertistas, that this insult to our flag presented the pretext for reprisals which the United States quickly grasped by seizing the important coastal city of Vera Cruz, thus cutting off from the Huerta Government all of the imports passing through that city. This huge loss of funds, from the impoverished Mexican Treasury, caused Huerta to resign in July, 1914. This was the fulfilment of President Wilson's threat "to cut him off from foreign sympathy and aid and from *domestic credit*, whether moral or material, and to force him out." While in the Mazatlan case in June, 1916, Carranza was the President of Mexico, placed in that position by his ally, the United States, and it would not have been good politics for the Wilson administration to have insisted that our insulted flag be suitable saluted, that the murderers of our sailor be adequately punished, or that we use the armed forces of the United States in such ways and to such an extent as might have been necessary to obtain from General Carranza and his adherents the fullest recognition of the rights and dignity of the United States, because this was the summer of 1916, on the eve of a presidential election, and to have used force to wipe out an insult to the Nation's flag, and to obtain justice for a murdered sailor, and to secure the fullest recognition of the rights and dignity of the United States would have caused war with the Carranzastas and this would have made ridiculous the democratic campaign cry: "He kept us out of war . . ."

Wilson's spineless and petulant Mexican policy is clearly pictured by Mrs. O'Shaughnessy, writing from Vera Cruz in April, 1914:

I think we have done a great wrong to these people, instead of cutting the sores with a clean, strong knife of war and occupation, we have only put our fingers in each festering wound and inflamed it further. In Washington there is a word they don't like, though it has been written all over this port by every movement of every war ship, and been thundered out by every cannon—WAR! What we are doing is war accompanied by all the iniquitous results of half measures, and in Washington they call it "peaceful occupation."

Chapter V

Carranza Becomes President

Mrs. O'Shaughnessy, in her very entertaining and instructive book, "A Diplomat's Wife in Mexico," says of Carranza:

Carranza is not a bloodthirsty villain, but the physically timid, greedy, conscienceless, book-reading kind. Those who have watched Carranza's long career, however, say that a quiet, tireless, sleepless greed has been his motive force through life, and his strange lack of friendliness to Washington is accounted for by the fact that he really hates foreigners, any and, all, who prosper in Mexico. He has none of the ability of Huerta and none of his force.

And Doctor E. J. Dillon in "Mexico on the Verge" says:

The circumstance should also be born in mind that in public affairs there is a kind of slowness which ripens and another which rots, and that the latter was a characteristic of the Carranza regime.

Although the taking of Vera Cruz by the United States was in the interests of Carranza, he resented this military maneuver and showed his resentment in a lengthy communication to our Secretary of State under date of April 22, 1914, in which he said in part:

But the invasion of our territory and the stay of your forces in the port of Vera Cruz, violating the rights that constitute our existence as a free and independent sovereign entity, may indeed drag us into an unequal war, with dignity, but which until today we have desired to avoid.

The reaction of Villa, Carranza's principal general, was just the reverse. Special Agent Carothers in a telegram to the Secretary of State dated April 23rd, said:

I have just dined with Villa. We discussed situation at length. He said there would be no war between the United States and the Constitutionalists; that he is too good a friend of ours and considers us too good a friend of theirs for us to engage in war which neither desired; that other nations would laugh and say: "The little drunkard has succeeded in drawing them in;" that as far as he was concerned we could keep Vera Cruz and hold it so tight that not even water could get into Huerta and that he could not feel any resentment. He said that no drunkard, meaning Huerta, was going to draw him into war with his friend; that he had come to Juarez to restore confidence between us.

My impression is that he is sincere and will force Carranza to accept his own friendly attitude.

Huerta resigned the Presidency in July, 1914, and a month later Venustiano Carranza made a triumphal entry into Mexico City and assumed the Executive Power of the Republic. His first act in his new office was to antagonize the Diplomatic Corps by ignoring them. The Constitutionalists, in the very hour of their success, disagreed. Villa, probably the most disinterested and purest patriot of the lot, suspected

Carranza of placing his personal ambition above the Revolution's cause. This suspicion became a conviction. In September, just one month from the entry into Mexico City, Villa repudiated Carranza and took the field against him.

Conditions in and around Mexico City grew steadily worse from the time Carranza made his triumphal entry in August, 1914. During the first three days of March, 1915, every business house in the city both large and small closed its doors, and the entire commercial traffic of a metropolis of over half a million inhabitants was completely paralyzed. This was due to the request of the military authorities that a special tax levy of twenty million pesos be paid for the ostensible purpose of relieving the poor whose situation had become really desperate due to the shortage of food stuffs. This shortage of food was due to the deliberate campaign of the military leaders desirous of starving the working classes into enlisting. In addition to a definite order forbidding the importation of cereals and other foodstuffs, all food possible to seize was shipped out of the city in furtherance of the scheme. When the merchants refused to pay this extraordinary tax General Obregon stated in a public address: "At the first attempt at riot I will leave the city at the head of my troops in order that they may not fire a single shot against the hungry multitude, as the merchants do not accept the invitation which was made to them to assist the people and prevent violence. . . I will not fire a single shot into any mob who may attempt to get what hunger has driven them to seize. Rather than to fire on my people I will evacuate the city leaving the selfish merchants who refused to contribute to their relief to manage their own defense."

This, of course, was an invitation by the authorities for the mob to loot the city.

This desperate situation was wired to our State Department by the Brazilian Minister to Mexico. The reply advised all Americans to leave Mexico. But the American citizens could not leave Mexico, because three times already they had left on the advice of our State Department. When the first advice came in 1911, many throughout the Republic left, some at complete sacrifice of the work of years. The first revolutions were victorious and many Americans returned. Another revolution occurred; the advice to leave was repeated and a second exodus took place with its inevitable hardships, losses and sacrifices. Optimistic reports published in the United States afterwards brought back many to their abandoned homes and neglected businesses where these had not been destroyed. There came a third warning to leave, which was still obeyed by increasing numbers and at greater sacrifices, immediately after the American occupation of Vera Cruz. After the Huerta regime and on encouraging advices as to peace prospects in Mexico many individuals and families again came back to resume the work that had been perforce abandoned and the Evacuation of Vera Cruz brought still more. A fourth exodus of our people was now impossible considering the large number in Mexico and the demoralized condition of public order and transportation. Financial difficulties were also too great for the average family to leave again on a voyage of thousands of miles. The Mexican peso had dropped from fifty cents American currency to *thirteen cents during eight changes* of the Supreme Power at the National Capital, since the overthrow of Porfirio Diaz in 1911.

Thousands of Americans and other foreigners scattered through the country found it quite impossible to leave their all, or abandon positions of trust in charge of properties or business of owners in the United States and elsewhere.

The Mexican political situation was more chaotic and helpless than ever. Foreigners of other nationalities, neighbors and friends of American citizens, all asked what course was open for them if conditions were such as to render it necessary for Americans to leave.

All foreigners—Americans, Europeans, and others were in Mexico under treaty and international rights by which their persons and property were assured of the protection usual in civilized countries. By subscribing to certain treaties and international rights the Government of the United States assumed an obligation toward Americans as its nationals, to the end that their persons and property be respected according to the letter of the obligation and international compacts by which the Mexican Government expressly agreed to give guaranties to foreigners residing in Mexican territory. These people were engaged in lawful and useful occupations. They asked from our Government effective guaranties of those rights and no more. This plea was based not only on the right of a citizen to protection in person and property when abroad but on that plank in the platform adopted by the National Democratic Convention, Baltimore, 1912, which stated: "Every American citizen residing or having property in any foreign country is entitled to and must be given the full protection of the Government of the United States both for himself and family."

Had our people obeyed this fourth summons to leave *en masse* such an exodus would have repeated the sad experience of the Belgians in 1914. For many it would have meant leaving behind the savings and other interests of a life time, and arriving in the United States or Europe virtually as charges on public charity or friends. Had all foreigners—business men, bankers, professionals—left on this fourth summons it would have paralyzed what remained of the country's commerce and industry. Innumerable business houses, banks, factories would have closed entirely; mines still working would have suspended; oil production would have ceased; many of the most important public service utilities could not have operated, and the general suffering already severe would have vastly increased. Such an exodus, advised by our State Department, would have thrown many worthy Mexican employees out of work and forced them to choose between starvation or joining some of the warring factions or plundering bands. The great majority of the fifteen millions of the Mexican people, unarmed and generally passive, who were the victims of violent deeds committed under the guise of revolution, prayed for an end to the reign of disorder, bloodshed, rapine and destruction into which the half measures of the Mexican policy of Woodrow Wilson had plunged them.

Owing to the rigid censorship of the mails and telegraph the above desperate condition of American citizens could not be communicated to their friends and relatives in the United States, so early in March, 1915, they sent the facts to our State Department through the Brazilian Ambassador, with the prayer that these facts be given to the press of the United States. They insisted that the experiences of the past four years pointed clearly to the fact that the time had come to accept the Mexican situation for what it was, and not for what it might be hoped it would become, or what interested leaders or warring factions might try to represent it to be. The record was written in facts which showed the true value of the pretentions of contending groups.

These people were sincere in their conviction, based on their illuminating if painful experiences of the past four years, that their duty required to take the people of the United States and of the civilized world into their fullest confidence and in the interests of humanity to lay before them the whole truth of the Mexican situation. In the performance of this duty they earnestly invited and ardently hoped and prayed for the aid and cooperation of the Wilson administration. They desired in so far as they could, to controvert the systematic misrepresentation of the Mexican situation, to put an end to evasion and repression of the truth in regard thereto, and especially as to their own situation and attitude. They were not surprised that General Carranza at this time should renew his promise "to exert himself to the utmost to protect lives and property of foreigners," but they insisted that the true value of this promise should be estimated by what General Carranza had done and decreed since his triumphal entry into the city of Mexico in August, 1914, viz: The arbitrary taking from Mexicans and foreigners of property including houses, horses, automobiles, carriages, furniture, money and crops; the issuing of decrees so in contravention of right, fairness and justice as to be almost incredible; the deliberate, persistent and ill-concealed attempt to starve a city of half a million inhabitants, depriving them of water, fuel and transportation; the shipping of defenseless women in locked cattle cars to Vera Cruz; the carrying away of the controllers of electric cars, thus paralyzing two hundred miles of city transit; the closing of the courts and schools; the holding of priests for ransom; the arrest and detention of 300 business men who had assembled at the request of General Obregon who was in charge of the City of Mexico; the persecution of Spaniards; the suppression of the mails and violation of sealed correspondence, both foreign and domestic; the removal of public archives and stripping of public buildings; the open invitation to riot and loot; the sacking of churches and desecration of images; the killing of men and outraging of women, both foreign and Mexican—were events too recent and well known to permit of their being overlooked in judgment. The wantonness of some acts rendered it impossible to accept the professions of these factions or their counsels as to the course to be pursued by foreigners.

It was the earnest desire of these Americans in Mexico to assist the Washington Government to find a solution for the perplexing international situation that existed, and to this end they requested that their efforts be regarded as made in good faith and that their knowledge

Francisco Villa

and experience of the Mexican situation be accorded full weight. They were willing to make sacrifices if through them any ultimate good might accrue to the Mexican people or American prestige, but they felt thus far the very opposite had been the result. They considered that American civilization was on trial and had a duty to humanity which no longer should be postponed.

Mexico was drifting toward total destruction from which a mistaken altruism was powerless to save her. This struggle did not represent the efforts of a people to secure liberty and civil rights, so much as a clash of personal ambitions and revenge. American citizens in Mexico looked to the administration for the protection which they believed it was their due to receive, and they further expressed the hope that their views might be given such publicity as might effectively assist the American people in forming a sound opinion of the Mexican situation; but President Wilson did not think "it would contribute to their welfare to grant their request to make public their appeal".

The stability of international finance depends very largely upon the security of private property wherever it may be located. Law and public sentiment in the United States have always made private property immune from government seizure, regardless of its ownership by our citizens, citizens of foreign countries or enemy aliens. In the case of enemy aliens international lawyers have many times pointed out that if a government permits foreign investors to place capital within its borders, it is morally obligated to protect such investments with the same care that it accords to the investments of its own people. If this concept of law and politics is not followed, bankers and investors would withdraw bank balances and new securities upon news of any international dispute. Such instability of foreign investments would make them highly speculative. In almost every address the President made up to our entry into the World War he made some reference to Mexico, dwelling upon the fact that 80 percent of her people had no part in any genuine participation in their government. He closed his eyes to the fact that Mexicans had never decided a presidential election without the use of bullets, and failed to realize that they could hardly be expected hastily to reach the decision to employ only ballots. Had he been as concerned over the international rights of American citizens resident in Mexico as he was over the hypothetical "liberties and permanent happiness" of the Mexican peon, the domestic quarrel in Mexico would have been settled in 1913.

As early as 1914 President Wilson tried to induce the warring factions to settle their differences through the agency of the "Niagara Conference", but this resulted in completed failure. Again in August, 1915, the United States and several South American countries issued an invitation to the various military factions to get together in the interests of peace and harmony. All approved but Carranza, so this also failed.

Chapter VI

Carranza and Villa

President Wilson was so absorbed in his altruistic theories regarding the "submerged 80%" that he failed to recognize the real peril and need of his countrymen resident in Mexico. He was entirely without experience with Latin American people, as his many notes to Huerta, Carranza, and others, conveying veiled threats which were never made good, indicate. He failed to discover that the Mexican diplomat was trained in a school which enabled him to lead one less sophisticated into a labyrinth of words away from the point at issue, only to end up at the beginning—nowhere.

Finally President Wilson showed his disappointment and exasperation over Mexico's domestic affairs in a statement issued for the consumption of the so called Mexican leaders dated June 2, 1915:

For more than two years revolutionary conditions have existed in Mexico. The purpose of the revolution was to rid Mexico of the men who ignored the constitution of the republic and used their power in contempt of the rights of the people; and with these purposes the people of the United States instinctively and generously sympathize. But the leaders of the revolution, in the very hour of their success, have disagreed and turned their arms against one another. All professing the same objects, they are neverless unable or unwilling to cooperate. A central authority at Mexico City is no sooner set up than it is undermined and its authority denied by those who were expected to support it. Mexico is apparently no nearer a solution of her tragical troubles than she was when the revolution was first kindled. And she has been swept by a civil war as if by a fire. Her crops are destroyed, her fields lie unseeded, her work cattle are confiscated for the use of the armed factions, her people flee to the mountains to escape being drawn into unavailing bloodshed, and no man seems to see or lead the way to peace and settled order. There is no proper protection either for her own citizens or for the citizens of other nations resident and at work within her territory. Mexico is starving and without a government.

In these circumstances the people and Government of the United States cannot stand indifferently by and do nothing to serve their neighbor. They want nothing for themselves in Mexico. Least of all do they desire to settle her affairs for her, or claim any right to do so. But neither do they wish to see utter ruin come upon her, and they deem it their duty as friends and neighbors to lend any aid they properly can to any instrumentality which promises to be effective in bringing about a settlement which will embody the real objects of the revolution—constitutional government and the rights of the people. Patriotic Mexicans are sick at heart and cry out for peace and for every self-sacrifice that may be necessary to procure it. Their people cry out for food and will presently hate as much as they fear every man, in their country or out of it, who stands between them and their daily bread.

It is time therefore that the Government of the United States should frankly state the policy which in these extraordinary circumstances it becomes its duty to adopt. It must presently do what it has not hitherto done or felt at liberty to do, lend its active moral support to some man or group of men, if such may be found, who can rally the suffering people to their support in an effort to ignore, if they cannot unite, the warring factions of the country, return to the constitution of the republic so long in abeyance, and set up a government at Mexico City which the great powers of the world can recognize and deal with, a government with whom the program of the revolution will be a business and not merely a platform. I, therefore, publicly and very solemnly, call upon the leaders of factions in Mexico to act, to act together, and to act promptly for the relief and redemption of their prostrate country. I feel it to be my duty to tell them that, if they cannot accommodate their differences and unite for this great purpose within a very short time, this Government will be constrained to decide what means should be employed by the United States in order to help Mexico save herself and serve her people.

This combined appeal and threat simply added to the contempt the Mexican leaders felt for the United States. About this time or shortly after, General Hugh L. Scott, Chief of Staff of the United States Army, was in El Paso, Texas, to confer with Villa. On his return to Washington he called at the White House to make his report to President Wilson. During the talk the General told Mr. Wilson there were rumors that he was going to recognize Carranza, and he urged him not to do it. The President did not reveal his intentions then, but he recognized Carranza a few months later, in October, 1915. General Scott never knew why. He asked the officers of the State Department, junior to the Secretary, why such a thing had been done and they said they did not know, for they had all advised against it a month previous to the recognition. The General said that information had always made the President's step a mystery to him.

Quoting from "Some Memories of a Soldier", written by General Hugh L. Scott:

The recognition of Carranza had the effect of solidifying the power of the man who had rewarded us with kicks on every occasion, and of making an outlaw of the man who had helped us. We permitted Carranza to send his troops through the United States by our rails to crush Villa. I did what I could do to prevent this but was not powerful enough. I have never been put in such a position in my life. After Villa had given up millions of dollars at the request of the State Department, expressed through me, they made him an outlaw. He was a wild man who could not be expected to know the difference between the duties of the State and War Departments, and might very well have thought that I had doublecrossed him, had he not had the confidence in me that he did. No white man, no Negro, no Indian, no Moro, nor any person, however humble, ever had as much right as Villa to believe I had turned against him, yet he telegraphed a mutual friend in New York that General Scott was the only honest man north of Mexico—he once included the President but now he dropped him out altogether.

This recognition of Carranza by Wilson was a contradiction of Wilson's Mexican policy, as outlined in his speeches from his message to the Congress in August, 1913, and in his letter of admonition to the factional chiefs of June 2, 1915. In all of his speeches on Mexico, Mr. Wilson emphasized that the only class of government he would recognize would be one organized in conformity with the constitution of the country.

On October 15, 1915, the United States recognized the Carranza Government as the de facto Government of Mexico, a military government with Carranza as the dictator—Carranza, who closed the tribunals of justice; who suspended the individual guaranties of the constitution; who permitted and authorized attacks upon religious liberty; who muzzled the press; who prohibited every political meeting or association; who issued no less than three decrees which *amended the Constitution of the Republic.*

In addition to these crimes against free government and the liberties of his people, crimes which Mr. Wilson pretended to abhor, during the month of September, 1915, one month previous to the recognition, and during the month of October, the month of recognition, the frontier of the United States along the lower Rio Grande was thrown into a state of apprehension and turmoil because of frequent sudden incursions into American territory and depredations and murders on American soil by Mexican bandits and Carranza soldiers, who took the lives and destroyed the property of American citizens, sometimes carrying American citizens across the international boundary with the booty seized. American garrisons were attacked at night, American soldiers killed and their horses and equipment stolen; American ranches raided, property stolen and destroyed and American trains wrecked and plundered. The attacks on Brownsville, Red House Ferry, Progreso Post Office and Las Paladas, all occurring during September, 1915, one month before recognition.

Not only were these murders characterized by ruthless brutality, but savage acts of mutilation were perpetrated. Representations were made to General Carranza and he was emphatically requested to stop these reprehensible acts *in a section which he had long claimed to be under the complete dominion of his authority.* Notwithstanding these representations and the promise of the local Mexican commander, General Nafarrate, to prevent attacks along the international boundary, in October, the very month of recognition, a passenger train was wrecked by bandits and several persons killed seven miles north of Brownsville, Texas, and an attack was made upon United States troops at the same place several days later. Since these attacks, leaders of the bandits, well known both to Mexican civil and military authorities, as well as to American officers, had been enjoying with impunity the liberty of the towns of northern Mexico. *The Carranzista authorities not only encouraged these murderers but gave them protection and aid as well.*

But apparently Carranza could do no wrong, for a few days following these murders the United States aided him to defeat Villa at Agua Prieta, a Mexican town opposite Douglas, Arizona, an important port of entry. Had Villa captured Agua Prieta, which he would have done had not the United States transported on American rails through United States territory a large Carranzista reinforcement to the Carranza garrison, he would have strengthened himself politically and added materially to his war chest.

The recognition of Carranza and the defeat at Agua Prieta so embittered Villa against all things American that he vowed vengeance. When we recall the concessions Villa had made to the demands of the United States we are forced to admit that he had cause for bitterness. Of all the factional chiefs he had proved himself the most friendly to the United States. As late as August, 1915, at the request of General Scott, he had returned to the owners more than a million dollars in property seized. When the United States seized Vera Cruz he said it was all right, and refused to get excited over the incident. Carranza was always our enemy: before recognition, at the time of recognition and afterwards; he showed no gratitude and was consistently antagonistic to the United States and her people.

After his defeat at Agua Prieta, thanks to the United States, Villa and his men drifted south across the desert and reorganized in the region of Rubio and Santa Ysabel, and started a campaign of harassment of both Carranzistas and Americans, which culminated in the attack on Columbus, N. M., in March, 1916.

Continuous bloodshed and disorders marked the progress of the Mexican quarrel, especially during the years of President Wilson's first administration. During these years the lives of Americans and other aliens were sacrificed; vast properties developed by American capital and enterprise were destroyed or rendered non-productive; bandits were permitted to roam at will through the territory contiguous to the United States and to seize, without punishment or without effective attempt at punishment, the property of Americans; while the lives of citizens of the United States who ventured to remain in Mexican territory or to return there to protect their interests, were taken, and the murderers were neither apprehended nor brought to justice. It would be difficult to find in the annals of the history of Mexico conditions more deplorable than those which existed during the period above mentioned.

The territory adjacent to our border towns soon became a favorite battle ground for Mexican revolutionists, as both sides knew our troops were forbidden actively to resent any damage to life and property which might result, and did result, from the wild firing of the battling forces. They also knew that if defeated they could find sanctuary on American soil but a few steps away. The many battles along our border resulted in our border towns being shot full of holes, and not only were buildings bullet scarred, but many of our people were killed and wounded by stray shots from Mexico, some of them in their own homes. These fights became so frequent that hotels in the border towns advertised their houses as bullet proof, thus assuring their guests safety from stray Mexican bullets. A good illustration of this state of affairs is the Siege of Naco.

Early in October, 1914, General Hill, commanding one faction of Mexican forces, took position at Naco, Sonora, separated from Naco, Arizona, by a broad street, threw up intrenchments to hold it, and was besieged by Maytorena. The two troops of the 10th U. S. Cavalry stationed there were reinforced by most of the 9th Cavalry, and on October 7th telegraphic orders were received for Colonel W. C. Brown, commanding the 10th Cavalry, to report with three troops and machine gun troop, 10th Cavalry, to Colonel Hatfield at Naco, Arizona. Troops left about two hours after receiving the orders and made the thirty mile march to Naco by night. The 9th Cavalry (Col. Guilfoyle) was assigned to the east section of the town and the 10th Cavalry to the west section, Colonel Brown marking the boundary with a row of flags. The fire of the contending Mexican forces was supposed to be parallel to the border line, but shots constantly fell on the United States side of the line. The

Mexicans secured ammunition without limit from United States sources: that for the besieged arriving at the railroad station on the United States side of the line. The fire, with the exception of a truce from October 24th to November 9th, was continuous until December 18th, being heavier by night than by day, and including fire from small arms, three inch shell, shrapnel, Hotchkiss revolving cannon, rockets, land mines, bombs, bugle calls and epithets!

Eight men of the 10th Cavalry were wounded and the regimental commander's tent was hit four times. As the situation became more grave, additional troops were sent, and as the Mexicans paid little attention to protests against their firing into U. S. camps, the latter about Oct. 14, were abandoned at night and eventually moved about a mile north of the line, along which outposts only, and these in bomb proofs, were maintained. The provocation to return the fire was very great, but so far as known not a shot was fired by the 10th Cavalry in retaliation. This high state of discipline called forth a special letter of commendation from the President, and the Chief of Staff in his Annual Report for 1915, page 18, referring to the conduct of the 9th and 10th Cavalry, said:

During the siege of Naco, Sonora, which was carried on for two and one-half months, the American troops at Naco, Arizona, were constantly on duty day and night to prevent the use of United States territory in violation of the neutrality laws. These troops were constantly under fire and one was killed and 18 were wounded without a single case of return fire of retaliation. This is the hardest kind of service and only troops in the highest state of discipline would stand such a test.

It would be tedious to recount instance after instance, atrocity after atrocity, to illustrate the true nature and extent of the wide spread conditions of lawlessness and violence which prevailed. From the middle of 1915, the date of the President's letter of admonition, to the Columbus raid, March, 1916, the frontier of the United States, especially along the lower Rio Grande, was in a state of constant apprehension and turmoil because of frequent and sudden incursions into American territory and depredations and murders on American soil by Mexican bandits and Carranzista soldiers.

Depredations upon American persons and property within Mexican jurisdiction were still more numerous. The American Government repeatedly requested in the strongest terms that the Mexican Government safeguard the lives and homes of American citizens and furnish the protection, which international obligation imposes, to American interests in the northern states of Nuevo Leon, Coahuila, Chihuahua, and Sonora, and also in the states to the south. For example: On January 3, 1916, the American Government requested the Mexican Government to send troops to punish bands of outlaws which had looted the Cusi mining property, 80 miles west of the city of Chihuahua, but no effective results came from this request. During the following week the bandit Villa with about 200 men was operating without opposition between Rubio and Santa Ysabel, a fact well known to Carranza authorities. Meanwhile a party of unfortunate Americans started by train from Chihuahua to visit the Cusi mines, after having received assurances from the Carranzista authorities in the State of Chihuahua that the country was safe, and that a guard on the train was not necessary. The Americans held passports or safe conducts issued by authorities of the de facto Government. On January 10, 1916, the train was stopped by Mexican bandits and 18 of the American party were stripped of their clothing and shot in cold-blood, in what is now known as the Santa Ysabel massacre.

General Carranza stated to the Agent of the Department of State that he had issued orders for the immediate pursuit, capture and punishment of those responsible for this atrocious crime. Yet, so far as known, but one man connected with this massacre was brought to justice by Mexican authorities. Within a month of this barbarous slaughter of inoffensive Americans it was notorious that Villa was operating within twenty miles of Cusihuiriachic (Cusi), and publicly stated that his purpose was to destroy American lives and property.

Despite repeated and insistent demands that military protection should be furnished to Americans, Villa openly carried on his operations, constantly approaching closer and closer to the border. He was not intercepted, nor were his movements impeded by the de facto Government, and no effectual attempt was made to frustrate his hostile designs against Americans.

While Villa and his band were slowly moving towards the American frontier in the neighborhood of Columbus, New Mexico, not a single Mexican soldier was seen in his vicinity. Yet the Mexican authorities were fully cognizant of his movements, for on March 6th, three days before the Columbus raid, as General Gavira publicly announced, he advised the American military authorities of the outlaw's approach to the border, so that they might be prepared to prevent him from crossing the boundary.

Villa's unhindered activities culminated in the unprovoked and cold-blooded attack upon American soldiers and citizens in the town of Columbus on the night of March 9th. The invaders were driven back across the border with heavy casualties by American cavalry, and fleeing south passed within sight of the Carranzista military post at Casas Grandes, no effort being made to stop them by the officers and garrison of the de facto Government stationed there.

These four years of humiliation for the United States were accurately epitomized by Senator Henry Cabot Lodge before the Lynn, Massachusetts, Republican Club, March 17, 1916, eight days following the Columbus raid, when he said in part:

The responsibility for the conditions in Mexico rests largely on the government of the United States. The present administration found Mexico and Mexican relations in bad condition. They have made these bad conditions infinitely worse.

The result of the President's war against General Huerta was the destruction of the only government that offered any prospect of order or peace or responsibility. Out of this miserable tragedy one thing commands our attention above all others: Americans have been murdered in Mexico, soldiers wearing the American uniform have been shot on the soil of the United States. The Americans robbed and slain in Mexico were entitled to our protection for their property and their lives. They have had none. Within a week Mexicans have invaded the United States, attacked an American town, and killed American citizens and American soldiers. This is the inevitable result of our failure to protect Americans in their rights both by land and sea.

We are told that the great cry of the Democratic party is to be that their President has kept peace. The virtue in keeping peace depends altogether on how it is kept. You can always keep the peace if you will submit to any wrong, to any outrage, to any oppression. The peace of this country would have been far better kept, we should have been in far less danger of war today, if we had kept it without humiliation, kept it in honor and without fear.

We all want peace. We are all against war if it can possibly be avoided; but we shall insist that American rights shall be protected at home and abroad.

Chapter VII

Events Preceding the Columbus Raid

From the time of Villa's defeat at Agua Prieta to the moment of the Columbus raid his movements were well known to the Carranzista authorities and in a general way to the United States authorities stationed along the border, but the American authorities had no knowledge of his intentions.

At the time of the massacre of the Americans at Santa Ysabel, January 10, 1916, by Villa bandits, Mr. George L. Seese, formerly correspondent of the Associated Press, was sent from Los Angeles, California, to El Paso, Texas, to assist in covering the story of this massacre.

While Mr. Seese was on this work, he was approached by a Mexican who represented himself as a personal representative of Villa, sent by Villa to the United States to assure the people of this country that Villa had absolutely nothing to do with the massacre of Americans at Santa Ysabel and that Villa deprecated it and intended to punish Pablo Lopez, a subordinate officer of the bandit forces, who had perpetrated the massacre. This Mexican stated to the newspaper man that Villa planned to come to the United States at some future time and bring proofs to this government that he had not ordered the massacre or countenanced it in any way. The Mexican and the correspondent had several conferences concerning Villa's coming to the United States in secret and going to Washington to see President Wilson in company with and under the protection of Mr. Seese.

Finally, about February 18, 1916, this alleged agent of Villa agreed to take a letter to Villa suggesting the wisdom of going to Washington and seeing the President. About a week later a verbal reply was received by Mr. Seese ostensibly from Villa, that he considered the plan feasible, and that he would be glad to accompany the Associated Press Correspondent to Washington, provided he could be assured of a safe conduct. On March 2nd, one week previous to the Columbus Raid, the Associated Press forbade their agent to continue with the scheme. Villa was so notified.

It should be stated here that Villa possibly fostered this scheme as a blind to his real intentions, as his private papers, found on the Columbus battle field, provided that he had planned as early as January 6th to make an attack on Columbus.

As regards Villa's guilt in connection with the Columbus Raid it is but fair to quote from pages 516-517, "Some Memories of a Soldier" by Major General Hugh L. Scott, who was Chief of Staff of the Army at the time of the Columbus Raid and was well informed of conditions in Mexico and on the United States-Mexican border in 1916. General Scott in referring to his influence over Villa, and Villa's confidence in Scott even after the recognition of Carranza by Mr. Wilson, said:

He (Villa) never lost confidence in me to the day of his death. The first thing he would ask after meeting Americans was after General Scott, although, when he sent an emissary to me at Washington I refused to have anything to do with him until I had proof from two Americans that he had cleared himself from his attack on Columbus. I have always believed he was too wise to make such an attack willingly.

It is certain that a member of the Associated Press made arrangements for Villa to come to Columbus with a view to conducting him to Washington, until Mr. Melville Stone, director of the Associated press, quashed the plan. Anyway, I have always believed that Villa came up to the border for the purpose of going to Washington, and found the plan quashed, that his men there, hungry and naked, got out of hand and started to loot the town against Villa's will. I am further guided in this belief by a surgeon of Albuquerque, N. M., who said that a Mexican boy, whom he took into the hospital and kept until he was well, told him that he had held Villa's horse while the raid was on, and that neither of them went into the town.

Mr. Seese had as complete and accurate information concerning Villa's movements immediately previous to his attack on Columbus as any American official on the border. Six days before the raid General Gavira, Mexican Commandant at Juarez, across the line from El Paso, informed him that his secret service had reported that Villa's intention was not to come across the border to make out a case in his own defense for the Santa Ysabel massacre, but to commit some act of violence that would compel the United States Government to intervene in Mexico.

This was reported to General John J. Pershing, commanding the 8th Brigade at Fort Bliss, close to El Paso. The General replied that he had heard similar stories so many times before that he was inclined to take them all with a grain of salt. All of the army officers stationed at Columbus felt as did General Pershing. For years, we of the border patrol, had heard many rumors which had never materialized. However, in this case, Colonel H. J. Slocum, commanding at Columbus, took all the precautions to intercept Villa which the reliable information available warranted. No one knew how many men Villa had with him. Our Government did not permit the United States Army authorities to send any experienced scouts or officers' patrols into Mexico. We had to depend upon Mexicans and Mexican renegades, a most unreliable source of information, as to the movements of Villa or any other Mexican bands.

The day before the raid a Mr. Riggs, head of the United States custom house at Columbus, told Mr. Seese that there had been any number of similar reports that Columbus was to be raided. He said that these reports had come in so often that the people of Columbus were inclined to discount them. Mr. Seese was kept informed of Villa's movements by General Gavira. As late as March 6th Gavira reported that Villa was at Palomas, six miles south of the border and about ten miles south of Columbus, a report obviously incorrect.

This report could have been easily checked by an officer's patrol from Columbus but the President's Mexican policy proscribed any such simple source of information.

As late as March 8th Mr. Seese, the Associated Press representative, received reports that Villa and his men were at the same time at three different and widely separated places, viz: at Palomas, about eight miles south of Columbus; on the Casas Grandes River, about forty miles southwest of Columbus; and at the Rancho Nogales, about sixty-five miles southwest of Columbus. This last report was entitled to consideration as it was wired in by the American caretaker of the ranch, who stated that Villa personally was at the ranch house with his entire force the afternoon of March 8th, but it has since been determined that this could not be true. At the time of its receipt the report was accepted by the army officers at Columbus and by Mr. Seese as correct. These reports are quoted to show the "fog of war" that surrounded Villa and his band a few hours before his attack on Columbus.

During the evening of March 7th a Mexican called "Antonio," referred to by the agents of the Palomas Land and Cattle Co. as an old employee, came into Columbus and reported to agents there that that morning he and forcman McKinney had seen Villa and about 500 of his men making camp on the Casas Grandes River. He stated that McKinney and another American namcd Corbett rode into the Mexican camp and were made prisoners, that the Mexicans chased Antonio but he managed to escape and made his way to Columbus. Antonio reported this to Colonel Slocum that same night.

Colonel Slocum, after much effort and the promise of money, succeeded in persuading Antonio to return to Mexico and find out all he could concerning Villa's whereabouts. Antonio returned to Columbus the evening of March 8th and reported to Colonel Slocum that Villa's main body had gone eastward from Boca Grande to Guzman, and that about one hundred men had taken the road towards Palomas, and later turned southward towards Vado de Fusiles. This report was made to Colonel Slocum in the presence of Major Elmer Lindsley and Captain George Williams, the regimental adjutant. Antonio was closely questioned but he was positive that his statements were correct. As this report of Antonio was contradicted a few days after the fight by high officials of the Palomas Land and Cattle Company it is of military importance to emphasize right here just what Antonio did report to Colonel Slocum. Colonel Slocum's Spanish had its limitations and Antonio's English was not equal to this occasion, so Major Lindsley acted as interpreter. The following is a quotation from Major Lindsley's signed statement:

Tuesday, March 7, 1916, McKinney was killed at Boca Grande in the forenoon, and the matter reported to Colonel Slocum that afternoon or evening. Wednesday, March 8th Antonio made his ride into Mexico and reported to Slocum that evening.

Antonio reported that he had gone to Boca Grande and found the place deserted. That Villa's gang had left about 3:00 A. M. that day, March 8th, as the ashes in the camp fire were still warm; that he had followed the trail as far as the Vado de Fusiles, where the trail split, some, about 120 more or less he thought, had gone towards Palomas and then turned south, and the rest had kept on down the river towards Guzman.

From a high point near the Vado de Fusiles he had seen through his field glasses two or three mounted men on the road down the river towards Guzman, and had deemed it best to return to the Gibson Ranch and report to me.

Slocum had sent him to me at the Gibson Ranch that morning early, with a letter to me to furnish him with a rifle and a pair of glasses, and told me what instructions to give him.

He reported back to me at the Gibson Ranch just at sundown, Wednesday, March 8th, and I took him in the Ford car to Slocum, who had no working knowledge of the Mexican language.

His report sounded intelligent and I believed it and still do—but not so strongly as I did then—I suspect that Villa was then on the Casas Grandes River between the Vado de Fusiles and the Vado de Piedras, resting until dark; and that if Slocum had had the authority to send a combat patrol instead of a hired spy we would have gotten definite knowedge of Villa's whereabouts then on the 8th. Slocum personally paid Antonio twenty dollars as he had promised him. I left Columbus about 11:00 P. M. in the car and returned to my camp at Gibson's.

In view of young Marshall's statement to his father (Marshall, senior, President Palomas Land and Cattle Co.) that Antonio reported to Slocum that Villa was on the Boca (Casas) Grandes River and "headed this way" it would seem wise to stress that Antonio actually did report, viz: that *Villa's trail led on down the river from Vado Fusiles,* and to insert right at this point a sketch (not printed) showing how the river runs easterly from Boca Grande to Fusiles, and then turns southward towards Guzman and *away* from the United States.

I well remember my anxiety during the night of the 7th and the day of the 8th. Antonio's report of the capture of McKinney, and of the presence of Villa with a large force at Boca Grande was evidently true. Antonio was too scared to be lying. It was the first *definite*, believable report we had had of Villa's whereabouts, and we were all wondering where he would strike next. My personal opinion was that it would be *west* of Gibson's, at the little ranches near the line, or at a railway train. I had no idea that he would strike my camp at Gibson's, though if he had we would have licked him, same as Slocum did at Columbus, only probably not so hard.

This information was all Colonel Slocum could get from Mexico. Carranza troops at the border gate to whom he appealed would do nothing to help.

Now let us consider how much territory Slocum was required to cover and what troops were at his disposal. The sector of ground assigned to the 13th Cavalry was along the border from Noria, N. M., on the east to Hermanas, N. M., on the west a distance in an air line of about 65 miles. The order assigning this sector to the Columbus command stated that it would be patrolled, but the manner in which the patrolling would be done, was left to the discretion of the commanding officer at Columbus. The force under the command of Colonel Slocum consisted of the Headquarters and Machine Gun Troops and seven Rifle Troops of the 13th Cavalry, aggregating about 21 officers and 532 enlisted men.

These forces were disposed as follows: Headquarters and Machine Gun Troops and four Rifle Troops (12 officers and 341 men less 79 non-combatants) in camp at Columbus; two troops (7 officers and 126 men plus a detachment of 25 men from other troops of the Columbus garrison) under the command of Major Elmer Lindsley, at Gibson's Line Ranch, 14 miles west of Columbus; one troop (2 officers and 65 men) under Captain Jens E. Stedje, at the Border Gate, about three miles south of Columbus.

These troops were ordered to take the following precautionary measures: The command at the border gate was ordered to send out patrols at irregular intervals, day and night, to the east as far as monument,

No. 19, a distance of six miles; and on March 7th was directed to send a special patrol 20 miles to the east, to remain out all night and to return next day, March 8th. This was less than 24 hours previous to Villa's attack on Columbus. This command was also instructed to establish an officer's patrol at Moody's Ranch, 4½ miles west of the border gate, and to require this patrol to send out smaller patrols as far as monument No. 27, about 4 miles west of Moody's, connecting at monument No. 27 with patrols from Gibson's Ranch six miles west of monument No. 27.

Major Lindsley's command, at the Gibson Line Ranch, was ordered to send out officer's and noncommissioned officer's patrols at irregular intervals during the day and night, covering about six miles to the east to monument No. 27 connecting with patrols from the Moody Ranch, and about ten miles to the west to monument No. 35, thus covering 44 miles of border line. The only weak link in this chain of precaution was the fact that the Mexican policy of the United States forbade patrolling south of the international boundary line.

In addition to the above exterior guards there was an interior guard consisting of three regular posts with their reliefs, a watchman, and, during the night, a patrol of one noncommissioned officer and three privates. This patrol covered the town and the outmost limits of the camp under the direction of the officer of the day, sometimes mounted and sometimes dismounted. There were about 30 men on duty along the line of stables.

From the early fall of 1915 to the raid on Columbus, March 9, 1916, the author was a Major in the 13th Cavalry, commanding the 3rd squadron and acting as executive officer of the regiment (in charge of all tactical training). My duties brought me in close and confidential touch with Colonel Slocum. I knew of the many reports coming in about Villa; I know of Colonel Slocum's dispositions of troops and approved of all he did. On the afternoon of March 7th I patrolled about 15 miles east of the border gate. Close to midnight of March 7th I accompanied Colonel Slocum to the border gate to interview the commanding officer of the Carranzista troops stationed there. When these soldiers heard our horses approaching, they sprang to arms and took shelter designed to offer protection from attack from the direction of the *United States.* Their conduct showed all the symptoms of a guilty conscience. I believed then and I believe now they were aware of Villa's movements and intentions and I am convinced some of them took part in the attack. In this interview less than 30 hours previous to the attack, this Carranzista officer denied any knowledge of Villa or his movements.

Colonel Slocum, denied by the Government the only sure method of locating Villa and determining his intentions, that is by contact through officers patrols, turned to other sources for information. In testifying before an investigating committee he stated in part:

I had a number of times questioned a number of supposedly friendly Mexicans in town, and among them a Mexican of the old type, a man who was far above the average, who was Spanish teacher for a number of my officers, and whose daughter was a Spanish teacher in my household, and who had every reason for being under obligations to the Americans at Columbus. My family paid the rentals for his house, and in affection and in every way we felt most kindly toward this Mexican and his family, but I could learn nothing. The civil authorities in town I frequently questioned.

The American Collector of Customs worked earnestly with me and endeavored in every way possible to get information from across the line. I lost no opportunity, however small, to get information. I was satisfied there were Villa sympathizers and spies in town, but they were constantly coming and going, as the supplies for the little town of Palomas, Mexico, and the Carranza Garrison (at the border gate) had to come from Columbus, so this opened up a constant communication, authorized and necessary for the Carranzistas. Getting information as to what was going on south of the border was almost an impossibility. The Palomas Land and Cattle Company, that controlled thousands of acres immediately south of the border, was just as anxious as I was to learn what was going on south of them. They had their cow men in there all the time, Americans and Mexicans, and they would frequently come to me for information, which, such as I had I gave them, but the fact that they, whose work took them south of the border with their cattle, knew nothing, shows how impossible it was for anyone else to get anything like accurate information.

The fact that Villa was assisted by spies in the town was shown by the knowledge the enemy had of the houses of officers. In the early part of the fight certain officers were cut off from the main camp. These officers heard voices in the dark pointing out certain houses of Americans and certain of Mexicans. The Mexicans houses were not attacked.

The whole situation as regards Villa's movements and intentions was clouded by so many conflicting reports that it was impossible for anyone to formulate a clear view of the situation. For example, in addition to the reports already quoted, on March 5th or 6th, Colonel Slocum received a confidential letter from Department Headquarters (General Funston commanding) stating that *reliable* information had been received that "Villa intended to cross the border and give himself up to American authorities; that there was another rumor that Villa intended to raid American towns along the border, but this had been received from *unreliable* sources."

Colonel Slocum's problem, and his solution of it, might be better appreciated by the reader if we present in brief form its salient features.

(1) For years the cry of "Wolf" had been heard along the border.

(2) The town of Columbus was known to contain a number of Villa sympathizers.

(3) The Carranza garrison at the border gate was unfriendly to the United States.

(4) The town and the camp of the U. S. troops were so nearly one and the same that free circulation of the civilian element had to be permitted both day and night.

(5) The small town of Columbus and the camp were unlighted: no electricity, no gas, and but little kerosene was used. On a dark night, such as the hour selected for this attack, a sentinel or member of a patrol could not see twenty feet in front of him. It was an easy matter for lightly shod Mexicans to sneak into the open stable sheds, in this darkness and cut the horses loose. A requisition for oil and street lamps to care for this situation had been previously disapproved.

(6) Colonel Slocum was forbidden to get in touch with Villa's band

or get any information from south of the border by the usual military methods, such as officers' patrols.

(7) Under these conditions it was an easy matter for an enemy to concentrate immediately south of the border without being seen or suspected, and attack the camp and Columbus when notified by spies of the most favorable opportunity.

(8) The United States was at peace with Mexico and all Mexican factions so that an attack from Mexico was not a logical thing to suspect.

(9) The long border line to be patrolled, 65 miles, contained many isolated ranches and small settlements, with women and children to murder, horses and cattle to steal; while the railroad paralleling the border but three miles north offered a splendid opportunity to Villa to indulge in his favorite sport of train wrecking.

(10) There were but 266 fighting men with which to protect life and property and repulse a night attack by a force estimated to be from 500 to 3000 men.

How did Colonel Slocum and his men meet this attack? After the alarm was given by the sentinel, the command assembled with commendable promptness and soon gained control of the situation, driving the Mexicans from the town and camp with a comparatively small loss: 7 soldiers killed and five wounded; 8 civilians killed and 2 wounded. Considerable loss was inflicted upon the Mexicans. Villa admitted a loss of 190, which speaks well for the discipline and morale of the American command.

In testifying before an investigating board Colonel Slocum tersely and clearly described the conduct of his men in this fight when he said "In my opinion, after 40 years service, a more gallant or plucky fight by American troops is not a matter of record."

CHAPTER VIII

Villa's Raid on Columbus, New Mexico

The actual fight is described in the official reports of the officers who participated. I shall quote a few. They are mostly in military form and do not dwell upon the many heroic acts of the troops, but the reader, knowing the terrible odds, can read between the lines and thrill with pardonable pride at the splendid response made by this small command of regular United States Cavalry to the challenge from the "Lion of the North" (Villa).

At the time of this attack Columbus was divided into 4 sections by the El Paso and Southwestern Railway running east and west and a wagon road running north and south from Guzman in Mexico to Deming in New Mexico. The town, consisting of scattered houses and stores, was located principally in the northeast section, while the camp lay in the southwest section. The distance from the international boundary to the railroad is about three miles. The camp was bounded on the west by the Deming-Guzman wagon road, and on the north by the railroad. The region consisted of a broad plain covered by mesquite and sloping gently to the south.

The headquarters building, the shack for the officer of the day, a shack occupied by the surgeon, and the quartermaster store house were on the west edge of the camp on the Guzman-Deming road; the guard house and stables were located on the east edge of camp, and the barracks and mess shacks lay in between. In addition to the Guzman-Deming road another road meandered through the eastern part of camp. These roads were open to traffic night and day.

The barracks were flimsy wooden structures, the stables were open sheds, but the mess shacks and hospital were bullet proof, made of adobe (mud) bricks. The Guzman-Deming road had a deep ditch paralleling it on its western side. Beyond this ditch to the west was a knoll known at that time as Cootes Hill, named for Captain Cootes of the 13th Cavalry. Between this hill and the ditch was a 'dobe house occupied by two officers. The other officers of the regiment were quartered throughout the village but not more than three or four hundred yards distant from camp. This arrangement had existed for several years.

The Mexicans crossed the international boundary line at a point about three miles west of the border gate. They sifted across in small bands, united at a point safe from observation from our patrols, then marched northeast until within about one half mile of the American camp when they split into two attacking columns. The first column moved to the south of camp, then east and attacked the stables from a southeasterly

Columbus, New Mexico, After the Raid. Showing the Burned Area

After the Raid. Results of Tompkins' Pursuit

After the Raid. Burning Buildings at Columbus

direction. The second column crossed the drainage ditch immediately west of the camp at the custom house, where they divided, the first half attacking the camp from the west and the second half moving into the town where they proceeded to loot, murder and burn.

Private Fred Griffin, Troop "K," 13th Cavalry, was the first man killed in the fight. Griffin was a sentinel on post No. 3, around the regimental headquarters, so he was nearest to the first point of attack by the Mexicans. He challenged a Mexican who answered by shooting the sentinel, but Griffin killed this Mexican and two others before he died.

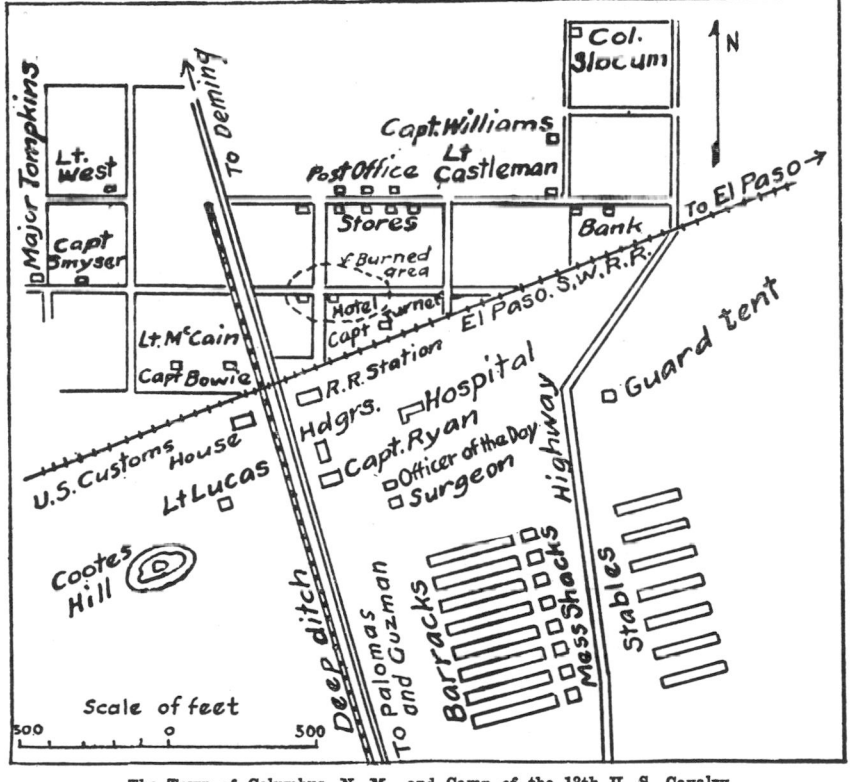

The Town of Columbus, N. M., and Camp of the 13th U. S. Cavalry

Lieutenant James P. Castleman, the officer of the day, hearing the firing, rushed out of his shack and as he turned the corner of the building, collided with a Mexican whom he promptly killed. Sizing up the situation at a glance, he ran to his troop barracks where he found his men formed. Sergeant Michael Fody of this troop ("F") describes what follows:

Just as we cleared the width of the barracks to the lane leading towards headquarters, Lieutenant James P. Castleman came running to me with his revolver in his hand and took command of the troop. We proceeded towards headquarters and after advancing about two hundred yards we encountered a heavy fire, so close that the flash almost scorched our faces.

Instantly every man in the troop dropped to the ground and opened fire. On account of the darkness it was impossible to distinguish any one, and for the moment I was under the impression that we were being fired on by some of our own regiment, who had preceded us to the scene. The feeling was indescribable, and when I heard Mexican voices opposite us you can imagine my relief. As soon as there was a lull in the fighting, Lieutenant Castleman ordered the troop on towards the town, where the heaviest firing was concentrated.

To my surprise, at the command "Forward march," every man jumped to his feet without a scratch and advanced. After crossing the railroad track we had our first man hit, Private Jesse P. Taylor, who was shot in the leg. I told him to lie down and be quiet and that we would pick him up on our return. Advancing about ten yards farther Private Revielle tripped over the barbed wire, discharging his piece in front of his nose, the concussion of which made his nose bleed. We made about four stands in about 500 yards. Private Thomas Butler was hit during the second stand but would not give up and went on with us until he was hit five distinct times, the last one proving fatal.

We advanced and took position on the main street near the town bank, having a clear field of fire. For over an hour we lay in this position but were unable to do effective work on account of the darkness. As soon as it began to light up our ammunition was getting low. I sent Private Dobrowalski to the guard house after some ammunition, he had to get three Mexicans who disputed his way before he could comply with his orders.

When the Mexicans set fire to the Commercial Hotel, the blaze illuminated the section. We were then in the dark and had the advantage. The group of which I was a member, numbering 25 men under Lieutenant Castleman, was the largest group under one command during the fight. Our forces were scattered in little bunches throughout the camp and vicinity but did very telling work. As soon as the light was bright enough we made every shot count and soon thoroughly discouraged the invaders. About 6:30 the Mexican bugler sounded "recall," it was a welcome sound. The Mexicans began immediately to retreat. Major Frank Tompkins obtained permission from Colonel Slocum to give pursuit.

While the sentinel on post No. 3 was killed at the start of the fight, Private John D. Yarborough, sentinel on post No. 1 at the guard house, was very badly wounded in the right arm when that side of the camp was attacked, but he fought through the entire action with his arm hanging useless.

The part played in this action by the machine gun troop is told by its gallant commander, Lieutenant John P. Lucas.

Lieutenant Lucas reported for duty to the 13th Cavalry in October, 1914, having just arrived from a tour in the Philippines. He describes his first impressions of Columbus as follows:

The town of Columbus, as seen at 4:00 A. M. did not present an attractive appearance. I found later that it also failed to do so in broad daylight. A cluster of adobe houses, a hotel, a few stores and streets knee deep in sand, combined with the cactus, mesquite and rattle snakes of the surrounding desert were enough to present a picture horrible to the eyes of one who had just spent three years in contact with the vivid colors and exotic atmosphere of the Philippines.

I was assigned to Troop "A," Captain Alexander H. Davidson. This troop had been sent temporarily to Douglas, Arizona, so I was attached temporarily to Troop "D," which was very ably commanded by Captain Walter C. Babcock. I served, however, very little with either "A" or "D" because in January, 1915, I was assigned to command the Machine Gun Troop of the regiment, and with that troop I remained for over two years. Life at Columbus was not exciting. There was little to do and plenty of time to do it in. As I look back on it, however, I forget the sand storms, the heat and monotony of existence in this sun-baked, little desert town. I forget the habit of the rattlers to occupy our houses. I forget also the fact that the nearest tree was in El Paso, 75 miles away. I remember only the pride with which I commanded my troop. Some job, too, because the Machine Gun Troop had been organized by transferring men from other troops, and it requires no unusual deductive powers to determine which ones I got. I loved them all, and the worse they were the more I loved them. They caused me considerable worry, and they were hard to handle, but they were fighting men all of them.

Three exciting events took place during my sojourn at Columbus. First the "Golden States" passed through every day going east. This occurrence was attended regularly by all those present for duty. Second, the "Golden States" passed through every day going west. This was attended also by all those present for duty. Third, Villa raided the camp and town on March 9, 1916. This, likewise, was attended by all those present for duty.

As to the events preceding the Villa raid I hesitate to give my views. Any statement I should make would be merely hearsay, as I spent the week previous thereto playing polo in El Paso.

I reached camp at 12:00 o'clock midnight, March 8-9, on the same old "Drunkard Special," going in the other direction this time, and went immediately to my quarters. I lived with Lieutenant Clarence C. Benson in an adobe house about 50 yards west of camp.

I found that Benson had gone to the border, his troop being stationed at the gate, and had taken all the ammunition out of my revolver. In order to reload it I had to open the trunk room, move a lot of boxes, and get some more ammunition out of my trunk. That I did this must have been due to pure "hunch" because ordinarily I wouldn't have taken the trouble; I had seen no one in camp and was not aware that conditions were at all serious. This was the second "hunch" that I had had that evening. The first had caused me to return from El Paso immediately after the last game of the tournament, not waiting until the following day.

About 4:30 A. M. I was awakened by some one riding by the open window of my room. I looked out, and although the night was very dark, I saw a man wearing a black sombrero riding towards camp. From the sounds I heard, it seemed to me he had quite a few companions and that the house was completely surrounded. I knew who they were because Villa's officers affected the type of headgear I had noticed. We heard later that this party was composed of Villa himself and 35 or 40 of his officers. They were the only ones who approached on horseback.

I got hold of my gun and stationed myself in the middle of the room where I could command the door, determined to get a few of them before they got me. I was saved, however, by a member of the guard, and I have always felt that I owed him a great debt of gratitude. Unfortunately he was killed. This soldier was posted at regimental headquarters, which was within sight of my house. He evidently saw the Mexicans approaching because he opened fire on them and they immediately left my house and charged him. They galloped right on through camp and down to the stables which were four or five hundred yards east of the barracks.

When the greasers left my house, I was able to get out and follow them on into camp to turn out my men. In the dark I was unable to find my boots so that I was forced to go barefooted for about an hour and a half and had very little skin left on the soles of my feet. It took me over six months to get all of the sand burrs out. The sentinel who had saved my life had gotten one Mexican but had been shot through the belly and was dying when I went by.

I reached my barracks and told the acting first sergeant to turn out the men and follow me down to the guard tent. The guard tent was near the stables and standing orders required that we keep the machine guns under lock and key in the guard tent as they could be sold to the Mexicans for five or six hundred dollars apiece. Without waiting for my troop I took two men, a corporal and the horseshoer, and proceeded immediately to the guard tent. My idea was to get a gun out and in action to keep the Mexicans out of camp. By this time the town was full of them.

So far I had seen no other officers. All those who lived in the town, and a majority of them did, had been surrounded in their houses and had been unable to get out. Two officers, Lieutenant Stringfellow and myself, lived in camp, and were the only ones present in the first phase of the conflict. (Note by author: Lieutenant Castleman, officer of the day was in the fight up to his neck at this time). The officer of the day was required to sleep in a small adobe house in the center of camp. I had looked into this house as I passed and had seen that it was empty. Lieutenant James P. Castleman was officer of the day and it developed later that he had turned out his troop, I have forgotten which one he commanded, and marched it over to town, where he took station in front of his residence. (Note by author: And opposite the bank).

The Mexicans were poor shots and to this fact we certainly owed our light casualty list. One of them fired at me with a rifle while I was on my way to the guard tent. He missed me, even though he was so close that I easily killed him with a revolver and I was never noted for my excellence in pistol practice.

We reached the guard tent and got out one of the guns. The sentinel on post No. 1 was lying across the door of the tent. He died later. The three of us set the gun up where we could command one of the crossings over the railroad. It was very dark but we could see the flash of the Mexican rifles. They burned up thousands of rounds of ammunition. As I remember the affair, the corporal acted as gunner while I loaded the piece. The gun was the old Benèt-Mercier, a very complicated weapon, which required perfect conditions in order that it might function. The conditions not being perfect the gun jammed after a few rounds, and we left it in position and went after another. The corporal's remarks were enlightening but not printable. The jam was reduced later and the gun returned to action.

By this time the remainder of the troop had arrived and I stationed the guns in what I considered to be strategic positions to fire on the Mexicans in town. Also about 30 men with rifles had shown up, and these I deployed along the railroad track to fire on the same target. Lieutenant Stringfellow also came up about that time, and, being senior to him, I sent him with some men to protect our left flank from any further invasion from the west.

This may sound like an account of "Alone at Columbus," but, as a matter of fact, none of the officers who were marooned in town were able to get to camp until our fire had cleared up the situation to some extent. About the time I got my "army" nicely deployed the greasers set fire to the hotel in town. This lit up the terrain so effectively that we were able to see our targets very plainly. Also Castleman's move to town with his troop proved to be strategically correct as it enabled us to bring a cross fire on the enemy. The Mexicans stood it for a few minutes only, when they commenced to fall back. Captain Hamilton Bowie was the first officer to be released and he immediately came to camp.

I turned over my command to Captain Bowie, and, taking a few men with me, worked around the enemy left into town. My idea was to clear the town and do what I could to protect the families of officers from the greasers. To my surprise I found Castleman and his men there already. I had no idea of his whereabouts before. It was just about daylight when I joined Castleman and a few minutes later the Colonel appeared. I then returned to camp and, after daylight, was sent by the Colonel with 15 or 20 men to relieve Captain Stedje at the gate and allow his troops to pursue the enemy who were, by this time, in full retreat.

I was criticised rather severely in the papers, and even in the halls of Congress for allowing my guns to jam. As a matter of fact the four guns used up about five thousand rounds *apiece* in the hour and a half they were in action, which was much more efficiency than the most sanguine had ever expected them to display.

The rumor that they had jammed was started by a private of the Hospital Corps who had been sent to El Paso with the wounded. This man could have known nothing about the circumstances because he, in company with some others of equal daring, had barricaded themselves in the hospital, and not only refused to join in the war themselves but also refused to allow some of my men to enter when the latter wished to replace a firing pin in a place where a light could be struck with safety. Needless to say the hospital was of bullet proof construction.

We were also criticised for taking so few prisoners. We did take, I believe, five wounded men and they were, I understand, later tried and hanged for murder. As a matter of fact no quarter could be shown with safety. I, myself, was fired at by a wounded man the bullet striking an adobe wall about six inches from my head, and I retaliated. This was not only the natural, but, I am convinced, a necessary thing to do.

I had five men in my troop on the casualty list. One of these men, Sergeant Dobbs, was shot through the liver but refused to leave his gun. He continued firing until he died from loss of blood. I recommended this man for the Medal of Honor, and later, for the Distinguished Cross, but have never heard from either recommendation. One man was shot through the jaw, and three others had minor injuries. Only one man, Dobbs, was killed.

We picked up about 67 dead greasers in the camp and town and burned them the following day. It is impossible to say what the Mexican casualties were, but they must have been heavy because the mesquite was full of them. Few of their wounded could have survived.

The above account by Lieutenant (now Major) Lucas, told simply and directly, leaves untold, except to the imagination, the splendid courage, devotion to duty, and clear grasp of a military problem on the part of this young officer and his Machine Gun Troop, whose conduct was true to the best traditions of our army.

The attack was delivered on the camp simultaneously from the west and east, and on the town from the west. Lieutenant Castleman, by his prompt action, drove the Mexicans from the western part of camp into town, and then circling to the east took up a position in the eastern edge of town with his right resting in front of his house and his left in front of the bank, facing west, and commanding the only business street in the town. He thus created a diversion from the camp, protected a large part of the business section from plunder and flames, drove the Mexicans to the western part of town where they set fire to the Commercial Hotel, a stupid move on the part of the Mexicans, as the conflagration furnished sufficient illumination to make them an easy target for our troops, and contributed to a prompt withdrawal of the enemy from town, which withdrawal soon degenerated into a rout.

The saying that "Self preservation is the first law of nature" does not apply to the trained and disciplined soldier. Witness Lucas, whose sense of duty was stronger than any thought of self. His place was with his troop and he took the one chance to join it by mingling with the Mexicans flowing past his door trusting to the friendly shelter of the night. He charged with them and when they dropped to fire he kept going. Fired at from time to time he returned the fire with deadly effect. Note the coolness with which he rallied his men and inspired them with his splendid courage, the promptness with which he got his guns in action, the intelligence with which he grasped the military problem which con-

fronted him, and his brilliant solution of it.   To John P. Lucas, now
Major, then Lieutenant, belongs more than to any other individual the
title of "The Hero of Columbus."

And in the press and in Congress he and his gallant men were criti-
cized because one or more machine guns jammed.   These critics had
probably never seen a machine gun and were certainly not familiar with
its many intricate parts and delicate adjustments.   Nevertheless they,
unhesitatingly at long distance and without proof, maligned these brave
men who were faithful, some of them even unto death, to the traditions
which have always upheld and animated the officers and men of the
regular army.   Guns of this make have always jammed, even at target
practice, but in spite of the jamming Lucas fired close to twenty thousand rounds from the four guns in less than ninety minutes, caused the
greater number of enemy casualties and kept down the accuracy and
power of their fire while our troops organized for the counter attack
with but few casualties.

Although Lucas rendered services on this occasion which could and
should be characterized as exceptionally meritorious and distinguished
in the performance of duties of great responsibility, nevertheless, up to
date, he has not received even a citation.   Then there was Sergeant
Dobbs shot through the liver and slowly bleeding to death, whose sense
of duty was so high that he chose to serve his gun until death claimed
him rather than seek shelter in the hospital where his life might have
been saved.   His troop commander recommended him for the highest
award our Government gives, the Medal of Honor, and later for the
Distinguished Service Cross, but in neither case did the War Department
deign to answer the correspondence.

CHAPTER IX

The Pursuit from Columbus

The reports of the activities of Lucas and Castleman give a clear picture of the fighting in town and camp. The pursuit of the defeated Mexicans should be described, to complete the picture. The following is taken from the report of Colonel Frank Tompkins, U. S. Cavalry, Retired, who at the time of the Columbus Raid was a Major of the 13th Cavalry, stationed at Columbus.

My quarters in Columbus were situated in the western edge of the town and about 300 yards from the Camp Administration Building.

About 4:15 A. M., March 9, 1916, I was awakened by the sound of rifle shots immediately outside my bedroom window, accompanied by shouts of "Viva Mexico" and "Viva Villa." I realized at once that Mexican military forces were attacking Columbus. I dressed and armed myself and intended to join the troops in camp, but this last was impossible, as my house was surrounded by Mexican soldiers, my wife and two other women were in the house, and I could not leave them to the mercy of these bandits.

Just before dawn the Mexican troops were driven back to the west of my house by the fire of our troops, so I considered myself justified in leaving the women alone while I proceeded to camp. I arrived in camp and found Colonel Slocum with a greater part of the command occupying Cootes Hill, immediately west of the Administration Building, the troops in the prone position firing on the Mexicans who were south of the railroad with their left flank resting on the railroad track, at a distance of about 500 yards. Colonel Slocum was standing in an erect position, very much exposed to the fire of the Mexican troops, but carefully observing the phases of the fight, in complete command of the situation, and an inspiration to the officers and men of his command.

Realizing that the Mexicans were whipped, I asked Colonel Slocum to allow me to mount up a troop and take the offensive. He authorized me to take Troop "H," commanded by Captain Rudolph E. Smyser, who had requested that his troop be the one selected to go. In about twenty minutes we managed to mount 32 men and left camp moving in a southwesterly direction. About one half mile out of camp, it not yet being broad daylight, we encountered Captain George Williams, Lieutenant William A. McCain, Mrs. McCain, Miss McCain, and a soldier. These ,people had been cut off by the Mexican forces and were trying to rejoin camp. They had just killed a Mexican soldier. I dismounted one of my troopers in order that Captain Williams, at his own request, might join my command.

We proceeded southwest, and in the dim light of early morning saw the Mexican column retreating south towards the border. We paralleled their march with the object of cutting off as many as possible as soon as we could get clear of the wire fences. We finally reached the border fence with the loss of one horse killed.

There was an isolated hill about 300 yards south of the fence between the Mexican column and my forces. This hill was occupied by Mexican troops, evidently a covering detachment for their left flank. We cut the fence to the east of this hill, deployed as foragers and advanced, increasing the gait until the command: "Charge!" when our fellows socked in the spurs let

55

out their charging yell and swept forward holding the alignment. The fire
of the enemy went high, but they held on until we hit the lower slopes of
the hill when they broke and ran. We galloped to the hill top, returned
pistols, dismounted, and opened rifle fire on the fleeing Mexicans killing 32
men and many horses.

Realizing that I was in Mexican territory in violation of War Department orders I wrote a note to Colonel Slocum stating that the Mexicans
had taken up a position on a ridge 1500 yards to the south of the international boundary, and asked for permission to take Troop "G", Captain
Stedje commanding, in addition to my 29 men of Troop "H" and continue
the pursuit. In about 45 minutes I received a reply to use my own judgment. I notified Captain Stedje to come with me. He replied he heard
firing at the border gate and would have to return there. At this moment
I saw 27 men of Troop "F" under Lieutenant Castleman following my trail.
I sent word to Castleman to come forward at a gallop. I then continued
the pursuit and in about 45 minutes struck Villa's rear guard. I had 29
men of Troop "H", 27 men of Troop "F", Captain Smyser, Captain Williams
and Lieutenant Castleman.

We deployed at wide intervals and advanced towards the enemy at a
fast trot, the enemy firing all the time but their shots going wild. When
we were within 400 yards of them, finding good shelter for the horses, we
dismounted, and opened fire, driving the rear guard back on the main body
and killing and wounding quite a few. It may be well to state here that
the men dismounted while extended, each man linking his horse to his
stirrup buckle thus keeping the animal immobile and allowing every rifle
to get on the firing line and get there fast. For this kind of fighting where
the horses were in a fold of the ground but a few yards behind their riders,
this method of linking enabled the men to dismount and mount with speed.

We again took up the pursuit, and in about thirty minutes overtook the
rear guard. This time we tried to turn their left flank, but became exposed
to their fire at close range. I received a slight wound in the knee, a bullet
through the rim of my hat, and my horse was wounded slightly in the head.
Captain Williams was also wounded slightly in the hand. To avoid this
fire we dismounted under cover, advanced to within view of the enemy,
and with the men of Troop "F" firing at the main body at 800 yards, and
the men of Troop "H" firing at the Mexican rear guard with battle sights,
we soon drove the rear guard back and again took up the pursuit. In advancing from this position we counted twelve dead Mexicans that had been
killed from their main body.

Thinking that the Mexicans were going to take up a position on an elevation, I detached Troop "F" to flank this position while I proceeded on the
Mexican trail with Troop "H". I again overtook the enemy, but this time
on a plain devoid of cover. They soon saw our weakness (but 29 men) and
started an attack with at least 300 men while the remainder of the Mexican
forces continued their retreat. We returned their fire until one horse was
wounded and one killed when we fell back about 400 yards where our
horses had excellent cover. But the Mexicans refused to advance against
us in this new position.

After waiting about 45 minutes I returned to Columbus. This was made
necessary by the fact that our ammunition was running low, that the men
were exhausted from fighting many hours without food or water, and the
horses were likewise becoming fagged as they had not been fed or watered
for 18 hours and they had travelled very fast over an exceedingly rough
country, under a hot sun, for 15 miles and with the same distance to return.

As a result of this pursuit my officers counted between 75 and 100 dead
Mexican bandits killed on *Mexican soil*, many killed and wounded horses
and mules, the abandonment of two machine guns by the Mexicans, many
rifles and pistols, much ammunition, food stuff and loot which had been
taken at Columbus, and most of all we took the fight to the Mexicans, all
of which must have had a very depressing effect in the ranks of the Villistas.

I returned to Columbus with my little command, reporting to Colonel

Slocum at 12:50 P M., having been gone seven and one half hours, covered 25 to 30 miles of rough country, fought four separate rear guard actions without the loss of a single man, and inflicted a loss of from 75 to 100 killed and actually counted.

Villa, "The Lion of the North," was not only defeated at Columbus, but he at once became a fugitive from American justice, and was chased by American troops for over 500 miles through his native country at terrific cost to his prestige and power. The fight at Columbus caused his star to wane, and it so continued until he was assassinated on the outskirts of Parral in 1923.

This victory was made possible by the superb training, discipline and spirit of the 13th Cavalry. This morale was due solely to our commander, Colonel Herbert J. Slocum. The victory added new laurels to the history of the United States Cavalry, and our Government has waited entirely too long to reward adequately¨ the man responsible, Colonel Herbert J. Slocum.

That Colonel Slocum was justified in permitting the pursuit of the bandits into Mexico in violation of War Department orders is supported by the telegrams quoted below, one from Collector Cobb at El Paso to the Secretary of State, and the other from General Funston to the Adjutant General of the Army, both sent the same date:

El Paso, March 10, 1916, 11 A. M.
Deputy, Columbus, phones that best information obtainable is that Villa had about 400 men in Columbus attack. This supplemented by statements of Villa captives brought north that Villa had large force, some say 2000, in reserve, which he has probably joined.

Cobb.

Fort Sam Houston, March 10, 1916.
Under circumstances I believed Colonel Slocum entirely justified in violating War Department's order relative to sending troops across border and am of the opinion that had he not done so Villa might immediately have returned to attack after being joined by his men left south of line.

Funston.

As I suggested the counter attack and commanded it Colonel Slocum was of the opinion that my action in this part of the fight was' worthy of the award of the Medal of Honor. I did not agree with him, but nevertheless he so recommended. I did not receive the award of the Medal of Honor but was awarded the Distinguished Service Cross with the following citation:

CITATION FOR DISTINGUISHED SERVICE CROSS

Frank Tompkins, colonel, United States Army, Retired, then major, 13th Cavalry, United States Army. For extraordinary heroism in action at Columbus, New Mexico, March 9, 1916. Major Tompkins requested and received authority to pursue a superior force of bandits into Mexico. Although wounded early in the pursuit, carried on a running fight with the bandits for several miles, inflicting heavy losses upon them and stopped the pursuit only when men and horses were exhausted and ammunition reduced to a few rounds per man.

Given under my hand at the City of Washington this 11th day of September, 1934.

Recorded in the office of the   George H. Dern,
Adjutant General   Secretary of War
James F. McKinley
The Adjutant General.

CHAPTER X

Incidents of the Fight at Columbus

There were certain incidents of the Columbus fight that were never reported officially, but are nevertheless interesting.

The kitchen shacks of the camp were of adobe construction, erected by the troops and bullet proof. The desert around Columbus was full of rabbits and quail. It was customary for each troop to keep in the kitchen a company shot gun with ammunition. This enabled one of the kitchen crew to go out in the afternoon and bring back a mess of quail or rabbits. When the Mexicans made their attack the unexpected resistance they met broke them up into small groups. The fire of the American soldiers was so hot and accurate that these small groups sought shelter behind the bullet proof kitchen shacks. The kitchen crews could hear them talking outside the kitchen windows—so they promptly fired into them with the shot guns. Those of the Mexicans who were not killed by this fire took back into Mexico some American shot under their hides.

One group of Mexicans broke in the door of a kitchen shack. The crew were waiting for them: one cook soused them with boiling water, while the other cook sailed into them with an axe. When the smoke of battle cleared the only Mexicans left on that particular spot were dead Mexicans.

Another group took shelter against a kitchen wall. They were located by one of the machine guns. The gun crew gave them a burst of fire at short range, firing low to get advantage of ricochets. Few of that party of Mexicans ever saw Mexico again. They were literally cut to pieces by these ricocheting bullets. On my return from the pursuit I took a look at this place and saw several pieces of human skull as large as my hand, with the long hair of the Yaqui Indian attached.

One soldier of the stable crew killed a Mexican with a baseball bat. As a matter of fact the Mexicans were getting it from all sides. In the darkness and confusion some soldiers became separated from their troops. These men carried on a private war of their own, shooting Mexicans whenever they saw one or more. This reception was so totally different from what they had been told to expect that the camp and the town too was soon cleared of the enemy.

Certain individuals had experiences that are worthy of notice. Captain Thomas F. Ryan, 13th Cavalry, occupied a house on the Guzman-Deming road near the camp headquarters. Behind the house was his adobe garage. At the time of the raid Captain Ryan was on patrol duty at Gibson's line Ranch. Mrs. Ryan was in the house alone. As the Mexicans rushed the camp from the west, yelling and shooting, Mrs.

Ryan made an effort to get to her bullet-proof garage. A Mexican grabbed her by the arm and asked "Adonde va?" (Where are you going?). She answered "Nowhere." He released her. The usual procedure would have been to kill her on the spot. Mrs. Ryan entered the garage and stayed there until the fight was over.

Captain Rudolph E. Smyser, with his wife and two children, occupied a house on the western edge of town across the street from my quarters. The Mexicans battered in their front door as Smyser and his family climbed out of a back window and took refuge in an outhouse. They heard the Mexicans talking of searching the place, so Smyser abandoned the outhouse for the mesquite and got pretty well filled with cactus thorns in the process. No wonder Smyser was eager to join the pursuit. His troop caused most of the Mexican casualties in Mexico that morning.

Lieutenant William A. McCain lived with his wife and little girl in a house near the southwest edge of the town not far from the railroad track. In the first moments of the attack this house was surrounded by a swarm of Mexicans. In the building at this time, in addition to the family, was a soldier, McCain's orderly. As soon as the first Mexican wave passed, the McCain party evacuated the house, moved south across the railroad, and hid in the mesquite.

When this first wave of Mexicans hit the camp, it acted as all waves act when they bang up against an immovable mass it receded. As this wave fell back it passed all around the bush under which the McCain party were hiding. Captain George Williams, the regimental adjutant, who had been cut off from camp, stumbled into McCain at this moment. McCain and his orderly had between them a pistol and a shot gun. Captain Williams had his pistol. It was still dark. The retreating Mexicans were thinning out; falling back in small groups, in pairs, and singly. They would halt, fire towards the camp and then continue to retreat. Finally an isolated Mexican discovered the Americans. Before he could give the alarm the man with the shot gun shot him but did not kill him. They pulled him under the bush. He struggled and tried to give the alarm. McCain did not want to shoot him again for fear that the shot might betray their hiding place. Something had to be done to silence the cries of the wounded Mexican. They tried to cut his throat with a pocket knife but the knife was too dull. They finally killed him by hammering in his head with the butt of the pistol. A horrible experience for Mrs. McCain and her young daughter, both of whom were close enough to the Mexican to touch him. Just as the Mexican was killed I rode onto the party with the pursuit column, and it was here that Captain Williams joined me.

It was also at this point that I saw something waving in the brush about 100 yards north. I sent a trooper to investigate. He reported it was a Mrs. Moore, shot through the leg. Her house was in flames a short distance away and her husband had been killed. She had managed to crawl to where I found her. I detached a soldier to look out for her. He managed to get her into camp, and later she was sent to a hospital in El Paso where she finally recovered from her wound, but the memory of her experiences of that early dawn will ever be with her.

Chapter XI

Colonel Slocum, U. S. Commander at Columbus, Attacked and Vindicated

After all major disasters by fire, flood, or battle, the sufferers immediately look about for some scapegoat to be cast out into the wilderness. The victim chosen in this case to bear not the sins of the people but the sins of the Mexican policy of the United States, was Colonel H. J. Slocum, commanding officer of the United States troops stationed at Columbus.

Senator Albert B. Fall, representing the State of New Mexico, without any evidence, but under the urge to make political capital for himself, saw fit to denounce Colonel Slocum for the Columbus affair. This man Fall, like many another politician, could not appreciate the fact that to such a man as Colonel Slocum his unsullied military record covering a period of over 40 years meant more than life itself. And Fall, without any justification whatever, attempted to blacken this honorable soldier's distinguished record. But the world has since learned of the caliber of Albert B. Fall. The world knows that in the oil scandals of 1926 and '27 the Supreme Court of the United States traced the passage of some $230,000 in Liberty bonds from the Sinclair interests to the hands of Fall, and, convincing itself of this passage, it records this damning judgment:

The clandestine and unexplainable acquisition of these bonds by Fall confirms the belief, generated by other circumstances in the case, that he was a faithless public officer. There is nothing in the record that tends to mitigate the sinister significance attached to that enrichment.—*Quotation from Boston Evening Transcript, October 11, 1927.*

Then there were two newspaper criticisms; one published in the Washington (D. C.) *Evening Star,* March 10, 1916, and the other in the New York *Times* of March 19th. The *Times* article consisted of a letter written by M. M. Marshall to his father E. J. Marshall, President of the Palomas Land and Cattle Co., whose two million acre property lies on the Mexican side of the line south of Columbus. The *Star* article assumed that the military at Columbus probably had no night guards in the camp and certainly no exterior guards, and then goes on to say in the most fatuous manner that: "It is one of the first principles of military work to guard against surprise." And this: "The necessity for security and information is a cardinal principle of the soldier's training, and seemingly this principle was forgotten at Columbus." This was offered before any investigation and without any knowledge of the facts, but it was poison that the reading public lapped up and to this day many people in all walks of life believe the garrison at Columbus was negligent in the performance of their duty. Young Marshall in his letter to his father and which the *Times* published stated that:

The blame for the Columbus affair should rest on the United States Army. It had been forewarned, not only by foreman Fondille and Antonio, our men, as to Villa's where abouts and the directions being followed by Villa on his march, but had information from several other sources. As I understand, there were no troops patrolling the border during that night— only sentries about the camp and Columbus. * * * The United States Army was extremely lucky in having so few soldiers killed—I believe seven in number—and luck is all that it can be called. A large part of their guns and ammunition was locked up. Overconfidence and the thought that Villa would not dare attack a detachment of United States troops no doubt lulled our soldiers into a feeling of security.

Such wild and loose statements based on gossip and unanalyzed were a cruel and cowardly injustice to the brave men who performed their duty so nobly at Columbus in the early hours of March 9, 1916.

That part of young Marshall's letter relating to the capture and death of McKinney and Corbett is interesting:

Antonio, one of the Mexican boys whom our company has raised and who was with foreman McKinney at the time of Villa's capture of Mc-Kinney's outfit, gives the following report:

"At about 8:00 o'clock on the morning of Tuesday we were coming down the Boca Grande River (Casas Grandes) when McKinney and myself sighted about 500 men beginning to make camp. They were unsaddling and starting to make coffee.

"McKinney wanted to go up and talk to them but I said to him, 'Arthur, please don't go, for they may be Villistas.' I told him this several times, but finally he turned to me and said, 'Well, I am going to talk to them, are you such a coward that you do not want to go with me?' I told him that if they were Villistas they would certainly kill us, so what was the use of taking such a crazy risk; that it would be better to stay where we were and wait to see what they intended doing. He went away, taking one of the other Mexican boys with him.

"I then went down toward the river to head off the other boys who were dragging up stream. I met Corbett and Juan and showed them the camp of horsemen. Corbett said he would join McKinney, for to him it looked as though Arthur was all right; but I warned Corbett also and told him to wait and see what would develop. He rode directly into the camp, how-ever, notwithstanding just at that time we saw a troop of about 20 horse-men coming in our direction.

"These men had sighted us, and we started north for the line. They gave us a hot chase, but we gave them the slip in a canyon, and came straight into Columbus, arriving here the same night. (March 7th.)

"On arriving here I notified the Colonel of the United States troops of the happenings during the day, and he sent me back the next day to locate the band and report to him. I reported that night, Wednesday, that Villa, with about 500 or 700 men was on the Boca Grande River (Casas Grandes) and was headed this way. The following morning the Villa outfit attacked Columbus."

This gives you quite full information of the capture of McKinney and the branding outfit. Bunk, the Negro water foreman of Oihital's Ranch, who was a captive with Villa at the time Villa took foreman McKinney and Corbett, together with the balance of the branding outfit, makes the following report on the death of these two men:

McKinney rode right into the camp of Villa, and as he rode through inspected the horses quite thoroughly. The Mexicans took him captive, and soon after took Corbett, who came into camp of his own accord.   Their capture was reported to Villa, who at the time was not in camp.   Villa ordered them hung.   McKinney laughed and joked with the men as they were making preparations, and shook hands with me and some of the men as he was pulled up on the limb of a tree, remarking that there was only one chance to die.

Corbett also shook hands with me when he came into camp, and at that time realized his time had come.   He took his death like a brave man.   O'Neil were also killed.   The cook was laid on the ground, and 60 horses lined up to run over him, for he was fighting every second.

The second horse went over him, but as the third jumped he grabbed the stirrup and swung himself up behind the rider.   He had almost choked to death the Mexican rider when a bullet pierced his heart and he fell.

Bunk and Mrs. Walker, who was also a captive, escaped from the Villa outfit during the retreat from Columbus.

Mr. Marshall's statement that the border line was not patrolled was false; the promptness with which American troops got into action and the heavy casualties of the Mexicans show his statement about guns and ammunition being locked up is also false; and as to being over-confident we certainly were not, though the results of the fight showed we well might have been.

Of course these criticisms were very carefully and thoroughly investigated, and the findings, which were bulky, were returned to Washing through the following military channels:

General John J. Pershing, Commanding Mexican Punitive Expedition;

General Frederick Funston, Commanding Southern Department;

General E. A. Garlington, Inspector General, U. S. Army;

General Tasker H. Bliss, Assistant Chief of Staff, U. S. Army;

General H. L. Scott, Chief of Staff, U. S. Army.

General Pershing commented as follows:

1. Returned, attention invited to the testimony of witnesses taken by the Inspector General of this Provisional Division, and to his conclusions in the premises.

2. Colonel Slocum seems to have made every endeavor to obtain accurate information of the whereabouts and intentions of Villa.   The information received from the usual Mexican sources was unfortunately, credited, when as a matter of course, under the circumstances it was entirely unreliable.   From Headquarters, both of the Department and of the Brigade, the information regarding Villa's exact whereabouts and his intentions were not such as to cause any particular alarm in Colonel Slocum's mind, although he did reinforce the troops patrolling the border line.

3. Although a brigand, Villa was not presumably an enemy of the United States, nor were Mexico and the United States at war.   Although Villa's approach to the boundary excited the curiosity of our officers along the border, it is not believed that many thought that Villa would have the audacity to attack a regimental garrison of American troops.

4. The very prompt action on the part of the officers and men of the garrison in meeting this sudden attack, the small loss incurred, and the very great loss inflicted upon Villa and his band, deserve full consideration in this connection.   To my mind the results present a good reason for complimenting the officer in command, instead of subjecting him to a technical criticism which could serve no good purpose.

John J. Pershing,
Brigadier General, U. S. Army,
Commanding."

Remarks by General Funston:

1. In my opinion Colonel Slocum meets quite fully the criticisms that have been made in connection with the alleged lack of precautions taken to guard the camp and town of Columbus. Especially significant is his statement that he had employed and sent across the line a presumably reliable Mexican who brought him false information to the effect that Villa with his main force had gone towards Guzman, leaving only a few men at Palomas. Another circumstance that deceived him was the persistent report which I had also seen in the press, to the effect that Villa's march north was for the purpose of seeking refuge in the United States.

2. The matter had not seemed clear to me before reading Colonel Slocum's statement, but it is now my opinion that there were not sufficient grounds for alarm to have made it incumbent on him to increase materially the guards at the camp and the town. Some precautions had been taken by strengthening the force at Gibson's Ranch and the patrols sent out from there. When the great distance to be covered by these patrols is taken into consideration, it does not seem strange that Villa's force was able to slip through them in the darkness. Doubtless, during the night he assembled his men immediately south of the line, which our patrols were not allowed to cross, and then, his scouts or spies having reported the patrol had passed, took his men over.

3. A partial surprise carried out by stealth and treachery in time of peace must not be judged by the same standards as a surprise in time of war. Had open hostilities existed between our forces and Villa's, and our scouting parties been able to go anywhere, Villa would never have been able to concentrate his band within a day's march of the border without his actions being known.

4. Further, last November, Villa, smarting under his defeat at Agua Prieta, (which he claimed was due to the fact that I told him that if he resumed the attack and any projectiles fell on the American side I would attack him with my entire force, openly threatened on several occasions that he would raid Arizona with his entire force. The fact that he did not when he had fully 10,000 with him for such an enterprise, made it naturally seem improbable that he would try a raid with one tenth of that number; and it must be remembered that until he made his raid our information was to the effect that he had only a small personal escort. Colonel Slocum, being at Douglas at the time, heard of Villa's threats and knew of his failure to carry them out.

Frederick Funston,
Major General, Commanding.

Extract of remarks by General Garlington:

7. From the facts before me I am of the opinion that Colonel Slocum followed correct military principles in the disposition of his forces, in the orders given to the commanders of the detachments on the boundary line, and in the organization of his interior guard. The fact that he was barred from sending patrols across the boundary line into Mexico deprived him of the only sure means of discovering the presence of bandits or others with hostile purpose in time to adequately protect his territory from sudden incursions by them.

8. After the alarm was given by the sentinel, the command appears to have assembled with a commendable alertness and soon gained command of the situation, driving the Mexicans from the town and camp with a comparatively small loss, (namely, 7 killed and 5 wounded), and inflicting considerable loss upon the Mexicans, which speaks well for the discipline of the command. These papers do not show the extent of damage done to the town of Columbus, but do show that there were 8 civilians killed and 2 wounded.

Approval recommended: E. A. Garlington,
H. L. Scott,   Inspector General.
Major General,
Chief of Staff

General Bliss states in part:

The best information obtainable indicates that Villa with from 500 to 1,000 men, assisted by darkness and the complete information he was able to obtain through spies, succeeded in evading the outpost patrols and made an absolutely unexpected attack on the camp of United States troops and the town of Columbus, N. M. That this attack was successfully repulsed, under most adverse conditions, testifies to the commendable bravery and staunchness of the officers and enlisted men constituting this command.

Tasker H. Bliss,
Major General, General Staff,
Chief, Mobile Army Division

And General Scott, after reviewing all the papers in the case, sums up as follows:

I recommend that Colonel Slocum be advised that no stigma rests upon his conduct of command at Columbus, N. M., at the time of Villa's attack, and that he and his command are highly commended on their prompt and valorous action in the repulse of Villa's force and in pursuit of same, and that this be given to the press.

H. L. Scott,
Chief of Staff.

Approved,
  Baker.

The "Baker" in above signature was the Secretary of War at that time.

I call that a pretty good bill of health, the Falls and the Marshalls to the contrary notwithstanding. But to this day I have had people say to me: "Oh, you were at Columbus where the machine guns jammed and the arms and ammunition were locked up." But no civilian has yet spoken of the epic fight that small body of regular soldiers made, to the honor and glory of their country's flag. The average mind is more receptive to and retains longer, unfounded and malicious gossip than news of worthwhile quality. Conscious of our own weaknesses, we are too prone to find consolation in the alleged weaknesses of others.

"Some of Our Prisoners"

Apache Scouts

CHAPTER XII

Diplomatic Exchanges Following the Raid

Villa's raid upon Columbus, N. M., immediately became the occasion for diplomatic exchanges between the de facto Government of Mexico and the Government of the United States. The United States took the position that Villa and his band must be captured or killed, or so thoroughly dispersed as to render them forever impotent as a threat to the safety of the American people in territory contiguous to the Mexican border. This position demanded prompt and energetic pursuit by the military forces of both countries. Mexico recognized the position of the United States *in principle*, but evidently not wishing the United States to capture Villa or have any hand in his capture, immediately started negotiations involving a delay fatal to the campaigns desired by the United States.

Carranza and his cabinet were past masters in drawing red herrings across the trail, so they now attempted to lead our State Department away from the point at issue into a wilderness of words, ever traveling in a gentle circle which would end at the point of beginning, get nowhere, and thus enable Villa and his band to make a clean "get away."

In other words they continued to "play horse" with Secretary Lansing and President Wilson, as they had been doing for the past four years. But this latest outrage proved to be the last straw, as is well indicated in the following telegram from the Secretary of State to Special Agents Silliman and Belt, dated March 9, 1916, 4:00 P. M., the same date as the raid:

Official reports just received from El Paso, state that General Villa with several hundred men early this morning attacked the American garrison at Columbus, N. M., setting fire to principal buildings in town and killing a number of soldiers and civilians. Other official reports from El Paso state that Villa's forces were well known to be in the Casas Grandes district several days ago, but that the forces of the de facto Government were said to be insufficient to pursue them; also that, about that time, the Mexican Consul at El Paso requested General Carranza to furnish additional troops for the State of Chihuahua.

Convey foregoing to General Carranza for his information and advise him that this Government is suspending judgment until further facts can be learned, but you may say to him that this appears to be the most serious situation which has confronted this Government during the entire period of Mexican unrest and that it is expected that he will do every thing in his power to pursue, capture, and exterminate this lawless element which is now proceeding westward from Columbus.

Lansing

Mr. Belt answered the above from Irapuato, Mexico, March 10, 1916, 11:00 A. M.:

Department's March 9, 4:00 P.M. At request of Mr. Silliman, presented this representation as soon after departure from Guadalajara as possible. General Carranza requested that I first present matter to Secretary Acuna (Mexican Secretary of Foreign Affairs), upon which I advised him that, owing to extreme importance of the matter, I trusted he would handle it personally. Secretary Acuna advised me that they were in receipt of news of the attack last night at 8 o'clock. After I had presented Department's representation, dwelling upon the very serious situation, his first remark was: "The fact that Villa and his forces have entered United States territory is evidence of the strength of the de facto Government's forces." I have conferred at length with him and have urged the necessity of a full reply to this representation inasmuch as the position of the de facto Government in the matter should be clearly set forth. He promised to immediately take up this matter with the Chief Executive. He further assures me that the two of us can jointly take up the matter with the Chief. I have asked for an answer to the six following questions as a basis for a fuller understanding of the facts:

(1) Was the de facto Government aware of the presence of Villista troops in the Casas Grandes district?

(2) Did the Mexican Consul at El Paso request General Carranza to furnish additional troops for the State of Chihuahua?

(3) Upon receipt of this advice what action was taken by the de facto Government to furnish additional forces?

(4) What effective action will be taken by the de facto Government to pursue, capture and punish this lawless element, especially as pertains to Villa and those responsible for the Columbus atrocity?

(5) Will the Chief Executive return to Queretaro direct owing to the seriousness of the situation?

(6) What expression does the Chief Executive care to make for the information of the Government of the United States pertaining to this serious question?

Secretary Acuna said he would endeavor to answer these questions.

John W. Belt

Carranza replied to the above through Special Agent Silliman, who immediately forwarded it to our State Department:

Irapuato, March 10, 1916, 11:00 P.M.

In reply to your courteous note of yesterday, forwarded today by Mr. John W. Belt, I have the honor to inform you that in making the said note known to the citizen First Chief of the Constitutionalist Army in charge of the Executive Power of the Nation, he directed me to say to you, who will have the kindness to repeat it to the Department of State of the Government of the United States, that:

The First Chief is pained to hear of the lamentable occurrence at Columbus, New Mexico, on the occasion of the attack upon it yesterday by bandits led by Francisco Villa.

Although there has been in the State of Chihuahua a sufficient force to restore order and afford guaranties to nationals and foreigners, since Francisco Villa began operations in the mountains of that State, the Chief Executive, at the request of the Governor of Chihuahua and of the Consul at El Paso, ordered 2500 men under command of General Luis Gutierrez to pursue the bandits who have just crossed into the territory of the United States, who made this move doubtless because they were driven to it by the persistent pursuit conducted by the said command of General Gutierrez.

The deplorable incident above mentioned bears some resemblance to the raids into the States of Sonora and Chihuahua by Indians from the reservations of the Government of the United States. The Sonora raid took place about the year 1880 when the Indian Geronimo with a large horde invaded a community in the northern part of Sonora, and committed a number of murders and depredations, taking the lives and property of Mexican families until, after a long and persistent pursuit by Mexican and American forces, the band was annihilated and the chief captured. The invasion of Chihuahua by the Indian Victor followed by 800 Indians took place from 1884 to 1886. At that time the bands went as far as the towns of Tejolochic and Tres Castillos, very near the capital of Chihuahua, committing many crimes. At their first real battle with the Mexican forces they lost their chief and scattered.

In both these cases an agreement between the Governments of the United States and Mexico provided that armed forces of either country might freely cross into the territory of the other to pursue and chastise those bandits.

Bearing in mind these precedents and the happy results to both countries yielded by the agreement above referred to, the Government over which the citizen First Chief presides, desiring to exterminate as soon as possible the horde led by Francisco Villa, who was recently outlawed, and to capture Villa and to adequately punish him, applies through you, Mr. Confidential Agent, to the Government of the United States and asks that the Mexican forces be permitted to cross into American territory in pursuit of the aforesaid bandits lead by Villa, upon the understanding that, reciprocally, the forces of the United States may cross into Mexican territory, if the raid effected at Columbus should unfortunately be repeated at any other point on the border.

The Government of Mexico would highly appreciate a prompt and favorable decision by the Government of the United States.

Accepted, etc.

    Acuna,
     In charge of the Department of Foreign Relations.
      Silliman

The reader will please note that in this suggestion from Mexico for reciprocal privileges in pursuit of outlaw bands the plan is *not* to become effective until there should be a *repetition* at some point along the border, of the Columbus outrage. This, of course, is merely a sample of the "red herring" game. But the United States was not to be fooled so easily, as is shown by the following reply to Special Agent Silliman:

Department of State,
    Washington, March 13, 1916, 3:00 P. M.

Your March 10, midnight. You are instructed to reply as follows to Secretary Acuna's note of March 10:

The Government of the United States has received the courteous note of Senior Acuna and has read with satisfaction his suggestion for reciprocal privileges to the American and Mexican authorities in the pursuit and apprehension of outlaws who infest their respective territories lying along the international boundary, and who are a constant menace to the lives and the property of the residents of that region.

The Government of the United States, in view of the unusual state of affairs which has existed for some time along the international boundary and earnestly desiring to cooperate with the de facto Government of Mexico to suppress this state of lawlessness, of which the attack on Columbus, N. M., is a deplorable example, and to insure peace and order in the regions contiguous to the boundary between the two Republics, readily grants permission for the military forces of the de facto Government of Mexico to cross the international boundary in pursuit of lawless bands of armed men who have entered Mexico from the United States, committed outrages on Mexican soil, and fled into the United States, on the understanding that the de facto Government of Mexico grants the reciprocal privilege that the forces of the United States may pursue across the international boundary into Mexican territory lawless bands of armed men who have entered the United States from Mexico, committed outrages on American soil, and fled into Mexico.

The Government of the United States understands that in view of its agreement to this reciprocal arrangement proposed by the de facto Government the arrangement is now complete and in force and the reciprocal privileges thereunder may accordingly be exercised by either Government without further interchange of views.

It is a matter of sincere gratification to the Government of the United States that the de facto Government of Mexico has evinced so cordial and friendly a spirit of cooperation in the efforts of the authorities of the United States to apprehend and punish the bands of outlaws who seek refuge beyond the international boundary in the erroneous belief that the constituted authorities will resent any pursuit across the boundary by the forces of the Government whose citizens have suffered by the crimes of the fugitives.

With the same spirit of cordial friendship the Government of United States will exercise the privilege granted by the de facto Government of Mexico in the hope and confident expectation that by their mutual efforts lawlessness will be eradicated and peace and order maintained in the United States and Mexico contiguous to the international boundary.

Sent in duplicate to you and Belt.

Lansing.

The *first* reaction to the American note was most favorable. Belt stated that it was plainly evident that the reply had created a most favorable impression and an already delicate situation had been remedied. Silliman stated that Mexican Secretary of Foreign Relations said substance of reply to American note had been agreed upon, but it would not be formulated or presented until excessively special message of confidential character had been sent to the Mexican Confidential Agent in Washington for delivery to our Secretary of State. Upon asking whether it could be said in advance what would be the attitude of the Mexican Government to the announced plan of sending American troops into Mexico for the immediate pursuit and capture of Villa, the Secretary of War and the other secretaries present said the attitude would be one of approval and acquiesence. The Secretary of War added that the Mexican commanders would be instructed to cooperate with the American commanders in the campaign.

In spite of the spirit of cooperation expressed in this diplomatic correspondence the excessively special message of confidential character sent to the Mexican Confidential Agent at Washington for delivery to our Secretary of State denied the right of United States troops to enter Mexico, denied any permission having been given for the entry of such troops, and denied the use of Mexican Railroads to United States forces. It did propose that the two countries agree upon the conditions under which the troops of one country might enter the territory of the other while in pursuit of marauders, should such necessity unhappily arise *in the future*. The whole note was designed for the purpose of delay, so that Villa could get so far south that by the time the "conversations" had ended there would be no excuse for the United States to send troops after him. It is very certain the de facto troops made no effort to capture Villa, nor did they aid the troops of the United States in effecting his capture. Quite the contrary. When it became evident that American cavalry were on the eve of capturing Villa the Americans were attacked by Carranza troops, and were recalled from the pursuit by President Wilson, to avoid war.

This diplomatic situation is put before the reader that a clear picture may be had of the problem which confronted General Pershing and his command at the very beginning of the campaign, when time was such an important factor of success. The American troops not only received no aid from the de facto troops of Mexico, but, under the guise of co-operation, were furnished with deliberately false information, made with intent to deceive and delay. We were not allowed the use of the railroads for the movement of troops or supplies. We campaigned in a wilderness which, save for wild cattle and corn, had been stripped bare of all food supplies, at the end of the dry season when grazing was poor and the water holes were drying up. At all times we were surrounded by enemies who were posing as friends; and we made our own roads and laid our own telegraph lines, both of which we guarded for several hundred miles of their length.

In spite of these obstacles, the treachery of Carranza and his officers, Pershing broke up the Villa bands, killed his principal lieutenants, and captured many of his followers who were sent to the United States, tried and hanged for their share in the Columbus raid. And in addition, in all the engagements, both large and small, with Villistas and with the de facto troops of Mexico, excepting the fight at Carrizal, Pershing was always victorious, though always outnumbered many times, and always inflicted overwhelming losses as compared to the American casualties. It is no wonder, with such a splendid achievement to his credit, that General Pershing was selected, a year later, to command the largest American army in the biggest war the world has ever known.

CHAPTER XIII

Orders for the Punitive Expedition

While the diplomats were writing notes the soldiers were getting ready for a campaign. Under date of March 10th General Funston wired to the Adjutant General of the Army:

It is the opinion of Colonels Dodd and Slocum, in which I concur, that unless Villa is relentlessly pursued and his forces scattered he will continue raids. As troops of Mexican Government are accomplishing nothing and as he consequently can make his preparations and concentrations without being disturbed, he can strike at any point on the border, we being unable to obtain advance information as to his whereabouts. If we fritter away the whole command guarding towns, ranches and railroads, it will accomplish nothing if he can find safe refuge across the line after every raid. Although probably not more than 1000 took part in Columbus raid, he is believed to have about 3000. Even if he should not continue raids, he has entered on a policy of relentless killing of Americans in Mexico. To show apathy and gross inefficiency of Mexican Government troops, an American woman held prisoner by Villa for nine days but who escaped in Columbus fight states that during all that time he was undisturbed at no great distance from the border, collecting a force of about 3000. The few Carranza troops in the region fled, losing all contact with him and not even informing us as to his whereabouts.

Funston.

This telegram had the desired effect and on March 10th, the same day replied as follows:

President has directed that an armed force be sent into Mexico with the sole object of capturing Villa and preventing any further raids by his band, and, with scrupulous regard for sovereignty of Mexico. Secretary War directs you telegraph exactly what you need in order to carry out foregoing general instructions, but you will not take any overt steps until definite instructions from War Department.

McCain.

And in further support of the intent of the United States to rid our border of the Villa menace, with or without the consent of Carranza, the following telegram was sent on same date by our Secretary of State to all American Consular Officers in Mexico.

The following statement has just been given to the press by the President:
An adequate force will be sent at once in pursuit of Villa with the single object of capturing him and putting a stop to his forays. This can and will be done in entirely friendly aid of the constituted authorities in Mexico and with scrupulous respect for the sovereignty of that Republic.

Lansing.

On March 13th the Adjutant General of the army sent a wire to General Funston enlarging somewhat on the telegram sent on the 10th.

The President desires that your attention be especially and earnestly called to his determination that the expedition into Mexico is limited to the purposes originally stated, namely the pursuit and dispersion of the band or bands that attacked Columbus, N. M., and it is of the utmost importance that no color of any other possibility or intention be given, and, therefore, while the President desires the force to be adequate to disperse the bands in question and to protect communications, neither in size or otherwise should the expedition afford the slightest ground of suspicion of any other or larger object.

McCain.

The above instructions were received by General Pershing less than two days before his Expedition crossed into Mexico. At the very instant these instructions were received General Pershing was informed by the commander of the de facto troops stationed at Palomas, a Mexican town six miles south of Columbus, that he would oppose the crossing with force. And at this time, and all during the campaign, Mexico was protesting against the presence of United States troops within her borders; while at the same time our State Department was sending sugar-coated notes to the effect that the expeditionary forces were in no way a menace to the sovereignty and dignity of Mexico, but, on the contrary, were the outward expression of the affection and friendship this country entertained for her sister republic, and were intended solely to help in the elimination of an irritation which threatened the harmony which existed, *and has existed for so long,* between the two countries.

Though from the very first Mexico protested against our sending troops after Villa, our country politely but firmly went ahead with the organization of the Punitive Expedition. On March 10, 1916, the day following the attack on Columbus, General John J. Pershing was named by the President as the Commanding Officer of the Expedition. He immediately began receiving telegrams from "higher authority" as to organization, equipment, etc., of his command. Supplementary to these instructions, a confidential telegram, dated March 16th, the day following our entry into Mexico, conveyed orders indicating the attitude to be observed toward troops of the de facto government, and the course to be followed in the event of a menacing attitude or actual attack on the part of the forces of the Mexican Government. This confidential telegram shows very plainly that while, in the exchange of notes between the two governments relative to our sending troops into Mexico to punish Villa, we assumed the attitude that this expedition was in accord with a friendly agreement between the two countries, proposed in the first place by Mexico, and planned to be of mutual benefit, with the troops of Mexico cooperating with the troops of the United States in crushing a common enemy, the position was false, not founded on fact, and was in danger of being challenged by the troops of Mexico.

CHAPTER XIV

The Expedition Enters Mexico

While the State Department had notified the press that an adequate force would be sent at once in pursuit of Villa with the single purpose of *capturing* him, the final instructions General Pershing received were to *pursue and disperse* his band or bands. So it will be seen that the information given to the press by the State Department and the orders given to General Pershing by the War Department were quite different. General Pershing accomplished his mission. He dispersed the bands of Villa, scattered them leaderless to the four winds, and rendered them impotent as a menace to our border states, but he did not capture Villa, though he would have done so had not President Wilson interfered at the eleventh hour and called off the chase.

The Punitive Expedition was organized in accordance with the following order:

Headquarters Punitive Expedition, U. S. Army,
Columbus, N. M., March 14, 1916.

General orders }
   No. 1.   }

1. The forces of this command are organized into a provisional division to be called Punitive Expedition, U. S. Army.
2. The following staff is announced:
   Chief of Staff: Lieut. Colonel DeR. C. Cabell, 10th Cavalry;
   Asst. to Chief of Staff: Capt. Wilson B. Burtt, 20th Infantry;
   Adjutant: Major John L. Hines, Adjutant General's Department;
   Intelligence Officer: Major James A. Ryan, 13th Cavalry;
   Inspector: Colonel Lucien G. Berry, 4th Field Artillery;
   Judge Advocate: Captain Allen J. Greer, 16th Infantry;
   Quartermaster: Major John F. Madden, Quartermaster Corps;
   Surgeon: Major Jere B. Clayton, Medical Corps;
   Engineer Officer: Major Lytle Brown, Corps of Engineers;
   Signal Officer: Captain Hanson B. Black, Signal Corps;
   Commander of the Base: Major William R. Sample, 20th Infantry;
   Aides: 1st Lieut. James L. Collins, 11th Cavalry;
        2nd Lieut. Martin C. Shallenberger, 16th Infantry.
3. The Provisional Division will consist of:
   (a) First Provisional Cavalry Brigade, Colonel James Lockett, Commanding.

   Troops:

   11th Cavalry   13th Cavalry
       Battery "C", 6th Field Artillery (attached)
   (b) Second Cavalry Brigade, Colonel George A. Dodd, Commanding.

   Troops:

   7th Cavalry   10th Cavalry
       Battery "B", 6th Field Artillery (attached)
   (c) First Provisional Infantry Brigade, Colonel John H. Beacon, Commanding.

Troops:

6th Infantry   16th Infantry
    Cos. "E" & "H", 2nd Battalion Engineers (attached)
(d) Ambulance Company No. 7, Field Hospital No. 7.
(e) Signal Corps Detachments, First Aero Squadron.
            Detachment Signal Corps
(f) Wagon Companies, Numbers 1 and 2.
4. Lieutenant Colonel Euclid B. Frick, Medical Corps, will report to the
   Commanding Officer (Major Sample) as surgeon in charge, Medical
   Base Group.

      *   *   *   *

11. (1) The following telegrams from Department Headquarters are
quoted for the information of all concerned and compliance therewith
is enjoined:

March 14, 1916.

The Department Commander directs that you inform all subordinates in
your command that they will report promptly by wire to proper authorities, who will report to these headquarters the names of all officers and
enlisted men accompanying your command who are wounded or killed in
action or who die of sickness while in the field. Commanding Officers of
base and cantonment hospitals will be instructed to make reports. "Dundy."

March 14, 1910.

The greatest caution will be exercised after crossing the border that fire
is not opened on troops pertaining to the de facto Government of Mexico
as such troops are very likely to be found in country which you will traverse. The greatest care and discretion will have to be exercised by all.
"Bundy."

(2) It is enjoined upon all members of the command to make the utmost
endeavor to convince all Mexicans that the only purpose of this expedition
is to assist in apprehending and capturing Villa and his bandits. Citizens
as well as soldiers of the de facto Government will be treated with every
consideration. They will not in any case be molested in the peaceful conduct of their affairs, and their property rights will be scrupulously respected.

By Command of Brigadier General Pershing:
DeR. C. Cabell,
Lieutenant Colonel, 10th Cavalry,
Chief of Staff.

Under orders from Department Headquarters the Expedition was to
enter Mexico in two columns. The west column consisting of the 7th
and 10th regiments of Cavalry and Battery "B," 6th Field Artillery,
was to have its base at Hachita and move by way of Culberson's Ranch.
On March 11th these troops were stationed as follows: 7th Cavalry:
Troops "A" and "B" at Alamo Hueco, N. M., Troop "C" at Culberson's
Ranch, N. M., Headquarters Troop, Machine Gun Troop, and Troops
"E," "F," "G," and "K" at Douglas, Arizona, and Troop "M" at Huds-
peth's Ranch, Arizona. 10th Cavalry: Entire regiment (less Troops
"L" and "M") at Douglas, Arizona, having left Fort Huachuca, Arizona,
on March 9th, arrived at Douglas on March 11th. Battery "B," 6th
Field Artillery at Douglas, Arizona. These troops were directed to proceed overland (by marching) without delay to Culberson's Ranch where
they had all arrived by the night of March 14th, except wagon transportation which came in early on the morning of the 15th.

The east column, consisting of all other troops of the expedition, was
to use Columbus, N. M., as its base and move directly south from there.
The stations of these troops at that time were as follows: 13th Cavalry at
Columbus, N. M., and vicinity (less one troop at Fort Riley, Kansas);

6th and 16th Infantry at El Paso, Texas, from which point they reached Columbus by rail on the night of March 13th and the morning of the 14th; Battery "C," 6th Field Artillery, from Nogales, Arizona, arrived at Columbus by rail on March 14th. Troops of the staff departments were scattered all along the border and arrived on various dates.

Under the proposed plan the two columns were to unite at Ascencion, Mexico, and thereafter take such course as circumstances might dictate. Information reached Columbus before our departure that Villa's band had passed Casas Grandes, moving south.

This changed the original plan as to union of the two columns because to meet at Ascencion would cause delay, and the use of Hachita as a base for the western column was inexpedient. It was therefore decided that the Hachita column was to push on through from Culberson's Ranch by the most direct route to Casas Grandes which should for the time being become the advance base.

On the night of the 13th it was learned that the Commanding Officer of the small detachment of de facto troops stationed at Palomas had received orders to oppose the entry of American troops into Mexico. Every argument was used to convince him that opposition would be futile, and he was advised that an understanding on the subject had been reached between the two governments. But he maintained that his orders made it imperative that he oppose us by force. As an armed clash at the very start was undesirable, Department Headquarters was notified of the situation, and was advised that the column would cross the line at noon on the 15th. Notification was also sent to the officer at Palomas that we would enter Mexico at the appointed time whether he offered opposition or not. The command entered as planned and found that the Mexican troops had vanished.

The Columbus troops received orders at 10:30 A.M., March 15th, to march at 11:30 A.M. Due to the splendid gallantry of the 13th Cavalry in the Columbus fight that regiment was assigned the post of honor—at the head. Troops were formed and moved out promptly at the hour designated. As a mark of appreciation for the part taken by Major Frank Tompkins in the pursuit of Villa on the morning of March 9th, he was designated as commander of the advance guard.

The regiment marched the three miles to the border in column of squads in the order: "K," "L," "M," Machine Gun Troop, and 2nd Squadron. The regimental standard was near the head of the column, and when the international boundary was reached the regimental standard with its color guard was the first to cross at 12:13 P.M. The head of the column then passed through and Troop "K" moved out at a gallop as the advance guard with one platoon covering the front and flanks and the 2nd platoon as support some 600 yards ahead of the main body, consisting of the 6th and 16th Infantry, Battery "C," 6th Field Artillery, and the 1st and 2nd Wagon Companies. The advance guard found Palomas deserted, with the exception of an old couple. As this was to be our first camp in Mexico the advance guard formed an outpost covering the rest of the command as they made camp.

Palomas consisted of about thirty adobe houses scattered about a spring which became a small alkaline stream, flowing into a lake a mile or so to the east.

For the benefit of those civilians who may read these pages let me say that a Wagon Company in 1916 consisted of:

1 Wagon boss, sergeant	27 Wagons
3 Assistants, sergeants	112 Mules
1 Cook	6 Horses
1 Saddler	
1 Blacksmith	
1 Blacksmith's assistant	
28 Enlisted men	

Total 36

It was a cold night. At reveille we found the water in our canteens frozen and ice in the stream. Fed horses at 5:30 A.M., had breakfast, and mounted up at 7:00 A.M. Due to the greater mobility of the Cavalry and Artillery the command separated, the mounted troops going on ahead and followed by the two infantry regiments. Company "C," 16th Infantry, was detailed as a guard for the two wagon companies. This permitted this company to ride on the wagons.

The mounted command now consisted of Headquarters and 7 troops of the 13th Cavalry, Battery "C," 6th Field Artillery, (Captain Tilman Campbell), Company "C," 16th Infantry, (Captain William G. Ball), and two wagon companies. We marched about 20 miles to Boca Grande without incident other than finding the body of a white man who had been murdered. He was dressed in drawers and an olive drab shirt, was blindfolded, and been shot in the head. Dead about a week. We paused long enough to bury the poor fellow and murmur a prayer for the repose of his soul. Our march carried us over a high rolling country for a few miles, then we entered a canyon which continued to Boca Grande. Shortly after leaving camp we passed over some of the ground I had traversed in my chase after Villa on the 9th.

On March 17th, we left camp at 7:30 and headed for Espia where we arrived shortly after noon, having marched 21 miles. A courier from General Pershing came into camp from Ojitas saying the General would reach Casas Grandes this same evening (March 17th) with the 7th and 10th Cavalry. We were to join him there, as he needed the wagon companies to operate from there as a new base. This courier took one of our fresh horses and proceeded to Columbus, where he expected to arrive that night provided he was not caught by roving bands of Mexicans.

On March 18th we left camp at 7:00 A.M. for Colonia Diaz, where we arrived at 11:10 A.M. This was once a prosperous Mormon Colony, but had long since been destroyed by one or more of the warring factions. At one time the population was 900 but few now remain. The houses consisted of brick and adobe—almost all in ruins. It was laid out in broad streets with sidewalks bordered with cottonwood trees.

We continued our march to Ascencion, where we arrived at 1:10 P.M., after covering 22 miles from Espia. Ascencion seemed well populated by people of both sexes and all ages. Their curiosity brought them out in great numbers to watch us go by. They were very apathetic, displaying neither friendship nor hostility. This was formerly a place of about 1500 people, and it looked as if most of them were still there, living in flat topped adobe houses, affording excellent vantage points from which they could observe us. This town is in the midst of a farming region which at one time was prosperous, prior to the numerous revolutions that have been played on the Chihuahua stage, each leaving behind it sights and memories of death and destruction, ruin and desolation.

At 10:00 P.M. Lieutenant Arthur E. Wilbourn came into camp with three motor trucks, via Gibson's Ranch from Columbus, having left Columbus at 11:00 A.M. this date. He reported 11th Cavalry, 6th and 16th Infantry, and one battalion, 4th Field Artillery behind us, coming along. The trucks will make one or two trips, relaying supplies forward from Boca Grande.

On March 19th the wagons left camp at 5:00 A.M.; cavalry at 7:00 A.M. Planned to water the horses at a lake about five miles from Ascencion, but guides sent word that the water was alkaline and would kill the horses. Reached Ojo[1] Frederico at 8:45 A.M. where we watered stock and grazed for an hour. Again started at 9:45, and two hours later Colonel Herbert J. Slocum, commanding officer, took the advance guard, and moving at a faster gait than the main body headed for the Casas Grandes River where he arrived at 2:00 P.M. The main body pulled in 50 minutes later. This camp is called Vuerte de los Alamos (Big Bend). Distance marched 30 miles. Country generally level except for three miles through Capuchin Pass. Everybody had a good bath in the river and some washed underclothing, the author amongst them. I was made responsible for the safety of this camp. There was no danger from any attack in force, but a skulking foe could do some sniping, if not discouraged. To guard against this I placed outguards at exposed points. The heavy brush across the river was an ideal place for the kind of annoyance we might expect, but this was guarded against by training a couple of the guns from the artillery on this place ready to fire in case of need. The night passed without alarm.

On March 20th reveille was at 4:00 A.M. Wagons left camp at 5:00 A.M., followed at once by the artillery. Cavalry left two hours later. This arrangement of splitting the column worked out to the advantage and comfort of all concerned. The cavalry being the more mobile could cover the day's march in less time than the others, so by starting late were in the saddle a shorter time. Marching in two short columns caused less dust and less "checks" on the road than when in one long column. The route carried us through Corralitos and continued on to a point about one mile north of Colonia Dublan, where we went into camp at 1:20 P.M., having marched 25 miles. We found here two troops, 10th Cavalry, Battery "B," 6th Field Artillery, and General Pershing and staff.

Now for the western column. On the 15th telegraphic orders were sent to Colonel Dodd at Culberson's Ranch to hold his command in readiness to start upon arrival of General Pershing, but owing to an automobile accident the General did not arrive until nearly midnight, the column having waited, ready to start, since 9:30 P.M., a poor prepa-

---

[1] Ojo, a well.

ration for a night's march. In view of the forced march planned for this column their wagon transportation had been sent to Columbus, pack trains being the only transportation to accompany the column.

This flying column was led in person by General Pershing. They crossed the border at 12:30 A.M., March 16th, and marched in the dark to Geronimo Rock, a distance of about 25 miles, where they arrived at 6:00 A.M. and went into bivouac. At noon they again took up the march and halted for the night at Ojitos, a distance of about 30 miles, at 6:45 P.M., having covered about 55 miles since midnight. They bivouacked at Ojitos that night, and took up the march at 7:00 A.M. the 17th for Colonia Dublan, where they arrived about 8:00 P.M., having marched that day 68 miles. This made about 125 miles in all since crossing the border and was an eye opener to the Mexicans. It was really remarkable marching when we consider the long distances these regiments had marched to reach Culberson's Ranch, the heavy loads carried, the rough country covered, and that neither men nor horses had any sleep the night of March 15-16.

The route taken by the cavalry of this command was so rough that the artillery, Battery "B," 6th Field Artillery, commanded by Captain E. H. Yule, since deceased, was ordered by another route more suitable for wheels but at least 20 miles longer. This battery crossed the line at 12:30 A.M., March 16th, by the battery commander's watch and arrived at the camp at Colonia Dublan at the same time as the cavalry column. In this march Captain Yule claims the following records for his battery:

(1) Distance for U.S. Horse Artillery in 46 hours elapsed time anywhere.

(2) Distance for U.S. Horse Artillery in 46 hours elapsed time in a foreign country.

(3) Distance for U.S. Horse Artillery in 46 hours elapsed time in foreign hostile country.

(4) Distance for U.S. Horse Artillery in 46 hours elapsed time following cavalry the first 18 hours and over rough unimproved roads all the way (when there *were* roads).

(5) Distance for U.S. Horse Artillery in 46 hours elapsed time at approximately 4000 feet altitude in a desert country.

(6) World's record for Horse Artillery of any country under similar circumstances.

(7) Distance for U.S. Horse Artillery in 46 hours elapsed time over unknown, unimproved desert country, led by a guide.

Whether these records will hold or not is immaterial, as the fact remains that this march of Battery "B," 6th Field Artillery, is an illustration of what troops can do under adverse circumstances when well disciplined, well trained and well led. As this battery marched 20 miles farther than the cavalry column their total distance was close to 145 miles in about 46 hours, an outstanding accomplishment.

CHAPTER XV

Campaign of the Three Cavalry Columns From Colonia Dublan. Operations of the 7th Cavalry, March 18 to April 3. The Fight at Guerrero

Upon the arrival of the western force at Dublan it was reported by natives that Villa and his band were somewhere in the vicinity of San Miguel, where they were gathering supplies, recuperating stock, and seizing new mounts from the people in that vicinity. It was at once determined to send south three separate cavalry columns with instructions to cooperate with each other to the fullest extent. It was believed possible, by moving these detachments, approximately parallel to each other, that Villa would be prevented from moving toward Sonora on the west, or toward the railroad on the east, with the additional chance of cutting his trail or getting ahead of him before he could move south of the railroad into the mountains back of Guerrero, to which section it was believed he would probably go.

One of the three detachments, consisting of the 7th Cavalry, 29 officers and 647 enlisted men, Colonel James B. Erwin, Commanding, left Colonia Dublan on the night of March 17-18 (a few hours after reaching that place from their forced march from Culberson's) with orders to proceed without delay by way of Galeana to the southwest of El Valle, thence to ascend the eastern slope of the Sierra Madre Oriental Mountains by trail to the eastern edge of the San Miguel plateau in the hope of striking Villa's band if there, or as he moved eastward with his spoils.

The second detachment, consisting of the second squadron and Machine Gun Troop of the 10th Cavalry, 14 officers and 258 enlisted men, under Command of Colonel W. C. Brown, was directed to proceed by rail and detrain at Rucio, and from there move direct to San Miguel.

The third column, consisting of the first squadron of the 10th Cavalry, 8 officers and 204 enlisted men, under command of Major E. W. Evans, was also ordered to proceed by rail to Las Varas, near Madera, cover the territory to the south of Babicora plateau, prevent Villa from moving southwest, and cooperate with the other two columns as far as practicable.

The reason for sending the two 10th Cavalry detachments by rail was that this regiment had already traveled from Fort Huachuca, Arizona, to Colonia Dublan, a distance of 252 miles, since March 10th, an average of over 30 miles a day, and the animals had begun to show the effects of the strain. Moreover, it was thought they could gain time on Villa's swiftly moving column. Upon General Pershing's telegraphic request to the general manager of the El Paso Southwestern Railroad, a train was promptly sent from Juarez for the use of this regiment.

Upon the arrival of the train at Colonia Dublan on the morning of March 19th the cars were found in very bad condition. The box cars had to be ventilated by cutting holes in the sides, and many repairs had to be made on all cars, causing considerable delay in departure.

The first of these three columns to hit the trail was the 7th Cavalry. This command had reached Colonia Dublan in the early evening of March 17th, after their memorable march from Culberson's Ranch. Before the animals had a chance to recover from this effort the regiment was ordered out as one of the three flying columns in pursuit of Villa and his band, and started at about 3:00 A.M. March 18th.

On March 21st Colonel George A. Dodd was ordered to join the 7th Cavalry and take command of its operations. He had further instructions to cooperate with the 10th Cavalry, and in case of emergency or pressing expediency to use that regiment or any part of it in the attainment of the object in view. He joined the 7th Cavalry in its camp about six miles south of Galeana and assumed command of operations. Colonel Erwin retained immediate command of his regiment.

On March 22nd the regiment proceeded southward, passing by El Valle about noon. Lieutenant Robert M. Campbell, 7th Cavalry, and Scout Tracy were sent with a message to the commander of the federal troops in that place, Colonel Salas, requesting an interview. Colonel Salas expressed a desire to see the American commander, but first sent his adjutant to meet the American troops, which had halted on the outskirts of the town. The trail followed by the 7th Cavalry led through a canyon, the sides of which were covered by Carranza troops. Colonel Salas met Colonel Dodd and asked by what authority the United States troops were in Mexico. The letter under which the United States troops were acting was interpreted to him, and he stated that he already had a copy of that letter, but that it had not been sent by his government.

Salas then confided that Villa was at Namiquipa with a large command; that three or four days before, Villa had beaten him badly and had driven him back through Cruces to El Valle, where he had taken up a defensive position in expectation of further attacks. Salas detailed a staff officer to accompany the American troops through the canyon. The command then pushed on as rapidly as conditions would permit, and bivouacked at Agua Zarca.

On March 23rd camp was broken long before daylight, between four and five o'clock, and the command followed the road to the crossing of the Santa Maria River about six miles north of Cruces. At El Valle, and during this day's march, assurances were received that Villa was still at Namiquipa, and that he had expressed his intention of remaining there until driven out. There were no troops in Cruces, though a strong anti-American sentiment prevailed there. The regiment left the main road in order to keep its presence unknown in Cruces, and followed an arroyo eastward, striking an indistinct trail leading south to the foothills of the mountains east of Cruces and Namiquipa, and nearly paralleling the general course of the river. The passage of the troops around Cruces was probably unobserved.

Colonel Dodd intended to remain concealed about 12 or 13 miles from Namiquipa, then proceed to and surround the place and take it at day-break the next morning, but before it was possible to act upon this plan, information was received from the scouts that Villa was no longer at Namiquipa; that on March 20th, immediately after Colonel Salas' defeat, Colonel Cano, another Carranzista commander, had attacked Villa and driven him from Namiquipa. It was uncertain whether Villa had gone south, west, southwest or east, and Colonel Dodd, bitterly disappointed at learning that he was too late to catch Villa at Namiquipa, ordered the command to bivouac at the nearest water.

After a study of the scant and conflicting information, the commander sent, on the following morning, a message to General Pershing, apprising him of the information just obtained, and also dispatched a note to Colonel Cano requesting him to guard certain passes, while the American column would swing westward in an endeavor to get south and west of Villa. This plan was based upon a report that Villa had passed through or near Oso Canyon, and gone to the south or southwest. Until the receipt of this report Colonel Dodd had believed that Villa had gone south or east, and had conducted his march accordingly.

The command swung into the saddle at 5:00 A.M., March 23rd, followed good road for ten miles to Santa Maria River, where they had plenty of good water which the animals appreciated. A few miles farther, opposite Cruces, a native stated that there were some Carranzistas at Ortega under Colonel Cano. Some Villistas had come to Cruces, the day before to get provisions to take to Villa, wounded in the hills just southeast of Cruces. No Villistas were in Namiquipa. He stated that Villa had left Namiquipa and gone no one knew where. The Villistas had scattered from Namiquipa on March 19th or 20th, after fight with the Carranzistas. There were two factions in Namiquipa, one of which threatened to fight if American troops entered the town. Villa made a speech here before going to Columbus saying he was going to hit a blow on the border, hurt Americans' pride and bring on intervention. The native stated there were no troops in Namiquipa and that people in the town did not know American soldiers were present.

The column continued south five miles to a valley running east and west and made camp. Water was good and plentiful. Hit camp about 12:45 P.M. after a march of 20 miles. The following men were reported by Mr. J. B. Barker (civilian scout and guide) as having gone away with Villa from Namiquipa: Nicholas Hernandez, Candelario Cervantes, Ramon Tarongo and two or three others. Lopez was wounded and in the hills.

Namiquipa was considered the most revolutionary town in Mexico, and had a population of 3,000 to 4,000 people. At 5:00 P.M. Tracy (scout and guide) was sent into Namiquipa for information. Nothing could be planned until his return.

At 8:15 next morning, March 24th, three Carranzista soliders came into camp. They were members of Colonel Cano's command, and were sent by Colonel Brown, 10th Cavalry, at Babicora, with information

GENERAL PERSHING AND STAFF

Left to right: Capt. W. O. Reed, Lieut. J. L. Collins, Lieut. Col. DeRosey C. Cabell, Gen. Pershing, Maj. John L. Hines, Col. Geo. O. Cress, Capt. Leon B. Kromer.

Wagon Trains at Colonia Dublan

that Villa had pretty surely gone south from Namiquipa to San Geronimo or south of there. Villa expected reinforcements from General Banderas to reach him from the south. The rendezvous was supposed to be Los Tanques, 23 miles east of Namiquipa. Villa had about 200 men, many of whom had been taken along by force. Carranza people thought he could increase this to about 800, many of whom would be impressed. Colonel Cano had about 100 men towards Babicora which place is about 30 miles from Namiquipa. Colonel Brown with his command arrived at Babicora March 22nd and was to wait there for Colonel Dodd and his command. These soldiers said Santa Ana had been looted and no supplies could be obtained there. That Chavez or Babicora were the best places from which to operate, (Santa Ana, Chavez, Babicora were properties of the American publisher, W. R. Hearst) as they had supplies, and Maximiliano Marquez, a Mexican agent for Mr. Hearst, had some 50 men, all good scouts. Cano would cooperate. These Mexicans were to find Cano and give him information of the American plan, which was to march to Chavez for supplies and to communicate with the 10th Cavalry at Babicora. From there two columns would go S.E., 10th to go farthest south, 7th to go S.W., Cano to guard Villa's northern exit at El Oso. A Carranza column then on N.W.R.R. was to go to Santo Tomas (just north of Guerrero) and await directions, which would be to march east and block Villa's southern exit. Cano was supposed to be at Santa Clara east of Namiquipa.

Dodd broke camp at 9:45 A.M. and marched into a cold gale, hard on man and beast. The command followed a trail going a little south of west across the hills and arrived at Las Cruces after going 12 miles. Watered the horses in irrigation ditch at south end of town. Tracy joined here and confirmed Villa's fight with Carranzistas on Sunday the 19th, and his fight with Cano a couple of days later at Las Animas. Tracy said Cano was reported at Namiquipa on the 23rd and Villa at Los Tanques same date. This checked up pretty well with the Mexicans' from Babicora. Continued the march, buffeted by the gale all day. Finally arrived in a canyon on the east slope of the Sierra Madre Oriental Mountains and made camp at 5:30 P.M., having covered twenty miles in cruel weather.

Broke camp at 6:20 A.M. Saturday the 25th. Travelled up the canyon, leading the horses up steep rocky trail and over the divide. Beautiful country, heavily wooded; tall pines, oak, cedars, junipers. The march continued through Chavez, half way to Babicora, total distance 20 miles. Camped close to Babicora where the troops secured plenty of supplies. Also received messages from Colonel Cabell and Colonel Brown, and sent messages to Brown by courier and to General Pershing by wire. Colonel Maximiliano Marquez, caretaker of Babicora, was very hospitable and cordial. The command remained in camp until 4:00 A.M. the 26th. About 5:00 P.M. the 25th 1st Lieut. Emil Engel, 7th Cavalry, who had left Dublan the same evening as Colonel Dodd but at a later hour, caught up and delivered three messages: (1) Colonel Cabell to Major Frank Tompkins directing him to establish base at El Valle; (2) Col. Cabell to Colonel Dodd, giving information we already knew of Colonel Brown's movements; (3) Colonel Brown to Colonel Erwin, addressed to San Miguel, stating he would move to Chavez.

Colonel Dodd here arranged to leave two troops to guard Jaral and Aramillo passes. Colonel Marquez got word about 5:00 P. M. that Carranza troops had moved to passes south of Los Tanques from southeast, and that Carranza troops were in Santa Clara. The 10th Cavalry was reported by messenger, at 9:00 P.M., to be close to Los Tanques.

We broke camp in the early morning of the 26th and marched down Potrillo Pass. Good road except for a couple of miles down hill. Reached Santa Ana at 11:30 A.M., 28 miles from camp. Everything ruined, burned and deserted—inclosed ranch buildings, great court yards, many rooms, etc. Villa burned it last February. Carranza messengers arrived at 1:00 P.M., and from them it was learned that the 10th Cavalry was still in El Oso Canyon and had thoroughly explored it without finding a trace of Villa.

The 7th Cavalry bivouacked overnight at Santa Ana. Late in the evening a messenger came from Lieutenant William C. F. Nicholson, 7th Cav., with messages from Colonel Brown which had been sent from Namiquipa on the 25th. In one of them was stated: "Villa's whereabouts unknown, but it is thought possible he has gone through the mountains towards Bachineva." The Colonel stated that this slight clue was somewhat in line with the conclusions he himself had arrived at, which was the probability of Villa striking for the Guerrero Valley.

From the Santa Maria plain two passes with good trails lead to the Guerrero Valley: the Piojo Trail direct from Providencia to San Isidro and Guerrero; and the Nahuerachic Trail from the same point, but farther west, through Nahuerachic Pass, leading southwest to Santo Tomas. In order to take either trail it would have been necessary for Villa to leave the mountains and at some point cross the plains. On March 27th Colonel Dodd marched to Providencia, looking for signs of the passage of Villa. Finding nothing, he was satisfied that all reports that had reached him of western and southwestern movements of the bandit chief after the Namiquipa fight were false, and that Villa had not crossed the plain toward these passes.

Accordingly, without lingering at Providencia, the column took up the march to Bachineva, making bivouac at a place called Soledad. No water was available here for the horses, so the command resumed the march early the next morning, March 28. At Delicia, the command was met by one of Cano's officers, Lieutenant Ismall Ontevera, and some of his men. Ontevera said that he had just driven off some of Villa's men who had been spying on the American column. He also stated that Villa had, on the previous night, passed toward the south some 25 miles farther to the east, and was now on the Mexican Northwestern R. R. near San Diego. Colonel Dodd did not attach much importance to this report.

A little later a native was captured who told Colonel Dodd that Villa had been in Bachineva two or three days before, had taken property and persons, and had made an inflammatory speech stating that the Americans were coming and urging everyone to join him; also that Villa had been in a fight at Guerrero the night just passed. Colonel

Dodd gave some credence to this report and pushed on to Bachineva, where it was confirmed, and where it was learned that Villa was wounded and was still, at last report, at Guerrero with 500 or 600 men. After receiving this information from the native and before reaching Bachineva, Lieut. Herbert A. Dargue, flying from the north, landed his plane alongside the marching column and delivered a message from General Pershing. This message acquainted Colonel Dodd with the fact that Major Robert L. Howze, 11th Cavalry, with a command of 240 officers and enlisted men of the 11th Cavalry, had been sent out to take up the chase, and conveyed instructions that Colonel Dodd should turn over to the fresh column his pack animals, should put his command in camp near Namiquipa, and should allow it to recuperate for further service.

Lieutenant Dargue took back a reply which included information of the situation, and disclosed Colonel Dodd's plans for the immediate future. "I am now satisfied," he stated, "that Villa is not far distant." And he adds, "I shall proceed farther south, and shall continue in such touch as is possible to attain (and attack if possible) with Villa. At any rate, until fresh troops arrive."

Colonel Dodd was now satisfied for the first time that he was on the right trail, for every indication and new rumor went to show that the immediate objective of Villa was Guerrero, military center of the Guerrero district, or some other important point in the Guerrero Valley. But what confused Colonel Dodd was that Villa did not go there by way of either the Piojo or Nahuerachic Trails, unless he was afraid to cross the valley on account of the troops west; or desired to reach Bachineva, which he could do under cover, for the purpose of securing supplies, impressing men and inciting the people against the American troops. Had Colonel Dodd only known it there were trails leading from near Bachineva to the Guerrero Valley, which if followed would have lessened the distance marched by the American Cavalry by at least one third, a consideration of the highest importance, as the command was practically without supplies, and had been living on fresh beef, frijoles, and parched corn for several days. Men and animals had already suffered severely from poor rations, and from the intense cold that had been endured on the high Babicora plateau, where canteens of water froze solid and whiskers grew icicles. The horses of the command were nearly worn out and the men were tired. From March 13th to March 28th (this date) the troops had marched 14 days out of 15, a distance of approximately 400 miles under most trying conditions, and with a shortage of rations and forage; and on top of this they had a night march ahead of them of about 36 miles over unknown mountainous trails, to be followed at dawn, as every man in the command hoped, by a battle with an enemy who not only knew the ground but outnumbered them at least two to one.

The weakest horses and men, quite a large number of the latter, and with them the only medical officer of the column, had been left at Santa Ana, and of the pack mules all but a few had already been sent back to the base. Bivouac was made for a few hours south of Bachineva, while men fed and horses grazed. Colonel Dodd consulted his maps and guides, and sized up the situation. The guides with the column knew nothing of the country, as they had gone beyond the limits of the territory familiar to them. Reliable native guides could not be secured, though large sums of money were offered. None of the natives would state whether a certain designated trail led to Guerrero or not. The only reply to inquiries being the usual "Quien sabe?" Mr. Barker, on whom the colonel had greatly relied for information and as a guide, had been in Guerrero but once, some years before, but had entered from another direction. He had had a trail explained to him which led from Bachineva to Guerrero, a long way around, which could be taken, and which he believed could be followed. This trail, or what was believed to be the trail, was indicated on the map.

Realizing that this juncture was a critical one, Colonel Dodd resolved to follow a moderate certainty rather than an absolute uncertainty, and in doing so made a forced night march, hoping to reach Guerrero next morning by or before daylight. After resting a few hours in bivouac the march was continued until dark, when bivouac was again made. At 11:00 P. M. the night march began. The uncertainty of the route caused many halts and delays, during which the men would lie down on the ground, in spite of the bitter cold, and to sleep holding the reins. At the last bivouac two guides had been impressed, who, as was feared, led the command the longest way round, though, as was known, in the correct general direction. Later, before daylight, the knowledge and the courage of these guides gave out simultaneously and others, probably equally unreliable, had to be found, all of which, together with the long circuitous route which we had followed during the night, consumed much valuable time. Finally at about 6:30 A.M. we had gained a position from which the town of Guerrero could be located, but it was probably 8:00 o'clock or later before the attack could be made, this delay being due to the treachery of the guides in leading us into an impossible approach.

Guerrero, military center of the Guerrero district, is located in the lower plain of the Guerrero Valley, and is not visible from the east until one is directly over it. On the east side there are precipitous bluffs, high and in most places impassable, cut by deep arroyos running well back into the upper plain. These arroyos are also invisible until one is practically at their edges. The main road from the east follows a steep spur or "hogback." On the west side are bluffs, not quite so abrupt, and these extend back to the mountains. This edge of the valley is also cut by deep, partly wooded arroyos, difficult of passage.

Colonel Dodd says of the approach march: "Had the main road been struck and followed, disposition for attack would have been quickly and more advantageously made." The correct road and the trail followed under the direction of the guide are shown on the sketch map by A and B respectively. "Finding myself misled," to quote the commander further, "and being ignorant of the corrugated character of the ground between the column and the town along the bluffs, I endeavored to correct the doings of the guide by following the bluff, but was stopped by the arroyos. These had to be headed in many cases, which necessitated extra distance and consumption of much time."

Colonel Dodd's plan of attack was to detach one squadron and order it across the river to the west side, so that it might, unobserved if possible, gain the foothills west of the town and block the arroyos leading out from the valley on that side. The second squadron, Major Edward B. Winans, was selected for this mission, and its advance is described by the commander of "E" Troop, Captain Samuel F. Dallam, as follows: (C on the map indicates the point at which the squadron was detached. "E" Troop was the last troop in the squadron, and was designated as rear guard.)

Our squadron turned off to the left, descended the bluff, crossed the river, changed direction to the right and pushed on to get between the town and the hills. As the squadron went over the bluff, it naturally became elongated, and I saw it was drawing away from me, so I dismounted my men in order to go down the faster. Arriving at the base of the bluff, I halted to assemble my troop and moved forward some distance in rear of the column. As I descended the bluff, looking to the right, I could see at the far end of the village, mounted men leaving it and galloping up the bluff on the same side that I was descending. I estimated that these men would encounter the head of the regimental column on that side.

Pushing along the rear of the column, I saw one of our troops had disappeared, then another, and finally I saw the third turn off to the left. Firing came from the hills on our left and not from the town. As our troops had evidently gone into action, and as the direction of the enemy was in my front toward the town, I pushed on to get between the town and our squadron. Just between me and the town was a ravine, and I decided to cross that, take position above it and cover our side of the town with mounted patrols. About this time the squadron commander rode up beside me and I gave him my plan, which he approved.

Securing the ravine and some houses beside it, which were used as shelter for the horses, a squad was detached to reduce an annoying fire coming from our left and rear. Another squad was sent up ahead outside of the town, and the balance remained in hand near the houses.

Shortly after we had taken this position, the Villista commander, with the rear guard and train, tried to rush the ravine but was killed in the attempt, and his troops and train and some Carranza prisoners captured. About this time Lieutenant Pearson Menoher appeared on the opposite side of the ravine with a detachment.

Lieutenant Albert J. Myer also appeared from that side of the ravine. He had been with the brigade commander on the bluff, and they had seen a large force of Villistas leave the town on our side before our arrival, and feared we would be ambushed. Lieutenant Myer had offered to inform the squadron commander of the situation, and had descended the bluff and ridden alone through the town and the Villistas for the purpose.

On the map the positions taken by the principal portion of the 2nd squadron (Troops "F," "G," "H,") and by Troop "E" were indicated, probably not very accurately, by F and G respectively. The Villista commander, General Hernandez, was killed by Captain Dallam's troop, which also captured two machine guns and other arms, and secured some Carranza prisoners, who were being held by the bandits.

No bandits escaped through arroyo G after Dallam had attained this position, while those who had already passed were pressed and driven westward. The balance of the squadron, arriving at arroyo F encountered a large body of Villistas moving in an orderly manner, not firing, and carrying the Mexican flag. They were consequently not molested, and this ruse undoubtedly saved the escaping party from

annihilation. This same use of the national flag was resorted to elsewhere but without such favorable results to the bandits.

In the meantime the main body had been pushing along the eastern
bluff. The arroyos caused much delay, and the command was still a

The Fight at Guerrero

great distance from the town when it became evident that the bandits
had been alarmed and were escaping. Attack had to be initiated at
long range. Fire with machine guns was opened at D and with rifles
at E.

As a number of the bandits were seen escaping at the north end of town whence they then struck eastward, Lieutenant Colonel S. R. H. Tompkins, then with Troop "C" at H was sent with that troop to intercept the escaping party. He was presently reinforced by Major A. L. Dade with "I," "K" and "L" Troops. Later, as the Villistas were moving toward the hills about Colera, "B" Troop, under Captain William B. Cowin, and the Machine Gun Troop under Lieutenant Albert C. Wimberly, were sent as further reinforcements.

The pursuit of the bandits was pressed vigorously, in spite of the exhausted condition of the horses. Several stands were made by the retreating parties, and dismounted fire action was resorted to. A pistol charge mounted was planned, but had to be abandoned because it was found impossible to urge the horses into a rapid gate. The poor beasts had given all they had and could do no more.

The running fight continued until the Villistas entered the mountains, which were rough and difficult to traverse. Here they broke into small detachments and scattered. The engagement had started shortly after 8 o'clock March 29th, and it was 11:30 A.M. before the regiment was reassembled.

The command that participated in this action consisted of 25 officers and 345 enlisted men, all of the 7th Cavalry except Colonel Dodd and his staff. The only casualties were five men wounded, none seriously. Villa's command numbered from 500 to 600. Their loss is not known. Colonel Dodd reported 30 killed and an unknown but large number wounded. He later estimated that the enemy loss was still greater. No prisoners were taken. The captured property included two machine guns, 44 rifles, 13 horses and 23 mules.

Francisco (Pancho) Villa, having been wounded twice in a fight with Carranzista troops several days previously, was not present with his band at Guerrero at the time of the action. His movements have not been accurately determined; but there was some reason to credit the report that he left Guerrero at two o'clock on the morning of the 29th, the day of the American attack. The doctor who had treated Villa in Guerrero was interviewed, and he confirmed the report of the wounded condition of the bandit leader. He stated that Villa's leg was broken. The sought-for Pancho was, then, probably effecting his escape in a wagon, accompanied by a small escort, while the 7th Cavalry column was feeling its poorly guided, uncertain, but determined way through the night from Bachineva to Guerrero.

During the night march the command, uncertain as to its route, halted at a road fork. The guide, Mr. J. B. Barker, preferred one route, while the advance guard commander, after consultation with some natives, desired to take the other. Later indications showed that if the column had taken the route preferred by the advance guard commander, it might easily have encountered Villa and his body guard. In any case, it is certain that Dodd's column missed the bandit chief at this time by not more than a few miles.

Villa's command at Guerrero was under orders to follow their commander, who knew of the near approach of the American troops and sought to avoid them. The bandit command was saddling up to leave when the 7th Cavalry struck them.

Colonel Dodd estimated that from March 22nd, when he took immediate command of the column, to the evening of the 29th after the engagement, the command had marched approximately 225 miles, an average of over 28 miles a day, much of it over very rough trails, on insufficient and at times practically no forage, without rest for a day; this marching, immediately following other marches from March 13th (for a portion of the command, and for the balance from March 9th) to the 20th of approximately 252 miles. And it might be well to add that much of this campaigning was at elevations around 7,000 feet above sea level with the accompanying hot days and freezing nights, a condition which soon consumed the vitality of man and horse.

After the engagement the command went into camp close to San Isidro until the afternoon of the 30th, when the entire body moved to Frijole Canyon, 10 miles toward the north. Here it rested over the 31st and while in camp endured a storm of hail and snow. Scouting was kept up continuously with the object of learning the movements of Villa and his adherents subsequent to their departure from Guerrero.

On April 1st the regiment left the 3rd Squadron at Frijole Canyon and marched to Providencia. Here the command received the first fresh supplies since leaving Galeana. Colonel Dodd visited General Pershing at the expedition headquarters at San Geronimo, and received instructions to send two troops to occupy Bachineva and to block the Mazana and Naheurachic Passes, then to return with the balance of the command to Frijole Canyon. Lieutenant Colonel Tompkins was sent with the two troops to Bachineva, Captain Dallam to guard Naheurachic Pass with Troop "E," and Lieutenant Henry E. Mitchell with Troop "F" was sent to Mazana Pass, somewhat to the north of "E" Troop's station. Headquarters and two remaining troops returned to Frijole Canyon on April 3rd.

A military commander, operating as was Colonel Dodd in an enemy country where all sources of information must be carefully weighed and sifted, where he had received one false lead after another until he found himself groping through a fog of war and getting nowhere, finally makes an estimate of the situation and then acts on his conclusions. On the evening of March 26th Dodd had about made up his mind that Villa was striking for the Guerrero Valley. Then this same evening he received a message from Colonel W. C. Brown, 10th Cavalry which stated "Villa's whereabouts unknown, but it is thought possible he has gone through the mountains toward Bachineva." Colonel Dodd stated that this slight clue was somewhat in line with the conclusions he himself had arrived at, so while Brown and his command were not in the Guerrero fight his energetic scouting furnished the information which decided Dodd to make that splendid night ride through the mountains with the 7th Cavalry, resulting in the crushing defeat to the Villista band at Guerrero on the morning of March 29th.

At this time Colonel Dodd was 63 years old, approaching his 64th birthday, when he must retire from active duty. When his victory at Guerrero was heard on the floor of Congress the members cheered and a few days later the President of the United States nominated him for promotion to the grade of Brigadier General, which nomination was quickly confirmed by the Senate.

CHAPTER **XVI**

Campaign of the Three Columns. Operations of the Second Squadron, 10th Cavalry, March 19 to 31

Of the three original columns General Pershing sent from Colonia Dublan we have just followed the fortunes of the first to start, the 7th Cavalry. We will now march with the other two: 1st Squadron, 10th Cavalry, under command of Major E. W. Evans, consisting of 8 officers and 204 enlisted men; and 2nd Squadron, same regiment, consisting of Machine Gun Troop and four rifle troops, 14 officers and 250 enlisted men under command of the Colonel, W. C. Brown.

Brown's orders were to entrain March 19th with such troops as could be loaded on cars placed at his disposal at the Embarcadero near Colonia Dublan, and to proceed to Cuevitas, there to disembark and take the trail for San Miguel, arriving there just before daylight. The trip by rail was given him as one of about three hours, and had it been so there should have been no difficulty in carrying out the order completely.

The column under Major Evans was also to go in this same train to Las Varas, near Madera, cover the territory to the south of Babicora plateau, prevent Villa from moving southwest, and cooperate with the other two columns as far as practicable.

The rolling stock was very bad. Holes in the sides of the box cars had to be cut for ventilation, and very considerable repairs made to floors of cars where burned through, doors improvised where missing, and fuel secured by tearing down stock pens and loading material on the tender. Twenty-five box, stock and three flat cars in all were taken, and subsequent events proved that the train was twice the size that it should have been. The train was loaded at 5:00 P.M. on the 19th, and started thirty minutes later. The command had two days rations, the only government supplies for any kind they were destined to receive until April 20th, 32 days later. They "lived on the country" for 32 days. More fuel being required, the train was to have stopped at Casas Grandes for this, but the conductor and engineer fearing a clash with Carranza troops, passed through without stopping until reaching Don Luis, where a large troop detail tore down part of the stock yard for fuel.

At 8:15 P.M. the engine's supply of water being practically exhausted it uncoupled from the train and went on to Pearson for water. This required several hours before the engine returned, hooked on to the train and took it on past Pearson to the loading place, uncoupled and then returned to Pearson, accompanied by Brown. This was about 1:00 A.M., March 20th, and Brown had some difficulty in arous-

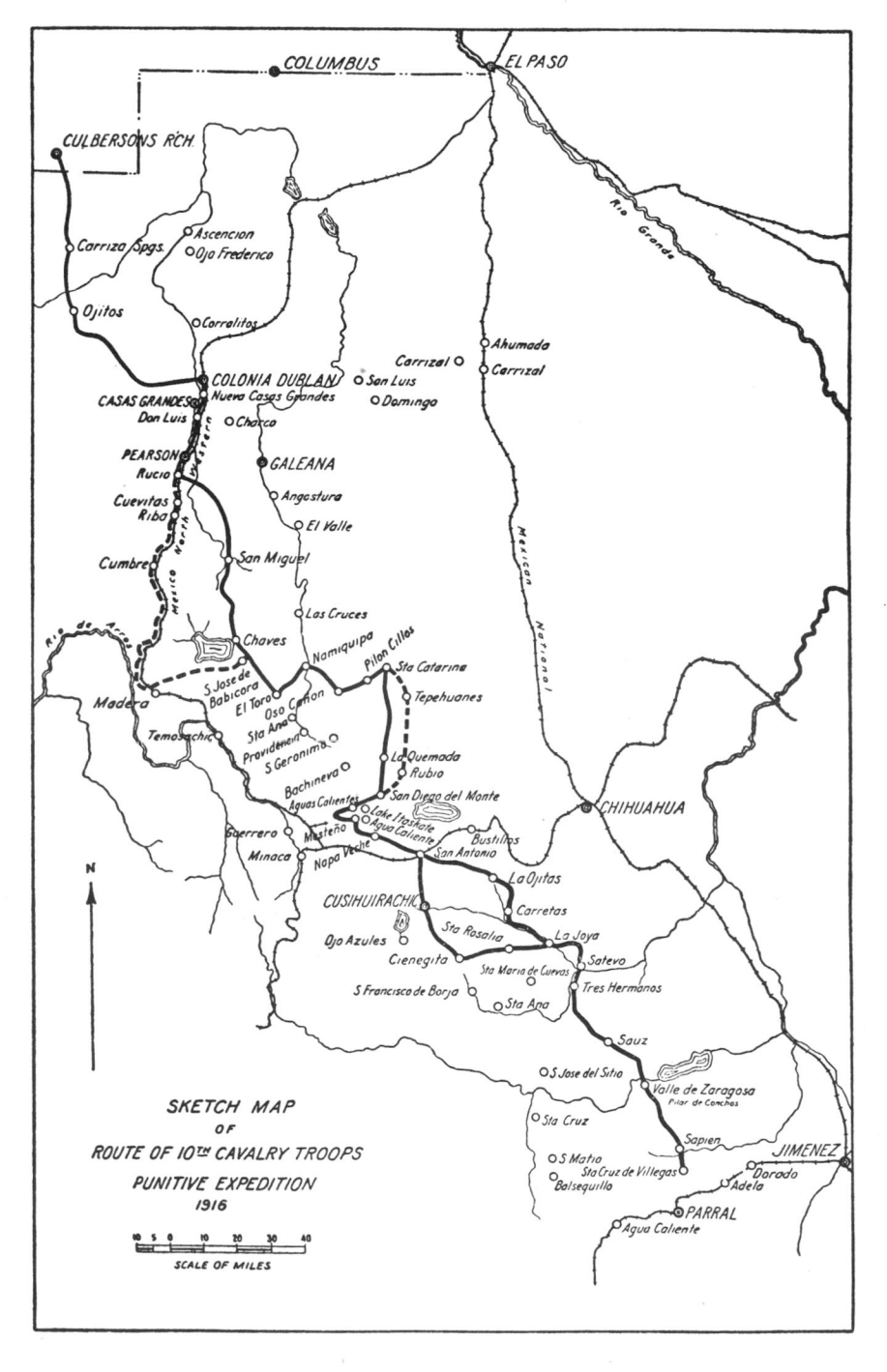

COLUMBUS   EL PASO

CULBERSONS RCH.

Ascencion
Carriza Spgs.   Ojo Frederico

Ojitos   Corralitos

Ahumada
Carrizal   Carrizal
San Luis
COLONIA DUBLAN   Domingo
Nueva Casas Grandes
CASAS GRANDES   Charca
Don Luis
PEARSON   GALEANA
Rucio
Angostura
Cuevitas
Riba   El Valle
Cumbre   San Miguel

Las Cruces
Chaves   Pilon Cillos   Sta Catarina
Namiquipa
S Jose de   Tepehuanes
Babicora
Madera   El Toro   Oso Cañon
Temosachic   Sta Ana
Providencia
S Geronimo
La Quemada
Bachineva   Rubio
Aguas Calientes   San Diego del Monte
Guerrero   Masteño   Lake Itzashate   CHIHUAHUA
Minaca   Napa Veche   Agua Caliente   Bustillos
San Antonio
La Ojitas
Carretas
CUSIHUIRACHIC
Sta Rosalia   La Joya
Ojo Azules   Satevo
Cienegita   Sta Maria de Cuevas
S Francisco de Borja   Sta Ana   Tres Hermanos

Sauz

S Jose del Sitio
Valle de Zaragosa
Pilar de Conchos
Sta Cruz   Sapien
JIMENEZ
S Matio   Sta Cruz de Villegas   Dorado
Balsequillo   Adela
PARRAL
Agua Caliente

Rio Grande

Mexican National

Mexico North Western

Rio de Aros

N

SKETCH MAP
OF
ROUTE OF 10TH CAVALRY TROOPS
PUNITIVE EXPEDITION
1916

10 5 0   10   20   30   40
SCALE OF MILES

ing the Division Superintendent, who stated that as no notice had been given to him of the prospective arrival of the train, no preparation had been made to forward it.

The conductor and the engineer put in a plea that they had had practically no sleep for three days and nights, but Brown assured them of a reward of fifty dollars gold if troops were put through all right. Brown made an urgent plea for two engines, but they failed to grant it, though they did give them coal. But it was 4:00 A.M. before they got started, and at 8:15 A.M. when they arrived at Kilometer 282, two miles north of El Rucio, when the train officials announced that they could go no farther with their heavy train, so took the forward half, 1st Squadron, on to El Rucio, and returning hauled the balance to the same point. Here Brown unloaded his command to march to San Miguel, while Evans, with the train thus lightened, went on to Las Varas.

After detraining at El Rucio Brown watered and fed his stock, had dinner for the command, and at 1:00 P. M., March 20th, started for San Miguel over a very hilly, rocky trail. The column was delayed by a pack mule getting lost, necessitating several men going back to find it, so Brown camped at 7:00 P.M. in a gulch on Cunnivie Trail. At about 4:00 P.M. the command met two Mexicans with corn from San Miguel, who said nothing had been heard of Villa. Reveille was at 5:30 A.M., March 21st, and the column took up the march for San Miguel over the difficult and rocky trail, where it arrived at about noon. It surrounded the place but found Villa forces had not been within 12 miles thereof. The manager of the ranch reported that he heard Villa was in the vicinity of El Valle on the 19th, two days earlier.

Lieutenant C. B. Drake, 7th Cavalry, came in late that evening with a dispatch from Colonel Erwin, from which it was learned that his guide had failed to conduct him to the point agreed upon. Next day, March 22nd, Colonel Brown sent Lieutenant Drake back to Colonel Erwin, advising him of his position and movements and suggesting that he (Erwin) march south while Brown marched on Chavez. Brown marched to Chavez, 27 miles, in a light rain, and found at his destination good hay and corn which the animals deeply appreciated. Mr. Fox, civilian guide, went on to San Jose de Babicora to send messages by wire and to get in touch with Carranza officers. He returned to camp about 8:15 that night with word about Villa at Namiquipa and Santa Clara, where Colonel Cano, Carranzista, had just had a fight with him and defeated him.

On March 23rd the command continued on south through San Jose de Babicora to El Toro, 27 miles, where it went into camp while Brown and Fox detoured via San Jose de Babicora. Here they found several Carranza officers who were very friendly. Brown sent a telegram from this place to Colonel Erwin (through General Pershing) to the effect that Brown was consulting the Carranza commander and that Major Evans would join Brown next day at noon. Brown then rode on to camp at El Toro. At about 7:00 P.M. Colonel Cano's adjutant came into camp and had a satisfactory talk with Brown, arranging for a meeting with Colonel Cano for the following day.

At 1:00 A.M., March 24th, Mr. Fox rode into camp from San Jose de Babicora with about 20 Mexicans, some to be used as guides by Brown. Later in the day Brown met Cano who agreed to cooperate with the American troops, so Colonel Brown sent a message to Colonel Dodd, the brigade commander, giving the location of Brown's command and Evans' prospective movements, and stated that the latest information indicated that Villa was in Oso Canyon or near Santa Clara (east of Namiquipa). Evans joined Brown at 2:50 that afternoon. Everybody, and the horses, suffered from a high cold wind which split lips, cracked the skin, formed ice in the streams, and froze the canteens.

Next morning, March 25th, at 7:00 o'clock, the command left camp for Namiquipa, where they halted for 2½ hours collecting corn, beans, flour, and other food supplies, while Brown conferred with Cano. A few armed men thought to be Villistas were seen in the hills two miles east of town, just before the arrival of the American troops. After the conference the command marched nine miles farther, to Oso Canyon where they went into camp, making 20 miles for the day. The Mexican Colonel, Cano, with 200 or 300 men took a northern trail and camped at the Cervantes ranch. Cervantes' father and mother lived there. Cervantes was second in command to Villa. Cano promised to send a scouting party to the east. In the evening he came to Brown's camp for some more talk. Brown suggested that they could best cooperate by the Mexicans locating Villa, when Brown by a night march would make the attack. Cano promised to do this, so Brown agreed to spend one more day in camp waiting for reports from Mexican scouting parties.

Next day, the 26th, the American cavalry remained in camp as per the agreement with the Mexican Colonel. Brown sent a dispatch to Colonel Dodd and one to General Pershing. Some of Brown's men found in a cache near camp a couple of rifles, Villista officers' clothing, and some expensive decorated china—all loot. Lieutenant W. C. F. Nicholson, 7th Cavalry, came into camp at about 4:00 P.M. with two dispatches Brown had sent out but which had not been delivered.

Next day, the 27th, Brown visited Cano's camp in the early morning and closely questioned the Mexican commander regarding the scouting parties he had agreed to send out, and the results. Brown left the conference satisfied Cano had lied in saying the country had been scouted to the east. Reports from the south toward Bachineva indicated no enemy in that vicinity. Convinced of Cano's treachery Brown broke camp and marched east for 12 miles to Pilon Cillos, where he found good water, grass and wood. This place is 8 miles southwest of Santa Catarina. He purchased some tobacco and soap and 200 pounds of flour in Namiquipa. Brown received a message from Major Frank Tompkins, 13th Cavalry, who was in Namiquipa.

On March 28th, the command broke camp at 3:30 A.M., and at daylight surrounded Santa Catarina and there learned of the presence at Rubio of Villa's forces, about two days previously. The telephone line was cut, and Major Evans and his squadron were sent to Tepehuanes, while Brown and his command went to La Quemada (a ranch), secured seven animals (including two 13th Cavalry horses stolen at

Columbus) which had been left by Villa. Subsequent to his arrival, Brown learned that a Villa lieutenant had been at the ranch and escaped just as the American soldiers arrived. The assistant manager in charge seemed disposed to give correct information but was timid about it. He reported Villa there six days earlier and said he had then gone to Guerrero via Rubio. Information was so indefinite that Brown decided to lay over at Quemada on the 29th, and to go with guide Fox to Rubio to secure positive information as to the whereabouts of the elusive enemy. Brown sent a dispatch to Colonel Dodd at Bachineva, but the guide returned reporting no troops there. Colonel Cano had loaned Colonel Brown a captain and several other men to be used in any way he might think best. Brown now learned that Pablo Lopez was in a canyon near Pilon Cillos and sent this information in a dispatch to Colonel Dodd. Lopez, one of Villa's principal lieutenants, was wounded in the Columbus fight.

Draft of dispatch from Colonel Brown to Colonel Dodd, dated Quemada, March 29, 1916:

Arrived here about 5:30 P. M. 28th. Villa left here March 22nd going to Rubio and from the latter place toward Guerrero. Am sending to Rubio today to secure more definite information. We surrounded ranch when we arrived here but Villa Lieutenant Valintin Avitia saw us coming and escaped. Villa left 6 or 7 horses here including two from 13th Cavalry. Am confiscating all that will be of service. I learned that Pablo Lopez is in the mountains back of Pilon Cillos, badly wounded. Suggest that about 30 men from Namiquipa with some of Colonel Cano's men be sent to search that locality wherever there is water, and effect his capture. Hope to get Villa's trail tomorrow. No use killing horses running about aimlessly until more definite information is secured. My march commenced at 3:30 this morning and ended at 5:30 this evening. The trail today one of the worst for rocks I ever saw. Horse shoes will soon be badly needed. Am satisfied we are making sincere friends among people, but Mexican currency for purchase of supplies *urgently* needed.

Brown's command remained at Quemada over the 29th while he and scout Fox, with a small escort, went to Rubio where he met Major Evans who arrived about 1:30 P.M., and learned that Villa was at Rubio in person on 25th with about 80 men, and had gone from Rubio probably to San Diego del Monte. Brown also learned that some of the men forced to join Villa at El Valle deserted at Rubio. Brown returned to Quemada, having marched 22 miles, and learned the dispatch sent to Colonel Dodd had not been delivered, as Dodd had left Bachineva for Guerrero.

March 30th Brown marched to San Diego del Monte, 13 miles, where he united with Major Evans' squadron and learned that Villa had passed through two days earlier going west, and had had a fight on the 28th at Guerrero with Carranzistas. In this fight Villa was shot through the leg breaking the bone below the knee. In the afternoon of this day Brown sent a dispatch to Colonel Dodd at Guerrero by Sergeant Allen and a private, both of the 7th Cavalry, guided by a local Mexican.

March 31st the command remained in camp. Brown sent Lieutenant J. F. Richmond with two soldiers and a local guide to San Antonio on the railroad with a dispatch to General Pershing asking for instruc-

tions as to where his command could be of most service. Richmond
returned late at night reporting that no trains had passed trough San
Antonio for four days, and that the line in both directions was out of
commission.

A heavy snow and high wind in the afternoon caused considerable
discomfort and suffering among men and animals. Colonel Brown had
lost touch with both General Pershing and Colonel Dodd and was much
concerned about it.

At the start this column was delayed nearly a day because of broken
down railway equipment. Then the Mexican Colonel Cano lied to
Brown about Villa's whereabouts and delayed him through the pretense of discussing plans of cooperation. Of course, Cano probably knew
where Villa was, but he played Carranza's game of obstruction while
pretending to cooperate. But Brown was an old Indian fighter. He
had served in the far west in the Indian country during some strenu-
ous campaigns, and he was a hard man to lose when he once hit a
trail. His marches during these 13 days were over rough country, at
high elevations, and some of them were very long. When his command
could rest in camp over a day he was in the saddle running down the
scent of the fleeing Villa, so when we consider the treachery and intentionally false information as a part of the Mexican plan to delay and
if possible nullify the American pursuit, it is indeed remarkable that
when he reached San Diego del Monte he was but three days behind
Villa. At this time Brown was over 61 years of age and Colonel Dodd
would be 64 in July. These two men were the old type of cavalry officer, who had learned every phase of Indian warfare in the hard school
of our western frontier, where a soldier was taught to consider his
horse first and himself last, where it was not unusual to campaign in
the zero weather of a Montana winter, or the burning heats of the
deserts in an Arizona summer, and furthermore these officers were true
to the cavalry tradition: once on the trail stick to it until the quarry
is run to earth.

CHAPTER XVII

Campaign of the Three Columns. Operations of the First
Squadron, 10th Cavalry, March 19 to 31

We carried Major Evans and his squadron on the same train with
Brown and his command as far as Rucio, where Brown left the cars
at 9:30 A.M., March 20th, and ordered Evans to proceed by rail to
Las Varas, his original destination. At this time Evans' command consisted of the 1st Squadron, 10th Cavalry, 8 officers and 208 enlisted
men, 1 Sergeant Hospital Corps, and 1 Sergeant Signal Corps. Progress
was very slow, being frequently interrupted for want of wood and
water.

On March 21st, at 6:30 A.M., at a point near Musica, on the Cumbre
switchback, two cars loaded with horses, with men and horse equipment on the roof, overturned, throwing men and horses down a steep
embankment. Eleven men were injured:

One Sergeant Signal Corps—name not known
Sergeant Doudy, Hospital Corps
Saddler Hudnell, Troop B, 10th Cavalry (later died)
Private Harrison, Troop B, 10th Cavalry
Sergeant Shivrell, Troop B, 10th Cavalry
Private Reynolds, Troop A, 10th Cavalry
Private Sitgraves, Troop A, 10th Cavalry
Private Warren, Troop A, 10th Cavalry
Private Woodfork, Troop A, 10th Cavalry
Private W. R. Thomas, Troop A, 10th Cavalry

After men and horses were rescued from this wreck, and the injured
attended to, Major Evans directed Captain William C. Gardenhire and
2nd Lieutenant Leo A. Walton, with 24 men and 38 horses, to proceed
to Las Varas by marching, where they arrived the same evening. The
injured men were cared for as far as possible in the caboose of the train,
Sergeant Doudy, Hospital Corps, being particularly efficient, notwithstanding the fact that in the accident he was severely cut and bruised
about his head and face. Musica was finally reached, but engine trouble
prevented further progress.

During the early morning of March 22nd Major Evans detrained
men and horses at Musica, and at 7:30 A.M. started to march to Las
Varas, where he arrived at 4:45 P.M., covering a distance of 26 miles
over a mountain trail. The injured men were taken by rail in the
caboose and were at Las Veras when the cavalry column arrived.

At Las Varas Major Evans met Colonel Maximiliano Marquez of the
Carranzista Army, who informed him that Villa was at Namiquipa.
Evans sent this information by telegraph from Madera (20 miles dis-

tant by courier) to General Pershing, and stated that if instructions to the contrary were not received he would march with his command to San Jose de Babicora. At this time Evans had received no information from either Brown or Erwin.

March 23rd Evans received a message from General Pershing at 4:50 P.M., as follows:

Major Evans   Casas Grandes 3/22 date 23
Las Varas via Madera.

10:30 P. M. Fox (Brown's Scout) reports from San Jose de Babicora that battle between Villa and Carranza forces at Namiquipa corroborated and Brown is doubtless moving in that direction. You are directed to proceed to San Jose de Babicora immediately and with all haste where you will probably get word from Colonel Brown as to situation. Fullest cooperation absolutely necessary. Am sending aeroplane to notify Dodd early 23rd and will instruct aviator to reach you if possible. Dodd is with Erwin's column and probably at Cruces tonight. Advise Brown. Wire full particulars of situation.
Pershing
9:40 A. M.

Also the following:

Nahuerachic 3/23
Major Evans
Las Varas.
Colonel Brown wishes that you go as far as possible on your road to Babicora today, say about Los Ojos.

Frank Black

In view of the above telegrams Major Evans left his injured men at Las Varas under charge of Sergeant Doudy, Hospital Corps, and Mr. Wagner, a guide, with the assurances that a doctor and an engine would arrive that day to conduct them back to Colonia Dublan, and started with Troops "A," "B," "C," and "D," 10th Cavalry, at 6:15 P.M. for a night march to San Jose de Babicora, four days out of Colonia Dublan, the loss of three days being due to the indifference of the railroad officials.

The command arrived at San Jose de Babicora at 1:20 in the morning of March 24th. At 8:30 A.M. a message from Brown was received as follows:

San Jose de Babicora, March 23rd noon.
To Major Evans:
I camp tonight about 13 miles west of Namiquipa. Join me as soon as you can consistent with keeping your command in good condition. Have advised Erwin to move to Santa Clara which is apparently center of disturbance at present.
Brown
Colonel.

Evans left San Jose de Babicora at 11:00 A.M., and arrived at a point in the Santa Maria valley near El Toro at 2:00 P.M. Here he found Brown's command in camp.

On March 25th the two squadrons left camp at 7:30 A.M. and marched to the south end of Namiquipa (12 miles) where a halt was made from 10:30 A.M. to 12:10 P.M. while Brown and Evans conferred with Cano, and the supply officer, Lt. R. F. Migdalski, and gathered in food stuffs for the men. At 12:10 the march was resumed to the east. Arriving at El Oso at 2:45 P. M. they went into camp after covering 22 miles for the day.

Next day, March 26th, Brown and Evans had another conference with the Mexican Colonel Cano as to the probable direction taken from El

Typical Mexican Troop Train. Soldiers on Top, Animals Inside

Oso by Villa. There were two passes open: one towards the east in the direction of Santa Catalina Ranch, and the other towards the south leading to San Geronimo, or, by crossing a mountain trail, to Carmen, Las Varas, and San Antonio. Colonel Cano said he would have the two passes scouted. It is known he had the southern trail scouted. He stated he had the eastern trail scouted. He evidently lied. Both commands remained in camp at El Oso this night.

On March 27th, after another conference with Cano the two American columns marched at 10:00 A.M., moving generally east through a canyon. Cano's command marched in advance of the American cavalry until 12:00 o'clock noon, when he left them. The Americans continued until 3:30 in the afternoon when they made camp near the peak called Los Pelon Cillos, having covered about 13 miles.

It was planned to leave camp at 3:30 the morning of the 28th so as to surround Santa Catalina by dawn. This plan was spoiled by a prairie fire which got the command up at 1:00 A.M. and so delayed the march that Santa Catalina was not surrounded until 6:15 A.M., and then by six troops under Brown while Evans took two troops to surround and search two smaller ranches about a mile to the west. It was here learned that Villa had been at Rubio on the 24th. At Santa Catalina the two columns separated, Evans and his four troops taking a parallel route farther to the east to Tepehuanes, while Brown and his command marched by the direct road to La Quemada. This made a march for Evans for the day of 23 miles. At Tepehuanes Evans found a telephone line connecting the Zuraga ranches in this valley: Santa Catalina, Tepehuanes, La Quemada, San Antonio, and Bustillo. This was fortunate, as it enabled Evans to talk to Brown, who was at La Quemada. Brown directed Evans to march to Rubio the next day.

On the 29th Evans left Tepehuanes at 7:30 A.M., and followed the telephone line to Saucito, where his column arrived at about noon. The manager of this ranch was not inclined to give information. He stated that he had just returned from Chihuahua and that he knew nothing of Villa's movements, so the march was continued to Rubio, where the command went into camp at 1:30 P.M., having marched a total distance of 25 miles. At Rubio Major Evans met Colonel Brown, who had ridden over from La Quemada. Brown ordered Evans to join him next day where the two roads met at San Diego del Monte.

Next day, the 30th, Evans' column left El Rubio at 7:15 A.M., arriving at Ojo Caliente at 9:15, where it was reported that Villa had not gone that way but to San Diego del Monte, part of his men by way of La Quemada and part direct from Rubio. The command proceeded generally southwest arriving at San Diego del Monte at 11:15 A.M., having marched a total distance of 14 miles. Mexicans reported that Villa had passed into the mountains from this place, going towards Guerrero, on March 25th, stopping only long enough to take some horses. It was also reported that Villa had had a fight at Guerrero with Carranzistas and had received a bullet through his leg breaking the bone below the knee.

On March 31st the united command remained in camp awaiting word from Pershing or Dodd.

Chapter XVIII

Survey of the Campaign of the Three Columns. False Information and Treachery Enable Villa to Elude the Americans. Four New Columns Take Up the Pursuit

We have just followed "The Campaign of the Three Columns": Dodd, 7th Cavalry, Brown, 10th Cavalry, Evans, 10th Cavalry. An analysis of this campaign should be of interest, especially if the reader will consult the map and note the location of Villa, Dodd, Brown and Evans on the same dates. Had the Mexicans really wanted Villa captured one of these columns would have certainly caught him. As it was ne escaped Colonel Dodd only by good luck. We recapitulate the principal events of this campaign.

Upon the arrival of the train at Colonia Dublan on the morning of March 19th, the cars were found to be in very bad condition, the repairs caused many hours delay in departure of the troops. After starting we have seen that there were many difficulties as to fuel, water, and unwillingness on the part of railroad employees to further the aims of the expedition, so that Colonel Brown's squadron did not arrive at Rucio until 8 o'clock on the morning of the 20th. He promptly detrained and proceeded to San Miguel over a rocky, mountain trail, arriving there on the morning of the 21st, to find that Villa had not been within twelve miles of the place. From this point Colonel Brown's column moved on the 23rd to El Toro, where he received information that Villa had recently fought Colonel Cano's command of Carranzistas near Santa Clara Ranch.

Major Evans' column continued by rail to Musica, where he decided to detrain and march overland to Las Veras, arriving there on March 22nd. A railroad wreck at the switchback over Cumbre Tunnel, in which two cars were overturned, killing Saddler Hudnell and injuring 10 others, caused a long delay.

In the meantime Colonel George A. Dodd was directed to join the 7th Cavalry detachment under Colonel Erwin, and take charge of the operations of both regiments with an especial injunction to establish communication with the other two columns, and endeavor to secure all possible cooperation among our forces.

On March 22nd Colonel Dodd got in touch with Colonel Salas, commanding the de facto troops near El Valle, who confirmed the report that the latter had encountered a detachment of Villistas on the 19th of March, and had been driven back through Cruces to El Valle. Colonel Salas' command was found to be in a demoralized condition, and had taken up a defensive position just south of El Valle, expecting another attack by the Villistas.

As it was thought that Villa was still at Namiquipa, Colonel Dodd's column continued south, crossing the Santa Maria River on March 23rd about 6 miles north of Cruces, and bivouacking for the night at a point about 15 miles northeast of Namiquipa. Later news apparently confirmed the report that Villa had recently been defeated by a detachment of Carranzistas near Namiquipa, but the information as to the direction Villa had taken was indefinite and confusing.

Reports to Colonel Dodd on the 24th indicated that Villa had passed through or near Oso Canyon and had gone south or southwest. In the hope of cutting ahead of him Dodd therefore moved westward to Santa Ana, arriving early on the morning of the 26th. It should be noted that the country was extremely dry and that it was next to impossible to follow a trail of any kind.

Upon information received at Expedition Headquarters by telegram from Colonel Brown, that Villas forces were somewhere between Namiquipa and Santa Clara, Major Evans was directed by wire to move to San Jose de Babicora and communicate with Brown. On the 24th of March, at Namiquipa, Brown had a consultation with Colonel Cano and was advised that Villa's band was either at Oso Canyon or near Santa Clara. Upon this report Brown telegraphed headquarters that he would attack Villa next day. He marched through Namiquipa to Oso Canyon, remaining the night of the 25th in Oso Canyon, Colonel Cano's command of 200 men camping near by.

Cano was to cooperate by sending out scouting parties to locate the enemy, while Brown was to remain at Oso Canyon and plan to move against Villa at night. Meanwhile Evans' column had joined Brown at a point in the Santa Maria Valley near El Toro, March 24th at 2:00 P.M.

Brown, with both columns, remained at El Oso, about 15 miles east of El Toro, on the 26th, and learning that Colonel Cano had not sent out scouting parties as promised, left on the 27th for Pilon Cillos. Being advised that Villa was at Santa Catalina, he surrounded the ranch on the 28th but found nothing. Here he heard that Villa, in person, had passed on to Quemada three days before. From here Evans' column went to Tepehuanes and on the 28th to El Rubio. Brown moved to Quemada where he remained during the 29th.

Dodd's column left Santa Ana on the 27th and camped east of Providencia, hoping to obtain news of Villa's whereabouts. But Dodd remarks in his report that he had about concluded that all information up to that time regarding Villa's movements after the Namiquipa fight was false, and cites a belated message from Brown, dated Namiquipa the 25th, stating: "Villa's whereabouts unknown, but it is thought possible he has gone through the mountains toward Bachineva."

Tracing Villa's movements from March 19th, the date of his fight with Carranzista forces at Namiquipa, it is now known that he left there on the 20th, camped at El Rosal, or Lujan's Wells, that night; that on the 21st he marched to La Cartucheva, 12 miles southeast of Lujan's Wells; that he was at Quemada on the 22nd; that he reached Rubio on the 23rd, leaving on the night of the 25th, and reaching San Diego del Monte on the morning of the 25th. From there he followed a trail leading southwest to Agua Caliente, thence changed direction to the westward, arriving the night of the 26th at San Ysidro near Guerrero, where he successfully fought with the Carranzistas on the 27th of March.

The movements of these various columns given in detail show that the information upon which they were acting was very conflicting. It had now become evident that the de facto government troops intended to prevent the Americans from overtaking Villa if possible. At the start the report that Villa was at San Miguel was unfounded. Practically every Mexican so far encountered had questioned our right to be in Mexico, and claimed there was no authority for our presence. Colonel Salas of the de facto forces said his government had not authorized us to be in Mexico.

A proclamation had been issued by General Obregon, Secretary of War, and published in several towns, copies of which our columns carried and displayed as evidence of an agreement between the two governments. This proclamation should have settled the mooted question in so far as the local inhabitants were concerned, but it did not change their views or their intentions, although it probably did prevent hostilities at the start.

Colonel Dodd, in his report of March 28th states: "But information having reached me too late, combined with misrepresentations, nullified what was done toward carrying out the plan." Brown learned while at Oso Canyon that Cano had not kept his word, and had made no attempt to ascertain the whereabouts of Villa. In his report Brown says: "Have just had a conference with Cano, who could not produce the man who saw Villa's trail. I fear he simply lied to me." No apparent effort was made by the various Carranzista commanders to keep in touch with Villa, nor was there any active pursuit of Villa's rapidly fleeing command. Many deserters from Villa were returning to their homes who must have brought back information, and it is idle to presume that the direction that Villa had taken, or his actual location, were unknown to the de facto commanders.

Convincing evidence of opposition was shown in the tissue of falsehoods presented to our officers. As the Mexican villages along the Santa Maria River are known as the "Pueblos de Los Indios," and the inhabitants are generally Villista sympathizers, and it was from these towns that Villa had recruited much of the force he led to Columbus, it was probably natural that they should mislead us. Namiquipa was the home of Cervantes, Villa's chief lieutenant, who planned and carried out the attack on Columbus. So there was among the people a resentment toward us that was clearly shown in the brazenly false news they disseminated. Practically all information from native sources was either entirely misleading, or if based on fact, located Villa's band at places several days later than the actual date. The people in general were but following Villa's well known methods in using this means in assisting his escape. Several Mexicans frankly said that they would consider it a national disgrace if the Americans should capture Villa. Nor was this attitude entirely confined to native Mexicans. Most foreigners, including some Americans with interests in Mexico, hoped we would not succeed, believing that the expedition would be withdrawn if we should succeed, and consequently no assistance came from that source.

In the meantime other pursuing detachments were organized to be held in readiness to move in any direction that circumstances might dictate.

The first of these detachments, Major Elmer Lindsley, 13th Cavalry, commanding, was the 2nd Squadron and Troop "L" of the 13th Cavalry, five troops in all, consisting of 11 officers and 275 enlisted men. This column was directed to occupy Chuichupa, about 16 miles in an air line west of Cumbre. It left Colonia Dublan on March 20th, marching mainly by night, by way of Colonia Pachoco, and reached Chuichupa March 22nd. The purpose of this move was to guard the trails leading westward in the event that Villa should evade the columns pursuing him and strike in that direction. As Villa continued to flee south, Major Lindsley's detachment was moved to Babicora plateau to cover the territory vacated by the 10th Cavalry. Leaving Chuichupa on the 24th, by way of Musica, he arrived at San Miguel de Babicora on the 27th, and continued on to San Jose de Babicora on the 30th of March.

Another detachment under Major Frank Tompkins, 13th Cavalry, consisting of Troops "K," "M," and Machine Gun Platoon, 13th Cavalry, with Troops "I" and "K," 10th Cavalry, 11 officers and 160 enlisted men, left Colonia Dublan on March 21st, with instructions to follow up the Santa Maria River and be on hand should his services be needed later in pursuit of any portion of Villa's force. In accordance therewith Major Tompkins went to Namiquipa where he was in camp on March 29th.

A provisional squadron was organized from the 11th Cavalry, composed of men selected from all troops of the regiment, and placed under command of Major Robert L. Howze, 11th Cavalry. This command consisted of 10 officers and 255 enlisted men. It left Colonia Dublan on March 24th and proceeded south along the line of communications to Namiquipa, where it was in camp on March 29th.

Another provisional squadron, from the 11th Cavalry, consisting of picked men from each troop, with two machine gun detachments, making a total of 10 officers and 292 enlisted men, was placed under Lieutenant Colonel Henry T. Allen, 11th Cavalry.

We shall now follow the movements of these four columns of cavalry up to March 29th, the date Colonel Dodd and the 7th Cavalry defeated the main Villista force at Guerrero, and thus terminate the first phase of the Expedition.

CHAPTER XIX

Operations of the Second Squadron, 13th Cavalry (Lindsley), March 21 to April 2

Major E. Lindsley was the next cavalry commander to hit the trail after Villa. At 5:00 P.M., March 20th, he received orders to proceed by two night marches to Colonia Chuichupa via Pacheco. He was supposed to start at dark but due to difficulty in securing a guide the column did not start until 8:00 P.M. I have read Lindsley's diary covering this march, but like the diaries of most soldiers it gives merely the framework upon which a complete official report can be built. This command experienced hunger, cold and deadly fatigue, but they carried on without complaint, as well disciplined soldiers always do, and in true accord with the splendid traditions of the Regular Army.

Fortunately, accompanying Major Lindsley was a Mr. John W. Converse, Sergeant First Troop, Philadelphia City Cavalry, who was with the "Expedition" as an authorized observer. During the World War Converse commanded a regiment of Field Artillery in the American Expeditionary Forces. The following is taken almost entirely from Colonel Converse's record of this march.

With the safe arrival of the supply train at Casas Grandes, the duties of the 13th Cavalry as convoy came to an end. It then developed upon this command to take an active part in the pursuit of Villa. The regimental commander was directed to detach a provisional squadron to be ready to leave at dark the same day we arrived at Casas Grandes. An attempt was made to secure railway transportation for this detachment, but this was unsuccessful. The following order was therefore issued to Major Lindsley.

Casas Grandes, March 20, 1916

Information has been received that Villa bandits are in the vicinity of San Miguel, to which place they retreated from Namiquipa, where they were defeated March 20th by Carranzistas with the loss of 70 men. Villa has with him about 200 men, worn out by recent defeats, and hard marching.

Our troops are as follows: Colonel Erwin, with the 7th Cavalry near San Miguel; Colonel W. C. Brown, with squadron of 10th Cavalry, disembarked near Rucio and marched on San Miguel; Major Evans with squadron of 10th Cavalry is near Laguna de Babicora.

In event of Villa's flight, it is believed his most probable avenue of escape will be west from San Miguel through Chico and Chuichupa.

The Commanding General directs that you start from here at dark tonight and proceed to Pacheco arriving there early tomorrow, the 21st instant.

You will ascertain at Chuichupa if Villa's column has passed, and if so you will take up the trail and follow it. If he has not passed Chuichupa, you will endeavor to find his whereabouts through messengers to the other columns.

J. A. Ryan
Major 13th Cavalry,
Acting Chief of Staff.

As the route lay over mountain trails, wagons were out of the question. The route covered was west of the Mexico North Western R.R. and from 20 to 16 miles distant from it. Each man was directed to carry five days rations for himself and two days forage for his horse on his saddle. In addition 150 rounds of ammunition were carried, 90 rounds in the belt and 60 rounds in the bandoleer over the left shoulder.

Right here one of the disadvantages of the new saddle equipment developed. Field rations consisted of two packages of hard bread per man per day, 12 ounces of bacon, and small amounts of coffee and sugar. Five days rations meant 10 packages of hard bread. Those troops who had the new equipment could only get six packages in their pommel pockets, three on a side, while those who had the McClellan saddle easily packed the rations, 5 packages of hard bread fitting nicely into each saddle bag, besides the bacon, coffee and sugar. Right here is where the Armour Emergency Ration, dehydrated, vacuum sealed, compact, weight one pound should have been issued. The McClellan saddle bags also had room for the mess kit, curry comb and brush. Oats were carried in a grain bag strapped across the pommel on both sides of the equipment. One troop left behind their shelter halves and slickers in order to lighten the load, but later had cause to regret this.

The squadron left Casas Grandes at 8:10 P.M., March 20th. Bear in mind that these troops had already covered 25 miles this day, convoying the supply train. It was quite dark the first part of the march as the moon had not yet risen, and shortly after leaving camp one or two of the troops at the rear of the column got on the wrong road. Fortunately they were heard by the guides who rode with the point, and soon got back to their places. Presently the moon rose and then the going was easier. Also it was possible to trot occasionally, which was a relief, as the night was cold.

Villages and houses were avoided and little used trails taken: sometimes the trails were abandoned entirely and the column filed across country. The guides showed a wonderful knowledge of the country and of direction. One of them had not been over it for five years, and the other not for ten. We marched thus but for one brief halt, mostly at a walk, occasionally trotting, and sometimes leading our horses down steep hills, until 1:00 A.M. Then we halted for half or three-quarters of an hour to water the horses and to allow them to crop a few mouthfuls of grass. When the march was resumed we found ourselves following the course of a railroad bed, projected and commenced before revolutions disrupted Mexico, but now abandoned until happier times. It wound around the side of the mountain range, part of the Sierra Madres, bordering a wide basin stretching for miles below us. For 12 miles it was a steady uphill climb. It was cold now, and officers and men got out their blankets and rode with them over their shoulders like Yaqui Indians. It would be out of place in this report to describe the beauties of that night ride and the agonies of trying to keep awake. Just as the sun was rising at our backs and the moon was setting before us we crossed the Continental Divide, and I sleepily tried to be appreciative of a verse from Omar, which the Major recited—something about the sun putting to flight the stars. Then after a short halt to allow the column to close up, we proceeded down the other side, jumping a bunch of white tail deer at which several of the men took a crack. They could not have been experts as the deer escaped, and we proceeded on downwards, until the bottom of the canyon was reached, about 9:00 o'clock. Here the Major consulted with the guides who said we had come 40 miles, and that Pacheco was eight miles farther. As horse and man had had about enough, it was decided to halt here until evening, in accordance with instructions. Outposts were placed, horses fed their grain and picketed so they could graze. The men cooked their bacon and hard bread in their mess kits, and lay down in the grass for a few hours sleep, which was not long in coming.

In the afternoon another meal was cooked and the march was resumed at 5:00 o'clock. The trail followed the bed of the canyon for eight miles to Pacheco. Frequent pauses were necessary to allow the column to close up on account of the rough going. Before dark we saw some old cliff dwellings perched away up on the walls of the canyon, which boxed here. Deserted ranches were passed and Pacheco, one of them, was reached at 10:00 P.M.—only 8 miles in five hours, if the guide's estimate of the distance was correct.

At 1:00 A.M. an hour's halt was made, then the march resumed. The way lay over rough, mountainous country, the moon was obscured, and frequently the troops in rear of the column would lose touch. Word would be passed up to halt, and a guide sent back to locate them and put them right. No formation was attempted. We pushed along in single file, mostly walking and leading, trying to keep touch with the man ahead. Towards dawn the going became a little better and sunlight was welcome indeed. At 8:00 o'clock a two hour halt was ordered at a spring in a pine timber country and man and beast fed and watered. After this the terrain permitted the alternate walk and trot by which cavalry can cover from five to six miles per hour, and after passing more deserted ranches, through a wonderful cattle country destitute of cattle, we came in sight of our destination, Chuichupa, at 2:30 P.M., March 22nd. A careful inspection through field glasses of the deserted village by the advance guard commander revealed no sign of life. Accordingly the column entered the village, and after further reconnoitering, passed through and camped in a grove of pine trees beside a stream which rose from the ground in little pools at this point, and where we were partially concealed, yet had a field of fire on three sides. Four o'clock was the hour when the saddles were taken from the horses' backs, and camp made. We had covered 100 miles in 44 hours, after a 25 mile march on the day we started. We had been in the saddle, or on the move, 20 hours out of the past 24. Every horse and man came in, a little groggy perhaps, but still able to go. During the entire 100 mile march we did not see a single human being outside our column, and no animal life except a few white-tail deer and some range mares. The guides were sent to circle the town and "cut" for signs of the Villistas, but reported no tracks. So after outposts had been placed, the command settled down to a well earned night's rest.

Chuichupa, the word meaning smoke in the Yaqui Indian language, proved to be an old American Mormon settlement, at one time probably having 500 or 600 inhabitants but now abandoned, since five years ago it was sacked by the "Red Flaggers" as the revolutionists are called, who sprang up all over the country when the iron grip of Diaz began to relax. The town is located in a rolling fertile plain, surrounded by pine forests in which turkey and wild deer abound. The inhabitants were evidently thrifty farmers and cattle men. Their homes were well built of frame, brick and adobe, in the American fashion, which is always a pleasing contrast to the squat adobe, or log hovels, which the Mexicans affect. Now the houses and fences are falling down, acequias, gardens, and fruit trees gone to ruin.

The next day was devoted to the business of locating Villa, getting in touch with headquarters and the other columns, and arranging for supplies. At 9:00 A.M., March 23rd, Major Lindsley sent a patrol, consisting of Lieutenant Franklin, one scout, one signal corps man, and two privates to Musica, to tap the wire and get in touch with Division Headquarters by buzzer. At the same time an officer's patrol with a scout and five privates, was sent four miles to the south, and thence around the meadow surrounding the town, keeping a mile away, to the point where we came into the town. They reported nothing.

At the same time another officer's patrol, with a scout and five men went to the trail leading to Sonora, to a pass in this trail that Villa must go through if he came this way. The patrol went around from north to east to the trail we came in on. They reported no tracks and no one had gone through the pass.

At 4:00 P.M. two N.C.O. patrols were sent to the trail we came in on with orders to work: one four miles to the south and the other four miles to the north, returning to camp at 8:00 o'clock.

At 9:00 P.M. an officer's patrol, consisting of one officer, one N.C.O., and four privates, was sent out on the trail to Cumbre to watch for Villistas. This patrol was to be relieved by another officer's patrol at 1:00 A.M., which was to stay out until 5:00 A.M.

Lieutenant Franklin returned alone about 1:45 A.M., March 24th, having left the signal corps man, privates, and scout, at Musica. Franklin took a big chance when he made this return trip alone, but he was always taking chances. He apparently had no idea of fear in his make-up. Lieutenant Franklin succeeded in getting in touch with headquarters, and got orders for us to proceed to the vicinity of Chico, a few miles south of Cumbre, where rations and forage would be sent to us. This was good news as we were all out of oats for the horses and with very little left for the men to eat. This date Major Lindsley sent out hunting parties. "G" Troop got a deer, and "F" Troop a turkey. The Major's orderly found a few frijoles in a shed, which helped a lot. Camp was moved about a mile to a more sheltered spot.

The night of the 23rd and 24th was windy and so cold no one could sleep. Men and horses suffered. The command woke in a hail storm, left camp at 9:30 A.M., and proceeded to Musica in a cold snow storm, where they arrived at 2:20 in the afternoon, a distance of 18 miles. This place consisted of a few shacks and box cars, on a switch of the Northwestern Railroad of Mexico, built after the revolutionists blew up the Cumbre Tunnel.

Major Lindsley got in touch with headquarters and learned that Villa had turned toward Namiquipa again, where he had the better of a slight engagement with Carranzistas. Colonel Brown was reported moving toward Namiquipa. Colonel Erwin was reported at Las Cruces on the night of the 22nd. Erwin had advised Brown to move toward Santa Clara. Villa was last reported at El Oso Canyon. Evans was reported at Babicora.

We learned that in the train carrying Major Evans' command two cars had overturned, 9 men being hurt, 2 seriously. A patrol reported finding a damaged aeroplane near Musica, with aviator's hat and goggles beside it. The scout of Lieutenant Franklin's patrol had remained at Musica and purchased two steers, which with potatoes and tortillas furnished two good meals for the command.

On the 25th an officer's patrol was sent from Musica to Las Varas with a hospital corps man to render assistance to the men of Major Evans' command of the 10th Cavalry, injured in the train derailment. The Mexican Government refused to allow these men to be transported by rail, although a box car loaded with supplies for us reached us this date. The vagaries of the Mexican authorities in this respect were past comprehension. An American cattle man, foreman of one of the Hearst ranches, took the injured men on a handcar to Casas Grandes, being two days on the journey.

A patrol was sent to Chico, 5 miles away, to guard the signal corps man who had remained there to keep on the wire to Division Headquarters. The rest of the squadron, those who were not herding horses that were grazing, busied themselves with matters pertaining to sustenance. The "F" Troop commander presented his men with a pig which they proceeded to barbecue, by transfixing it whole with an iron pipe and slowly turning it over a fire. A beef was killed and the steaks distributed. Tortillas (corn meal cakes), frijoles (beans), eggs and potatoes, were purchased in quantity from the Mexicans. I assisted at a liver and bacon luncheon given by Captain Stedje of "G" Troop. We were like wolves after our short rations of the past few days. I can readily understand how Villa kept the loyalty of his followers by occasionally well filling their stomachs when he looted a town or isolated ranch. Their usual food is "jerky" and "pinole." Jerky is strips of beef dried and salted. Pinole is made out of parched corn ground to a powder. It is eaten mixed with milk or water, and contains a great deal of nourishment. We took to it later on as a breakfast food, making it ourselves, and found it very palatable.

The thermometer was below freezing here at night, and some ingenious devices were resorted to to get some sleep. One was to dig a shallow trench, the width of a man's body, build a fire in it, and when the ground had become thoroughly heated, rake the coal away, put the shelter half over it, and crawl under both the saddle and sleeping blankets. One man who tried this said it was too warm.

Another method was to make what the woodsmen call a "lean-to." This was done by swinging a shelter tent half between two trees, starting a fire under a good long log placed parallel to the shelter tent and as near as danger from sparks permitted, and then making one's bed beside the fire under the tent.

March 26th. Orders came this afternoon to proceed at once to San Miguel. The orders came just as I was taking a bath and washing my underclothes. I felt just as I used to, when as a rookie at Mt. Gretna or Gettysburg, orders seemed always to come when one was doing something like that. However, the operation was all finished except drying, so I put them on wet and hurried into camp to pack and saddle up.

Camp was broken at 6:30 P. M., but the night was so dark, and the trail so rough that at 9:00 o'clock we had gone only 4 or 5 miles. So the Major decided to bivouac and wait for the moon to rise. On the way we passed the camp of the cavalrymen injured in the railroad accident. They were camped beside their handcar in which they were working their way to Casas Grandes.

The moon did not rise until 4:00 A. M. We saddled up and left at 4:30. We followed the bed of a narrow canyon until at dawn we found ourselves at one end of the long Cumbre Tunnel, a fine piece of engineering, blown up by the revolutionists. Thence, after a brief halt to close up the column, we ascended along the canyon which headed in the Continental Divide. During this ascent, the troopers with the new equipment were constantly falling out to adjust their saddles, which do not seem to stay in place so well over rough country as the McClellan. Then down the other side, down a long point, down a canyon, where at noon March 27th we halted for lunch. Here I nearly lost my saddle and equipment, as a prairie fire got started while I went to the stream to fill my canteen. Fortunately someone rescued it, else I would have been out of luck. In spite of precautions we seemed to be continually setting fire to the country wherever we went. The grass was dry as punk and if it got a good start with the wind blowing, it was almost impossible to put it out. We left a big cloud of smoke behind us, and after crossing two or three good sized canyons, came out on a big mesa, from which we could see our destination, San Miguel, in the plain, two or three miles below. The squadron was formed in line of troops in column of squads and halted while the advance guard went forward to reconnoiter. The coast was clear and we went into camp at the San Miguel Ranch at 4:00 P. M., having covered over 40 miles of as rough country as, I venture to say, cavalry has ever operated in.

San Miguel is a Terrazas ranch, situated in a beautiful rolling cattle country. Around it is the best cattle range I have ever seen and it is far understocked. In fact, the whole state of Chihuahua has possibilities of becoming the beef producing section of this hemisphere.

San Miguel has a fine old hacienda built around a court yard, or patio, and surrounded by stone corrals, stables and vaqueros' quarters. The ranch was confiscated from Don Luis Terrazas by Carranza and Villa. It is said that it is one cause of the split between Carranza and Villa, as the former wanted to give it back to the big land baron, while the ex-bandit was opposed to returning anything. There was a Mexican administrator, or foreman, and some vaqueros at the ranch, but they had no news of Villa.

On March 28th at 8:30 A. M. an officer's patrol was sent to El Valle for supplies and orders. The patrol consisted of Lieutenant William W. West, a corporal, 4 privates and a scout. Horses about all in. Rations all gone. Living on corn and beef. No coffee or sugar. Some hard bread. I (Converse) accompanied the patrol. We arrived at about 5:00 P. M. having covered 32 miles, but we stopped an hour and a half for lunch. El Valle is a good-sized adobe town in a wide valley, and a river, from which are taken the irrigation ditches, furnishes water to the town and apparently to each inhabitant, as each house has its own little garden or field, surrounded by an adobe wall, and water from the irrigating ditch which flows down the middle of the street outside.

At the camp we found the machine gun troop of the regiment and a battalion of the 6th Infantry. We learned that a pack train of 76 mules had been sent to the squadron, which should arrive today. We learned also that an auto-truck base had been established at Namiquipa, and that the other two troops of the 13th had gone on south under Major Frank Tompkins.

General Pershing arrived in camp after dark by automobile, and told the officers in command of the patrol that instructions for the squadron were being sent with the pack train.

March 29th. I had my first glimpse of the work of our aeroplanes, as two or three arrived, or left with messages, while we were at these headquarters. We left headquarters at 10:30 A. M. and stopped in the village to change some American money and for some Mexican tobacco for the men. American tobacco had not yet come down. After these commissions had been filled we returned to San Miguel and arrived there at 6:30 P. M. to find an abundant supply of rations and forage which a pack train had brought in. There were also orders for the squadron to proceed to San Jose de Babicora.

March 30th. In accordance with instructions the command left camp at San Miguel at 7:00 A. M. and proceeded to San Jose de Babicora, arriving at 4:00 P. M., distance 35 miles. The pack train which arrived the day before accompanied the column. This ranch is one of a chain belonging to the Hearst estate. The old hacienda was built in 1770 by the Jesuits. In 1840 they were driven out by the Apaches and the place was abandoned until 1882 when an adventurous Arizonian, named Jack Gilbert, appeared and bought the land in the big basin for a song. He became Don Gilberto. The Mexican vaqueros thronged to him and he built up a big outfit. This in time passed into the hands of the New York family, the present owners.

The administrator is a colonel in the Carranza army; while the book-keeper and factotum is a Mexican-American, named Simpson, whom we called Don Pedro, when we got to know him. We fell into good hands here, and anything that the ranch afforded in the way of guides and supplies for man or horse was gladly furnished. Whether the Mexicans here were of a better type than those we encountered else-where, or whether it is only the Mexican who does not come into direct contact with the "Gringo" who hates him, I do not know. At any rate no one could be more cordial than the people of this ranch were to us.

We learned that a troop of the 7th Cavalry was camped 13 miles to the east at a place called Potrillo, guarding El Toro Pass. Major Lindsley sent a message to the commander by a vaquero of the ranch to be forwarded to the General at Namiquipa, the new base. Lieutenant R. W. Barker, 10th Cavalry, came in at 9:00 P. M. with a message from Frank Tompkins at Namiquipa. Purchased beef and corn from the ranch. Three or four horses died this date, the victims of short forage, hard marches and freezing nights. The poor beasts drop by the trail, the equipment is removed, the column goes on, and the circling buzzards are eloquent of the end of long and faithful service.

March 31st. In the evening a courier came from Captain Augustus C. Nissen, 7th Cavalry, at El Toro Pass, relaying a message from General Pershing. This was an order for Major Lindsley to stay at Babicora with three troops, sending one troop to El Toro Pass to relieve Captain Nissen, and one troop to Babicora Canyon, 18 miles to the west and south. This seemed to indicate that we were to sit down here and play fullback in the chase for Villa, who, we learned, had gone on south towards Guerrero, closely followed by Major Frank Tompkins with two troops of the 13th Cavalry, and Colonel Dodd with parts of the 10th and 7th. It snowed this afternoon. Weather very hard on horses and men. Cleared at night, but continued cold.

This terminates the interesting account of Colonel Converse covering the movement of Major Lindsley and his gallant men. It is almost exactly as written by Colonel Converse, but the author has seen fit to interpolate from time to time. It gives a clear picture of the difficulties and hardships these soldiers met and overcame, and the sufferings they cheerfully endured. Words cannot describe the tedious effort demanded of the tired trooper when he is forced to dismount and lead his weary horse over a difficult trail on a dark night, making effort to keep in touch with the horse in front, for to lose contact in the dark means going astray, causing long delays in reassembling the column. The soldier is burdened with a belt filled with ammunition in addition to the heavy Colt pistol attached thereto. He also has a bandoleer of sixty rounds slung diagonally across his body. He must carry his rifle in one hand and lead the horse with the other. Many times the horses are so played out that they hang back and make the troopers pull them along. The soldier is animated by the prospect of meeting the enemy, but the poor horse has nothing to stimulate him to abnormal effort except the instinct of service which is born in him. It is too dark to see the trail, so horses and men go stumbling along, drunk with sleep and fatigue, with the horse sometimes on top of the man. No wonder it is a common saying "he swears like a trooper." The trooper learns to swear when leading his mount in a long column, on a night march, over a rough trail.

CHAPTER **XX**

Operations of the Provisional Squadron, 10th and 13th Cavalry (Tompkins), March 21 to April 2

The next flying column to leave Colonia Dublan was under command of the author. On March 21st I was given command of the provisional squadron composed of Troops "K" and "M" and Machine Gun Troop 13th Cavalry, and Troops "I" and "K," 10th Cavalry.

The officers of the 13th Cavalry accompanying this column (I will not mention those of the 10th Cavalry, which appear in an appendix, as those two troops were soon detached) were:

Major Frank Tompkins, 13th Cavalry, Commanding
Captain Frederick G. Turner, Troop "M"
Captain Aubrey Lippincott, Troop "K"
1st Lieutenant Clarence Lininger, Troop "M"
1st Lieutenant Wm. A. McCain, Troop "K"
2nd Lieutenant Horace Stringfellow, Jr., Troop "K"
2nd Lieutenant James B. Ord, 6th Infantry, Interpreter and acting Squadron Adjutant
1st Lieutenant Claude W. Cummings, Medical Reserve Corps on active duty
1 man Hospital Corps
Scouts and Guides: Haney and Jorgensen.

My instructions were to follow up the Santa Maria River, be on hand should my services be needed later in the pursuit of any portion of Villa's force, and act as a support to the 7th Cavalry.

We had the usual cavalry equipment except the sabers and the curb bits. I knew we didn't need sabers in chasing Indians, and I knew the horses were too tired to call for the use of a curb bit. Every ounce saved in weight on an expedition of this kind adds much to the prospects of success for the undertaking.

I was issued two days' rations for men and horses; these were carried on the saddle. No wagon or pack mule was allowed us. There was nothing to cook in but the soldier's mess kit. A kettle for each troop in which to make coffee would have been a godsend and saved much waste of coffee and sugar. I had no map of the country—a slim equipment with which to ride into an unknown and unfriendly country, for an indefinite time, but each man had a belt full of ammunition with an extra bandoleer over his shoulder, so I rejoiced, for we were after Villa and I had real soldiers at my back.

I received my orders at 2:00 P.M. and was on the road at 4:00 P.M. We marched from Colonia Dublan via Nueva Casas Grandes to the southeast headed for Galeana. As we approached Casas Grandes we could see the Carranzista garrison turning out under arms, and one of their officers rode rapidly to meet us, saying that if we entered the town we would be opposed by force. This did not look much like a friendly cooperation so I skirted the town and avoided a clash with our allies at the very start. To experience such positive opposition and animosity from Carranza forces within a mile or two of General Pershing's headquarters heralded the futility of counting on assistance from de facto troops. Even at this early stage in our campaign the Mexican people and the Mexican troops looked upon us as invaders, and encouraged this sentiment until it resulted in open attacks upon our forces. What we needed in the White House was a Cleveland, a Roosevelt, or a Coolidge. Had we had such a President there would have been no Columbus Raid, there would have been no need for a Mexican Punitive Expedition, because the Mexicans would have held the United States in respect instead of contempt.

As long as daylight lasted we trotted, then marched at the walk until 11:30 when we bivouacked on the bank of a little stream, watered the horses, stretched lariat picket lines in the tall grass so that the horses could graze, posted necessary sentinels, and slept until just before daylight. Our route on this first march took us through Chocolate Pass, near the summit of which we encountered a radio section about 20 miles from Colonia Dublan, which had been sent out by Colonel Erwin, 7th Cavalry, to try and get in touch with Colonia Dublan. They could get nothing out of the air. This detachment was commanded by 2nd Lieutenant William O. Ryan, 7th Cavalry, and they joined our column.

We had reveille just before daylight on the 22nd, fed oats, each man cooked his breakfast (an awful waste of time and food), after which horses were groomed and allowed to graze; men looked over arms and equipment, and at 7:30 A. M. swung into the saddle and headed for Galeana, where we arrived an hour later. We found Galeana to be an adobe town of about 100 houses, fairly prosperous looking. The people viewed us with mild animosity. We continued on and camped in a grove of trees on the river bank, at about 11:25 A.M. Our line of march carried us through an irrigated section where the people were working peaceably in the fields. Our camp was near Galera Lopena (Angostura), and on the left or west bank of the Rio de Santa Maria, which has its source many miles south of here beyond Namiquipa near Providencia, and empties into the Laguna de Santa Maria near Guzman. Three or four miles west of us rise the Sierra Madre Oriental Mountains. We found here three officers and about 100 men of the 7th Cavalry left by our brigade commander, Colonel Dodd. They let us have some rations and oats, so we gave the horses three feeds of oats this date, besides letting them graze all day. The grass was bone dry but there was plenty of it and the horses seemed to like it. There was no danger from colic in it anyway, and it was good "roughage."

Our rations were limited to hard bread, bacon, potatoes and coffee. We got some flour from the 7th Cavalry and made tortillas or cowboy bread by making a dough of flour, water, and a pinch of salt and frying in the meat can in bacon grease. It tastes pretty good when one is hungry.

The air was filled with rumors of Villa. Heard yesterday that the day before he had been defeated by the Carranzistas somewhere near Cruces and driven north. Heard today he may be going south or east, so there is no use in getting excited over that. My little Arab stallion raised hell during the night. He took a notion he wanted to eat "Sheep" my second horse, so I had to leave my blankets long enough to tell him he not only had the wrong idea about "Sheep" but that his noise was disturbing the camp. After this all was quiet.

March 23rd. As the sun rose the wind came up with it until by 8:00 o'clock a howling gale was blowing, drenching all with a blinding dust. At 8:30 saw an airplane coming from the north having a very rough time of it. When near our camp it was seized in the arms of the wind, turned over several times, and then plunged towards the ground. We lost sight of it behind the tall trees, when we all rushed toward the meadow expecting to find the ship wrecked and the aviator mangled beyond recognition. What we found was the ship rightside up uninjured, and 1st Lieutenant Arthur R. Christie, Signal Corps, walking toward us as nonchalantly as you please. I was the first to reach him and exclaimed: "By God, my boy, I thought it was taps for you! How did you get out of it?" He answered: "I don't know unless God had me by the hand." And added, "Got anything to eat?" He brought orders for us to move south to El Valle. I noticed he had a map, which he very kindly gave to me when he learned I had none.

We left camp at 2:00 P. M. to establish new base at El Valle. Reached the northern edge of El Valle about 4:30 and went into camp on the river bank. Sent an officer's patrol under Lieutenant Lininger, accompanied by Lieutenant Ord and Scout Haney, to ascertain the temper of the people of El Valle and anything else they might pick up by way of information. There was a rumor earlier in the day that these people intended to resist our advance. The patrol returned at 8:00 P. M. and reported as follows:

Trotted most of the way. After going through the first little suburb, we went through an open space and then entered a narrow street inclosed on each side by adobe houses or adobe walls. This continued for two and a half or three miles, there being no way of escape to either side. Then came a short open space and we went through another tunnel to the church. Here the Padre told me 300 soldiers had left that morning to report to General Herrera at Chihuahua. He also said the town had 40 soldiers, and that the sympathy of the townspeople was with Villa, but that he was Spanish and did not like him. The chief of police, or assistant, showed up with a letter from the Alcalde of Galeana to the Alcalde of El Valle saying United States troops had authority to pass through the towns. This was sent through Colonel Erwin, 7th Cavalry. This man was dressed in leggins coming well above the knees, in Stetson hat, bandoleer of ammunition, etc., and looked very impressive.

We stayed there about 15 minutes and left, going out of town by the first street north of the church that runs west, crossing the river and returning by an open road on the left bank. Unfortunately the guide turned off this road too soon, and we wandered about the fields for about two miles, finally getting to camp at 8:00 P. M.

We marched 12 miles this date. The gale continued with increasing violence, making it impossible to cook as the wind not only blew over the tin cup, filled the meat can with sand and gravel, but blew the

THE U. S. CAVALRY IN MEXICO
13th Cavalry En Route to El Valle

Major Tompkins on "Kingfisher"

fuel from the fire. We munched a little hard bread, covered our heads with our blankets and prayed for gentler weather for next day.

We left camp the morning of March 24th at 9:30 and marched through El Valle bivouacking two miles south of that town at noon, distance about 8 miles. Motor trucks that stopped at our camp the previous night followed us up and left supplies at this place as the nucleus for a new base.

General Pershing, Major Ryan, and Lieutenant Patton arrived about 1:00 P. M. in Ford cars and other kinds. Here we left the two troops of the 10th Cavalry and our Machine Gun Troop, and started at 3:00 P. M. to escort General Pershing to Colonel Dodd's headquarters somewhere south of Cruces. About 5:15 P. M. we met Lieutenant Nicholson, 7th Cavalry, with dispatches, so General Pershing and party went back while we continued on for two more miles and camped near the top of the pass, against the side of the mountain, where we found water. Elevation about 7000 feet, wind strong and cold. The two guides ran a wild steer into camp and killed it. We butchered it and all had fresh meat for supper. What was left we hung high. In the morning it was frozen stiff. We tied our horses on a picket line, and when they had eaten the grass bare we moved the line to another place. As we had no hay it was most important to give the horses every chance to graze. We covered about 24 miles this date. I was up during the night inspecting and got so chilled that I shivered and shook until morning, finding it impossible to keep warm. Everybody else was in the same fix and so were the horses, poor brutes. This was one of the real hardships of the campaign—hot days followed by freezing nights. Many times we experienced a difference of 90 degrees between noon and midnight. Sometimes it was so cold no one could sleep, man or beast, and still we must push on after the elusive Villa.

March 25th was the 11th consecutive day of marching. Most of the horses had the appearance of being in good condition, but the lack of grain was making itself felt. After marching a few miles we began to go through canyons, some of them very narrow with steep grades. I remarked to Ord that if trucks or wagons ever got through these places it would be a miracle. Later on wagons and trucks went through here regularly, the army engineers in a few days having made the trail a negotiable road.

This bad going continued until 3:00 P. M., when we returned to the Santa Maria River, in the meantime having crossed but one mesa two miles wide, the others being trifling.

At the highest point of this day's march we must have reached an elevation of 8000 feet, as we were among the oaks and conifers. At 4:45 we passed the plaza of Cruces, and at 5:15 went into camp south of the town on the river bank. The camp was threateningly dominated by hills across the stream to the east, but it contained more grazing than I had seen in the past ten miles; and any way, I sent for the head man of the town and told him that at night I had guards posted who were ordered to shoot first and challenge afterwards, so to notify his people to keep away. I also told him that should anyone throw a shot or two into my camp during the night, that in the morning I would

burn the house of his honor. These head men did not like this arrangement and put up the plea that they could not possibly know in advance
of any such hostile intent toward my camp. I would only reply: "Then
you are out of luck," and terminate the conference. I used this method
when camping near any settlement and never had my camp disturbed.
Other commands were not so fortunate.

Just before reaching Cruces we met a Mexican with a load of oranges.
I bought enough for the two troops, each man as he passed put 5 or 6
in the bosom of his shirt. This was a real treat. The people of Cruces
were very Indian in appearance. They have well irrigated and well
tilled fields in the narrow valley along both sides of the river. The
town has a populous center, but for the most part extends for about
four miles along the river. The people were cordial, differing very
much in their attitude from those at El Valle. They had never seen
any airplanes until ours passed. They called them eagles and were
very much afraid of them. We fed corn this evening. Covered 42
miles over rough country.

March 26, left camp at 8:30 and almost immediately struck a trail
up and down hill, over rocks, and so difficult that wagon transportation,
if we had had any, could not have passed. However, wagons and trucks
did pass a week or so later after the army engineers had worked on it.
This continued off and on all day. We reached Namiquipa at 1:30 P. M.
and went into camp across the river east of the town 20 minutes later,
having marched 17 miles.

We picked up a couple of horses the 7th Cavalry had abandoned as
played out. These poor beasts showed every evidence of joy at seeing
once more a cavalry column. They followed us into camp where they
were properly cared for.

After getting camp established, I invited all officers to take lunch
with me in town, having first notified the head man to have the meal
cooked. We all rode back to town and enjoyed a hearty meal of eggs,
tortillas, frijoles, jerked beef, and coffee made of the green coffee bean
roasted. When I paid for this meal with Mexican silver there was not
only surprise but joy expressed by the Mexican.

Just a week ago Villa caught a Carranza battalion straggling through
here and killed some 18 and captured about 40. Only 40 fought, the
rest ran when the attack came.

Troops "I" and "K" of the 10th Cavalry came in just as we were
finishing our meal, so I had some more prepared for them. They
brought with them 2000 pesos with which to pay for food, forage, etc.
When we asked for forage and food, the Mexicans said there was none
as the Mexican troops of both factions had taken it all; but when they
learned they were to be paid for it in Mexican silver and not with some
of the Mexican rubber stamp money, we got plenty of grain and food
stuffs.

Horses were allowed to graze some when we fed corn for the evening
feed. Our camp was on the side of a hill. It had two parallel depressions. As night came on we placed the picket lines in the bottom of
these depressions, thus affording some protection to the horses in case
of hostile rifle fire. I also sent for the jefe and made my little speech
about what would happen to him in case my camp was disturbed.

We spent the 27th in camp awaiting instructions. About 7:00 A. M. a Carranza scout arrived, on his way to El Oso, where Colonel Brown was with a part of the 10th Cavalry, and where the natives say Villa is. The scout was riding a roan pony that if fed up would have looked good. The man carried a carbine and two belts of ammunition, and came in wrapped in a black, green and salmon colored serape. He left a little before 8:00 A. M. with a note from me to Colonel Brown. Lieut. Engel, 7th Cavalry, came in late this afternoon with a message from Colonel Dodd, who wants the motor trucks sent to him with supplies. About every one down here is out of rations, or nearly so, and living off the country—which is "slim pickings" for man and horse.

These towns are full of men, showing that Villa has not taken them all. It may be that the very men we look upon may be his—yet where are the horses? We must rely upon our wits and training, the justice of our cause, and the splendid quality of our enlisted personnel.

About noon Major Howze arrived with a provisional squadron of the 11th Cavalry, composed of 20 picked men and horses from each troop. They expect a pack train of 75 mules and some wagons to arrive tomorrow when they will take the pack train and go into the hills after Villa. We who have been given nothing, not even a map, or a mule to carry a few cooking utensils, look with envy upon this superbly equipped outfit, and make sarcastic remarks to the effect that Villa's last chance of escape is gone, now that these hand picked soldiers are on his trail.

March 28th, we were still in Namiquipa, but moved camp a couple of hundred yards. At 3:00 P. M. a motor truck came in loaded with supplies for Howze's command. As I was out of food for man and beast I asked Howze to give me some from his ample store, but he refused. However, when he left on the morning of the 30th I seized what was left and gave my men and horses a square meal. The trucks brought some mail, but none for us. However they did bring us a little news: that the 1st Squadron, 13th Cavalry must remain in the Big Bend country of Texas to watch our "allies," the de facto troops of Mexico; that the 5th Cavalry and 24th Infantry were coming to Columbus; that the House bill for increase of the army has passed the House and the Senate bill the Senate; that the attack on Verdun continues; and that Mexico is taking our invasion calmly.

March 29th was our third day of rest at this place, but all we can do for ourselves is to shoe our horses, as our forges and some shoes came with the trucks yesterday. We also got a little dab of rations, but the coffee is all gone. Some of the officers went over to town in the morning and got an early lunch of native coffee, jerked beef, tortillas, and eggs, and arranged for some tortillas for the troops and a little pinole for the officers.

General Pershing, Major Ryan, Lieut. Patton, and Mr. Rurn (war correspondent), and small escort arrived sometime before sunset from El Valle.

On March 30th at 7:00 A. M. Major Howze and his command left for Bachineva, about 35 miles to the south. They made an impressive sight with some 200 fighting men, followed by the long pack train. General Pershing left for the south two or three hours later.

Our horses had been getting two feeds of corn daily and were now beginning to refuse it, probably because their mouths were getting sore. Much of this native corn has little pebbles in it, so each soldier must carefully spread each feed on his blanket and pick out the stones before putting on the nose bag. Once a horse bites a stone he stops eating regardless of his hunger. The grazing land around this camp was about all cleaned off and we had no hay. Our horses were looking better than those of the 10th Cavalry, probably because the latter made four long marches; two before crossing the line into Mexico and two after. We had marched farther, but had not been forced as much.

Captain Claude H. Miller, Quartermaster Corps, bought a couple of big porkers for the command today. We were now reduced to what we could buy locally, and that was not much. We were camped on a bare elevation and the wind is a constant torment. As officers and men have but one blanket each we were doubling up at night. Ord and I slept together. He is skillful in making a sleeping bag out of the two shelter halves, placing one blanket under us and one over, with the two slickers on top, after that we crawl in and cover up, including our heads. Sometimes when it was not so cold we would remove our spurs, but nothing else not even the pistol belt. This meant remaining in one position all night. We became quite skillful in locating stones and other rough places before making our bed.

At 1:00 P. M. I sent Lieut. Franklin, 24 men and a civilian guide to El Oso, here I had heard Candelario Cervantes, one of Villa's chief lieutenants, had taken refuge. Seven miles from camp the patrol met his brother Jose who said Candelario had not been at the ranch since the night of March 21-22, when Villa camped there. Jose said Candelario went with Villa next day to the Santa Catalina country and had not returned. The patrol continued on to El Oso, searched several houses without finding anything incriminating and returned to camp with Jose, getting in at 5:35 P. M., distance covered, 20 miles.

Some trucks with supplies came in about 8:30 P. M. Around 9:00 o'clock Lieut. George S. Patton arrived with orders for my squadron (Troops "K" and "M," 13th Cavalry) to proceed at once to Providencia, to arrive there at daylight, to scout the mountains around Providencia, and to return to Geronimo at dark. Patton told us that Dodd, with the 7th Cavalry, had hit the Villistas at Guerrero at 7:00 A. M. the 29th, yesterday, and it was thought some of the defeated Villistas might head for Providencia.

I drew two days rations and two days grain and left camp at 11:30 P.M. The night was very dark. We could see no trail, so laid a course by the stars and held it. In the darkness we lost a couple of men who failed to keep closed up, but learned later that they found their way back to Namiquipa. We hit Providencia just after daylight having marched 20 miles. It was now the morning of March 31st. There were no signs of the enemy. We watered the horses, gave them a feed of grain, and all hands cooked breakfast—coffee, bacon and hard bread. When all had been fed I got out the map, called the officers together, made an estimate of the situation, and stated I intended to scout the mountains toward Bachineva, reconnoitering that town, and reach San Geronimo about dark. Lieut. Patton at once spoke up and said he was representing General Pershing and that General Pershing wanted me to scout the mountains farther to the north. I told Patton he must assume all responsibility, and this he agreed to do.

We remained at Providencia in all about an hour and a half when we again hit the trail. I sent Lieut. Lininger with a squad along a ridge of the mountains to the southeast, while "K" Troop took the valley to the right and "M" Troop to the left. We cut no trail of man or horse. Saw plenty of cattle. A high wind accompanied by snow caused some suffering. Had I gone to Bachineva as I had planned we would have caught General Beltran and 200 of his men who had taken shelter there from the snow storm. Such is fate.

General Pershing was justly provoked with me, but quickly exonerated me from all blame when Patton came forward and assumed full responsibility. Major Ryan, acting Chief of Staff, told me I should have followed my judgment even though the General's aide had given me orders in the General's name. I believe to this day I followed the correct military procedure.

We marched about 57 miles from Namiquipa to San Geronimo via Providencia through the night, snow, wind and over a mountain range. On top of this the General sent me off with a patrol to search a ranch a few miles away. I was glad that night to crawl into the sleeping bag alongside of Ord. In the morning our bed was covered with snow. Lininger got lost in the snow storm but found his way into San Geronimo. It is almost impossible to lose a good soldier.

On April 1st we left camp at 9:30 A. M. and marched across country to Bachineva, a distance the way we went of about 20 miles. We entered the town from two directions. Here I learned that Beltran with 200 Villistas had taken shelter here from the storm last night and had left early this morning. Again heard reports that Villa was wounded in an engagement with Carranzistas at Guerrero, previous to Dodd's attack on that place.

We went into camp at 4:30 in the afternoon, alongside the 11th Cavalry on the south edge of Bachineva, with orders to be ready to leave at 6:00 P. M. Gave a feed to the horses, and had some bacon, hardtack and coffee. We did not move, however. Ord, who speaks Spanish like a native, and who has a most sympathetic manner, rustled a lot of fodder last evening for our horses. This is the first real roughness in way of feed they have had since leaving Dublan. The poor beasts waded into it with gusto and filled up for once. I noticed a big improvement in them next morning.

General Pershing came in during the evening. He sent for me and we sat on a couple of mantas before a fire and talked things over. He finally said: "Tompkins, where is Villa?"

I answered: "General, I don't know, but I would like mighty well to go find out where he is."

He asked: "Where would you go?"

I replied: "I would head for Parral and would expect to cut his trail before reaching there."

He said: "Why?"

I answered: "The history of Villa's bandit days shows that when hard pressed he invariably holes up in the mountains in the vicinity of Parral. He has friends in that region."

The General remained silent, so I enlarged upon my statement to the effect that my small command (a half squadron of two troops), with a few pack mules, could move with greater speed and less effort than a command more than three times as large, that it could conceal itself when concealment might be necessary when a larger command could find no shelter, that it could live off the country when a larger command would starve, that its very size might tempt the Villistas to give battle when with a larger force they would avoid any such issue, and that Villa, if suffering from a shattered leg, was certainly headed south where he could have a chance to recover from the wound. I also added that in my opinion, the Villista bands in our immediate vicinity were here to keep the American troops occupied until Villa made his getaway.

He asked: "How many mules do you want?"

I replied: "Twelve."

The subject was dropped and not referred to again that evening.

About 4:00 A. M. on April 2nd two troops mounted and two dismounted, all of the 11th Cavalry, left camp and moved south to investigate a report that 200 Villistas had formed an ambush in a pass which they expected United States troops to traverse. The command returned about 11:00 A. M. They saw nothing except 14 fires at the place where the ambush was supposed to have been.

We were up at break of day. After men and horses had been fed, I ordered the saddles packed, arms looked over, clinches on horse shoes tightened and preparations made for a "quick getaway" should orders come. I had a hunch the General was going to send me on some mission, and if I was right I was determined to start before he could change his mind. After the above preparations were made I took one of the guides as a guard and went to a nearby house to arrange for a bath. Had a fine hot tub and felt greatly refreshed. Returned to camp as the 11th Cavalry outfit were coming in from their early morning scout. About noon the General sent for me and said: "Go find Villa wherever you think he is." He gave me 12 pack mules from the 11th Cavalry, 500 Mexican silver pesos, 5 days rations, and grain for two days: all from the stores of the 11th Cavalry. This was a roving commission, though a very dangerous one due to our small numbers, but a job any cavalryman would rejoice in. As soon as the pack train was loaded we started, 1:50 P. M. Crossed the range east of camp, then marched south on mountain trails following footprints of ponies made by the Villista band that left Bachineva yesterday morning after the snow.

Chapter XXI

The Situation After the Fight at Guerrero

When General Pershing arrived at San Geronimo Ranch on March 30th, Dodd's report of the Guerrero fight reached him there. This victory was promptly reported to Washington, and the reply was published to General Pershing's command as follows:

Headquarters Punitive Expedition, U. S. Army,
In the field, Mexico, April 4, 1916.

General Orders ⎱
    No. 17 ⎰

1. The following telegram from the War Department is published for the information of the command:

Fort Sam Houston, Texas,
3-31-16

General Pershing, Columbus, New Mexico.

Number eighty-four period Following just received from Washington quote Secretary of War desires you convey to General Pershing, Colonel Dodd, and command, his hearty commendation of exploit mentioned in your eleven seven six Scott Chief of Staff unquote

By direction of the Department Commander
Bundy.

2. All officers and enlisted men of the command are cautioned against a feeling of overconfidence as to the final result to be achieved by this expedition. The Commanding General appreciates most highly the work already performed by this command, and considers it exceptional in many respects to anything heretofore recorded in the annals of the army. All members of the command are urged to put forth renewed energy both as individuals and as organizations in an effort to accomplish successfully the mission entrusted to the expedition by our people.

By Command of Brigadier Pershing:
DeR. C. Cabell,
Lieut. Colonel, 10th Cavalry,
Chief of Staff.

After the fight at Guerrero the detachments of Villa's command scattered to the four winds, some being reported as returning north to the mountains of Bachineva, others to Providencia, while others were hurrying south. Rumors, reports, and even positive assertions by natives indicated Villa's departure to all points of the compass, and his presence in several places at once.

On March 29th Brown was at Quemada, Evans at Tepehuanes, Howze at Namiquipa, Lindsley approaching San Jose de Babicora, Tompkins at Namiquipa, and Allen at Colonia Dublan.

When General Pershing received Dodd's report of the fight he immediately ordered Dodd to scout the country thoroughly, and make every effort to locate Villa or any of his followers left in that section. These instructions reached Dodd at Providencia, where he had returned in the belief that much of Villa's force, if not Villa himself had moved toward the mountains in that vicinity.

Howze's column, which had been gradually moving south, arrived at San Geronimo on March 30th. Upon information that Villa was then hiding west of Bachineva, Howze was sent to scout the mountains from the east, returning to Bachineva from the south; and Tompkins moved by night march to Providencia via Santa Ana as stated in previous chapter, and covered the western slope, both columns uniting on April 1st at Bachineva.

Upon receiving in person at Bachineva reports from these officers that no trace of any bandits had been discovered, it seemed possible to General Pershing that Villa had gone into the mountainous country southeast of Guerrero, or possibly had moved south. Howze was therefore ordered to Guerrero, at which place, in lieu of further instructions, he was to govern himself according to information he might obtain; and Tompkins was directed to follow the Villistas that were reported to have been at Bachineva under Beltran on the 30th.

In case it should be ascertained that Villa was moving generally south, the plan was again to use parallel columns converging near the Durango line, in an effort to overtake or cut off Villa's forces before they could get that far south.

Colonel Brown was to take the road farthest east, with Tompkins in the middle, and Howze farther to the west, while Dodd was to guard the trails leading into the mountains to the west.

Brown had left Quemada on the 30th for San Diego del Monte, where he was joined by Evans, remaining there during the 31st, sending an officer to the railroad in a futile effort to reach Dodd or General Pershing by telegraph. Leaving Evans to guard the pass, Brown, the following day, directed his course through the mountains by way of Agua Caliente, where he unexpectedly encountered a band of Villistas, and an engagement followed.

Evans remained at San Diego del Monte guarding passes as directed, and, upon receiving information that a band of Villistas was passing northward, moved to Quemada on April 2nd, thence to Tepehuanes through Santa Catalina to San Geronimo on the 5th, where he was given verbal orders to continue on to Namiquipa and cover the Santa Clara-Oso country, which duty was performed by his various detachments until the reorganization of commands on May 9th.

Four of the cavalry columns that chased Villa following his defeat by Colonel Dodd at Guerrero were commanded by Major Frank Tompkins, 13th Cavalry; Colonel W. C. Brown 10th Cavalry; Major Robert L. Howze, 11th Cavalry; and Lieutenant Colonel Henry T. Allen, 11th Cavalry. We shall now accompany these four columns on their hard ride to the south.

We have been with Tompkins and Brown from the time they left Colonia Dublan up to the first of April. We shall now accompany Howze and Allen from the same starting place.

CHAPTER XXII

Operations of the Provisional Squadron, 11th Cavalry (Howze), March 24 to April 2

A provisional squadron had been organized, made up of four provisional troops of 60 men each, one squadron sergeant major, one hospital corps man, two orderlies, and the following officers:

Major Robert L. Howze, 11th Cavalry, Commanding
Captain George B. Lake, Medical Corps
Captain Eben Swift, Jr., 11th Cavalry
1st Lieutenant John A. Pearson, 11th Cavalry
1st Lieutenant Alden M. Graham, 11th Cavalry
1st Lieutenant Emil P. Laurson, 11th Cavalry
1st Lieutenant James A. Shannon, 11th Cavalry
1st Lieutenant James L. Collins, 11th Cavalry
1st Lieutenant Sumner M. Williams, 11th Cavalry.
2nd Lieutenant Joseph W. Viner, 11th Cavalry

This squadron left Colonia Dublan at 9:00 A.M. March 24th for the south in pursuit of Villa, under special verbal instructions from General Pershing. Howze had a most difficult situation to face in that his horses were in no condition to start on any such campaign.

The horses of this regiment, the 11th Cavalry, got off to a bad start. They arrived at Columbus, N. M. from Fort Oglethorpe, Georgia, on the 16th of March after five days in the cars. During this journey they had no rest, only what sleep they could get standing packed like sardines in the cars, little water and feed, with all the accompanying nerve strain which animals experience when traveling by rail in cattle cars.

The 1st Squadron, under command of Lieutenant Colonel Henry T. Allen, started for Colonia Dublan the morning of March 17th, less than 24 hours after unloading, and before the horses had recovered from the long railway journey. The remainder of the regiment left Columbus 24 hours later. Due to short forage, hot days and freezing nights, and the recent long car journey, this march proved to be too much of a strain on many of the animals. The 1st Squadron arrived at Colonia Dublan on the 21st, and the other on the 22nd, and went into one of the windiest and dustiest of camps where they "rested" during hot days and freezing nights.

The reader must picture these horses starting for Colonia Dublan before the fever caused by their rail journey had subsided, sick and weak, marching in a long dusty column across the Chihuahua desert in the heat, hot wind, and dust of the day and the freezing cold at night, each carrying a load not less than 250 pounds (taking the average trooper at 150 lbs.). This was asking too much of flesh and blood. Ten horses from this regiment died between Columbus and Colonia Dublan, a distance of about 120 miles, made in five marches.

On March 24th, less than three days after the 1st Squadron arrived at Colonia Dublan and less than two days following the arrival of the rest of the regiment, Major Howze started on his memorable campaign, and on March 30th Lieutenant Colonel Allen started with his flying column.

These horses, in a weakened condition at the start, carrying maximum loads, on short forage, traversing a terrain of deserts and mountains almost devoid of vegetation and with but little water, were making longer marches than cavalry makes under normal conditions, and many of these marches over almost impossible country and at night. It takes but little carelessness to disable a horse under the best of conditions. Who but the best of leaders with a command of old and proven troopers' could have accomplished what Allen and Howze accomplished under the conditions they accepted and overcame? The leader rides as far as and often farther than any man in his command, he gets less sleep than any soldier under him; he carries the lives of his men in his hands; the success of the expedition depends upon his judgment and decisions. These conditions call for a steady nerve and a clear brain, but now both brain and nerves are at war with fatigue, loss of sleep, and poor food.

Howze, of course, was fully aware of the poor condition of his stock, but he accepted this mission with gladness, relying upon his skill as a cavalry leader to overcome the difficulties of his path. So he started, and after a cold march through a snow storm, camped on the Santa Maria River 8 miles south of Galeana at 7:00 P. M., a distance of about 35 miles. Next day he went 25 miles farther to Boka on the Santa Maria. On the 26th he continued south through the El Valle-Cruces canyon to a point on the Santa Maria River three miles south of Las Cruces, where he went into camp at 6:30 P. M., having covered 32 miles. On the 27th Howze marched to Namiquipa, where he arrived at 11:20 A. M. Here he met Major Frank Tompkins with two troops of the 10th Cavalry and two troops of the 13th Cavalry. Howze remained here until the morning of the 30th. On the 29th Pack Train No. 11 reported to him, and on the 28th some trucks brought him rations and grain.

Being now "all set to go," this column left Namiquipa at 7:00 A. M. on March 30th, and started for Bachineva, but when within six miles of this town the column was met by General Pershing, who ordered them to countermarch to San Geronimo, where they arrived at 7:00 P. M. having covered 38 miles.

Immediately after midnight, March 30th, Major Howze's column left camp under verbal instructions of General Pershing, scouted the mountains to the southwest of San Geronimo, and went into camp at 6:00 P. M. in a heavy snow storm within 5 miles of Providencia, having marched 36 miles over the most difficult trails. At 6:00 P. M. this date, March 31st, two civilian guides brought a message from Major Ryan to Major Howze, substantially as follows: That he had Villa located in a ranch which he had pointed out to the two guides in a general way, to the southeast from where he had entered the steep mountains. That he, Ryan, would wait for Major Howze until midnight, and if Major Howze did not reach Ryan by that time that he, Ryan, would attack at daylight.

As the command was thoroughly exhausted, and the mountains were far too difficult to move over at night, Major Howze decided to camp where the guides overtook him.

Next day, April 1st, the command left camp at daylight, crossed the mountains again to the east in search of Major Ryan, who had returned to San Geronimo without leaving word for Howze. Howze then camped 2 miles south of Bachineva at 2:30 P. M. having marched 22 miles over a mountain range.

On April 2nd Howze's command left camp at 3:00 A. M.

The mounted contingent of this force scouted in the mountains to the southeast of Bachineva in search of Beltran's forces, which were reported to have moved north after the Guerrero fight, going as far as Bustillo Plains. The camp of the bandits was found, which appeared to have been left by them 24 hours earlier. The command then returned to Bachineva and rested during the remainder of this day, having covered 26 miles through the mountains, mostly in the dark.

We shall now return to Dublan and bring Allen and his men south.

Chapter XXIII

Operations of the Provisional Squadron, 11th Cavalry (Allen), March 30 to April 15

On March 29th the commanding officer of the 11th Cavalry received orders from General Pershing to form another provisional squadron composed of four provisional troops. This was done by selecting 20 men and horses from each troop of the regiment, especial attention being given to the condition of the horses. To this was added 1st Lieut. Carl H. Muller with 25 men and two machine guns, Captain John R. Bosley, Medical Corps, one hospital attendant, and one civilian guide. The following were the other officers:

Lieutenant Colonel Henry T. Allen, 11th Cavalry, Commanding
Captain Julien E. Gaujot, 11th Cavalry
Captain John E. Hemphill, 11th Cavalry
1st Lieutenant Edwin L. Cox, 11th Cavalry
1st Lieutenant Seth W. Cook, 11th Cavalry
1st Lieutenant Charles McH. Eby, 11th Cavalry
2nd Lieutenant Harding Polk, 11th Cavalry
2nd Lieutenant John F. Crutcher, 11th Cavalry
Also Pack Train No. 10, and part of Pack Train Battery "C", 4th Field Artillery (mountain) making a total of 88 pack mules.

This provisional squadron set out from Colonia Dublan the next day, March 30th, at 6:30 A. M. The pack mules carried five days field rations, 2 days reserve rations, and 8000 pounds of oats for Namiquipa, where additional orders would be received. The distance marched was about 100 miles, which was covered in four days. The last day's march was the hardest because of steep grades and rough going. On arrival at Namiquipa on April 2nd, Colonel Allen received orders to send two troops to investigate the locality of Canyon del Oso and Los Tanques. He started at 2:00 P. M. this same day with two troops commanded by Captain Gaujot and Lieut. Eby for El Oso. Just before the start he took on a Mexican, ... Rico, an ex-Lieut. Colonel of Villa, as additional guide to the regular guide, Mr. Pratt, who did not know the country. It developed later that this Rico was formerly commander of all the men of Candelario Cervantes, and that the latter was his brother-in-law, they having adjoining ranches at El Oso.

Six miles out of Namiquipa the rear of the column was fired on by snipers from the foot hills to the south. The snipers were chased and lost after a pursuit of about two miles. There was nothing to indicate that there was any force of importance at El Oso, therefore the command proceeded the following day, April 3rd, to Los Tanques, 22 miles from Namiquipa. This cul-de-sac in the mountains offered a fine secluded camp, from which exit north, east or south is over precipitous hills. There was one house which Villa had used for his personal requirements, and the camp site for his men while organizing the force for the Columbus Raid. He also stopped here during his retreat south.

As it was evident that only the Cervantes contingent of the Villa Columbus column had remained in this section of the country, and in accordance with instructions received by courier, Colonel Allen hastened on to San Geronimo over a mountain trail for further orders from the Division Commander. The entire distance thus traveled from Namiquipa to San Geronimo was only 35 miles.

On April 5th Colonel Allen's command, including the part left at Namiquipa, which had joined at San Geronimo, remained in camp at San Geronimo.

On April 6th General Pershing ordered Colonel Allen to cut out the weakest animals, and leave Lieut. Muller and his machine gun detachment in charge of them. The medical officer and Lieut. Crutcher were also left behind. After the weaklings were cut out the new detachment was formed. The new command consisted of 7 officers and 169 enlisted men, and set out April 6th for San Antonio, marching 21 miles the first day to Lake Itascate. This day's march carried them through the Sitio Las Varas. Lieut. Polk and the pack train were fired on from the houses. The following morning Colonel Allen sent back Lieut. Eby's troop with Lieut. Polk to secure the culprit or culprits. As no one knew anything about the firing two leading citizens were seized and taken to camp as hostages; one of whom had a rifle. Since this experience no column has been fired on along the Namiquipa-San Antonio line of communications.

Next day, April 7th, the command marched to Rancho Delores, 18 miles; and on April 8th 14 miles to San Antonio, where they arrived at 11:00 A. M. This point is approximately 300 miles south of Columbus. Later this date General Pershing came in. It was reported that Pablo Lopez had the preceding night been at Bustillos but had left for the south.

General Pershing and Colonel Allen had a conference at which it was decided to reduce the size of Allen's command in the interests of greater mobility, and to hit the Lopez trail and follow it with all speed. So the detachment was again culled, and the troop commanded by Captain Hemphill was left behind. This left Colonel Allen a force of four officers and 84 enlisted men.

With this small force Colonel Allen left San Antonio the morning of April 9th, proceeded beyond Rancho Laguna, 9 miles, then returned to it as a feint to await darkness before surrounding the sitio of Santa Lucia, 16 miles south, whither Lopez's horse tracks (American horse with one shoe missing on right front foot) and information indicated he had gone the preceding night. Nothing was gained by this search. Colonel Allen decided to pursue the investigation at the very large hacienda Bustillos, where it was known Lopez's parents lived. The column reached there, an additional 11 miles, after midnight, and had the information confirmed that Lopez had gone south—probably to the caves of Santa Rosalia.

The next day, April 10th, the command continued the march to the south, hoping to cut the trail by following the San Juanita River through the sitios along it towards Carretas. About 7:00 P. M. they again hit the trail of Lopez about two miles southeast of Cienega; it doubled on itself and it was impossible to tell which was his later course. The one leading in the general direction of the caves was assumed to be the fresher of the two and so they followed that toward Carretas, camping three miles northwest of the town, where in the darkness water was found by mere chance.

On April 11th Colonel Allen's command were marching to the limit of their animals' endurance, and chiefly at night, believing that the chances of surprise were thus increased. There was good reason to believe that Lopez had gone to the caves and that Villa might also be there. This little command followed a branch of the San Pecho River, passing through various small village and ranches, including Carretas, San Bernardino, and San Lorenzo, and camped in the canyon of the San Pedro River at 10 P. M.

At Carretas the Jefe de Armas was Lieutenant Colonel David Barrios with a detachment of about 40 men. Except for the saber carried on his rather richly caparisoned saddle, there was absolutely nothing to indicate that he was a soldier. He seemed not to have the slightest knowledge of maps, and very little indeed of the surrounding country.

On April 12th, leaving the San Pedro, Colonel Allen's march was towards Satevo on the San Pedro (La Joya) River where the command arrived at 4:30 P. M., having covered 26 miles. Here they found General Pershing with a very small staff and an aero section. General Pershing here gave Allen instructions to send an officer's patrol of one officer and 10 enlisted men to find Colonel Brown in the region of Parral and get an immediate report from him of his operations. This dangerous mission was entrusted to Lieut. Eby, who most creditably made the distance to Santa Cruz, 81 miles, in 37 hours elapsed time, rather remarkable when we consider the condition of his horses. Colonel Allen had orders to follow up this patrol to the same section of country. It was supposed that Majors Tompkins and Howze were in that general direction.

It was on this date, April 12th, that Tompkins had his battle with Carranzista troops at Parral, and Colonel Brown moved forward while Tompkins made a slow retreat until the two forces, uniting 16 miles north of Parral, turned back the de facto troops of Mexico, and held their position until ordered to move north by General Pershing.

While Colonel Allen, under his new orders, would continue towards Santa Rosalier de Cuevas, his chances for looking farther for Lopez in the cave region, were, for the time, eliminated, and his efforts were to be transferred to the search for Villa.

On April 13th Colonel Allen's command left camp at Satevo at 11:00 A. M., and marched via Tres Hermanos to Santa Cruz de Valeria, going into camp at 7:30 P. M., having covered a distance of 26 miles. At Tres Hermanos, one of the Zuluaga ranches, it was evident from the conduct of the people that the community was wholly sympathetic with

Villa. About 8 miles farther south at Santa Cruz de Valeria the attitude of the people towards the American troops was friendly.

Next day, April 14th, the column started for Zaragosa (El Concho de Pilar) on the Conchos River, a tributary to the Rio Grande. When about 4 miles from that town the command was overtaken by an automobile section commanded by Captain Wm. O. Reed, 6th Cavalry, who was carrying orders to Colonel Brown, supposed to be in a delicate position at or near Parral. Captain Reed showed to Colonel Allen the instructions he was carrying to Colonel Brown. This decided Colonel Allen that the only proper procedure for him was to hasten to Colonel Brown's assistance as fast as possible. This was the 16th consecutive march for this column, without a break for a single day, and this new situation meant a march of 57 miles to the relief of Brown and his command at Santa Cruz de Villegas, about 18 miles north of Parral. Later developments showed that it was Major Tompkins' command that was involved in the affair at Parral and not Brown's. Colonel Allen and his command reached Santa Cruz de Villegas at 6:00 A. M. April 15th, having been on the road 21 hours. The short forage rations and the long and successive marches were telling heavily on his stock.

A few hours after the arrival of Colonel Allen Major Howze came in with his column, which had made a remarkable march to the south and west, and had reached Santa Cruz de Villegas, coming from the southwest of Parral.

The above shows how splendidly General Pershing's plan for supporting his flying columns worked out. Major Tompkins, with his little command of less than a hundred men, formed the spear-head of the advance. Colonel Brown covered Tompkins' left rear about a day's march behind; Major Howze covered the right rear at an equal distance; and Colonel Allen was about three marches directly to the rear. When the clash came at Parral on April 12th, Tompkins fell back slowly for 18 miles, stopping from time to time to bump off a few Mexicans as a warning to them not to get too aggressive, and Brown joined him at Santa Cruz de Villegas that same evening. Then on the morning of the 15th Allen and Howze came in. There was now a force strong enough to cope with anything the Mexicans might muster.

Throughout this narrative the reader has probably noticed that General Pershing is always turning up at unexpected places and unexpected hours. He covered the whole field of operations by moving quickly from place to place, using three automobiles for the purpose. This meant a small escort and taking big chances, but he took the risks and he knew at all times when and where to move his men.

We shall now return to the other flying columns: Tompkins, Brown, and Howze and bring them forward to Santa Cruz de Villegas.

Chapter XXIV

Operations of the Provisional Squadron, 13th Cavalry (Tompkins), April 2 to 12

On April 2nd we left Major Frank Tompkins striking into the mountains east and south of Bachineva. We shall now follow the fortunes of this command, which led the advance and fought with the Carranzistas at Parral. This action marked the turning point of our southern advance, and initiated the slow withdrawal of the American troops to the north. This terminated a month's campaign, marked by peril and extreme hardship, and conducted with a dash and celerity in keeping with the best traditions of the U. S. Cavalry. The campaign came to an indecisive conclusion as the American troops, defied and attacked under orders from the Carranza Government, retired to San Antonio, then to Namiquipa and to Colonia Dublan. They finally recrossed the border, February 5, 1917, without having captured Villa, all for reasons better known to our State Department than to the writer of these lines.

At 1:55 P. M., April 2nd, with Troops "K" and "M," 13th Cavalry, and 12 pack mules, Tompkins' column left Bachineva, moved to the east, and crossing two mountain ridges cut a trail which showed shod native horses and mules, probably 150 in number. In view of the information received at Bachineva and vicinity Tompkins decided that this trail had been made by some 150 Villistas under Beltran and Jose Maria Rios. The trail was two days old. Tompkins decided to follow it. At 3:50 P. M. he came across a camp showing some 30 old fires. Here were found parts of uniforms and equipment and two native mules. This camp had been made by the party being trailed. The American cavalry followed the trail to Santa Maria, where they camped, having covered about 10 miles. The trail led on through the high altitude flora such as juniper, manzanita, many oaks and some pines, resembling the jeffery, the yellow, the bull and others. The rest and feed the horses had at Bachineva had put them in very good condition.

On April 3rd, after the animals had been watered, grazed and given a feed of grain, the command saddled up and hit the trail at 6:50 A. M. moving at an alternate walk and trot. The column headed south and arrived at the barrio of Agua Caliente, 7 miles, at about 8:00 A. M. At this place there are three big adobe buildings capable of defense. In one was a store where we managed to get corn, potatoes, cigarettes, matches, etc. We also learned that two days ago the 10th Cavalry met a band of Villistas at this place and drove them southeast into the pedregal.

Tompkins, having decided to support Brown, left Agua Caliente at 9:00 A. M., moved south a mile to a prosperous hacienda at the junc-

Typical Road Scene, North of Namiquipa

Difficulties of Motor Transport. The Trucks Could Not Move in Wet Weather

tion of two beautiful, clear little streams, and then turned southeast into the pedregal, going up hill and down dale until 5:20 P. M. Most of the time there was no trail except the tracks left by the fleeing Villistas, who were evidently trying to shake their pursuers. About 1:00 P. M. Tompkins came to a place where Brown had lost contact with the enemy. Scouts Haney and Jorgensen could track like Apaches. They located numerous pony trails and decided they would unite where the mountains made a break in the horizon, so we headed for that point and sure enough cut Brown's trail without losing any time hunting for it. We followed this trail until we camped at 5:20 at Napavechic.

It was a hard day on the horses—both their bodies and their feet were tired. The trail much of the way was over round stones that rolled when stepped on. The command must have reached an elevation of 10,000 feet or more. The rough mountain scenery was magnificent beyond description. We camped in a grove of oaks by a pool, the grazing was good, but it was a poor place to defend. We covered about 40 miles this date, of the hardest going yet encountered.

Haney and Jorgensen ran a young steer into camp and slaughtered it. Not wishing to fire a shot, Haney grasped the animal by the horns while Jorgensen took it by the tail. The animal tried to gore Haney, but he tripped it and it fell so that the horns pierced the ground each side of him. Quick as a flash Jorgensen tripped the hind legs, and as the creature fell kept it from rising. Haney extricated himself from between the horns and forced one front leg over a horn, thus making it impossible for the animal to rise. These two men were expert cow punchers, bronco busters, and rodeo performers. They looked upon this steer act as nothing unusual. To me it was thrilling.

On April 4th we left camp at 7:40 and took up the trail which leads to San Antonio on the Mexican Northwestern Railroad, where we found Brown and the 2nd Squadron and Machine Gun Troop, 10th Cavalry. Brown and his command had been here about 24 hours. Here I heard that Villa, badly wounded, was moving from San Borja to Parral and that his bands were moving, some south and some east from San Borja. I decided to move on San Borja.

After purchasing some corn the command left San Antonio at 11:30 A. M. and reached Cusihuiriachic about 3:15 P. M. This place is down in a canyon, and the reason for its existence is the Cusi Mining Company and its mines. It was to this place that the 16 Americans were coming when they were taken off the train at Santa Ysabel and murdered by Pablo Lopez on January 10, 1916, less than three months ago.

The advance guard, under Lieutenant Lininger, reconnoitered the town. He discovered that the garrison was composed of Carranzistas, located their outposts, and arranged for our entry. Major Tompkins had a long conference with the Jefe de Armas, Major Reyes Castanada, and a doctor Seyffert, a resident physician. After verifying all the information received at San Antonio earlier in the day, Tompkins sent a telegram to General Pershing, through Brown, asking Brown to relay by courier.

Most of the garrison was 40 miles south under General Jose Cavazos, who was reported to have defeated Villa twice yesterday, but who was unable to pursue due to lack of ammunition.

The people of this town appeared curious, friendly, and accustomed to Americans. The Carranzistas seemed very friendly, and gave us three soldiers as guides to Cavazos. Dr. Seyffert also accompanied us. We camped about 5 miles south of the town at 6:00 P. M., having marched about 30 miles this date. During my conference with Castanada a a woman took part. She was small, thin, about 30 years old, dressed in the uniform of a Carranza officer, and wore pistol and belt filled with ammunition. She seemed to have considerable authority.

On April 5th the command marched at 8:05 A. M., followed by the pack train and rear guard at 8:50. Marching over these mountain trails, our advance guard consisted of a point under an officer, and was accompanied by the civilian scouts, and followed anywhere from 50 to 200 yards depending upon the configuration of the terrain, by the main body in column of troopers. Major Tompkins marched at the head of the main body. The narrow trails made this formation necessary. In the event of a sudden attack from either flank the command would be immediately deployed by moving to the flank. Attack on the head of the column would be met by each troop forming line to the front on its own head thus quickly forming the leading troop as the attacking line with the second troop as its support, about 200 yards to the rear (the head of the second troop was always about 200 yards in rear of the head of the leading troop). The command moved always at a slow trot (about 7 miles an hour) when trotting was possible. The point regulated its march on the head of the main body. Many times during each day it would be possible to trot not more than two or three hundred yards at a time. As the leading squad hit the level it would take up the trot, followed in turn by each succeeding squad at the same place. This would tend to elongate the column somewhat, but checked much of the backing and filling so tiresome to marching troops. No effort would be made to close up until the leading squad would reach rough going or a grade up or down, when they would again take the walk, each succeeding squad holding the trot until reaching the spot where the first took the walk. When the head of the column halted, the column would close up, form fours, and dismount, with a march outpost caring for our safety. This method of marching enabled us to cover a maximum of distance with a minimum of effort. This slow trot involved little more effort than the walk, and caused but little more violence to the rider and the pack, an important item when the horse is carrying 250 pounds.

When the march extended beyond the noon hour, a halt was always made at noon, march outposts established, horses allowed to graze, and the commander made an estimate of the situation. As a result of this estimate the destination for that day might be changed to another place.

About 11:20 this date we had a chance to water the animals in an arroyo containing occasional pools. About noon we went through a deep gorge fully half a mile long, in the center of which was a village and smelter. In the side of the cliff was a cave large enough to hold 50 horses. This place can be avoided by going farther to the east.

In the middle of the afternoon as we were approaching San Borja, we were met by a party of mounted Mexicans who delivered a note of which the following is an accurate translation:

On the third of April I telegraphed you, advising you that I thought it prudent to suspend the advance of your troops until we both receive orders on this subject from the Citizen Military Commander of the State. As I have just received knowledge that your forces are advancing in accordance with the itinerary which I have, with those under my orders, I would esteem it very much if you would suspend your advance until you receive the order to which I refer, by which means there can be avoided a conflict which may occur by reason of your advance. As I do not doubt that you are aware of the reasons which move me to write this, I hope that we can arrive at an agreement, for which I sign myself

Your attentative and true servant
General Jose Cavazos.

I showed the bearers of this message a copy of the letter I had from the President Municipal at Casas Grandes, and they agreed that it would be advisable to continue forward. I did so. Upon approaching the town I sent Lieutenant J. B. Ord and two men in advance to explain our presence and ask for a conference with General Cavazos. Ord signalled for me to come on, and soon after I met the General and his staff, with the Mexican colors flying. This rendezvous was on the edge of the town in a depression where a stream crossed the road. Before riding into this low place I took the precaution to have a troop of cavalry dismount and line the crest thus retaining military control of the situation in case our Mexican friends should think of indulging in any little act of treachery. I conferred with Cavazos and verified my information that Villa had gone south through San Borja. Cavazos told me that Villa was dead, and buried at Santa Ana, and that he, Cavazos, was leaving for that place to search for the body. Cavazos said he had no authority for us to pass through and could not answer for the conduct of the townspeople (they appeared friendly). He seemed to fear trouble between his soldiers and mine. I jollied him up a bit when he finally pulled out a quart of brandy took a drink from the bottle, and handed it to me. I took a good long pull and handed it to Ord who got his share and handed it to another of my officers who all helped to lower the line. When the bottle got back to Cavazos he took one look at it, made some exclamation in Spanish which sounded like strong language, and threw the bottle in the bush.

My orders forbade any clash with Carranza troops, and though the temptation was strong to continue on Villa's trail which was hot, to avoid trouble I moved back four miles to Cieneguita. As we parted the General shook hands and said in fairly good English, "Be good."

We camped at Cieneguita, having marched in all 32 miles. This experience with Cavazos confirmed our impression, which had been growing for some time, that the Carranzistas were against us, that we could expect no help from them, and that they would jump us at the first favorable opportunity. I had good reason to believe that Villa was at or near Santa Ana, 22 miles south of San Borja, so I decided to go around Cavazos to the east and come back to the trail below him.

At Cieneguita I received information as to the movement of the force under Beltran and Jose Maria Rios. They had gone east from Cieneguita two days earlier, April 3rd.

On April 1st Villa was here on a litter. His brother-in-law, Manuel Corral, killed one of the overseers and wounded his wife because he protested against Corral handling her so roughly. He pushed Corral through the door and shut it, when Corral fired five shots through the door killing the man and wounding his wife. When the rest of the band came they robbed the place of 2500 pesos in money and other property. This ranch furnished us with corn and fodder. The fodder was much needed. This morning in crossing an arroyo we passed an overturned spring wagon in which these people say Villa was riding. It is supposed the chase has become so hot that Villa did not want to wait for the slight repairs necessary to put the wagon in commission and so took to the litter.

On April 6th we started for Santa Rosalia. Left camp at 9:20 A. M. and took the trail heading in an easterly direction, guided by an old Mexican on foot. This old man guided us through the mountains for 12 miles. No matter how much we hurried, he always kept ahead and never seemed to tire. For 12 miles the trail was over rocks, up mountain sides, down through deep canyons, and in dry stream beds—heart breaking for man and horse, except the old Mexican.

At 1:40 P. M. we reached a village of about 75 houses. The name of the place was Cuarachic, or something like that. Here we left the old Indian and took a well defined road to Santa Rosalia de Cuerriavaca, about five miles farther along. We marched through the town and camped on the far edge in a grove of poplars.

The hillsides about here are apparently worth something for grazing, while the valleys are irrigated and cultivated. The people seemed timid at first but soon flocked to our camp in utter confidence. Quite a number of them have grey eyes, a type different from any we have yet encountered. We also passed a very good looking school building bearing the sign "Escuela Official Saragassa." There was a large man in the doorway to bid us "Buenas tardes" as we passed.

The Jefe de Armas was a young Carranza officer who had an ugly wound in his arm received two days ago when Pablo Lopez and his gang went through. Our surgeon gave him the attention which he needed badly. This boy certainly had nerve. He rode into our camp, explained his official position and offered us any help in his power. He asked our surgeon to look at his wound. He stood up while the surgeon probed, cleansed and dressed the torn flesh, and never quivered.

Reports of natives say that two forces of bandits met here and proceeded northward. If this is true it looks as though they were circling back to get out of the ring of Carranza troops. These people have suffered much from the operations of Pablo Lopez. They told me where 150 Villistas under Beltran could be found. It was a temptation to follow this lead. But so much information had been false, and then I could not spare the time and energy from the Villa pursuit.

Fed corn and fodder. Many of the horses do not care for corn and eat it only in small quantities. Most of them are thinning down more or less, but still, with very few exceptions, are going strong. Their satisfactory condition is due to our scheme of marching, dismounting to lead in mountainous country, and great care in saddling.

On April 7th we remained in camp at Santa Rosalia, shoeing horses, purchasing supplies and getting information. In the afternoon Colonel Brown with Major Young's squadron and Phillips' Machine Gun Troop of the 10th Cavalry passed my camp. The Colonel stopped long enough to exchange news. He informed me that he was enroute to Parral by way of Satevo—Valle de Zaragosa—Sapien.

The following amusing incident occurred while we were having our talk. The 10th Cavalry is composed of colored men, and it is well known that this race has a weakness for chicken. The Colonel rode up to where I was standing, followed by his orderly. Both dismounted, the orderly holding the Colonel's horse. We were immediately surrounded by children and idlers in general. Chickens, which are members of the Mexican family, were underfoot. The colored orderly, while the colonel was busy with me, reached down, grabbed a chicken by the neck, gave it one skillful snap, and placed it in his saddle bags. I said to myself: "The Colonel will have chicken for supper tonight and he won't know where it came from."

The horses got three good feeds of corn and fodder this date, and the men also filled up on hash, tomatoes, salmon, bacon, hardtack, tortillas and eggs. Each soldier was issued four eggs. This feed took the wrinkles out of their bellies and added to the cheerfulness which permeated this command during the entire campaign, regardless of the many vicissitudes experienced.

Most of us got a bath and washed our underclothes. We were rapidly losing all outward resemblance to regular troops. We were ragged, shoes almost gone, and nearly everyone had a beard. We certainly presented a hard-boiled, savage appearance.

I took advantage of this layover to sum up the situation as follows: *Villistas:* Beltran with 150 men at Santa Maria de Cuevas, and Cienega de Ladrones; Hernandez with 120 at Santa Ana, San Jose del Sitio, and Veile de Zaragosa; Villa with his staff and 50 men near La Gabilana. This made a total of 320 Villistas within striking distance of us.

Carranzistas: General Cavazos moving to Santa Ana and San Jose del Sitio; General Herrera, strength unknown, closing the passes in the mountains to the east of Santa Rosalia; General Garza with 1200 at Santa Maria de Cuevas moving on San Juan and Tres Hermanos; Colonel Cano with 400 moving east from Guerrero; Major Reyes Castanada at Cusihuiriachic with 200 men. This made a total of between 2000 and 3000 Carranzistas, either on our flanks or between us and the United States. In view of this summing-up I decided to move to Parral via Fresnitos and San Jose del Sitio, unless I received further word of Major Howze's movements.

On April 8th we left camp at 7:30 A. M. Our horses and men were much refreshed. The wounded Carranzista Lieutenant rode with us for a couple of miles. We started in a generally southerly direction. Until 3:15 P. M. the trail led parallel to a range of mountains, crossing innumerable narrow and deep arroyos. The footing was rocky in places, but the rocks were no longer volcanic but of the water worn variety. When the earth was exposed it was filled with water worn pebbles and rocks. At one place there was a stretch of a mile or so of granite.

This rough going made it necessary for the trooper to dismount and lead his horse. At 3:15 we turned south and camped at 5:00 P. M. on the banks of Rio San Pedro, a fine little river with a rocky bottom. We had marched about 32 miles. This place is called Las Secones or Fresnites. There is absolutely no grazing for horses.

On April 9th we left camp at 7:30 A. M., moving due east. At 8:30 we were fired on by some 8 Carranzista soldiers, a part of General Garza's command. We pursued them for three miles and captured from them a herd of bronco horses and mules, which I turned loose, except two mules. I then moved to San Juan de Bautista and thence south, and halted from 11:30 to 2:30 while our horses grazed.

Carranza troops are all about us. Several of their officers rode up to my column and asked where we were going to camp. I told them, but we did not camp where I said. After we lost the Carranzistas our line of march lay over a huge mesa with lots of grass. We passed two haciendas and finally went into camp at Sauz at 5:45 P. M. This is a fine camp. We turned the horses and mules loose in a large field inclosed by a high stone wall. This gave the animals a splendid chance to graze all night and rest undisturbed. Needless to say the place was well guarded.

We ordered the hacienda people to cook up a large copper boiler of frijoles for breakfast. Last night we heard there were 25 Villistas to the north of us, and this morning before leaving camp we heard there were 400 at San Juan de Bautista, six miles south. When we were fired on we gave credence to this last report. However, the presence of Garza's command in the neighborhood explained it all.

While the horses were grazing at the noon hour I made another estimate of the situation. I concluded that Major Howze would move from San Borja to San Jose del Sitio and that Colonel Brown would move to Satevo and on to Parral: that I was three marches ahead of Howze, and one and one-half marches ahead of Brown, and midway between their columns. I figured my best move would be to go rapidly to Parral, resupply and march to Rosario, about 30 miles south of Parral, and then work north between the other two flying columns, or close the two passes through the Sierra Madre Cuchilla into Durango and Sonora. We covered about 26 miles this date.

On April 10th we left camp at 8:30 A. M., and proceeded in a southerly direction for about 10 miles over a rolling and rocky country to a fairly good water hole in an intermittent river. Reached the barrio of Aguacito de Chaves at 12:45 P. M. over a mountain road. We bought some fodder here, watered the stock, fed the fodder, and after an hour's rest marched 8 miles to Concha on the Concha River. The official name of this place is Valle de Zaragosa or San Zaragosa, but the ancient name of Concha clings to it in common parlance.

The river is clear and swift but easily fordable. As we crossed the river 25 Villistas scattered out the other side of town. These men were under Montoya. They were looting a factory and had one mule already packed with loot. We captured the loot and returned the property to the owners.

We heard here that Hernandez had moved southwest with 100 Villistas to Valle de Rosario, about 32 miles in an air line. This confirmed my belief that the general movement of the Villista forces was southward toward the Durango line. It is reported that Hernandez has 100 or more led horses.

The people report that 90 Villistas went through here two days ago, killed six Carranza soldiers, took lots of supplies and departed. None of the people seem to know where Villa is. These are the best Mexicans we have seen: more intelligent and better dressed than any others. Some of the women wore fitted skirts, shirt waists, etc. while most of the children wore shoes and stockings.

I found that I could get some clothing for my men: canvas trousers, shoes and socks, and made arrangements to get the stuff by sending one troop at a time. As the first troop to go picked up their rifles and fell in, the women and children, of whom a good many were in camp, ran screaming. They thought we were going to sack the place, and their fright caused us to believe for a second or two that an attack was imminent.

At about 11:00 P. M. a Captain Antonio Mesa, Carranzista from the garrison at Parral, came into my camp, and after some conversation of a very friendly nature, told me that he would send word to Parral of our coming, by telephone, so that we could be met, pastured, fed, supplied, and camp site arranged for. Next morning this captain took breakfast with me. Upon leaving the town Captain Mesa told me the telephone would not function and that it was necessary to send the message by courier. He showed me the saddle mule all ready to carry the messenger, so that if I should see this mule again I would know it. The man was to go through in one day while I was to take two.

We got some fodder here which the horses enjoyed as usual. Shortly after our arrival I had a conference with the head official of the town. When this talk was over, I asked him to have enough beans cooked for the command for breakfast to be delivered at daylight. He assured me there was not a bean in the community, and besides there was nothing to cook them in. I told him we would have nice hot beans for breakfast or his house would burn. The beans came at the time ordered, and were paid for in Mexican silver. There were enough for breakfast and luncheon too.

Next day, April 11th, we left camp at 8:40 A. M. and marched southward. For 15 miles the country was almost useless for any purpose. For several miles the road lay through a deep, narrow and dangerous canyon. After marching 20 miles we found water for the animals. Ten miles farther on we camped at the barrio of Santa Cruz de Villegas at 4:00 P. M., having covered 30 miles this day.

There is a tank of water here covering about two acres, also a pleasant little stream. The last ten miles was over mesa land pretty good for grazing. Along this little stream grow a line of beautiful trees called Los Alamos, beneath which we spread our blankets.

There has been a very pleasant change in the weather. For the last three days the hours of daylight have been warm but not too hot, while the nights are decidedly warmer, making it possible for man and horse to sleep without being awakened by the biting cold of the higher altitudes.

We have supplemented our government ration of hardtack, bacon, coffee, and occasional tomatoes, salmon, and prunes, with what we could buy of native foods. Almost every night we have a big copper boiler of frijoles cooked for the next breakfast. Once or twice we have bought bread and flour. There is a native coffee which must be merely corn or wheat, highly parched and then ground. Eggs are plentiful and good everywhere. Chickens may be bought, but they are troublesome to prepare with only a mess kit to cook them in. Tortillas are always available, and occasionally we kill a steer.

It was a grave oversight not to supply these flying columns with plenty of Mexican silver. The people all over Mexico have been so consistently robbed by all the military factions over a period of years that when we pay in silver for services rendered and supplies furnished they nearly drop dead with surprise. After Parral, when the American troops were moving slowly north, this matter of money was rectified and the poor downtrodden Mexican peon looked upon the American soldiers as a blessing from heaven and furnished much in the way of service and supplies until frightened off by the Carranzista officials of the de facto Government of Mexico.

But on the march south most of the food for man and horse was purchased from the private funds of the officers with the flying columns. Colonel W, C. Brown of the 10th Cavalry was especially generous in this matter of paying government bills from his private funds. In order that his advance should not be delayed through lack of funds, he dipped into his personal supply to the extent of close onto seventeen hundred dollars. It was fortunate for my command that he did so, for it was his prompt reinforcement on April 12th that turned back the Mexican attack and prevented a real battle, with the accompanying casualties, especially on the Mexican side. Had the Mexicans made a determined attack on my column at Santa Cruz de Villegas, their losses would have been heavy. This might have infuriated the people to such an extent that war would have been inevitable—a war that President Wilson was so determined to prevent. But Brown's prompt action on the evening of April 12th turned the Mexicans back and probably prevented war. To the best of my knowledge and belief his action on this occasion has never been adequately recognized.

The change from oats to corn, the lack of long forage, the constant marching involving violent changes in elevation, hot days and freezing nights, had tended to thin down our horses so that their ribs, backbones, and withers were becoming prominent. Some were getting sore backs. Two horses had been abandoned and their riders mounted on native ponies which seemed to thrive under conditions in which the American horse wilts. One reason is that the native pony is NATIVE, and another reason is that the soldier gives him care a Mexican would never give. Our horses were not down and out by any means. They had plenty of latent strength, and when occasion arose for us to call upon them they were able to and did respond. We have been blessed with good water almost continuously since coming into Mexico, but some days it has been a long time between drinks. Operating largely in the mountains, we have been able to find running streams upon which to make our bivouacs.

On Wednesday, April 12, we left camp at 7:10 A. M., watered the horses in the irrigating ditch, and followed a well defined road to Parral, a distance of 18 miles. Here we arrived at 11:45 A. M. As we rode along Ord, Lippincott and I talked of the good time we should have in Parral. Captain Mesa had led us to believe that we would be received with friendship and hospitality. We understood that the place had a population of about 20,000 with a good hotel and a good club (Canadian I think). We pictured the hot baths we should have, the long cool drinks, and the good food. Mesa told me we could get money, clothing, food, forage, and even railroad transportation to carry us one march south of the city, as I had planned.

Upon reaching the town there was no official to meet me as Captain Mesa had promised, so I took my advance guard and went to the guard house near the railroad station, where I asked for permission to enter the town, and for a guide to the headquarters of the Jefe des Armas. Permission being granted and a Carranza soldier being detailed as a guide, I proceeded to headquarters where I met General Lozano and requested a private conference. This he granted and we went upstairs to his office. He first informed me that Villa was north in the vicinity of Satevo. He then asked me why I had come into town. I said: "By your invitation extended through Captain Mesa." He replied that Captain Mesa's messenger had never reached him; that he had probably been captured by Villistas. He reiterated that I should not have entered the town. I replied that I would get out just as soon as he would designate where he wanted me to camp. This he agreed to do. Then I mentioned the need of supplies, so he sent for a Mr. Scott, who claimed to be an American merchant but who spoke English with a strong Mexican accent and looked more like a Mexican than an American. Scott agreed to furnish my command with corn fodder and provisions. After all my business was completed General Lozano delayed about an hour before he was ready to lead me to the camp site.

The room in which we conferred had French windows opening onto a balcony overlooking the street where my squadron was formed in line facing the building. They made a very impressive sight. At one time we heard a great racket in the street when we all rushed onto the balcony to discover that a mule hitched to a heavy cart had been made to bolt down the street evidently with the intention of causing confusion in the ranks of my soldiers, but a big Yank grapped the mule by the bit and stopped that little act. This incident was so indicative of treachery that I slipped my holster in front in anticipation of immediate need.

By the time Lozano was ready to start, a big crowd had formed, and as we passed the plaza there were cries of "Viva Villa" and "Viva Mexico." As we approached the outskirts of town the rabble was pressing us pretty close, so I dropped back to the rear of the column to keep an eye on the situation. As our rear cleared the plaza the crowd followed us. I noticed a small, compactly built man, with a Van Dyke beard, riding a fine looking Mexican pony, who seemed to be trying to stir the people to violence. He was well dressed in grey clothes and looked like a German. He would ride into the crowd and yell "Todos! Ahora! Viva Mexico!" I watched this bird very closely and made up my mind to fill him full of holes should the break come as he evidently wanted it to. At one time I yelled "Viva Villa!" at which the people laughed. Mob psychology is amusing—sometimes.

Lozano and his staff were at the head of the column so were in ignorance of what was going on in rear. When a few hundred yards north of town Lozano led the column across the railroad track through a gap between two hills into a hollow beyond. I halted the rear guard under Lieut. Lininger behind the railroad embankment, and had Captain Turner occupy with his troop the hill immediately west of the saddle. I also notified Lozano that his people were firing upon us, as they were at this moment. He and his staff hastened back to stop the firing. Before going I asked him for an explanation. He denied all responsibility. I could have killed him at this time as I was convinced he was leading us into a cul-de-sac, but I let him go as his pistol was still in his belt. There was a third hill across the railroad track to the south. This was about 600 yards off. The Carranza soldiers continued to congregate on this hill, and soon they brought up a large Mexican flag.

A Mexican messenger arrived from Lozano, requesting our immediate withdrawal, giving as a reason for this request that he could control neither the soldiers nor the people. I agreed to move north if he would have delivered to me the forage and food I had contracted for. This man wanted merely to locate our positions because when he started back instead of going to town he went to the hill occupied by the Mexicans, who immediately began firing at us.

The Mexican soldiers on the hill now attempted to cross the road and turn my left flank. I was still making every effort to obey my orders and avoid a conflict with these de facto troops of Mexico, so I stood up on the railroad embankment and yelled to them to go back. They refused so I sent a combat patrol of four men to drive them back and ordered Captain Turner to fire when he had a good target. When I stood up to yell to these Mexicans they fired at me and missed, but killed Sergeant Richley. He was lying down behind the railroad track with his head just enough exposed to let him see over the rail. It was impossible for the Mexicans to see him. A bullet intended for me hit him in the eye passing out through the back of his head. He never knew what hit him. I had just asked him to let me have his rifle as I wanted to take a shot at the Mexican with the flag, but the flag disappeared, and as I turned to hand the rifle back to Richley I saw he was dead.

On observing that a force of a hundred or more were moving around my right flank, west, I decided to move out of the hole Lozano had led me into. We moved northeast across country until we reached the road Parral—Santa Cruz de Villegas, where we halted, put the pack train at the head of the column and checked up as to the situation. We found that Sergeant Richley was killed and Corporal McGee and Private Ledford wounded. Both men could ride but at a cost of much pain. McGee was shot in the mouth and Ledford through one lung. First Lieutenant Claude W. Cummings, Medical Corps, displayed bravery of a high order in dressing the wound of Ledford while under fire. I watched this operation, which excited my admiration. Both men became the target for a number of Mexicans. Their shots fell about the surgeon and his patient like rain, but Cummings cooly attended to his job, put the man on a pony, and took him to the rear.

Most of our firing was done by the rear guard of 8 men under Lieutenant Lininger. He handled his men well, keeping the Mexicans at a distance by very accurate fire. I learned later that at this time the Mexican loss was 25 killed and a number wounded. This close shooting on the part of our rear guard, coupled with a lack of coordination on the part of the Mexicans, allowed us to withdraw in leisurely fashion. I started our withdrawal at about 1:30 P. M. and arrived at Santa Cruz de Villegas at about 4:15 P. M., three hours to cover the 16 or 18 miles, a rate of march we had maintained daily on the way south.

When the Carranzistas turned against us at Parral, I naturally assumed that all American forces had been or were to be likewise treated. I knew that the garrison at Parral amounted to 500 or 600 men, and that the population of that town was rated as 20,000, many of whom were armed. I knew that Santa Cruz de Villegas was a small fortress admitting of easy defense by a command of the size of mine, including our animals, and that it was well stored with food for man and beast. I knew also that Colonel Brown could not be far behind me. In view of the foregoing it did not take me long to decide upon Santa Cruz de Villegas as our immediate objective, where we could withstand a long siege and then, if necessary, fight our way north. I had learned that General Garza had occupied Concha or Vaile de Zaragosa shortly after we left it, which looked as though the Carranzistas were trying to cut us off in that direction.

Remember that this little command of American soldiers numbered less than 100 all told. Our food and forage were gone, and our supply of ammunition was none too plentiful. We were surrounded by Carranzistas as well as by Villistas, both ready to unite in a common cause against the American invasion. We had penetrated 400 miles into the heart of a hostile country. We had lost touch with all supporting bodies and could only estimate where our nearest help might come from. Fortunately I guessed right, for Colonel Brown was but 8 miles north of Santa Cruz de Villegas.

The road from Parral to Santa Cruz de Villegas was a well defined wagon road, permitting us to march in column of twos. It led over a rolling country bordered by large fields, separated by stone walls about 4 feet high and four to six feet thick. Shortly after our taking up the retreat the civilian element of the attacking force, being mostly on foot, became exhausted and fell behind. The Mexican troops, being mounted, kept trying to flank our column by paralleling the road to the west. We watched them gallop madly across a field until stopped by a wall, when they would dismount, pull the wall down, and then race across the next field, and so continue until they finally awoke to the fact that this method was not getting them anywhere, and was wearing them out.

Finally some bolder spirits came closer, when I took Lininger and his 8 men and rode towards this approaching body. We dismounted behind a stone wall and opened fire. We got a hot fire in return. I stood up using my glasses to call the shots. Each trooper had his arm through the loop in his bridle rein. Two men in my immediate front had trouble with their horses. These animals would toss their heads every time the men would aim. One soldier said: "Hold my horse, Major," whereupon the other trooper sounded off: "Hold mine too." Even in the tenseness of the moment these informal *demands* caused me to smile, but I did as requested. Shortly after I became horseholder for these two privates the horse on the right was shot through the head and the one on the left got a bullet through the rump. Our men were shooting

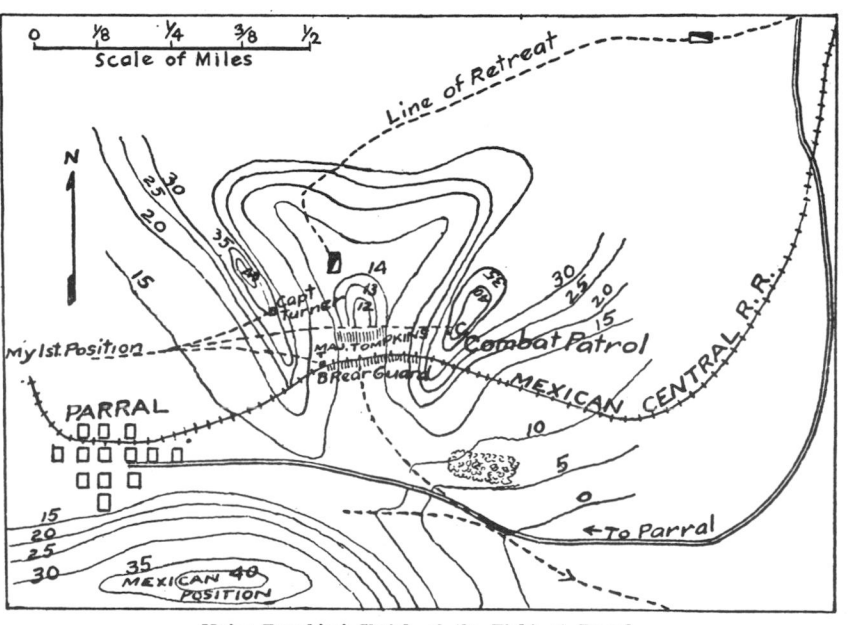

Major Tompkins' Sketch of the Fight at Parral

straight and drove the Mexicans back. The horse shot in the head broke from me and ran off. Ordering Lininger to fall back I jumped on my own horse and chased the runaway, which I soon caught. Just as I seized his rein I received a bullet in the left shoulder, but not a serious wound. I returned to the dismounted man and we both got safely back to the column. In falling back Corporal Proffit had his horse shot in the neck and hindquarters, which put Proffit on foot between the lines. Lieutenant Lininger wheeled, galloped back to Proffit and as he circled him the soldier grabbed the officer's left elbow, made a flying mount and landed behind the Lieutenant with his rifle in his hand, and both returned to the column unscathed though the horse was slightly wounded. This was a gallant rescue. I recommended Lininger for the Medal of Honor, our highest military decoration, but he was awarded the Distinguished Service Medal instead.

Shortly after this rear guard action we came to an adobe house with a wall around it. We halted here for the doctor to dress the wounded, while the enemy was kept at a distance by a dismounted skirmish line.

As we again took up the northward march, the enemy getting bolder, I dismounted a troop from time to time to keep them at a safer distance. In one of these engagements Sergeant Major D. McD. Juno had his horse shot from under him. My orderly, Private Charles D. Radcliffe, was leading my extra mount, a rather tall horse named Sheep. This horse carrying a McClellan saddle packed with some of my belongings filling the seat of the saddle. Radcliffe, seeing the sergeant's trouble, rode up to him under fire and said: "Here, Sergeant, mount Sheep." The sergeant could not mount the horse as the stirrups were crossed over the saddle and under the pack, and the sergeant was short and not as young as he used to be. Radcliffe, a much younger man, dismounted, gave his own horse to the sergeant and made a flying mount landing on top of Sheep's pack. During this change of horses the Mexicans concentrated their fire on the group between the lines but we all got back intact. The Mexicans are very poor rifle shots. They are not so bad with the pistol, but with the modern military rifle they are hopeless.

This ride back from Parral was punctuated by gallant deeds. There is one more which came under my personal observation. My adjutant, James B. Ord, was shot through the ear. Shortly after receiving this wound he noticed that the man Ledford, who had been shot through one lung, had fallen from his horse. Ledford and the horse were in the path of the advancing Mexicans. Ord rode back to Ledford, dismounted, lifted Ledford onto his horse, and led the horse back to our column. All this time the Mexicans were very busy shooting at Ord and Ledford. This rescue had been made after Ord had been wounded. I recommended him for the Medal of Honor. He was awarded the Distinguished Service Medal.

Shortly after getting Ledford safely back to the column we both noticed that his horse was lagging. Ledford was too far gone to urge the beast forward. He had all he could do to stay in the saddle. So Ord grabbed the reins and pulled the horse while I rode slightly in the rear and beat the beast with a rawhide whip. Ledford begged us to go on and leave him. His agony was great. Remember that he had been shot through and through, and was riding a Mexican pony we were trying to make lope. I gave Ledford a pull from my canteen, told him the ranch was just ahead, to hold on for five minutes more and we would have him where the doctor could make him comfortable. The man had courage, and held on, in spite of pain and loss of blood, until another bullet hit him back of his shoulder and came out in front just above his belt. He was dead when he hit the ground. Ord and I galloped on to join the command.

Turner's troop was in the rear. As we passed over a ridge and dipped down out of sight, I told Captain Turner to dismount 20 men, deploy them across the road and kill as many Mexicans as he could, for they evidently were getting ready to make one desperate charge to cut us off from the shelter that was just ahead. In a minute or two they came, without formation, hell-bent-for-election, firing in the air, yelling like fiends out of hell, and making a most beautiful target. When they were about 200 yards off Turner's men fired one volley; ponies and Mexicans rolled in the dust, some of those in rear tripped over the fallen, the balance checked their ponies quicker than any polo pony ever stopped, wheeled and raced to the rear. After our first volley our fellows sprang to their feet and gave the enemy a taste of rapid fire. We heard later, from Mexican sources, that we had killed 42 Mexicans including Major Orozco, and wounded many, including a colonel.

After this check the Mexicans pulled off, we watered our horses in the irrigating ditch, and marched into Santa Cruz de Villegas, which we seized, placed the horses under cover, put expert riflemen and sharpshooters on the roofs, from which vantage points they dominated the country, had the wounded cared for, placed barricades to block any sudden rush of the enemy, sent out dismounted reconnoitering patrols, and waited for the enemy to make the next move.

When our men had occupied the roofs with Captain Aubrey Lippincott in command of one troop and Captain Frederick G. Turner in command of the other, I took post on the ground between the two buildings within easy hailing distance of either roof. There was little firing on the part of the enemy and none by us, as the Mexicans were about half a mile away, probably thinking over the surprise Turner had so recently given them. They finally decided to advance. Their leaders, or what looked like leaders through our glasses, were mounted. Now Captain Lippincott was one of the best rifle shots in our army, especially at long range. When he saw the enemy advancing he estimated the distance at 800 yards (80 yards short of half a mile), set his sights accordingly, estimated the direction and force of the wind, took careful note of temperature and atmospheric conditions, and set his windage to correspond, took careful aim at one of the mounted men and fired. The shot evidently was a bull's-eye for the man fell out of his saddle. Lippincott then leaned over the wall surrounding the flat roof and called to me: "I got one at 800 yards, Major." The Mexicans must have concluded that that kind of shooting was too good for them so they fell back and sent in a note under a flag of truce from Lozano, which I quote as translated into English:

Sir Major Chief of the Expeditionary Column
Presente.
I have just arrived at this camp and I have been able to sustain (sic) my troops a little bit.
I supplicate you to leave immediately and not bring on hostilities of any kind. If on the contrary I shall be obliged to charge the greatest part of my forces. I pray you then to retire as soon as possible and if you wish to confer send me word. If it is that you leave send me word by the bearer so that I can withdraw my soldiers.

The General Chief of Arms,
Ismall Lozano.

I replied to this in Spanish of which the following is a translation:

To the General Commanding the Constitutionalist Forces in Parral:
I have just received your letter and regret very much that you were unable to control your soldiers.
We came to Mexico as friends and not as enemies. After you had left us,

I awaited in good order the grain and fodder contracted for. When your soldiers, without any provocation, fired upon mine, killing one and wounding two, as from this moment it became a question of self-defense, I also opened fire to permit my main body to retire, it still being my intention to avoid a general fight.

It was your soldiers who followed me five leagues firing at every opportunity. I did not answer their fire until those who fired came dangerously near.

I am prepared to continue to the north if you can assure me that I will not be molested. If not I will remain here to await the arrival of other American forces.

Awaiting your answer.

Frank Tompkins,
Major 13th Cavalry

So long as Lozano had started this note writing I was prepared to carry it on with enthusiasm. Just at this stage I was only too glad to spar for time. If Brown was near I knew it would not be long before he would show up, because as we neared Santa Cruz de Villegas three of our men continued on in an effort to locate his command. They found his camp 8 miles farther north at 6:30; and Brown with Major Young's squadron and the machine gun troop reached our outposts at 7:55 P. M., a mighty quick response. As Brown approached our position, as a precaution against being mistaken for the enemy he had his trumpeter sound "Attention," followed by "Officers' Call." Our trumpeters answered, Brown, marched in and Lozano and his gang beat it for Parral.

While we were in Parral Lieutenant Lininger saw a poster on a wall, signed by a Carranzista official, to the effect that American troops were in Mexico by authority of the Mexican Government, that we were not at war with Mexico, but merely in pursuit of the bandit Villa, and that the people should remain calm.

Many months later I had a letter from Lieutenant Lininger under date of Dublan, Mexico, January 2nd, 1917, in which he says in part:

Levi Brown has just come back from leave, and while in St. Louis he saw an uncle of Mrs. Brown, a Mr. Thatcher, who lived in Parral years ago and employed a man by the name of Mathews who was in the town when we entered last April.

He says the Carranza commander planned to put us in camp at the point to which he led us and then shoot us up that night.

Mathews says the first shots were fired by a woman whose brother had been killed by Lozano, and who hoped that by firing these shots she would bring on trouble and Lozano would be killed.

We left a very decided reputation for marksmanship behind us, even an exaggerated one, I think. For instance, they say that the first two Mexicans that lay down to fire were shot through the head by pistols.

Mathews says also the people of Parral were very much frightened when they found that we were followed by other troops as they thought that we were entirely alone.

Our casualties in this fight were as follows:

Killed in Action

(1) Jay Richley, Sergeant Troop "M," 13th Cavalry.
(2) Hobart Ledford, Private Troop "M," 13th Cavalry.

Wounded in Action

(1) Frank Tompkins, Major 13th Cavalry, commanding Squadron, flesh wound left breast and shoulder slight. Gunshot Mauser rifle bullet.

(2) James B. Ord, 2nd Lieutenant 6th Infantry, acting as Adjt. and Intelligence Officer, flesh wound lobe of left ear, slight. Gunshot Mauser bullet.

(3) Benjamin McGehee, Corporal Troop "M," 13th Cavalry, gunshot wound in mouth, severe, Mauser Rifle bullet. (Died later).

(4) Walter E. Willingham, Corporal Troop "K," 13th Cavalry, gunshot wound, calf left leg, moderate, Mauser rifle bullet.

(5) Richard Tannous, Corporal Troop "K," 13th Cavalry, gunshot wound, forearm, severe, Mauser rifle bullet.

(6) L. M. Schonborger, Private, Troop "K," 13th Cavalry, gunshot wound of hip, slight, Mauser rifle bullet.

(7) One man, Chas. H. Eichenberger, Troop "K," 13th Cavalry, missing, 7 horses killed and 16 wounded.

About 1500 men comprised these four flying columns when they left Casas Grandes late in March. A little more than half that number remained at the front the day of the Parral fight. The others had dropped out, because of shortage of food, the deaths of horses, their own semi-nakedness due to the wear and tear of day and night riding and occasional fighting among jagged mountain rocks, wildernesses of thorns, and the bitter snow and cold of the mountain altitudes.

It was a hot little campaign of less than two weeks, essentially cavalry and typical of our cavalry campaigns against the Indians immediately following the Civil War. It was well planned and gallantly executed. While the future will see other cavalry campaigns, the mechanicians to the contrary notwithstanding, it will never see one like this, operating completely cut off from the base. The airplane and the radio have changed all that, and for that reason if for no other this campaign is entitled to historical prominence. It was the last appearance of the Old Cavalry.

Adobe Huts at Colonia Dublan, Winter of 1916-17

General Pershing, Officers and Guides Consulting War Maps
Gen. Pershing in center, seated. Lt. G. S. Patton, Jr. at extreme left.

CHAPTER **XXV**

Operations of the 10th Cavalry, March 31 to April 15.
The Fight at Aguas Calientes

We left Colonel W. C. Brown, 10th Cavalry, at San Diego del Monte on March 31st, trying to get in touch with both General Pershing and Colonel Dodd. Failing to locate these officers, he decided to move towards Guerrero.

The afternoon and night of March 31st the command suffered from a violent snow storm accompanied by high wind. Next morning, April 1st, the command left San Diego del Monte for Guerrero. Near noon one of the horses dropped dead from fatigue. The cold nights are a terrible drain on the animals' strength.

About 1:15 the column came to Aguas Calientes, about 8 or 10 miles north of the railroad, and struck about 150 Villistas at the ranch. Troop "E," the advance guard under Captain S. D. Smith, encountered them first and exchanged a few shots. The enemy retreated south and east. Major Young with Troops "H" (Troxel) and "F" (Valentine), got on their left flank, Troop "F" killing two. The enemy abandoned some equipment, including a machine gun pack saddle. In the mixup a Pacifico was killed. Troop "G" (Rodney), "E" and the Machine Gun Troop (Phillips)[1] went on through the village. The pursuit continued for a couple of hours, and as the Mexicans scattered, the troops were not reunited until dark, when they met at El Mesteno and bivouacked.

Colonel Brown sent a dispatch to Major Evans, but as the native guide ran at the first fire he probably got there first. An interesting episode of this fight was the mounted pistol charge executed at Colonel Brown's order by Troops "F" and "H" against some Mexicans posted behind a stone wall in a ravine on the left flank of the Americans.

These Mexicans could not be dislodged by rifle fire, so Colonel Brown directed Lieutenant R. F. Migdalski, a member of his staff, to order Major Young to mount up and charge the enemy in flank. Young no sooner received the order than his two troops dropped back from the firing line, ran to their horses, mounted up and formed line of foragers with drawn pistols. The troops started down a steep hill. At a signal the gallop was taken and the forward movement continued in a direction

---

[1] Machine Gun Troop, 10th Cavalry. This troop, commanded by Captain Albert E. Phillips, 10th Cavalry, after making a six day march to the assembly point at Culberson's Ranch, New Mexico, made the forced march of 110 miles with General Pershing's column to Colonia Dublan, Mexico, and then continued south with Colonel Brown's force of the 10th Cavalry to the outskirts of Parral, Mexico, being the only Cavalry Machine Gun unit to reach that far south. In the engagement of 10th Cavalry troops at Agnas Calientes, Mexico, April 1st, 1916, Captain Phillips employed "Overhead Machine Gun Fire" to advance the attacking troops to the position held by the Mexicans. The position was captured with no loss to the American troops. This was the first use of overhead machine gun fire by the United States Army.

145

threatening to envelop the enemy's right flank. Not a shot was fired by our men, but at the signal to charge the troopers started to yell, at the same time increasing the pace. The Mexicans refused to meet the charge; they ceased firing and disappeared in the woods back of the stone wall long before the moment of impact. We lost one horse shot through the stomach.

Beltran was said to be the Villista commander. An "H" Troop horse died this night. Little food, hard marching, heavy loads, constantly changing elevations, hot days and cold nights are hard on horse flesh. It takes more than skill, experience and tender care to keep the poor beast going. They give all they have, uncomplaining, suffering untold tortures until the heart stops ticking. After the shoes are removed the brave horse is left for a buzzard's feast. One of the traditions of our cavalry service, bred in the days of our Indian wars, is that the trooper must care for his horse first and himself last. The men of this campaign were certainly true to that tradition.

On April 2nd Brown marched 15 miles to Napavechic Ranch, trailing Villistas. Very slow work. There were two main trails. Young followed the northernmost, indicating about 50 men, while Brown followed the other of about 80 to 100 men. When two miles out of camp at the top of a mountain Brown's column ran into two natives who claimed to be escaped prisoners, and said Beltran was short of ammunition. They also reported two companions over the hill not far away. Colonel Brown sent two troopers with one of the Mexicans as guide to bring in the rest of the party, and and to join the command in the canyon, to the east. As the trail Brown was following shortly changed direction to the south he tried to recall the two troopers by trumpet signals; this failing to bring the men in he sent Lieutenant Henry R. Adair and two men to find them. At 10:50 the first two rejoined the command without having seen Adair, so the Colonel left a sergeant and two men on the trail to wait for Adair and guide him back to the column. They did not join until just before making camp, 2½ or 3 hours having been lost in this operation. The first two men sent out returned with four rifles, three mules and one pony, and two more men, one of whom was thought to be a Villista and was sent back with the pack train. The others were, on the 3rd, released on the suggestion of one of the Carranza officers with Brown.

The trail of the fleeing Villistas led south and southeast. At times there seemed to be 50 to 80 men on it. As it came out of the mountains onto the plain it went in various directions, and was very hard to follow on account of slight traces left in heavy grass. Brown was now of the opinion that the main trail went nearly due south of Napavechic and crossed the railroad some five to eight miles west of San Antonio. About 4:00 P. M. one of Brown's guides reported many mounted men around Napavechic Ranch. Investigation disclosed Major Young, who had lost his trail, camping there.

People at this place were very unfriendly and reluctant to sell supplies, even refusing the customary receipts, but the command managed to get a third of a feed of corn fodder.

Colonel Brown sent a dispatch from here to Major Evans with orders to march to San Antonio. The dispatch was sent to San Diego del Monte, as that was where Brown had left Evans, but finding him there was another thing—detachments moved so quickly in this campaign. Late on April 1st Brown sent two native guides (Pacificos) on two of his mules to Major Evans, advising him of the fight at Aguas Calientes and to look out for enemy debouching on the big plain. There was no way of finding out whether this message was received. Guides and messengers were hard to get and very unreliable, as they feared retaliation by Villa for serving the Americans. Major Young had to deposit his watch and diamond ring as security for return of a messenger he sent to Brown on the night of April 1st. At San Antonio Brown found it impossible to send telegrams unless they were prepaid, though urgency of matter was represented. He sold a $2.50 knife to a soldier for fifty cents to get money to send one short official telegram.

Brown here learned, via telephone to Cusihuiriachic through Major Castanada, that General Jose Cavazos left Cusihuiriachic April 2nd with 600 men in pursuit of Villistas, destination in vicinity of San Borja. He also learned that General Gaza unloaded at San Ysabel this date for same destination as Cavazos.

On April 3rd Brown marched 13 miles to San Antonio on the railroad. Here he secured the telegraph line and wired to General Pershing to have all military telegrams sent collect. He also strongly urged the General to send money with which to pay for supplies, as the natives were more than reluctant to accept receipts which were written on any kind of paper, lacking even the dignity of the conventional cheque.

The question of lack of funds had now become serious. The securing of supplies by means of receipts was clearly not a workable arrangement, and sooner or later was likely to bring on open hostilities with the civilian population. A Cusihuiriachic citizen described the receipt method as follows:

You Americans pay for food all right, but you give receipts only. Now you buy a cow from a man who lives a hundred miles from any railroad. Even if that railroad were operating it would be six months before he could get his mail. You take that cow and you kill it and you give him a receipt. He mails that receipt to the Quartermaster at San Antonio in Texas. It takes, maybe, six months for it to get there, if it gets there at all. When the Quartermaster gets it he cannot pay for it. He returns duplicate vouchers to be signed. They take another six months to reach the man, and then he cannot write and he cannot read English. If he can do all these things and signs in the proper place—even then he gets, about 18 months later, a check that he cannot cash.

The above is no exaggeration. The same conditions prevail today in the United States, except that postal facilities are not quite so slow, which explains why our government must pay a much higher price for all contract work than is paid by civilian firms for like work. All business of the War Department is so hedged in by rules and regulations, made by civilians, that the army accounting officers must scan very closely all vouchers presented to them for payment, for should they settle an account that is in any way defective the comptroller of the treasury will disallow the payment and then the officer is stuck for the amount. This is known as "Red tape," which is the popular name given to army procedure in our country by the civilians who created it. As an illustration, long after the campaign was over, Lieutenant Migdalski, who was acting as quartermaster for Colonel Brown, received a letter from the office of the Quartermaster General in Washington requesting an explanation as to the reason why the hides of slaughtered animals were not sold as required by Army Regulations, and why he bought so many cheeses at Santa Cruz de Villegas and issued them to the troops. No consideration was given by "higher authority" to the fact that these purchases were made in a region that was practically uninhabited, and that the command was constantly on the move. I am only surprised that "higher authority" did not ask why these hides were not advertised for sale for ten days.

Colonel Brown writing to General Pershing from Parral on this subject said in part:

The greatest care has been taken to do no injustice to natives of this country. The chief difficulty from the outset has been to do this and still secure the necessary supplies from a country which has been raided in turn by Villistas and Carranzistas. To maintain my command on this expedition I have already advanced the Government over $1,453.00 of personal funds. Other officers have advanced several hundred dollars. How and when we will ever be reimbursed is problematical.

One thing in my opinion is certain, and that is that to seize supplies, whether the owner is willing or not, will sooner or later result in hostilities. Major Tompkins agrees with me most emphatically.

No officer who took part in this campaign displayed greater loyalty to his military superiors, was less unselfish, or was truer to the ideals and traditions of the United States Army than Colonel W. C. Brown.

Brown wired General Cavazos at Cusihuiriachic asking for an interview to plan a cooperative campaign against Villistas. A reply came from Major Castanada stating that Cavazos had gone in direction of San Borja. A Mr. Locke, an American hotel keeper of Minaca, came into camp and told of the attack at Minaca at 4:00 A. M. some days previous. Two of his companions were killed but he escaped. He also gave an account of the fight at Guerrero, and news of Villa's being badly wounded in both legs above the knees. Of course we knew later that Villa was wounded in but one leg below the knee. But the fact that he had a broken leg made his capture easier than when his legs were whole.

Migdalski bought several cords of wood at $15 per cord. It was difficult getting wood for cook fires. Individual cooking took more wood than if the cooking were done over one or two fires for the whole command. Major Tompkins' column was started off without even a camp kettle or coffee boiler, so each man had to cook for himself having only the soldier's mess kit and tin cup. Bacon, meat and other solids were fried in the meat pan and coffee boiled in the cup from which the coffee must be drunk when cool enough. This involved an enormous waste of wood, food and time, and was simply another obstacle to be overcome.

On April 4th Brown received orders from Division Headquarters to send his pack train with disabled men and horses back for supplies. Lieutenant John Kennard was sent in charge. Six pack mules, one for each troop and one for the quartermaster were retained, and these constituted the **sole transportation** of the 10th Cavalry from San Antonio south. This allowed each troop to carry a few improvised cooking uten-sils (5 gallon oil cans for boiling coffee), a half day's ration of fresh beef and such other food supplies as might be purchased. They were thus able to carry out their mission and **keep going.**

On April 4th Colonel Brown's command remained in camp, for on this date a message from the Mexican General Cavazos said an advance of the American troops would be considered a hostile act, and would be resented accordingly. The telegraph line to Chihuahua went out of commission. Major Frank Tompkins with his half squadron (Troops "K" and "M," 13th Cavalry) passed through San Antonio this date, headed for Parral. Tompkins and Brown compared notes and checked up on information.

Reveille was at 4:45 April 5th. Brown with Mr. Fox preceded the command to Cusihuiriachic to confer with the Mexican Jefe des Armas Castanada, and to arrange for the American column to continue south. Shortly after arrival at Cusihuiriachic Captain B. D. Foulois came in by airplane from Colonia Dublan with instructions from General Persh-ing for Brown to render a report of operations, especially of the fight of April 1st at Aguas Calientes. This was done. Foulois also gave the Colonel a map. For the section south of here this was much needed as the guide Fox had never visited that section. It might be remarked here that Fox was an excellent interpreter and invaluable in Brown's contacts with the natives.

In Cusihuiriachic Colonel Brown not only had a satisfactory interview with Major Castanada, but he met a Mr. Lopez, the manager of the Cusi Mining Co., who sold supplies to the troops and accepted Brown's per-sonal check in payment. The supplies included flour, bread, coffee, sugar, etc.

The Colonel also met Mr. Salamon Rahaim, who furnished Mexican silver and Cusi Mining Co. checks to the amount of $1,100 gold, due to the patriotism of Colonel Brown. From this sum the Colonel loaned each of his officers $10, and turned over the balance to Lieutenant Migdalski, who was quartermaster of this column. The total amount contributed by Colonel Brown at this time amounted to nearly $1,700, money which the United States should have furnished but did not.

After attending to this business the command marched about three miles south of town and went into camp, having covered about 20 miles for the day.

Next day, April 6th, reveille was at 6:00 A. M. As Brown had not finished his business in Cusihuiriachic, he and Fox left camp early, plan-ning to ride to town and back by the time the command was ready to leave camp. On the way back they saw an airplane which, failing to observe Brown's camp, landed about ¾ of a mile to the northeast. The Colonel hurried to the landing place and found Lieutenant Ira A. Rader with the machine, Lieutenant Herbert A. Dargue having gone to town on foot to find Colonel Brown, which caused serious delay. When con-tact was finally made with Dargue, Brown received the following message:

Camp at San Geronimo, April 5, 1916.

Colonel W. C. Brown,
Tenth Cavalry,
Enroute South from Cusi.
Sir:

1. Colonel Dodd, with 7th Cavalry, is near Santa Tomas. Major Evans arrived at Namiquipa today. Major Howze is near Guerrero and moving southeast toward San Borja. Lieutenant Colonel Allen, 11th Cavalry, leaves here tomorrow for San Antonio and points south.

2. From all information received it is believed that Villa with an escort, is going to Parral, being carried on a stretcher or carriage.

The Commanding General directs that in order to cut Villa off you proceed from Cusi to Parral via Bavans Nava, Satevo, Valle de Zaragosa, Sapien. You are reminded that Colonel Cano has moved in that direction and from him guides may be procured who will be of great assistance.

Your movement may also shield movements of Major Tompkins and Major Howze, who are following Villa's trail.

3. On arrival at Parral you will be guided by the information you secure.

4. An advance sub-base will be established at San Antonio, on the rail-road, from which a pack train will be sent you carrying horseshoes, nails, salt, money and other supplies.

5. Exhausted men and worn out animals will be sent to San Antonio where they will be cared for until fit for service.

6. Every effort possible should be made to reach Parral without delay.

7. It is not understood why you have not been able to send reports of your column, and the Commanding General directs that his orders on this subject be strictly complied with.

8. You are authorized to employ guides, interpreters, secret service men, or other individuals who may be of service to you, and to purchase all kinds of supplies that you may need. Money will be furnished you from here and an effort will also be made to send you money through the American Consul at Chihuahua.

9. You will make every effort to cooperate with our columns, and those of the Carranza forces operating in your vicinity, with a view to accomplishing the object of your mission.

10. Send reports to San Antonio.

J. A. Ryan
Major, 13th Cavalry, I. O. Acting Chief of Staff

Colonel Brown in going back to town and chasing the airplane marched fully 30 miles and was in the saddle 12 hours; more serious, however, was the fact that this caused the loss of nearly a day in getting the command on the road assigned it by the above order. All of which shows that airplanes are not infallible. The column marched 22 miles to Cieneguita where they camped for the night.

On April 7th Brown had difficulty in getting guides at Cieneguita. One started and then tried to leave but was forced to stay until the first town with a Presidente was reached—Tutiaca. Three miles farther on they came to Major Tompkins' camp at Santa Rosalia. Three horses passed out this date, two shot to prevent suffering and one abandoned. The trail for most of the day was up and down hill and over rocks; very hard on animals. They were 12 hours making 34 miles, and camped at La Joya after dark.

Shortly after reaching camp a young man came in and told the quartermaster that about 50 Martin Lopez bandits had passed through La Joya a day or two ago and were now at Cieneguita. (Not the place just left). He was sent home to change his clothes in order to act as guide and that was the last of the young man. It was noticed that there were a large number of men in town whose actions were suspicious.

On April 8th a native blacksmith shop was found at La Joya, so the march was delayed until 11:00 A. M. to get the horses shod. Men and animals were very tired and showed it.

The next camp was a short march away, 14 miles, at Satevo. The people at Satevo had been looted by both Villistas and Carranzistas, the latter taking even women's clothing. Colonel Brown and Mr. Fox, the Colonel with some Mexican silver, hunted up the principal inhabitant of the little village and asked for corn and fodder, at the same time displaying the silver with some ostentation, saying: "Nosotros pagamos todos" (We pay for everything). The place had been raided until there was little left, but when it became known that the hated "Gringos" were actually paying real money for the supplies, their astonishment knew no bounds; one native telling the interpreter: "Why, it is like seeing Christ come down from heaven, to see you pay for what you want."

The cash was the secret password all right, for the quartermaster was taken across the creek to a little adobe hut, and upon the door being unlocked a sight met his eyes which caused him, for the moment, to forget his troubles. For there were two rooms filled with corn fodder! It is needless to say that for once the hungry, tired horses got a good feed. The news that the Americans paid for things spread, and in the course of a couple of hours these hungry and weary men had more eggs and chickens offered for sale than they could buy.

The natives crowded into camp intent on seeing everything carried and worn by the Soldado Americano. In fact, they got so chummy that some one borrowed (?) Lieutenant Henry R. Adair's field glasses and forgot (?) to return them! The people were especially impressed with the size of the cavalry horses.

On this day's march, as at other times, the column passed through and by whole square miles of fields formerly under cultivation, and although this was the planting season no preparations were being made, save in the gardens about the houses, for raising a season's crop. No explanation was needed for this neglect of the ground, for the better the crop the surer it was to be levied on by one or the other of the contending factions, so: "What was the use?"

The fact that farm hands have been impressed in so-called armies; that farm animals have been utilized for like purposes; that leaders of roving bands of marauders under banners containing fantastic legends about "liberty and the rights of man" which they use as a blind to facilitate robbery, pillage, and murder, has so reduced the crop acreage that there is an estimated shortage of 39 million bushels of corn alone. Corn is the staff of life in Mexico as is wheat or its products in other countries.

Not only has the taking away of man and farm animal from the land produced this dire calamity, but many instances have been reported where the different military commanders have actually permitted their horses and mules to feed on young and growing corn in those sections where it may have been planted. Stored grain has also been burned in considerable quantities by these vandals, and the records show that in the face of all this some selfish military leaders have actually exported grain to enrich themselves. Is it any wonder that the peon refuses to attempt a crop?

Colonel Brown's command found here, as at other places where they happened to get close to the Mexican peon, that by treating him properly the American could expect an approximation at least of the same treatment in return, and that he was quite as appreciative of a square deal as his more intelligent neighbor.

On April 9th the friendly natives of Satevo, to the number of 30 or more, came to bid the American troops farewell. This in itself was remarkable, as the town and district have strong Villa leanings. The march this date was 16 miles to Tres Hermanos. The column habitually marched with an advance guard, flankers, and with patrols at times a mile from the column.

When within a mile or two of camp, the right flankers signalled "Mexican troops." The column halted and displayed their colors. As the Mexicans approached, Colonel Brown, his staff and interpreter, went out to meet them. They proved to be General Garza and staff, with about 200 men.

General Garza created a far more favorable impression than did Colonel Cano. He appeared to be frank and straightforward and agreed to cooperate, asking that the Americans stay over a day at Tres Hermanos until he could hear from a detachment which he had sent out to trail a suspicious band. At Colonel Brown's request he detached Captain G. F. Trevino to serve as guide and liaison officer for the Americans. Captain Trevino remained with Brown's command for nearly a month, rendering valuable service. He was a gallant officer, having been in many actions, and wounded some ten different times.

General Garza and Colonel Brown had their conference under a mesquite tree, after which the Colonel sent for his officers and presented them to the General, and as an additional courtesy and in the interests of the entente cordiale mounted up his command and passed in review before the General and his staff, enroute to camp.

On April 10th Colonel Brown and Captain Trevino rode 7 miles to General Garza's camp on La Mangu Ranch in Torreon Canyon. The General was in camp, but the party sent out to trail the suspected Villistas had not returned.

Brown paid a Mexican two pesos to carry a message back to Major Young to march the command forward, as Brown had decided to push south instead of delaying a day.

The Colonel bought a horse for 100 pesos from one of Garza's men for Major Young to ride. The command left the hill above Garza's camp at one P.M. and marched through Valeria to Sauz (willow tree). Soon after leaving the Mexican camp the column struck the trail made by Major Tompkins the day before and followed it to camp, where they found the two horses left by Tompkins.

Four horses were shot this day to prevent further suffering. This was a short march, only 11 miles. The horses were turned loose in the same field used by Tompkins 24 hours earlier. This opportunity to graze and rest was of much benefit to them.

On April 11th the command marched 18 miles to Valle de Zaragosa and camped in a beautiful grove on the banks of a stream. The Americans found the people friendly and better dressed than others they had seen. Captain Mesa, who was so friendly with Tompkins the day before, was equally obliging to Brown's command, and aided greatly in getting supplies. A check-up revealed that the command had lost 28 animals to date.

On April 12th at about 2:00 A.M., 300 Carranza troops arrived at Valle de Zaragosa. Brown's command left this place at 7:30 the same morning. Brown had hired a ten mule Carranza wagon and loaded it with all impedimenta intended for the pack train. This day's march was 28 miles to a ranch a few hundred yards west of the road, Media Ranch, near Sapien. Shot a mule and horse to prevent suffering. This made 30 so far.

About 6:30 P.M., three troopers of the 13th Cavalry marched past camp without seeing it and on being hailed returned, reporting that Major Tompkins' command had been attacked at Parral and had retreated to a ranch about 8 miles south of the 10th Cavalry camp.

Brown immediately had "boots and saddles" sounded; in ten minutes he and his men were in the saddle; and an hour later they rode into Tompkins' outposts. As the night had settled down, vision was restricted, so the guide announced when the command was close to Santa Cruz de Villegas. Brown halted and had a trumpeter sound "Attention," and "Officers Call." Ears were strained for the reply, which came a few minutes later, faint it is true, but as only one of *our* trumpeters could sound it.

The enemy had ceased firing about two hours earlier, but still held the hills to the south. Brown and his men rode into the defenses, and being the senior he took command.

He immediately sent Lieutenant H. R. Adair with a picked platoon of 40 men back to his camp to bring in the pack train and weak horses left behind under Lieutenant J. F. Richmond when Brown made his fast ride to the rescue. These came in about 3:00 A.M. on the 13th. The reader will note that this extra duty for Adair's detachment meant, with short rests, about 20 marching hours—distance between 45 and 50 miles.

Brown was up all night getting the "low down" on the Parral affair and then sending dispatches to General Pershing. Here is where the Mexican Captain Trevino came in. He carried Brown's dispatches to Parral to be wired by General Lozano, our recent enemy, to the American Consul at Chihuahua to be relayed by him to Pershing. As the Mexicans were pretty well scared, this channel of communication was used with moderate success. Brown also sent word to Pershing to Media Ranch to be forwarded through Valle de Zaragosa. The dispatches follow:

Santa Cruz Ranch, 8:20 P. M. April 12th

U. S. Consul, Chihuahua
General Pershing, San Antonio

Advise General Pershing at once that Major Tompkins' squadron was attacked today in Parral by Carranzistas. Tompkins and Lieutenant Ord both slightly, 4 soldiers more seriously wounded and two killed. Have just arrived here to his relief from Media Ranch 8 miles north of here. Situation serious and calls for immediate action by Carranza Government.

Brown, Commanding.

Another note was sent to General Lozano expressing surprise at the action of his troops, and inviting him to talk over matters under a flag of truce, half a kilometer south of camp at 10:00 A.M. the 13th.

On April 13th a mixed command of the 10th and 13th Cavalry under Colonel Brown and Major Young went back towards Parral for about two miles to get the body of Private Ledford. The body was found lying in the road where it had fallen with shoes and outer clothing gone and looted of all valuables.

The body had not otherwise been abused. It was guarded by a little white dog, which on the march south had "enlisted" in the 13th, and had been befriended by Ledford. As this dog had marched 36 miles the previous day, and had been without food or water for 20 hours, he had shown a degree of faithfulness and a sense of his responsibilities that was touching. When the body was placed on the wagon brought from the ranch for the purpose, the little dog, head and tail up, trotted along with an evident sense of relief, as much as to say: "My duty is now finished!" This animal merited his subsequent adoption as the Mascot of Troop "M," 13th Cavalry.

This same afternoon the Presidente of Parral, Senor Jose de la Luz Herrera, with an interpreter, arrived instead of General Lozano, and in the presence of the American field officers the occurrences of the previous day were discussed for several hours. Brown's request for a conference was made to the military commander in Parral. *Why* the civil head of the city came has never been explained.

Senor Herrera repeatedly expressed his evidently sincere regrets, claiming that Tompkins should not have gone into Parral unannounced; that Lozano had no knowledge of the invitation which had been extended to Tompkins. He attributed the trouble to the civilian population, which greatly outnumbered the military and could not be controlled. He did not explain why the soldiers persisted in the pursuit after the civilians had ceased, nor the deaths of the two military Mexican officers of high rank.

Colonel Brown, on behalf of the Americans vigorously denounced the treacherous conduct of the Mexicans, stating that the latter had lit the match which had started the fire, creating trouble which could now be settled only by the heads of the respective governments; that our flag had been hoisted at Santa Cruz de Villegas, and that there would be no withdrawal until so ordered by the American Government; and that in the meantime he demanded that our messages be forwarded by telegraph from Parral—for which he would give receipts.

Colonel Brown also demanded that the body of Sergeant Richley, who was killed just outside of Parral, be placed in a coffin and delivered to the American troops at Santa Cruz de Villegas. This was done the next day, April 14th.

He also presented to the Presidente a list of food, clothing, and horseshoes, needed by the American garrison, and informed the Presidente that these supplies must be delivered and would be paid for.

Just as the sun was setting we buried Private Ledford. Having no coffin we wrapped him in his blanket, put his name and record in a sealed bottle, and buried him with military honors. Having no chaplain I selected in lieu thereof Lieutenant Clarence Lininger, who had commanded the rear guard in the action in which Ledford had received his death wound, and who acted on that occasion with gallantry "above and beyond the call of duty."

The entire command turned out and marched to the cemetery adjoining the ranch, where Lininger read from his own composition the following:

For 100 years or more little bands of hardy adventurous Americans have gone forth from their land, where existed peace and plenty, law and order, justice and equality for all men. They have gone among savages and hostile peoples, into the wilderness and the unknown mountains, to the far islands of the seas, and even to the soil we now tread.

Many were the motives that actuated them, but beneath all was the glorious foundation of patriotism and love of country. At the peril of filling a distant grave in a far land they have turned their backs upon their homes that their country might grow and become strong, that their race might wax mighty upon the face of the earth, that greater comforts and greater happiness might come to the loved ones behind, and that the blessings of liberty might be shed upon less fortunate peoples.

Such is the group congregated today to do the last rites and honors to one of our number who died a soldier's death—than which none is more honorable. Grievously wounded at the first moment of hostile contact, he bore himself in a stoical and soldierly manner, firm and manly under the most trying and painful conditions, until again wounded—this time mortally.

His conduct calls for our emulation and highest admiration, and should instil in our breasts pride that he has been one of us in body and will continue with us in spirit.

Let us, in our humble way, consign to a temporary abiding place all that is mortal of our comrade Hobart Ledford.

The body was then placed in the grave, Lieutenant Lininger recited the XXIII Psalm, while Captain Turner dropped a handful of earth in the grave. Then all present repeated the Lord's Prayer in unison. This was followed by three volleys and taps.

Next day the Parral officials returned the body of Sergeant Richley in a coffin, borne in a hearse. At 5:00 P.M. we buried him with military honors, Lininger again officiating. He read as follows:

Some are born to tread the paths of peace, to walk among the sheltered ways, to dwell in the midst of tranquillity, and when their allotted race is ended, to look back from the sunset of life upon an even and uneventful course.

But others come forth into the midst of trials and tribulations, to be surrounded by perils, and to be tossed by the storms of life. Of such are they who step forward at the call of their country in its hour of need. With soul fired by the glorious spark of patriotism, animated by the desire to see their people wax strong upon the face of the earth and to spread the blessings of liberty, equality and justice to all men and to less fortunate peoples, they have offered and some have laid down their lives in defense and in furtherance of their high and righteous ideals.

We have congregated today to do the last rites and honors to one of that noble class. His comrades knew him as one possessed of the highest sense of duty; a brave soldier, and a strong man in time of danger. Instantly killed in the first moment of hostile attack in a foreign land, upon him falls the unique honor of being the first to lay down his life, to die the most honorable death of a soldier, for the success of the righteous enterprise upon which we are now engaged.

Let us with humble and contrite spirit consign to its temporary abiding place all that is mortal of our comrade in arms, Sergeant Richley.

The body was then consigned to the grave, Lieutenant Lininger recited the XXIII Psalm, while Captain Turner dropped a handful of earth in the grave. After that all present recited the Lord's Prayer in unison, the firing squad fired three volleys and the trumpeter sounded taps.

On April 14th about dark, Captain William O. Reed, 6th Cavalry, and Lieutenant James L. Collins, 11th Cavalry, both of General Pershing's staff, arrived in four automobiles from Satevo, 83 miles north. General Pershing had received by airplane from Chihuahua one of Colonel Brown's dispatches, when he immediately sent these two officers to the "front" for first hand information.

Captain Reed told Colonel Brown that he, Reed, was empowered by the General to make all arrangements with Colonel Brown, and whatever the two agreed upon would be confirmed. General Pershing was under the impression that it was the 10th Cavalry column that had been first fired on instead of the 13th Cavalry under Tompkins. The General was annoyed at getting no messages from Colonel Brown, not realizing the efforts the latter had made to get information back and the difficulties involved in sending dispatches.

After Brown and Reed had discussed the matter from all angles, Brown expressed the opinion that General Pershing should come to Santa Cruz de Villegas as the clash at Parral had changed the entire character of the campaign. Captain Reed expressed himself as believing the General would come. The practicability of establishing a sub-base on the railroad between Santa Cruz de Villegas and Jiminez was discussed, neither officer knowing at that time the positive objection to our use of the railroads by the Carranza Government. Mr. Floyd Gibbons, a correspondent for the Chicago *Tribune*, came with the party. I let him have a copy of my report of the fight in exchange for a side of bacon. Reed and party left at 10:00 P.M. expecting to get back at 6:00 A.M. the 15th.

On April 15th about sunrise, Colonel Allen, with two troops of the 11th Cavalry, and pack train, arrived. Two hours later Major Howze, with four picked troops of the same regiment also arrived. We now felt as though our force was strong enough to conquer Mexico, and we were hoping the order to "go" would come soon.

About 10:00 A.M. wagons with supplies came in from Parral. This wagon train seemed to be under the charge of Ramon Terrasas. The supply of this large cavalry command (13 troops) and communication with Division Headquarters had now become factors of such importance that a change of base to the railroad, both for telegraphic communication and for supply was regarded as most essential.

Colonel Brown, wishing to know if any suitable site for camp and new base was available on or near the railroad, sent Lieutenant Orlando C. Troxel, Mr. Fox, and 20 men to reconnoiter in the vicinity of the railroad, and especially to examine Adela on the railroad, about 16 miles to the southwest.

Troxel, when near Morita, met a Carranza major with a small detachment, who insisted that Troxel go with him to Dorado, which Troxel flatly refused to do. The most important part of his mission was to get information about Adela, and this was cleverly done by Fox going alone to Adela, while Troxel and his platoon, about which the Mexican major was so solicitous, kept to the north, and finally returned by the same road used in leaving camp at about 8:00 P.M. Troxel's mission was a delicate one and well executed.

Colonel Brown sent a note to Presidente Herrera explaining his desire to change his base to the railroad in order to facilitate supply from Chihuahua. The Colonel also asked the Presidente to put a telegraph office in at Adela, or such point as might be selected as a sub-base. Brown also sent a wire to the U. S. Consul at Chihuahua, explaining this plan and asking that he notify Peters & Johnson (merchants) to be prepared to send us a supply of hay, corn, flour and other provisions on receipt of wire.

The American force at Santa Cruz de Villegas now consisted of 34 officers; 606 enlisted men; 702 horses and 149 mules, requiring 6 tons of hay and over 9,000 pounds of grain each day; to say nothing of the rations for the personnel of the command amounting to about 2,000 pounds of food daily! This explains Brown's desire to establish a base which would make possible the relatively easy supply of his troops.

Senor Herrera sent Colonel Brown a wire to the effect that the military governor of Chihuahua had forbidden any movement of U.S. troops one foot south unless permission be given by the Mexican Secretary of War.

We will now go back to Bachineva, where we left Major Howze with his provisional squadron on April 2nd, and march with him to Santa Cruz de Villegas, where he arrived the morning of April 15th.

CHAPTER XXVI

Operations of the Provisional Squadron, 11th Cavalry (Howze), April 3 to 15. Evidence and Speculation as to Villa's Whereabouts

We left Major Howze at Bachineva. On April 3rd he sent Captain Eben Swift with the first and third provisional troops to San Geronimo. The command followed at 4:30 P.M., arriving at San Geronimo at 9:00 P.M., having marched a distance of 18 miles.

Next day, April 4th, the column left San Geronimo at 9:30 A.M., marching southwest and arriving at Providencia Ranch at 1:00 P.M., where the horses were fed and grazed. At 2:00 P.M. the march was resumed, heading southwest, and camp was made within six miles of Guerrero at 7:00 P.M., after a march of 26 miles. Wood was plentiful in this camp, but the water was poor and no grazing was found; the animals suffered accordingly. Before leaving San Geronimo it was found necessary to relieve the command of those men and horses not physically fit. 15 men were left here.

April 5th the command left camp at 7:00 A.M. and marched to the camp of Colonel Dodd and the 7th Cavalry, where they arrived at 9:00 A.M. After a halt of 45 minutes they continued south to a ranch southeast of San Ysidro, and from this point to Rosario, where they arrived at 6:00 P.M. The distance marched this date was 30 miles through the mountains. This camp furnished good water, but little wood.

Next day Howze left Rosario at 7:15 A.M., heading southeast, and arriving at Cusihuiriachic at 6:00 P.M., making the third American cavalry column to pass through this place in as many days. The distance covered was 36 miles. Water was good but scarce for a command of this size. There was no grazing and wood was very scarce.

On the 7th the command left camp at 9:00 A.M. and marched over a hard trail to Cieneguita Ranch eight miles north of San Borja. Brown had camped here the day before and Tompkins two days earlier. The distance for this day's march was 27 miles. There was good water and a plentiful supply of corn and fodder.

On April 8th Howze and his men left camp at 7:30 A.M. and continued their march south, passing through San Borja three days after Major Tompkins had turned back from that city to avoid a clash with Carranza forces under General Cavazos. Howze states in his diary:

At San Francisco de Borja, a place 8 miles south of Cieneguita, I got from a Principal the best information yet received, and information that was later confirmed, viz: That Villa was slightly wounded in the calf of the leg, that he could ride and was riding; that the seriously wounded man was

Pablo Lopez, and that Lopez had just died in the Cuevos region which suggested to Villa to announce his own death; that the main organized band of Villa was headed eastward for the purpose of diverting us towards Parral; that Villa with about 50 selected followers and plenty of extra mounts and pack animals was following untraveled routes towards the Sierras Puras, southward in the general direction of Durango, and that he had important wounded with him.

I struck southward with the utmost vigor possible and near Casa Colorado struck Villa's trail, then 6 days old, we followed it through the mountain fastness over the nearly impassable Cabilana trail and in three days gained nearly three days on Villa.

At a place called Aguahe he went into the Sierras Puras Mountains, mountains devoid of food, without plants or cultivation, over a trail nearly if not quite impassable for American animals.

If I had had Apache scouts I should have attempted to follow him. Instead I skirted the mountain wall as far as San Jose del Sitio, a community practically wholly Villista, disposed to fight us and determined not to aid us in any way. Our camp was fired upon. As I did not want to kill the people if it could be avoided, I refrained from returning the fire, as I delayed to the last the taking of food, etc. I allowed our animals to go on short food, hoping our humane and civilized methods would bear fruit, hopes which never materialized.

This information Howze received of Pablo Lopez was wrong, as Lopez was later captured by Carranzistas, in the place where Colonel Allen had located him when Allen was diverted to go to Parral, taken to Chihuahua and executed.

As to Villa's whereabouts at this time there are several "eye witnesses" who made statements contrary to each other. However, I believe Howze was on his trail. Three days earlier had the Mexican General Cavazos helped Major Tompkins instead of blocking him there is every chance Villa would have been caught, for he was badly hurt and could not ride but was carried on a litter borne by men on foot and traveling slowly.

After leaving San Borja the march was continued in a southeasterly direction over the roughest of mountain trails, and finally camp was made in a deep canyon at Los Estados at 6:30 P.M. after a march for the day of 28 miles, which was severe on account of the rough going. This was a poor camp. The water was scarce and hardly fit to drink.

During this day's march the Americans narrowly avoided a clash with General Cavazos. Major S. M. Williams, Quartermaster Corps, who in this campaign was 1st Lieutenant, 11th Cavalry, and a member of Howze's command, has the following to say of this incident.

At a meeting with Cavazos on April 8th, south of San Borja, I was with the point of the advance guard when these two forces met. Major Howze was quite correct in his report that a disaster was narrowly avoided at that time.

Cavazos was in a very ugly mood, and as he rounded a point he evidently thought he had come upon a very small force of our troops, as we were well strung out and only the advance guard, about 8 men, were in sight at the time. His force took up a gallop and started towards us. I put the advance guard in an arroyo and prepared for action. We would have opened fire had we not seen Major Howze dash ahead of us waving his hat. He wore a black sweater on this entire trip, and it being the only one in the column it attracted our attention immediately. Otherwise an engagement would have been inevitable, and would have resulted disastrously for the Mexican force, because our four troops closed up very rapidly and we would have quickly wiped out the Cavazos force.

On April 9th the column left camp at Los Estados at 7:15 A.M., marching southeast to San Jose del Sitio, where it arrived at 5:30, after covering 27 miles over mountain trails, a terrible pull on the stock. The camp was fired into this night but no damage done. The community was wholly Villista in its sympathies. People would sell neither food nor forage.

On the 10th Howze left San Jose del Sitio at 7:00 A. M. As a ruse he marched east-southeast towards Valle de Zaragosa, then west as far as the Concho River, when the column turned south-southwest and marched over a most difficult mountain trail to La Joya de Herrera, where it arrived at noon. The advance guard was fired on and the fire was returned. Captain Silva, Villista, was killed and the band completely dispersed. After resting and feeding the animals, the advance south was continued at 2:30 P.M.

At about 4:30 this afternoon the pack train was fired into from the canyon sides. Two mules were wounded and later died. At about 5:30 the column received a vicious attack from two sides of the canyon. The fight lasted about 20 minutes. The advance guard, Lieutenant E. P. Laurson commanding, received the brunt of the attack. One man, Private Kirby, Troop "M," was killed and three men wounded.

Private Kirby was buried on the site of the fight. Night coming on it was impossible to determine the damage that was inflicted upon the enemy. The command bivouacked until 10:00 that night, having marched 25 miles exclusive of the distance covered in the fight. At 10:00 o'clock the command was formed and moved through the darkness to surround, quietly, the town of Santa Cruz de Herrera, which was accomplished at about 3:00 A.M. April 11th. This night march in the mountains covered 16 miles.

The Villistas were evidently on the alert for they tried to escape before our men had completely encircled the town. In making their getaway they exchanged shots with some of our fellows, resulting in the killing of one Villista and wounding Lieutenant Beltran, son of General Gorgonia Beltran, who died later. The horse of Gorgonia was killed, and natives reported that Gorgonia was severely wounded. The Americans then proceeded up the Balleza River three miles, and men and animals being exceedingly weary, a halt was made for the remainder of the day, April 11th.

At daylight a search of the town was made and some arms secured. All of the natives were extremely nervous and noncommunicative. Major Howze endeavored in vain to find some one in the town who would give him information as to the identity of the Mexican force that had escaped from him.

Again quoting from Lieutenant Williams:

While bivouacked south of this town, I was sent during the afternoon with the pack train into the town to requisition corn and such other supplies as could be obtained. While in the town I saw coming from a ranch house about a mile distant, 14 Yaqui Indians, in full war paint but unarmed. When they came into the town the natives were tense with excitement. I

Villistas in Action

Graves of Private Ledford (left) and Sergeant Richley at Santa Cruz de Villegas

returned rapidly to camp and reported this to Major Howze, and several of us urged him to send a troop to this ranch house and search it, but he would not do so. No one of us could get him to listen to the possibility of Villa and a small band being in hiding in this house. He prohibited any of us from going to this ranch house, and the following morning we marched south.

I have always believed that Villa broke up his band at this place, and this belief is confirmed by an article that I read a year or two later in which Villa stated that he was hiding in a' ranch house within a mile of this squadron of cavalry, and that he was greatly relieved when he saw them march south the following morning without anyone of the column visiting the ranch house. I fully believe that this is where Major Howze and his column lost Villa and also lost our great opportunity.

This seems the appropriate place to discuss the movements of Pancho Villa during the first two weeks of April, 1016.

Each of the commanders of the flying columns was straining forward to the same objective—the capture dead or alive of the bandit chieftain.

Each knew that he must travel fast, though the trail lead over an almost impassable country lacking in wood, water and food for man and beast. Each knew he must conserve the strength of men and animals, especially the horses, so that should the great moment come he would find he had not "shot his bolt" but, to the contrary, had a reserve of energy for one last supreme effort—an effort which would place Villa in his grasp.

The principal anxiety was for the animals of the command. The men were inspired to supreme effort by the ardor of the chase and professional pride. The horses had no imagination to support them. They did their duty as called upon until they dropped dead by the trail. Day after day they covered the distance, heavily loaded, over mountains, across arid plains, sweating in the noonday heat and shivering in the freezing temperatures of the nights, always on short forage, never with sufficient sleep. Is it any wonder these horses weakened from day to day? Major Howze, thoroughly aware of the condition of his stock very wisely refused to pursue the few men seen fleeing from La Joya the morning of April 10th.

As to Villa's presence close to Santa Cruz de Herrera on April 11th, the following statement of Modesto Necares, who was the driver of the wagon in which Villa was carried after he had been wounded in the Guerrero fight, is of interest, and especially so when read in connection with the movements of Majors Tompkins and Howze in the vicinity of San Borja.

This statement of Modesto Nevares was interpreted by a Mr. Brown while the 11th Cavalry was at El Valle in June, 1916, and is as follows:

When Villa came through El Valle, going south, after the Columbus Raid, he stopped there and sent out his men to collect the people of the town to hear him make a speech. In his speech he asked for volunteers to help him fight the Americans who, he said, were in our country and would probably be here that day (this was late in March).

He then asked the rest of us if we were not going to join, and when we refused, he stood us up in line, dismissed the old men, and took the rest as prisoners under guard.

We went from there through the mountains and came down to the river again at Cruces, and from there we went to Namiquipa, where we had a fight and took some Carranza prisoners.

We then went to Quemada, then to Rubio, then to San Diego del Monte, then to Guerrero. When we reached Guerrero, he gave us arms and a small amount of ammunition so that we could take part in the fight against the Carranza forces, who were there.

We entered Guerrero about 4:00 A. M. and started fighting. The fight lasted until nearly noon when the Carranza forces gave way and the town fell into our hands.

During the progress of the fight we were lined up in an arroyo facing the Carranza forces. General Villa and his personal staff went forward towards the enemy on foot, leaving us in the arroyo, and when he became exposed he was shot from behind by one of the men who was with us as prisoners; in fact, it was our intent to kill him and go over to the Carranzistas. But just at the time he was shot the Carranzistas gave way and ran, leaving us with no possible way to escape, so we again assumed the pretense of loyalty and declared that if he had been shot by any of us it was purely accidental.

He was shot with an old fashioned Remington rifle which takes a very large lead bullet. The bullet entered his right leg from behind just opposite the knee joint and ranged downward, coming out through the shin bone directly in front and about four inches down. I account for the bullet ranging down by the fact that he was running forward on foot and his leg must have been in a forward motion. The bullet made a big hole where it went in and a much larger one where it came out. The shin bone was badly shattered and I afterwards saw them pick out small pieces of bone from the hole in front.

I know very well about the wound as I was appointed to drive the wagon in which he was carried from Guerrero to the south. I saw his wound every day.

The day after the fight at Guerrero he prepared to leave for the south, as we had already learned that the Americans were in Namiquipa. He left Beltran with the principal part of his army at Guerrero and started in the direction of Parral where they said they were going.

They took 150 men commanded by Nicholas Hernandez and they always kept a guard of about 50 men close about the wagon in which Villa was carried and which I was driving.

On being more carefully questioned about Villa's wound Nevares said:

After Villa was wounded at Guerrero, they sent to the house of a foreign doctor for medicine, and got some cotton, some cotton bandages, and some kind of coarse grain drug of a dark blue color which, when they put a few pieces in water, would turn it red. He used this to bathe his leg and would then wrap it in cotton; place splints on four sides over the cotton and wrap it tight with the bandages. The legs of his pants and drawers were cut away nearly to the hip, leaving his leg bare, and after some days it turned very black for about twelve inches above and below the wound.

I noticed that after that he nearly lost his courage, and at times seemed to be unconscious. He would cry like a child when the wagon jolted and curse me every time I hit a rock. After we passed San Antonio and started south through the mountains, he got so bad that he could not stand the wagon any longer.

They then made him a litter by cutting four small poles, two long ones and two short ones. They tied the short poles across the long ones making a frame just big enough for him to lie in and leaving the four ends of the long poles sticking out in front and behind enough for four men to carry the litter on their shoulders. They wove this litter with a net work of rope and placed his bed on it. They detailed 16 men to carry it in turn, but did not trust it to any but his staff officers and friends. His brother-in-law rode close by him, leading Villa's horse, a beautiful roan pinto, with Villa's empty saddle, and he seemed to have personal charge of the patient.

He is a very strong, well built man, and he lifted Villa around in his arms like a child.

For some reason they had me drive the wagon close behind them, and they traveled almost day and night. When they wanted to stop General Villa would not stand for it. He was the worst scared man I ever saw. When I last saw him, his big, robust, fat face was very thin and pale. His staff officers procured everything dainty that they could find for him to eat. He ate very little, and seemed to grow gradually weaker day by day.

The next day after they made the litter was a very bad day. It was snowing hard and the ground was slippery. On going down a steep hill I lost control of the horses on account of the condition of the road and the wagon turned over and was broken so that it was left behind. (Major Tompkins' column passed this wagon on April 5th so could not have been far behind Villa on that date.) I was left working with my wagon and got into camp (at a hacienda named Cienegita). They had already executed a man, who, I heard, was the ranch owner. (This was Saturday, April 1st, less than four days ahead of Tompkins.)

From there we went to a place called Santa Ana, near San Borja.

The interpreter asked him if Villa was the only man being carried in a litter, and Nevares said "No," that General Pedrosa was also in a litter; that he had been shot in the foot in the Guerrero fight.

At a little place we passed after leaving Santa Ana, the name of which I did not know, General Pedrosa bundled his lame foot in a blanket and again mounted his horse. They threw the litter in which he had been carried on top of a house. General Pedrosa was very friendly and communicated with me, and told me one day that the General's name was not Villa but was Dortello Arango.

On leaving there the command was split in two, one part going east under command of Nicholas Hernandez, and we turned back to the southeast through the mountains. This was done with a great deal of secrecy. In fact, I did not go with them, Villa, but when I got into camp late that night at a place called Rancho Casa Colorado he was there.

When asked how he knew Villa was there: "Did you see him?" he answered: "No, but I saw the litter."

"How did you know it was the litter in which Villa was carried?"

"Because it was entirely different from the other. It was made of nice straight poles, and the other was made of crooked poles and not nearly so well built."

"Are you sure that this was not Pablo Lopez?"

"Oh, yes, Lopez was left way back in the mountains before we reached San Antonio. He went a different way and we never saw him any more."

"Was there any other wounded man with Villa at that time?"

"Yes, General Pedrosa was there, and a black man with curly hair and thick lips; he looked like a Negro. His surname was Laso."

"Would the presence of the litter indicate that Villa was there?"

"Yes, they would often take him out of it, and they always hid him at night. They would always bring him out in the morning from an entirely different place from where he was at night."

"Where did you go from there?"

"I deserted that night and went away in the darkness accompanied by a boy named Benito Valdez, and we walked all the way back to El Valle through the mountains."

"What do you think became of Villa? Where is he now?"

"I give you my word I believe he is dead, but if he is not dead he is in the State of Durango, as I know he was trying to go there through the mountains. I learned this from General Pedrosa and General Jose Rodriguez, a man of the same name as the Rodriguez who was killed at Madero. The man was a native of Parral, at least he told me so."

"Describe the camp at Rancho Colorado."

"I did not camp right at the ranch."

The interpreter then told Nevares that he had been there with his colonel, and began describing the vicinity when Nevares said: "Yes, a big black oak."

The interpreter told him he had seen cotton and cotton bandages near the tree, when his eyes at once brightened. He said those bandages and cotton were off the General, that they did not have much and never used any on the other men who were not so badly wounded. He was then cross-questioned about the General, but he insisted that he was there and still alive at that time.

When asked about Silvas, or Silvia, or Sivas he said that he was there and wore a big broad-brimmed, lead colored hat and rode a heavy set grey horse, but he did not know his rank, describing him as a young fellow of rather slender build, of the cowboy type.

There have been many accounts of Villa's movements immediately following his fight at Guerrero with the Carranzistas on March 27th. The foregoing story by Nevares has stood up under close investigation. It is known that Villa was at Cienegita the night of April 1st and 2nd; that General Hernandez moved east from Cienegita; and that Villa did have a broken leg caused by a gunshot wound received at Guerrero.

When Major Tompkins reached San Borja at 4:00 P.M. on April 5th his intention was to camp 5 or 10 miles farther south of that town, which would have placed him one march nearer to Villa than the camp at Cienegita, and not more than one or two marches behind Villa.

It is ridiculous to assume that Cavazos did not know of Villa's movements during the first ten days of April. Had the Mexican Government been truly sincere in their desire to aid the American troops in the capture of Villa, Cavazos would have co-operated with Tompkins when they met the afternoon of April 5th, and within another 48 hours Villa would have been a prisoner.

Progress of a litter carried by four men, even with four reliefs, cannot be faster than two miles per hour when moving. This was rough country, and the wounded man was badly and painfully hurt, both of which combined to slow up the march. It took Villa five marches to move from Guerrero to Cienegita, travelling in a wagon, while Major Howze covered this distance in three marches. After taking to the litter, April 1st, Villa's rate of flight was necessarily slower.

Although Howze was three days later than Tompkins at San Borja, he nevertheless quickly picked up Villa's trail and gave him a close run. Had Cavazos combined with Tompkins on the 5th, or even granted Tompkins permission to continue south, with the great advantage that three days would have given, Villa's capture, in his crippled condition, would have been inevitable.

Six months after the above happenings I received a letter from my old adjutant, Lieut. James B. Ord, who was intelligence officer (secret service) and in a position to know much of what was not common knowledge. In writing from El Valle under date of October 3, 1916, he said in part:

Had a talk with a Villista who was with Villa when he went south. He told me that *they saw the American troops going into Parral*, so I guess we were pretty close on the trail.

Villa was in the Santa Ana Mountains within sight of us while we were talking with old General Cavazos that day at San Borja (April 5), and Major Howze's outfit passed by him near San Borja. The main body was ahead of us. They went clear south into Durango as far as Mapinsi via Camargo, Santa Rosalia—the place we were headed for. It is some satisfaction, anyway, to know we didn't make any mistakes about where our man was.

Here is another statement as to the movements of the elusive Villa. It is written by a business man with offices in El Paso, Texas and Canada, to General W. C. Brown, U. S. Army, Retired, under date of August 26, 1927.

General W. C. Brown,
875 Marion Street,
Denver, Colorado.
My dear Sir:

I beg to acknowledge your letter of August 8th, and to thank you for the inclosed map. The Consul in Chihuahua was good enough to show me the history of the participation of the Tenth (Cavalry) in the Punitive Expedition.

With your permission I am going to question the information in that pamphlet with reference to the wounding and retreat of Villa on and after March 29th (1916).

My intimate acquaintance with several of the leaders who were in that retreat, the fact that I spent three months as a prisoner of the Villistas in the early part of 1924, when they went out in favor of Huerta, and the fact that a number of them have been working for me during the past three years, has given me an opportunity to get the story from their side.

In the fight at Guerrero, the day before the arrival of the 7th (Cavalry), Villa had not been in the thick of the fight, but was wounded by a stray bullet fired by one of the soldiers under the Carranza General Cavazos. He showed me the scar, about six inches below the knee, when he was in my camp in the early part of 1920, and several months before his amnesty by Huerta.

He was unable to travel far after that wound and took refuge in a small cave high up on the side of a mountain not far from Guerrero, where he was taken care of by two or three faithful followers. He remained in that locality in hiding for nearly two months. The main body of Villistas under Martin Lopez and Nicholas Fernandez retreated rapidly south spreading the story that Villa was with them. Hernandez was reported killed by American troops at Guerrero. Nevares says Hernandez went south with Villa until a short distance south of San Borja when the party was split, Hernandez going east. (This is true, means Hernandez was not killed at Guerrero as claimed by Colonel Dodd. The Author). They proceeded by forced marches and made no considerable halt until they crossed the state line and dispersed in small bodies through northern Durango, Nicholas Fernandez on the Rio Florido near Camitillo and Martin Lopez in the mountains farther to the west.

The followers of the two leaders say that it was fully two months later, or early in June, before they next heard from their leader. He had sent a small commission to get in touch with them and to arrange for a rendezvous.

With reference to Villa's cave retreat near Guerrero, his men tell me that he lay at the mouth of the cave and saw your column (probably Howze) go by in the distance, on its forced march south in the direction of Parral.

You may make whatever use you wish of this information but without reference to its source.

Here are four possibilities as to Villa's whereabouts early in April, 1916:

(1) Lieutenant Williams has reason to believe that he was near Santa Cruz de Herrera.

(2) Nevares says he was with him until south of San Borja (which supports Williams) and believed he reached Durango. Navares and the writer of the above letter state Hernandez or Fernandez went south from Guerrero, while Colonel Dodd claims his men killed Hernandez at Guerrero.

(3) Ord states he has evidence Villa was in the Santa Ana Mountains watching our conference with Cavazos on April 5th.

(4) And the writer of the letter quoted above says he has excellent authority for believing Villa to have been in the mountains near Guerrero. But he does not say Villa told him so. His information is from Villa's followers and not from Villa.

I am inclined to think Nevares furnished the correct information, and Ord supports this.

In sifting the above evidence as to Villa's movements early in April we must consider any testimony from Villista prisoners in connection with General Pershing's policy in sending to New Mexico for trial any Villista found guilty, beyond a reasonable degree of doubt, of participation in the Columbus Raid. Several of these men were sent to the United States, tried, convicted and hanged. Naturally they would all try to prove an alibi of one kind or another.

At any rate, the energetic pursuit of Villa and his bands by the four flying cavalry columns under Tompkins, Brown, Allen and Howze, a pursuit made in the face of Carranza opposition and treachery, was a surprise to both Villistas and Carranzistas, and although Villa was not caught his force was compelled to disintegrate and seek shelter in obscure mountain retreats.

Now let us return to Howze.

The information which governed Major Howze's movements from April 11th to the date he joined the other columns at Santa Cruz de Villegas, is shown by an extract from his war diary dated April 10th, 1916.

I proceeded up the Balleza valley and when we entered well into its upper regions, I found that we were in Carranzista country, and as far as determinable Villa had not debouched from the mountains which we had so closely skirted from Aguaje, the point where he had entered.

Our animals were low in flesh, lame and footsore; our men were nearly barefoot; the country was nearly devoid of food, and wherever we turned we found less horse feed. So I decided to move to Parral, skirting the northern foot of the range of mountains which separates the states of Durango and Chihuahua.

We marched east-northeast for two and one-half days, a distance of about 70 miles, and when about 5 miles from Parral, April 14th, we were met by a delegation from that city bearing a white flag, which informed me of the attack which had been made upon Major Tompkins' small command and begged and warned me not to go into the city, instead urged that we join Colonel Brown at Santa Cruz de Villegas.

We were further informed that it would be impossible to get grain at any other locality, and that if we camped so near the city serious trouble might follow.

The need for grain, of which we had had none for 36 to 48 hours, and my desire to do everything reasonable to avoid complicating an already difficult situation, and to prevent loss of life due to the foolish acts of ignorant Mexicans, decided me to join Colonel Brown, a decision arrived at with great reluctance.

My command reached Colonel Brown at Santa Cruz at 8:30 A. M. April 15th. It had covered 691 miles since leaving Columbus, a great part of the distance over difficult mountain trails, some of which was as difficult as ever passed over by American cavalry.

The country passed through after leaving San Geronimo was nearly devoid of food articles except in the small Guerrero and Cusi regions, which we simply marched through. We have lost altogether 32 horses and 5 mules.

On the 14th, an airplane, trying to make contact with Howze, landed in rear of column and was wrecked. Pilot had a letter from General Pershing, but it contained nothing new.

Chapter XXVII

Rendezvous at Santa Cruz de Villegas. Conferences With the Mexicans

Now that all of the "dramatis personae" have assembled on the stage at Santa Cruz de Villegas, let us return there for a few days.

The combined strength of the four flying columns was sufficiently impressive to obviate any concern as to what the Mexican forces, regular or irregular, singly or combined, might do, but the question of food for man and beast had become serious, as we needed for our daily requirements 6 tons of hay, 9000 pounds of grain, and 2000 pounds of food for men. The Mexicans would doubtless have been glad to starve us out and would have done so had they not been afraid of reprisals from us. The authorities in Parral no longer wanted to issue merchandise in exchange for "receipts" which could be cashed in Chihuahua at the American Consulate. Colonel Brown sent foraging parties to scour the country for grain and beans, and on April 17th issued his personal check in favor of Constancio Ochoa for $226.60 gold for miscellaneous supplies. The Colonel was certainly doing all in his power to prevent this part of the expedition from becoming a flat tire.

Colonel Brown on this date sent a note to the Presidente of Parral demanding an apology and disavowal from the Mexican authorities for the outrage at Parral of April 12th. Reply to this was evasive and truly characteristic of Mexican diplomacy—"just drawing a red herring across the trail." However the threat, somewhat veiled, in Brown's note produced some supplies on the 18th, including some trousers which were much needed, as many of the men were beginning to get sun burned.

On April 20th Colonel Brown received a note from General Herrera stating that he would meet Colonel Brown at Santa Cruz de Villegas for a conference at 10:00 A. M., April 21st.

Captain Rutherford arrived at about 4.00 P.M., April 20, with 36 pack mules, carrying among other things $2,300.00 Money talks in this country, as everywhere. Mail also came in, the first I had seen since crossing the line. Rutherford also delivered to Colonel Brown instructions from General Pershing, dated April 15th, of which the following is an extract:

1. The Commanding General directs me to acknowledge receipt of your report as well as the reports of Major Frank Tompkins, 13th Cavalry, on the events at Parral, April 12th, 1916. He desires to congratulate Major Tompkins on the very patient and forbearing manner in which he handled a most delicate situation.

2. He directs that on account of the difficulties of supply in your present locality you move your force, which now includes Major Tompkins' squadron and Lieutenant Colonel Allen's squadron, by easy marches to Satevo,

taking advantage of any supplies or grazing along the line that may be necessary to put your command in better condition.

* * * * *

J. A. Ryan,
Major 13th Cavalry, I. O.,
Acting Chief of Staff.

April 21st. Generals Herrera, Lozano and two other Mexican Generals, with an escort of about 35 mounted men came in at 10:00 A.M.

Colonel Brown invited the field officers to be present at this conference so that included me. The meeting was held in a room with a long table occupying one end. Colonel Brown sat in the center on the north side facing south, with his field officers grouped on either side as in a general court-martial; behind him on the wall were the national colors and the regimental standard of the 10th Cavalry.

General Herrera sat in the center of the south side of the table facing Brown, with his generals grouped about him.

When I met Lozano he gave me a doubtful look as though he was not at all certain of the reception he would get from me. I was rather the worse for wear, being lame, with my arm in a sling. But I hobbled up to him and addressed him as "Amigo mio," shook hands, clapped him on the shoulder, when we both laughed.

Colonel Brown presented to General Herrera the following which he first read aloud:

Santa Cruz de Villegas,
Not dated. Handed to General Herrera
at meeting April 21, 1916.

General Luis Herrera,
Commanding Carranzista Forces in Parral.
Sir:

1. I am in receipt of a letter from General Pershing Commanding the Villa Punitive Expedition of which the following is an extract relating to the unprovoked assault upon our men in the town of Parral on the 12th instant:

Ascertain if possible whether the attack was directed by the local military commander of the de facto Government, demanding of him a disavowal of this base act. If the attack was directed by the local civil authorities, demand the immediate arrest of the responsible parties.

2. When all the incidents of the unfortunate affair of April 12th are sifted down they resolve themselves into the following:

3. When Major Tompkins was in Concho (he means Vaile de Zaragosa) enroute for Parral, he was visited by a Captain and Lieutenant of Carranzista forces and in the most friendly manner invited to visit Parral; they said that they would notify the civil and military authorities of the coming of the U. S. troops and that they would be welcome. It was arranged that Major Tompkins would arrive at Parral about 11:00 A. M. April 12th.

4. Upon arrival at the outskirts of Parral at the hour designated and finding no one there to meet him, Major Tompkins did the only thing he could do under the circumstances—he went into the city guided by a Carranzista soldier and went direct to the house of headquarters of General Lozano.

5. No warning was given Major Tompkins by General Lozano that any trouble would result, either intentionally or unintentionally, from the American troops coming into town, but the General went to show Tompkins a camping place, riding at the head of the column.

6. After leaving the city limits enroute to camp the American column was fired upon by citizens of the town and Carranzista soldiers. Upon this being reported to General Lozano, he returned to prevent further firing.

7. This fire was not returned until the American troops were again fired upon some 10 or 15 minutes later.

8. Shortly after General Lozano left Major Tompkins a civilian who seemed to be an official came to Major Tompkins and begged that he leave town to avoid a conflict. To this Major Tompkins made the very reasonable reply that as soon as he received the supplies ordered from some of the Parral merchants he would withdraw to the north, but notwithstanding this assurance he was a few minutes later fired into by Carranzista troops and Sergeant Richley was killed.

9. Major Tompkins used only sufficient force to keep his assailants at a distance and prevent a general massacre of his entire command.

10. Major Tompkins' assailants, not content with having caused him to withdraw from the vicinity of Parral, pursued him north some 20 miles to Santa Cruz de Villegas, killing one additional soldier and wounding 6 more, including two officers.

11. The assailants were not irresponsible civilians or simple private soldiers but were soldiers of the de facto Government under their officers as was shown by the admission of the Presidente that one Major was killed and a Colonel wounded, and they were led by General Lozano himself.

12. In one of his notes written to Major Tompkins at Santa Cruz, General Lozano states that if he (Tompkins) does not withdraw still farther north he (Lozano) would "be obliged to charge with the greater part of my (his) forces."

13. I am sure that you will realize that our government cannot pass over lightly actions such as these narrated above which call for the most ample disavowal and apology, and I have gone into detail hoping that you may do so in your reply. It will save both of us time and trouble in the end. I trust you will in your reply take up the subject matter of this letter by paragraph.

14. Your reply will be sent to General Pershing to be by him forwarded to our government authorities in Washington.

W. C. Brown,
Colonel 10th Cavalry, Commanding.

General Herrera received this letter, stating he would reply to it at a later date. Colonel Brown replied that he intended to start his northward march early the next morning and that he would like to have the reply before leaving Santa Cruz de Villegas. Herrera assured him the reply would be forthcoming early next morning. The conference then proceeded to other business.

Herrera agreed to transport our wounded to El Paso by rail, probably knowing full well the Mexican Government would not consent to our use of the railroad for any purpose. He suggested that we use Vaile de Zaragosa as a base, stating that Adela was too near Parral, as our presence in the Parral region was adding to Villa's strength. He denied that Mexico was responsible in any way for the Parral outrage. He also stated that we would be permitted to move north, but not south, east, or west. Then Colonel Brown pointed to the United States flag and said: "that flag does not move one step north until I have orders from my General to so move it." The conference then broke up.

The following extract from Lieutenant Colonel Allen's diary covers briefly but clearly the "story" of our stay at Santa Cruz de Villegas:

The story of Parral, conferences at Santa Cruz between the American and Mexican authorities, and the search for supplies, especially forage, during our encampment at this little ranch, constitute one of the most interesting, characteristic, and peculiarly delicate situations, within my knowledge, of the Punitive Expedition. The attitude of the people at Parral; prohibition by a major of the Carranza forces, the day after the Parral fight, of Lieutenant Troxel's visit to the railway north of Parral; the instructions from General Gutierrez *not to go a step farther south;* the dictatorial manner of General Luis Herrera at the conference on April 21st, and his reply to the request for a disavowal of the unprovoked attack ending with "no hay lugar a satisfaccion por mi parte" (there is no reason for an apology on my part); all these go to show the character of the cooperation this expedition was receiving from the authorities and the people.

And General Pershing in his report states:

At first it was thought best to retain the troops in the vicinity of Parral, but the strained relations between the two Governments that resulted from this fight brought the whole matter into the sphere of diplomacy and it was soon deemed advisable to withdraw for the time being.

Fortunately the dispositions made of the various columns, and the orders under which they were operating naturally brought them to the vicinity of Parral at the same time.

The four columns in that section were united soon after the fight under command of Colonel Brown, making a force sufficiently strong to have given a good account of itself under any circumstance likely to arise immediately.

But to have retained troops there would have required an extension of the line of communications 180 miles from San Antonio, (Mexico) and the road was difficult. To supply such a force with the transportation then available would not have been an easy task. These rapidly moving columns had outrun the means of supply, and as there was neither food nor forage obtainable in that district, withdrawal was the best solution of the problem.

There were no serviceable airplanes left by which to communicate with Colonel Brown, and as he had evidently taken the view that he should not withdraw, it became necessary to send Colonel Cabell, the Chief of Staff, there to investigate the situation and, if advisable, to direct the retirement of the force.

Upon his arrival the above conditions as to supply were found to exist, and as Colonel Brown had made every effort to obtain needed supplies and had been unsuccessful, the command was ordered to return to San Antonio.

Previous to the conference Major Howze had received orders to move north, so Colonel Brown authorized Allen and Howze to start at midnight following the conference, while Brown and Tompkins would leave about seven hours later.

General Herrera's reply to Colonel Brown's letter was received the morning of the 22nd shortly after the American column had left Santa Cruz de Villegas. Brown read it, then forwarded it to General Pershing. What satisfaction he derived from it can best be left to the imagination of the reader. Here it is:

Hidalgo del Parral, April 21, 1916.
Colonel W. C. Brown,
Commanding 10th Cavalry,
Santa Cruz de Villegas.
Dear Sir:

1. Referring to your official letter of today in which you make mention of extracts from letter of General Pershing relating to lamentable happenings on the 12th, I pass to answer:

2. I have reliable information and statement of Chief of Arms General Lozano, that forces under his command did not take part in what occurred, but on the contrary he as well as the civil authorities, tried to prevent same.

3. After a minute examination of happenings of April 12th, I have gathered the following: That the Chief of Arms of this place had no knowledge of the Captain and Lieutenant referred to by Major Tompkins (I am forced to call your attention to the fact that no official has the right to

effect the entrance of forces without first having taken the necessary steps with the commander of such place).

4. That General Lozano agrees in all its parts with statement referred to in paragraph marked four in your extract.

5. With greatest insistence both General Lozano and the Municipal President pointed out to Major Tompkins the fatal consequences of his presence in the Plaza, General Lozano calling attention to the multitude gathering in front of the cuartel.

6. General Lozano corroborates the affirmation of Tompkins, that the American troops were fired on upon leaving the town by the inhabitants, but has no knowledge whether soldiers off duty took part in the meeting of the populace.

7. General Lozano agrees to statement that American troops did not answer fire in those moments.

8. In regard to party who presented himself to Major Tompkins begging that his forces withdraw, Lozano manifests to have no knowledge, and that if fire was continued he does not know whether by populace solely or in company with soldiers already mentioned.

9. I am informed that Major Tompkins only used force under his command.

10. In regard to all this, we lament the accident, the same which could not be prevented notwithstanding the efforts of General Lozano and his chiefs, who tried to placate the populace, resulting a Colonel wounded and a Major dead of our forces. We regret that the American soldiers far from withdrawing, fortified themselves in advantageous points augmenting the indignation of the people.

11. Interrogated in this respect General Lozano protests with all energy that it is not true that soldiers or officers of his command opened fire on the American army, that if the Municipal President admitted that a Colonel had been wounded and a Major killed, it was in the manner already explained in the foregoing paragraph, having received the General himself various volleys fired by the Americans who were fortified on the roofs of Santa Cruz de Villegas.

12. General Lozano does not deny to what is referred to in yours of this paragraph stating that only in this way was he able to prevent situation from becoming graver, notwithstanding the hostile attitude of the people. I manifest to you that having discovered one of the instigators of the meeting, he has been shot.

13. Regarding this paragraph I offer to your intelligence that on account of the explanation for any part there is no room for apology.

Constitution Y Reforma
Luis Herrera
General Chief of Operations.

At 5:00 P.M. the 21st, Colonel Cabell, General Pershing's Chief of Staff, arrived by motor with orders for us to move to Satevo with ultimate destination Carretas. This would place us on the line of communications which would give the animals hay of which they were in sore need. On account of Tompkins' wound Colonel Cabell offered to take him back in his automobile, but Tompkins declined stating that he was fit for duty.

Chapter XXVIII

Operations of the 7th Cavalry Near Guerrero. The Fight at Tomochic

On April 3rd we left Colonel Dodd at Frijole Canyon about 10 miles north of San Isidro. On the 7th he received a message from General Pershing's Headquarters to take 175 men and the best horses available and move into the country south of Guerrero.

When Major Howze passed through Frijole Canyon on April 4th, Mr. Tracy, a scout with Colonel Dodd's column, was assigned to the command of Major Howze, but left the latter after two days and returned to his former command, bringing dispatches from Howze and information, received from a telegraph operator, that Villa was reported dead, that Carranza troops were advancing from the south at Parral and Camargo, and that Luis Herrera was in the vicinity of San Diego del Monte.

Colonel Dodd at once formulated plans for active operations of all the American columns in the country to the south, and communicated them to Headquarters. The orders received back from Division Headquarters at San Geronimo authorized him to carry out his part of these plans, and assured him of the proper activity of the columns of Howze and Brown.

Division Headquarters also furnished to Colonel Dodd at this time a new guide in the person of Dr. F. E. Gatens, to work with Tracy and Barker. Gatens was familiar with the country south and west of Guerrero.

Dodd's command had been without a medical officer since leaving Santa Ana, but upon establishing the camp at Rancho Frijoles the force acquired a surgeon in Major W. R. Eastman, U. S. Army. He made a valuable addition to the little force that was about to penetrate into the mountain fastnesses of the Sierra Tarahumara.

On April 8th, with a command consisting of 15 officers and 175 enlisted men, Colonel Dodd marched to Minaca, passing by the outskirts of Guerrero, occupied by Colonel Cano with some 300 men. While the command halted nearby, Colonel Dodd visited the headquarters of the Mexican commander. While there General Herrera, who had been placed, so he reported, in command of all operations in the bandit infested region, arrived with an escort of about 300 men.

The General informed the American commander that he intended to push large forces of federal troops into the district, and would in a short space of time destroy all bandits. He protested that the presence of American troops and their movements farther southward would in-

173

terfere with his plans. He urged Colonel Dodd, consequently, not to move in that direction.

Dodd explained that he was acting in accordance with instructions from General Pershing whom Herrera had met at Geronimo, and asked him why he had not laid the matter before Pershing at that time, to which he replied that when he saw General Pershing his plans had not been matured. Dodd then asked him what his plans were, which question he partially evaded, but repeated his former statement that Carranza troops would be rushed into the district by rail; but that he could not give his full plans until he had received Colonel Cano's report. After further unimportant conversation he said he would give Dodd a letter setting forth conditions, which he requested be forwarded to General Pershing. This letter by no means covers the conference, nor does it express the attitude of Herrera at that time. Dodd, thinking that something might have arisen that had not reached him, at any rate believing that Pershing should be informed of this new attitude, immediately dispatched a letter to Headquarters, and joined his command in camp near Minaca.

Just before the departure of the column from Rancho Frijole word was received to the effect that a party of Mexican federal soldiers under the command of Major Erviso had mutinied at or near Matachic or Tejolocachic (on the railroad northwest of Guerrero) and intended joining the Villistas.

Troops "K" and "M," 7th Cavalry, under Captain William J. Kendrick, were ordered to those points to investigate and take appropriate action. At daybreak of the next day, April 8th, this command, while saddling up in their bivouac a few miles south of Tejolocachic, heard firing to the north. The troops mounted up and rode to the sound of the guns to find at the Agua Zarza Ranch about 30 Mexicans surrounding and firing upon two Americans and nine Carranzista soldiers who were defending the ranch house. Both troops advanced against the besiegers, and a short engagement ensued, which resulted in the dispersal of the latter. The detachment kept up the pursuit as far as Matachic, but the mutineers kept well concealed in the ravines and underbrush. It was believed that two of them were wounded. The detachment suffered no casualties.

The two Americans at the ranch, Mr. W. Henry Acklin and Mr. Wallace C. Mebans, as well as Major Erviso and 8 soldiers of his command, were escorted by the American cavalry to Matachic. The besiegers of the ranch turned out to be part of Erviso's force that had deserted from him a few days previously, on account, so it was reported, of their hatred of the Americans, in which their commander apparently did not concur. Captain Kendrick, in reporting the incident, stated that, in his opinion, "the sentiment of the people in this section is growing stronger and more bitter against Americans on account of the presence of U.S. troops in Mexico."

The detachment returned to camp at Rancho Frijole on the 9th. In this little expedition Lieutenant T. K. Brown commanded Troop "M," and Lieutenant E. B. Lyon commanded Troop "K."

On the night of the 9th, Major J. A. Ryan, 13th Cavalry, Acting Chief of Staff, visited Dodd's camp at Minaca, and on the next day he and Dodd went to see General Herrera at Guerrero, when the subject of Herrera's letter was brought up and explained by the General, but by no means in the same manner or to the same purport as the explanation given Dodd on the 8th. He withdrew his former objections to the movements of the U.S. Cavalry. At Dodd's request he gave him an order directing a certain commanding officer to furnish him with an officer and 10 men to accompany Dodd's command in order to prevent the Americans from "mistaking Carranza for Villista soldiers." The order was not used, though later Colonel Bustillos furnished Dodd with a Carranza captain (Hernandez) who acted as scout and guide and rendered most excellent service. Dodd continued to send out scouts in an endeavor to locate a large number of Villistas which he was satisfied were west of him. All information seemed to confirm a widespread understanding that a large body of Villistas had concentrated at Ariseachic and Agua Caliente, the most firm believer in this being the Mayor of Minaca, who, after some persuasion, volunteered to act as guide to those places. Dr. Gatens, who claimed to know the trails and localities named, was likewise sanguine as to his knowledge of the whereabouts of these concentrated bands. Everything justified the trip being made, which Dodd knew was to be a hard one. At about 5:00 P.M., April 13th, he left camp and by marching continuously all night over a rough trail, passing through an arroyo, arrived at Ariseachic before daybreak, making a distance of about 35 miles, where nothing was found. The command then proceeded to Agua Caliente, where a fresh and heavy trail was struck, leading northeast. This was followed until it disappeared a little south of, and about 10 miles west of Minaca. Leakage of the trail showed that small parties, usually no more than two, three or four, left it from time to time. This, from subsequent developments, was undoubtedly the trail of Julio Acosta, and, possibly, the members of other bands many of whom left the trail going to the south and west, joining Cervantes command that later looted the town and mine of Yoquivo, and which Dodd afterward fought at Tomochic on the 22nd of April.

The command went into camp on the 15th near where the trail "petered" out, at a place called Tonachic, sending into Minaca for such supplies as could be obtained, and of which they were in great need.

In this night march Colonel Dodd rode, as was his custom, well forward with the advance guard. He was thus in a position to get the earliest information of any new developments, but jeopardized his personal safety, of which at all times he appeared completely careless. The presence of the commander, accompanied by the guides and the officer personnel of rather a large staff, intermingled with the advance guard, on difficult trails, and in the darkness, made the position of the advance guard commander an unenviable one.

At the other end of the long drawn out column was Captain Dallam, who says of this march:

Once again I had the rear guard. The route passed through deep, wooded canyons, and along rough narrow trails. The moon was bright and the night intensely cold, as usual. All that troop commanders knew was that we were off again on another night march. Neither distance, direction, nor destination was given. We had our place in the column and our duties to perform: to keep in place and to be ready when called upon.

Darkness came on quickly in the canyons, which were deep and narrow. The trails twisted and wound among the trees. At times we would suddenly come to the head of a canyon where three or more possible trails or directions might be followed. At times it was necessary to dismount and look for tracks of the preceding troops. The moon threw fantastic shadows across the path and distorted all objects. The intense cold and weariness numbed the faculties, and the utmost vigilance was required to keep in place. Sometimes a glimpse would be caught of the horses ahead; they would disappear and then, strive as one would, it seemed that they never could be found again. The pace was a forced walk, the trail rough, the horses stumbled, and the cold grew more intense. One's legs became numb from the knee down but there was no halting. Not until nearly midnight did we make our second and last halt. The squadron was still complete. The small pack train was up and my rear platoon close behind it.

A few minutes and we were off again, pushing all the time, pressing the horses to their fastest walk. Urgency required our arrival before dawn. The pack train fell behind, and each time as the necessity arose I' dropped a connecting file behind until the first platoon was all but used up.

Suddenly we stopped. We had reached our destination. Troops were assembled. Orders went back to bring together Troop "E." It seemed they would never arrive. The other three troops surrounded the town and advanced. The packmaster began to ring his bell to call the train together; the troop was assembled. The town was rushed—the enemy had gone. We had marched 30 miles. At daylight our scouts went out. We watered, fed, and slept until the arrival of further orders.

This maintenance of contact is the problem of the rear guard commander. Hampered by the trains, pushing off into the unknown, assuring himself of contact out in front and in the rear, requires the utmost vigilance and efficient, reliant, noncommissioned officers. Here were no roads, no sign posts, and no guides, nothing but rocky trails and thick woods, and a deceiving moonlight.

A rumor reached Colonel Dodd to the effect that the Villista force he had been tracking was at Yoquivo, had looted that place, and were holding for ransom a Frenchman named Seyffert, and an unnamed American.

Major Gonzales, commanding a federal detachment numbering some 40 men (most of whom were boys) offered to accompany the American force with his command on an excursion to Yoquivo. Colonel Dodd agreed to this enterprise, and Major Gonzales' detachment passed through the American camp about midnight of the 17th of April.

Without waiting for further supplies Dodd sent 17 men dismounted and the unserviceable horses into Minaca, and followed Gonzales at an early hour in the morning. Terrero on the Kansas City, Mexico and Orient railroad was reached at 10:45 A.M., and shortly afterwards the detachment struck off to the west of the railroad and traversed the Arroyo Ancho.

After traveling in a southwesterly direction all the afternoon bivouac was made toward nightfall in a pretty canyon that was very inviting after the long day's march, which had covered about 28 miles. March was resumed at daylight the 19th, and the trail led southwest through the Sierra Madre Occidental Mountains over a difficult trail. Napuchic, a camp of log huts, was passed about mid-afternoon, and the command arrived at Aguachic just after 5:00 P.M. and bivouacked there, after a day's march estimated at 30 miles.

The command was up before dawn of the 20th, and in the saddle at 5:45. The direction of the march now changed to the northwest, and at the end of some 10 miles junction was made with Major Gonzales. The two commands continued together along the very difficult trail until 1:00 P.M. when bivouac was made in a deep canyon at Basogachic, some 8 or 10 miles east of Yoquivo. Here the combined forces remained, well concealed it was thought, until the moon rose at 11:00 P.M. Then, instead of taking the direct and short route to Yoquivo, in order to effect a surprise the command marched by a little used and abominable trail over the mountains. It was steep and rocky and wound along the edges of precipices; the altitude was high and the wind piercingly cold.

Yoquivo was reached about an hour before dawn, and at the first sight of daylight the troops advanced to attack the place. The first sign of life was a bright light in a small stone house; it was Gonzales and his troops. Gonzales was stretched on a couch, resting, and a huge fire was going to keep him warm. Half a dozen of his men were ministering to his comfort. The bandits had departed.

From the inhabitants and the released prisoners it was learned that word of the approach of the combined American and Mexican forces had been received in the middle of the previous afternoon. It is not unlikely, and Colonel Dodd was convinced of the fact, that the march was betrayed by the Mexican "allies" themselves. The prisoners (the American and the Frenchman) had been released on partial payment of the ransom demanded. The Villista band, numbering about 200, commanded by Candelaro Cervantes, including among its leaders Manuel Baca, Rios, and Cruz Dominiguez, had vacated the place about 8:00 P.M. the previous evening, after having tarried there five days.

Our troops bivouacked in the vicinity, and sprawled in the sun to warm up and rest, while some welcome small supplies were gathered from the village. Colonel Dodd, instead of being discouraged and chagrined, felt an assurance that he was rather hot on a sure trail, and determined to follow to the end.

He requested Major Gonzales to accompany him farther with his little detachment. The Mexican commander excused himself, however, so plans were made to continue the expedition without his assistance. No signs of those plans were given to the inhabitants or any spies who may easily have been lurking in the vicinity.

The troops loafed first in the sun until it was too hot, and then hunted the shade, as if to remain indefinitely. About 3:30 P.M. orders were given to march, the command taking the trail shortly afterward, heading northeast. The few pack mules were loaded with supplies of all kinds which had been purchased at Yoquivo. The trail proved to be about the most difficult this outfit had yet encountered, while it seemed as if the horses could not stand another day's march.

The trail wound through a rocky chasm, then turned about in the opposite direction, and corkscrewed up the steep wooded slope of the mountain, the top of which was attained about midnight. Darkness prevented further travel.

After a hasty breakfast at dawn the march was resumed following the tortuous trail as rapidly as possible until about 3:00 in the afternoon when, from the crest of a hill, a view was obtained of the valley of Tomochic with the little village nestling in its plain. Some 30 or 40 bandits were at the same time seen taking to the hills north of the village. This first observation was made from what was really a high mountain, with elevation of over 8,000 feet, and the trail leading down to the valley was steep and difficult, so that considerable time was consumed in getting down to the level of the town, which was entered about 4:30 P.M.

Tomochic is a small but very old town, founded there, it is reported, when the Spaniards first came into Mexico. It consists of a dozen or so scattered buildings with a small mixed population of Mexicans, half-breeds, and Tarahumara Indians, all of them living in indescribable squalor. The town is located in a small valley or pocket (rincon) opening into the valley of the Tomochic River (locally so called, but noted on the maps as the Aros, and at some points the Rio Verde.) It is approached from the southwest by the Yoquivo trail, while the Campo-Minaca trail passes through it nearly east and west. It is surrounded by high and rugged mountains, clothed with splendid pine forests, and scarred with battlemented canyons. Some points on the Yoquivo trail were found to be higher than 9,000 feet, and the town itself lies at an elevation of 6,625 feet.

The aneroid barometer carried by the command was found to be practically useless, as it registered no more than 6,000 feet. Over these high trails the command had marched in single file, sometimes mounted, often on foot, each man holding to the tail of the horse ahead. Horses and men alike were rapidly becoming unshod. To the suffering from this cause, and from very short and inadequate rations, was added the extreme discomfort to both men and horses due to the high altitude, which caused very noticeable difficulty in breathing, headache, and bleeding at the nose.

After leaving the summit (A), the trail followed by the command, from the southwest, became concealed from the town by the ridges (B), one of which terminated at a point (C) near the river. Level ground was reached in a clear space or pocket (D), where the troops were massed and concealed. A machine gun was placed at (E) in such a position as to command the town and cover the advance of the attack.

From the position (D), Troop "L," commanded by Captain Moffet, closely supported by Troop "E" commanded by Captain Dallam, all under the command of Major Winans, were ordered to gallop rapidly around the point (C), charge into and take possession of the town.

The march-weary horses had to jump down from a high bank into the river bed, and when across the river had to jump upon a rocky shelf to get out. The advancing troops drew fire from several directions but continued on into the village, which the bandits had completely evacuated. Their rear guard was seen to scatter. Some mounted, some on foot, they took to the nearby hills to the north and south of the village, from which they opened fire.

The balance of the command, less a platoon sent to the north to cover the plain (F), followed closely in support of Major Winan's squadron, and patrols were sent out which dislodged or killed the enemy parties which had occupied the hills to the north and south. A considerable number of the bandits took flight toward the east, along the Ocampo-Minaca trail.

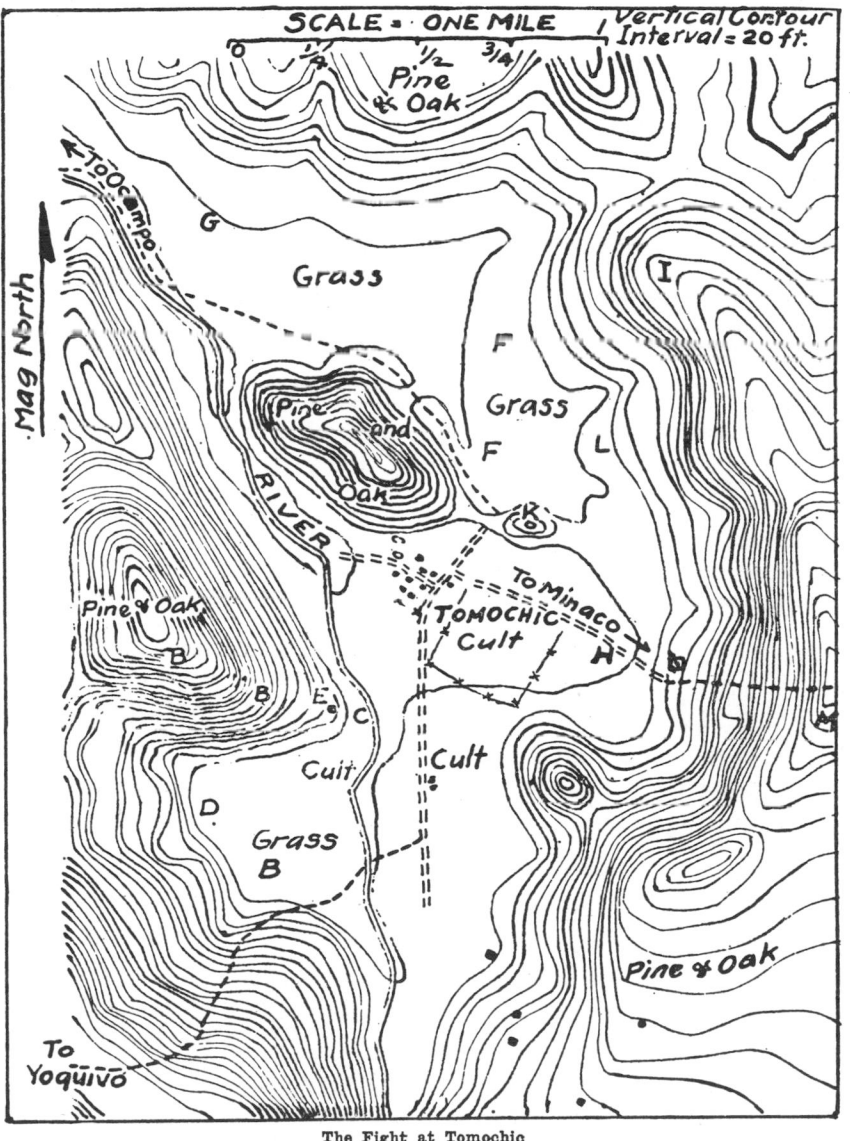

The Fight at Tomochic

From the first point of observation (A) a large herd of horses and also what appeared to be a column of troops, were noticed in the distance at (G.) As it seemed probable that the enemy main body might be in this locality, Major Dade was sent with Troop "H," Captain Wells, and Troop "I," Captain Gillem, Captain Leary accompanying, in the direction with orders to attack any forces found there and to capture or kill the herd. This force was accompanied by the machine gun originally stationed at (E.) The herd proved to be brood mares, and no considerable force was encountered in this direction. The troops received some fire from the hills, but found only small parties or individual bandits against which to operate. The absence of half of the command on what proved to be a useless mission was felt as a serious handicap when the principal resistance developed in another quarter.

A machine gun, under charge of Sergeant H. H. Rogers, was advanced to an abandoned adobe house at (H), in order to secure a more raking fire on the trail up which some of the enemy were fleeing. A platoon was sent in support, and later the remainder of the troop "L," under Captain Moffet, was sent to the same position.

Until the departure of Major Dade the enemy firing had been rather light and scattering, and had ceased altogether from the nearby hills. But soon after, a heavy fusilade was received from the circular hills to the east. This came from the enemy main body which, it was later learned, had advanced some three miles up the trail which could be plainly seen where it passed over the crest at (M.) Upon learning of the attack upon their rear guard, they had returned and now scattered along the crest and sides of the mountains, extending from about the point (I) at the northeast to (J) at the southeast. They had a decided advantage in position, and there was no way of getting around them in the short time that remained before dark.

Upon receiving this heavy fire the knoll (K), although dominated by fire from the hills, was immediately occupied by a dozen men of Troop "E" under Major Winans. The headquarters party advanced under fire to the knoll and joined them. From the knoll a well directed fire was kept up upon the head of the trail. The position (L) was occupied by a small detachment of Troop "E" under Lieutenant W. O. Ryan, which did very effective work.

As darkness set in the enemy withdrew, and retreated two or three miles along the trail from which they subsequently scattered. Pursuit was quite impossible after nightfall, consequently the command assembled and occupied the village.

Continuance of the action was half expected at daybreak, Easter Sunday, April 23rd, but nothing developed. The enemy force had put many miles behind them.

The American casualties were two killed: Saddler Ray of "L" Troop killed outright, and Private Bonshee of "H" Troop who died during the night from a shot in the abdomen. There were also three wounded. Several horses were lost, dead of exhaustion. "E" Troop alone lost three horses from exhaustion on the day of the fight, and one died that night on the picket line.

At least 30 of the Villistas were killed and wounded, and it is quite probable that their casualties were still larger. A number of their horses and mules and some arms were captured. Their defeat led to a thorough disintegration and demoralization of the Cervantes force. It had numbered between 150 and 200 on April 22nd, the date of the fight at Tomochic. A few days later Cervantes had scarcely a dozen men with him, according to report.

A story was subsequently current at Matachic that the Tarahumara Indians, who had no love for the marauding Villista bands, found and gathered in one place all of the bandits, presumably wounded, and being unable to care for them, poured pitch over them and set them on fire.

After resting over the 23rd, the command returned by easy marches to its former camp (San Pedro) near Minaca.

The dead were taken along and interred in the cemetery of that place, and the wounded were sent through as rapidly as possible to Namiquipa. The squadron proceeded by easy stages to Providencia, where it arrived April 28th, and joined the headquarters of the regiment.

During the absence of this squadron, a minor action had occurred

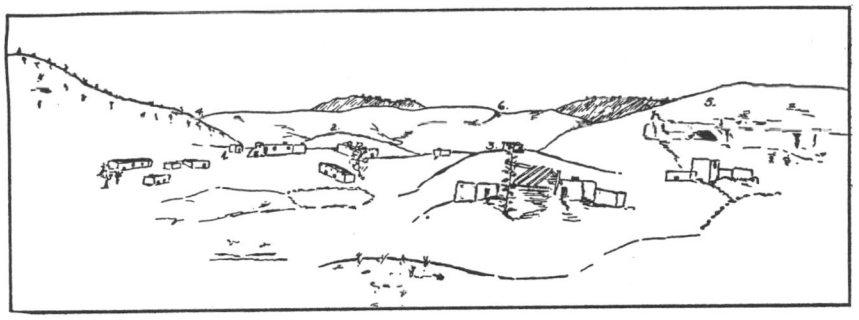

1. Adobe hut. Gen. Dodd's headquarters after the fight.
2. Hill which headquarters party reached under fire. Here Maj. Winans with some ten men engaged in long range fire (1000 yards or more) with enemy at 6. Here the Mexican commander was at times conspicuous on a white horse.
3. Machine gun position. Several casualties sustained here.
4. Pass into valley where a considerable number of animals was found. Capt. Leavy and two troops endeavored to capture this herd. They proved not to be Mexican mounts.
5. Cave in hillside from which fire was received. A sergeant with 6 men dislodged the enemy from this position.
6. Point on trail toward Minaca. This was the center of the Mexican position.

on April 20th. A patrol of two enlisted men and a civilian guide, while scouting in the country south of the camp of the 7th Cavalry, then established at Cocomorachic, encountered a band of 10 Villistas, who were waiting in ambush behind the stone wall of a corral. The patrol opened fire at short range, upon discovering the bandits, and then retreated under sharp fire to shelter. Information was sent back to the regimental commander, Colonel James B. Erwin, who sent "M" Troop under Lieutenant Thoburn K. Brown to the scene. Before the arrival of the troop, however, the bandits had scattered, after losing four of their number mortally wounded by the fire of the patrol.

The regiment remained at Providencia, inactive except for patrolling, for more than a month, and, on June 3rd marched a short distance to the north and took station in Raspadura Pass, where much needed re-mounts were received. Two days later Colonel Dodd was ordered to El Valle. He assumed command of the large camp at that place, where troops of all arms of the service had been assembled. He was created a brigadier general during his service at this camp, and left it and retired from active service on account of age, 64 years, July 28, 1916.

A high meed of praise must be accorded this officer, for the unflagging determination and energy with which he prosecuted the pursuit, in the face of great difficulties, that resulted in the rout of Villa's principal band at Guerrero, and the consummation of the task at Tomochic.

Where only a surmise was had as to the course taken by Villa, where every story contradicted the preceding one, and all reports and rumors were vague and misleading, where roads and trails were unknown, and the country rugged and difficult, where supplies were depleted, with small store in the looted countryside to draw upon, where horses gave out and men fell sick—he was not daunted nor drawn aside from a dogged, persistent determination to find the trail of the bandits and follow it.

For General Dodd no clue was too faint or improbable to follow down, no trail of pony tracks too slight to examine. No marches were too long and no way too rough for him to undertake. He scorned hardships, and was ever a splendid example of hardihood to officers and men. Red-shirted Tracy, the invaluable guide and scout, said of this cavalryman, whom he observed at close range for several weeks of vigorous campaigning: "Colonel Dodd ate less, slept less, and worked harder than any other man in the command."

General Dodd, in his report to General Pershing, stated in part:

Our casualties were as reported, two dead and three wounded as follows: Killed: Saddler Ralph A. Ray, Troop "L" 7th Cavalry. Shot in head. Died instantly. Private Oliver Bonshee, Troop "H" 7th Cavalry. Shot in abdomen. died several hours later.

Wounded: Q. M. Sgt. Louis Craink, Troop "H" 7th Cavalry. Shot in right arm. Private William F. Matthias, Troop "L" 7th Cavalry. Shot in right side. Private Thomas Henry, Troop "L" 7th Cavalry. Shot in ankle.

My first report by messenger showed the casualties of the bandits as 25 killed and wounded. Next day it was definitely known that this number was 31, and, on arriving at this point, it is understood that this number, on the acknowledgments of the bandits engaged in the fight, has been greatly increased. The behavior of the command on the march and during the fight was most excellent, without exception.

Property captured: 3 rifles, 20 sticks of dynamite, 10 horses, 15 mules, 7 saddles.

In consequence of this fight Cervantes' command was entirely disintegrated and scattered, and ceased to exist as a fighting force.

Officers who participated in this engagement were:

Colonel George A. Dodd, Cavalry, Commanding 2nd Cavalry Brigade.
2nd Lieutenant Jerome W. Howe, 10th Cavalry, personal staff of the Brigade Commander.
Captain Edmund M. Leary, 7th Cavalry, Acting Brigade Adjutant.
1st Lieutenant Emil Engel, 7th Cavalry, Statistical Officer.
2nd Lieutenant Albert J. Myer, Jr., 7th Cavalry, Acting Brigade Quartermaster.
Major William R. Eastman, Medical Corps, Surgeon.
Major Edwin B. Winans, 7th Cavalry, Commanding 2nd Squadron.
Major Alexander L. Dade, 7th Cavalry, Commanding 3rd Squadron.
Captain Samuel F. Dallam, 7th Cavalry, Commanding Troop "E."
2nd Lieutenant William O. Ryan, 7th Cavalry, on duty with Troop "E."
Captain Rush S. Wells, 7th Cavalry, Commanding Troop "H."
1st Lieutenant Horace M. Hickam, 7th Cavalry, on duty with Troop "H."

Captain Alvin C. Gillem, 7th Cavalry, Commanding Troop "I."
Captain William P. Moffet, 7th Cavalry, Commanding Troop "L."
1st. Lieut. Robert M. Campbell, 7th Cavalry, on duty with Troop "L."
Our command actually engaged numbered about 150 men. Cervantes command numbered between 150 and 200, though it has been definitely stated that his command numbered 200.

I wish to call attention to the fact that from the day of starting, the 18th, until the night of the 22nd, the day of the fight, the march of every day or night, (two night marches were made) was a forced march in the strictest acceptation of the term. The distance in miles is difficult to estimate, as all distances in these mountainous localities are indicated by "hours of travel," and in order to gain any distance forward it is necessary to travel nearly twice that distance or more in ascent or descent. In other words, it is necessary to traverse "both sides of the ground." These trails are more difficult than any of those thus far encountered by this command.

The population of the locality passed over, consisting largely of Tarahumara Indians, seemed friendly enough, willing to act as guides, but "exist" in a state of squalor, disease and filth incomprehensible and never before met with among Indians or people of any nationality. Smallpox existed in many places, while in some so-called towns (rincons) typhus fever was found.

Many of the animals captured in both fights were utterly useless, and were either killed or abandoned. Those that could be made of any use were brought to this point (Providencia), when two pack mules were selected and assigned to each organization for pack animals, and the balance sent to Namiquipa. Many of the arms captured in both fights were also useless, and such were broken up and destroyed as lack of transportation made it impracticable to carry along worthless material.

I wish to commend my regular guides, by whom excellent service was rendered under all conditions. Mr. C. E. Tracy was with me during the entire period of these operations, and I commend him as a trustworthy, fearless, enthusiastic and efficient scout and guide—as good as I have known anywhere, and the best I have found on this expedition; under fire he cannot be excelled. Mr. James Barker did excellent work while on or near the Hearst property, with which he is, or was, connected. Outside these limits he has little knowledge of the country, but is an excellent interpreter, and understands the Mexican character well. Dr. A. E. Gatens, sent me as a special scout, is acquainted with many of the principal trails through and in the vicinity of Ocampo, Yoquivo, the Green Road, etc, is an excellent interpreter, and on the trails taken in these localities rendered very satisfactory service; excellent in action. Captain Abigael Hernandez, Carranzista officer, allowed by Colonel Bustillos to accompany me from April 18th to May 15th, was invaluable as a guide and scout. To him I entrusted the entire charge of native guides, which he handled with marked success and satisfaction.

Chapter XXIX

The Cavalry Withdraws to the North. End of the Chase

The inglorious ending to a gallant beginning was consistent with Mr. Wilson's Mexican policy, which was a hodge-podge of interference and non-intervention, of patience and petulance, of futile conferences and abortive armed invasion, which has been described as the idealistic policy in the treatment of Mexican affairs.

Mr. Lester H. Woolsey, writing in *Current History* for December, 1928, an article entitled, "Robert Lansing's Record as Secretary of State," endeavors to excuse our cowardly patience in bearing with the insolence of the *de facto* Government, and thus maintaining a policy of peace. with Mexico under any and all forms of humiliating aggravation, under the plea that Germany was working to involve Mexico and the United States in war, and to avoid such a war at that time, 1916, we were justified in the course pursued.

As a matter of fact, war with Mexico in the spring of 1916 would have been a splendid preliminary to our entrance into the World War. Half a million men would have cleaned up Mexico in short order, and then this veteran army would have been available for service in France in the early summer of 1917, instead of which we had to wait a year in order to train men. During all of the World War we kept an army on the Mexican border of sufficient strength to act as an army of occupation after the army of conquest had gone to France.

During this month of campaigning actual armed clashes may be summarized as follows:

On March 29th, fourteen days after the pursuit of Villa began, American cavalry under the command of Colonel George A. Dodd attacked a band of Villistas at Guerrero, scattered them to the four winds, killing over 30, with four American soldiers wounded and none killed. Near San Borja, on April 8th, a force of mounted Carranza troops charged upon the command of Major Howze, who, putting his men in formation to receive them, galloped forward alone to meet the charge, waving his hat, thus stopping the Mexican advance within 50 feet of him and avoiding what would have otherwise been a bloody conflict. A brave deed.

At Parral, on April 12th, Major Frank Tompkins permitted a considerable Mexican force to pursue his command for several miles in an effort to keep peace with all Mexicans except Villistas. But the pursuit grew too hot for American honor. Major Tompkins stopped, wheeled his men and killed over 42 Carranzistas.

Colonel Dodd's column at Tomochic, on April 21st, broke up a band of Villistas, killing between 30 and 40 with a loss of two American soldiers killed and three wounded.

184

Then there were a few minor engagements such as that of Brown at Agua Caliente, and Howze in the mountains southwest of San Borja, in which the Mexicans lost a few men, making the aggregate Mexican loss for the 30 odd days of the campaign well over 100 killed, while the American forces suffered less than 10 killed, an impressive balance in favor of American valor and training.

Colonel Allen and Major Howze left Santa Cruz de Villegas shortly after midnight on April 21st and marched to San Antonio on the railroad, where they arrived April 28th with nothing unusual occurring on the way. Water was found in sufficiency along the route, but there was practically no grazing anywhere southeast of the vicinity of San Antonio.

Major Howze's command up to this time claimed to have covered a total distance of 845 miles. Colonel Allen's command had marched not quite so far. The author cannot vouch for these distances as there is nothing in the records to show whether the start was supposed to have taken place at Colonia Dublan or Columbus. The author believes the latter place. The 10th Cavalry under Colonel W. C. Brown marched considerably farther than either of the 11th Cavalry columns, as their start was made at Fort Huachuca, Arizona, and was practically continuous.

Major Howze's losses during the time he was detached from his regiment at Colonia Dublan on March 24th to the date of his arrival at San Antonio on April 28th was one man killed, 4 horses wounded in action, 2 horses died from wounds, 30 horses died from sickness or exhaustion, 2 mules died from wounds and 3 from exhaustion.

There was a shortage of forage in both of the 11th Cavalry provisional squadrons throughout the campaign. Both commands were able to secure sufficient quantities of beef and beans. The country passed through had been devastated by all Mexican factions, and supplies of all kinds in the towns were scarce.

Supplies were sent to these commands at Satevo, Carretas, and San Antonio. Colonel Allen states in his report: "There was no instance requiring special mention on the return to San Antonio other than the exceptional and continued goodwill of the officers and men in the command in spite of the fact that the retirement was a reluctant act. The conduct and general behavior of the entire command from start to finish left little to be desired."

These two provisional squadrons left Dublan with money, rations, forage and a pack train. They received supplies at three different places. Colonel Brown left Dublan five days ahead of Howze with two days' rations and a pack train, but not a cent of government money. He received no more supplies until April 20th, just 32 days from the time he left Dublan. In addition, on the way south his pack train, except six mules, was taken from him at San Antonio, but he kept going and joined Tompkins at Santa Cruz de Villegas in time to turn back the Mexican attack, and three days ahead of the other two columns. I have always felt that the conduct of Colonel Brown in this campaign has never received the recognition it was entitled to. My trail crossed his on several occasions, and I know the quality of his work. I saw him under most trying conditions performing in a

way decidedly creditable to his country and the army, doing his job
in a workmanlike manner without any thought of reward, but with
the knowledge that he had done his duty and done it well.

The columns of Colonel Brown and Major Tompkins left Santa Cruz
de Villegas at 6:30 A.M., April 22, and marched to Satevo via Valle de
Zaragosa (Conchos), Sauz, Tres Hermanos, Satevo. They arrived at
Satevo April 25th. Colonel Brown here received orders to go to Carretas by trail, so he ordered me with my two troops to take the longer
but easier road via Santa Ysabel, making three marches of it. I had
a couple of wounded in a spring wagon, and Colonel Brown ordered
what was left of Troop "C," 10th Cavalry, Captain Pritchard commanding, to join my command. This troop consisted of about 14 mounted
men, with 20 or 30 men on foot leading disabled horses or marching
by themselves.

On April 26th I left camp at 7:00 A.M. and continued my march
northward. Troop "C" left camp an hour earlier with the sick and
disabled horses. After a few miles the country became rather flat and
was a mixture of good grazing and cultivated land. About 12 miles
from camp we dropped into another valley and just avoided Cienegas
de Ladrones, farther down the valley. This is said to be very Villista
in its sympathies and to contain "malos hombres." At all events there
were no people in sight, which was very strange. We left the valley
for a couple of miles and then returned to it a mile below Guadalupe.

These people may be bad, but they have a beautifully cultivated
valley, and they appear to be prosperous. Maybe they are prosperous
because they are so bad that none of the roving bands dare attack
them. Their river is the Santa Ysabel, which flows towards the east
and south, and no doubt unites with the La Joya and San Pedro.

On April 27th we left camp at 7:00 A.M., Pritchard and his cripples
having started an hour earlier on account of their slower rate of march.
After about half a mile the road led us up on the Mesa and proceeded
north through cultivated and grazing land. About 11:00 A.M. we
dropped into a deep valley at a little barrio called San Chapel where
we watered the stock and caught up with Pritchard, having covered
about 16 miles since leaving camp. This was good going for the dismounted men in Pritchard's troop.

Soon after resuming the march we struck the Mexican Northwestern
Railroad and turned west towards Santa Ysabel. It was necessary to
march over some plowed ground which was hard on our wounded.
We soon crossed the railroad and found a Carranza outpost on herd
guard. Our sudden appearance was a surprise to the Mexicans. They
began running the herd into town, and we could hear bugles blowing
the alarm. We took up a position on an elevation commanding the
town and the ford just ahead and awaited events.

A Mexican officer came to interview me. He wanted to know by
what right I was there and where I was going. I told him I wanted
to cross the river and camp on the other side. He said I could not
cross until he had permission from Chihuahua for me to do so. I
strung the talk out until Pritchard and his cripples came up, when
I ordered Pritchard to cross the river (the ford was in the northern

part of the town) and keep going until he reached Carretas about 13 miles away, because it looked as though we might have a run in with the Mexicans. After Pritchard had cleared the ford I told the Mexican officer that I also would cross since it would be just as easy to wait for the permission from Chihuahua on the other side.

So we crossed without opposition. On the other side I selected a camp site which dominated the town but made no effort to make camp. We were soon surrounded by many Mexicans, all armed. Our men had their magazines, both rifle and pistol, full, and we were ready to cut loose at the slightest sign of treachery. A number of our men spoke and understood Spanish fairly well. One of my officers reported that he heard the Mexicans planning to kill us and then take our pistols—mine in particular, for it was silver mounted.

One official, in a jeering manner, asked me why we had not caught Villa. "Because the dog ran too fast." This reply seemed to satisfy him.

Colonel Brown had sent a truck from Carretas with rations and forage because he had expected me to camp at Santa Ysabel. But my experience at Parral was enough, so I put the wounded in the truck with a hospital corps man and told them to go back to Carretas with information that I would camp at Carretas, and that should there be a fight I would send in a courier.

When Pritchard and his men had a good start, I asked the Mexican official what news there was from Chihuahua. He answered that there was none but that he expected some any minute. As this was the same old manana stuff I replied that I could wait no longer and must be moving. He said I could not go without permission. I laughed and said "Watch me."

We started at 3:30 and covered the 13 miles to Carretas in three hours. Here we found the 10th Cavalry. We had to cook supper in the dark and we had but little wood.

Colonel Brown had sent the wounded on to San Antonio. We covered close to 35 miles this date—a mighty good job for the dismounted men. And the infantry say that cavalry cannot march dismounted!

There was mail at Carretas—the first since March 21st. We rested here until Sunday the 30th. Received some oats and hay for the horses and some clothing for the men. Our rations consisted mostly of hard tack, bacon, coffee and sugar. We killed a steer once in a while for fresh meat, but it was thin and tough and too fresh, though providing exercise for the jaw muscles.

We left Carretas at 7:50 the morning of April 30th and marched 11 miles to Ojitos where we had a very pretty camp. Next morning we started for San Antonio, 17 miles distant where we arrived at noon. Here we found General Pershing, most of the 11th Cavalry, and two battalions of the 6th Infantry. There were also some settlers of whom we bought pies, etc. They were deadly, but tasted good to us.

It was nice to be in a big camp once more with no danger of being shot up during the night. I noticed a pile of hay near my squadron picket lines, guarded by some 10th Cavalry soldiers. As I had served in that regiment as a captain they knew me. I asked if I might sleep on the hay that night. They said they would have to see the officer, of the day. I told them I was lame, had a bullet in my shoulder, and would certainly appreciate a soft bed as I had had none for a month and a half. They said they would take a chance, so I crawled under the paulin and literally "hit the hay." I look back on that sleep as one of the most luxurious and comfortable of my life, except perhaps once in the Philippines, during the Malvar campaign, when I slept on a wooden bench after a week of sleepless campaigning in the rain on Banajo Mountain.

On May 2nd, the 11th Cavalry with headquarters came down from Lake Itascata, joining the two provisional squadrons under Allen and Howze, and they started to reorganize the regiment on normal lines. The Colonel of the regiment, in commenting on this provisional squadron scheme, stated in his official report:

By this time it was strongly impressed upon all of us that the breaking up of troops in order to form provisional troops, as was done when Major Howze's and Colonel Allen's provisional squadrons were formed, is very apt to lead to great trouble in the future in the matter of records, the loss of Government property, and the lowering for the time being, of the efficiency of all organizations, even though the greatest care is exercised. In making up the provisional squadrons of Colonel Allen and Major Howze, legal troops were left in some cases without officers, and in other cases without first sergeants and troop clerks. In order to care for Government property and to insure that proper records were kept by all organizations of the regiment, the officers and men remaining behind were organized into four provisional troops. * * * All officers in the regiment are practically unanimous in believing that better results will obtain, unless it is for a short period of a few days, by taking complete organizations into the field rather than by breaking up regular organizations to form provisional troops. Both men and officers in provisional organizations lose the esprit pride and team work necessary to make any organization a success.

On May 3rd we were informed that we were to feed our horses seven pounds of hay, five of oats, five of corn, and graze them two hours every morning and afternoon. This change from the starvation ration of the past month rejoiced the heart of every trooper. As our horses suffered we suffered with them. Now that they could rest and eat we were glad.

That afternoon five troops and the machine gun troop of the 13th Cavalry came in from Rubio, together with the regimental headquarters. We were glad to see them, but from a selfish standpoint we were more glad to see our bedding rolls from which we had been separated since March 21st. I located my shaving tools and got busy at once—quite a job.

We also received the men we had left behind, extra horses, and best of all the troop cooks and the troop kitchens. Individual cooking, with its waste of food, fuel, and poor grub, was, for a time at least, a thing of the past—Thank God!

This camp was now filling up. Earlier in the day a squadron of the 5th Cavalry came in. We now had all or parts of the 5th, 10th, 11th and 13th Cavalry, and the 6th Infantry, making a very respectable force, considering that they were all veterans.

CHAPTER **XXX**

The New Plan. The Country Divided into Districts. The Fight at Ojos Azules

Upon the retirement of these southern columns to San Antonio, the various detachments of troops that had been moving southward along the line of communications were pushed to the front preparatory to the resumption of active pursuit, *or such other action as might be desired.* Meanwhile it was known that Villa's forces, although scattered in different directions and under separate leaders, were still within the State of Chihuahua, and that Villa himself was in hiding in the mountains to the south of San Borja.

In accordance with this view, a plan of action was ordered by which the territory infested by these bandits was divided into five districts, each patrolled by a regiment of cavalry, with the larger part of the infantry and artillery close in support in case their services should be required.

In pursuance of this plan the following order was issued:

Headquarters Punitive Expedition, U. S. Army
In the Field, Namiquipa, Mexico, April 29, 1916.

General Orders }
No. 28. }

1. As the result of the ardous and persistent pursuit of Villa by various columns of this command, his forces have suffered losses of approximately one hundred killed with unknown number wounded, and have been broken into smaller bands and scattered to different sections of the State of Chihuahua and elsewhere. The situation has changed to the extent that our troops no longer pursue a cohesive force of considerable size, but by surprise with small, swiftly moving detachments they must hunt down isolated bands, now under subordinate leaders, and operating over widely separated portions of the country. For this purpose the country to be covered for the present is accordingly divided into districts and apportioned to organizations available for such duty.

2. The commander of each separate district will organize his own agents and establish as far as possible his own service of information. Every assistance will be given from these headquarters in providing guides and interpreters and in furnishing information. It is also directed that this office and adjacent commanders be furnished with all information of importance that comes to the knowledge of district commanders, especially such as would influence operations of troops in adjacent districts. Each district commander will act on his own initiative on any information that seems likely to lead to the capture of any of the participants in the Columbus raid, and will keep the Commanding General and, as far as practicable, the Brigade Commander, advised of all movements in his district.

3. All officers are reminded that this expedition is operating within the limits of a friendly nation, whose peaceful inhabitants should be treated with every consideration. It is also desirable to maintain the most cordial relations, and cooperate as far as feasible, with the forces of the de facto

189

government. Experience so far has taught, however, that our troops are always in more or less danger of being attacked, not only by hostile followers of Villa, but even by others who profess friendship, and precaution must be taken accordingly. In case of unprovoked attack, the officer in command will, without hesitation, take the most vigorous measures at his disposal, to administer severe punishment to the offenders, bearing in mind that any other course is likely to be construed as a confession of weakness. 4. The following districts to be covered are embraced within the limits prescribed. The boundary lines are to be understood as indicating in general the territory over which district commanders are for the present to operate, but will not limit their efforts to secure information, often otherwise unobtainable, nor confine their activities when in actual pursuit of Villista bands. In locating their headquarters, district commanders, under direction of their brigade commanders, will give due consideration to the question of supply.

Namiquipa District:
Commencing at a point north of Alimo on the 13th parallel, thence east to the Mexican Central Railroad inclusive, south to Sauz, generally west through Tepehuanes, San Miguel, Madera to Tio Chico, north to the 13th parallel, thence east to Alimo.

Bustillos District:
Commencing at San Miguel, thence along southern boundary of Namiquipa district to Sauz, south to near Salas, west to San Andres and San Antonio, and excluding both towns, thence southwest to Mal Paso, thence north to Bachineva and San Miguel, including both towns.

Satevo District:
Commencing at San Antonio, thence east through and including San Andres to Mapula, thence along the Mexican Central Railroad to Jimenez, Parral to Santa Barbara, thence northwest to San Lorenzo and San Antonio.

San Borja District:
Commencing at San Antonio, southeast to San Lorenzo and Santa Barbara, west to Guachochic, north to Garichic, northwest to Rancho de Santiago, northeast to San Antonio.

Guerrero District:
Commencing at San Miguel, thence south through Bachineva to Mal Paso, southwest to Rancho de Santiago, southeast to Carichic, south to Guachochic, west to third meridian west of Chihauhua, north to a point west of Madera, thence east to Madera, thence southeast to San Miguel.

By command of Brigadier General Pershing,
DeR. C. Cabell,
Lieutenant Colonel, 10th Cavalry,
Chief of Staff.

Official:
John L. Hines,
Major, Adjutant General,
Adjutant.

Pursuant to the plan laid down in this order cavalry regiments were assigned to those districts where they had had the most service, and with which the personnel was the most familiar, viz:

District	Troops	District Commander
Namiquipa	10th Cavalry	Major Elwood W. Evans
Guerrero	7th Cavalry	Colonel George A. Dodd
Bustillos	13th Cavalry	Colonel Herbert J. Slocum
Satevo	5th Cavalry	Colonel Wilber E. Wilder
San Borja	11th Cavalry	Colonel James Lockett

Before proceeding to the districts assigned them, the cavalry regiments were busy in repairing the wear and tear of the campaign they had just finished. In the evenings the officers hunted up old friends they had not seen for years, in some cases not since West Point days. I experienced real joy in meeting the men of Troop "G" 11th Cavalry. I organized this troop in the spring of 1901 and commanded it until June, 1910. We campaigned together in the Philippines and later in Cuba. We were together through cholera and yellow fever epidemics, through fair weather and foul. My wife knew every man in the troop, my son "served" in the troop from the time he was five years old until he was fourteen. The old timers taught him to shoot, ride, box, wrestle and swear, and convinced him that the life of the soldier was the only life. Needless to say that these men with whom I had served around the world were very close to my heart, so when the mess sergeant hunted me up and said: "Sir, the men would be honored if the Major would eat dinner with them tomorrow," I accepted with much enthusiasm.

Now an invitation to dinner, as we were situated at San Antonio, meant beans, bacon, coffee and war bread, so what was my surprise to find that I was served with a plump chicken, most delectably prepared. I asked, "Where did you get this chicken, Sergeant?" He made some evasive answer, so I had sense enough not to pursue the subject. Of course some "rustler" had been detailed to rob a hen roost for the Major's dinner.

That was a touch of the old army which then was fast giving way to the machine-like service of to-day. Major General Harbord expresses what I felt in the following words:

The sun had already set on the Winning of the West. The charm of an army life that the present generation can never know, but which those of us who lived it can never forget, was fast giving way to change. Talleyrand said that only those who had lived in France in the years just before the revolution could know the real sweetness of life. So, too, it might be said of those Army days before the Spanish-American War, when regiments were regiments, and the army, remote from civilization, depended upon itself and its own social resources. Soldiers spent a lifetime in a single unit. Children were born and grew to adolescence following the fortunes of the old regiment. Chivalry, courtesy, hospitality and consideration were characteristics of that old army.

During the evening of May 4th, before all of the regiments had moved to their "Districts," General Pershing received a report that Julio Acosta and Cruz Dominiguez, two Villista leaders, were in the vicinity of Cusi (Cusihuiriachic), with 120 men, threatening that town and the small Carranzista force in the vicinity. The people of Cusi sent two representatives to San Antonio requesting of General Pershing protection for their town. As these bandit leaders had previously given it out that they had 1,000 men, and that they intended to attack the American camp at San Antonio, and had already frightened the inhabitants in that district by their attitude, the time was opportune to teach them a lesson.

Accordingly, Major Howze with six troops and the Machine Gun Platoon of the 11th Cavalry, numbering 14 officers and 319 enlisted men, was dispatched to Cusi with instructions to move against this band as circumstances might indicate. Howze reached Cusi about midnight May 4th, and learned that the hostile band was then in camp at Ojos Azules. After procuring guides he started in that direction, arriving at Ojos Azules shortly after daylight. His arrival and the attack that followed were almost a complete surprise, resulting in the total rout of the band, whose losses were 61 killed, as ascertained later, and a large number of wounded, without the loss of a single American soldier. Major Howze's report of the fight is as follows:

General Pershing:
We made an all night march to Ojos Azules, distance 36 miles. Reached here at 5:45 A.M., unfortunately one-half hour after daylight. We surprised Julio Acosta, Cruz Dominiguez and Antonio Angel; and jumped them. Had a running fight for two hours. Drove their band into the hills between here and Carichic. Killed 42 (later verification increased the number to close to 80) verified by officers, captured several and some 50 or 75 horses and mules. It is believed we killed Angel though identification not complete. We rescued a Carranzista Lieutenant and four soldiers just before they were to be shot. We followed the enemy, consisting of about 140, until our horses were wholly exhausted, but the chase did not stop until the enemy left unhit had been broken up entirely. In fact, those who escaped us did so as individuals.
Our approach was discovered by the Villista's herd guard, which fired at our Indians (Apache scouts), and also alarmed the sleeping enemy who ran pell-mell, half dressed, firing at us in their flight. The remarkable part is, although the clothing of several of our men was hit, not a single man was wounded, thanks to the utter surprise and confusion of the enemy. We lost three or four horses. I had to wait two hours at Cusihuiriachic for guides, hence my inability to get here earlier than 5:45 A.M., to do which we had to ride as hard as our horses could go. It is needless to say that the officers and men behaved as would be expected. I intend to rest here.

Howze,
Major 11th Cavalry.

Ojos Azules, Mexico,
May 5, 1916.

In commenting on this action General Pershing stated:

Major Howze's action showed enterprise and good judgment and resulted in the destruction and disintegration of Acosta's band. Since that time Acosta has never been able to assemble more than 20 men, and he has kept his band and himself hidden in the mountains back of Guerrero, where he is reported at the present time (October 7, 1916).

This cavalry fight was written up by First Lieutenant S. M. Williams 11th Cavalry (Now Major, Quartermaster Corps, U. S. Army), and published in the *U. S. Cavalry Journal*, January issue, 1917. I quote from this article as follows:

At 8:15 P.M. the provisional squadron moved out in the following order: Detachment of 20 Apache Indians, First Lieutenant James A. Shannon, 11th Cavalry, commanding; Troop "A", First Lieutenant A. M. Graham and Second Lieutenant Kenneth P. Lord; Troop "C", First Lieutenant C. McH. Eby; Troop "D", First Lieutenant John A. Pearson; Troop "E", First Lieutenant Emil P. Laurson and Second Lieutenant Stafford LeR. Irwin; Troop "F", Captain Guy Cushman; Troop "G", Captain William Renziehausen; Machine Gun Troop, First Lieutenant Carl H. Muller; Adjutant and Quartermaster, Frist Lieutenant S. M. Williams; Surgeon, Captain George B. Lake; Second Lieutenant Joseph W. Viner, assistant to the Quartermaster, in charge of the pack train.

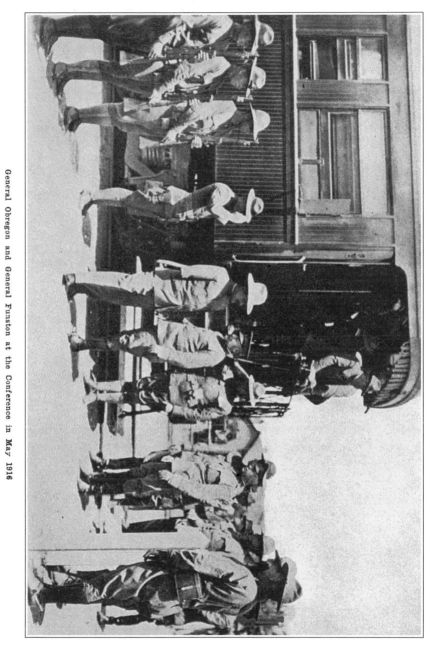

General Obregon and General Funston at the Conference in May 1916

It was an exceedingly dark night, but the road was good and the troops arrived within one mile of Cusihuiriachic about midnight. Here the Carranzista force was encountered, in a more or less intoxicated condition, and from them an account of the Villistas and of the day's battle was obtained. It appears that they fought desperately, all day, with an hour off for luncheon, and had both retired in good order at nightfall, casualties zero for both sides.

Inasmuch as the Villistas had moved back to the Ojos Azules Ranch, the location of which was not known, especially in view of the darkness, there was a delay of nearly three hours here while guides were obtained from Cusihuiriachic. The Carranza force flatly refused to furnish any guides. At 3:00 o'clock the squadron started out again, and moving at a fast trot a greater part of the time, and without any halts, arrived in sight of the Ojos Azules Ranch at about 6:00 A.M., distance 20 miles. The advance guard, which included the Indian scouts, observing the great activity at the ranch, took up a fast gallop and when within a thousand yards of the ranch deployed and advanced as skirmishers.

Major Howze had previously given orders for the attack, the general plan being for the leading troop to push ahead, while the troops in rear went alternately to the right and left to cut off the enemy's retreat, the plan being based on the well established fact that the Mexicans will not stand where their line of retreat is endangered. Unfortunately a barbed wire range fence on the right of the road prevented the rapid accomplishment of this formation, and resulted in a different deployment at the instances of the troop commanders themselves.

The Mexicans had sent the greater part of their horses some distance to the south of the ranch for grazing, and they now swarmed out of the ranch, and fled up the slopes of the hills to the southwest, a few mounted, but the greater part on foot. A force of about 30 remained on top of one of the ranch buildings and poured a heavy, but inaccurate fire on our leading troops, while another force was in position behind a stone wall on a hilltop on our left flank.

As soon as the advance guard took up the gallop, the troops in rear followed their example, and when firing commenced the gait was increased to the extended gallop. Troop "A", the leading troop, dashed through the ranch under fire from the men on the roof top, and catching up with the last of the Mexicans, commenced a pistol fight which lasted for several minutes and resulted in the killing of five or six of the enemy. The formation of the attack was with the troop in column of fours, deployment being impossible under the circumstances.

After advancing about 300 yards, a deep arroyo was struck, causing a delay in the pursuit. By that time Troop "C" had come up on the right and was immediately deployed in the arroyo, fire being opened on the retreating Mexicans at about 500 yards. Troops "D" and "E" had gone to the left, in the meantime, occupying a shallow ditch which ran south from the ranch. Troop "F" a little later came up on the left of Troop "A", while Troop "G" was held in reserve. The Machine Gun Troop was still far in rear, having lost much distance due to the exhaustion of the pack animals and inability to keep up with the troops at a gallop. All troops opened fire, the three left troops being under fire from the party on the hill. After five minutes firing, the troops were mounted again and the pursuit resumed. Troop "E" moved directly in pursuit while the other troops moved around the flanks of the hill.

Troop "A" moving around the right of the hill kept up the pursuit for several miles, capturing several of the enemy, while the troops that went around the south of the hill, catching the dismounted men coming down the reverse slope, killed quite a few of them.

The Machine Gun Troop got into action late and was able to fire at extreme ranges only.

By about 9:30 all of the troops had abandoned the pursuit and had returned to the ranch, which was searched for any concealed Villistas, resulting in the finding of a few rifles and antiquated pistols, which were destroyed. The men found on the ranch were lined up, but, as it was impossible to differentiate between the pacificos and the enemy, they were finally all released. Among these men were four Carranzista prisoners who, it appeared, were to have been executed that morning, and who were, therefore, overjoyed at their escape, one even offering personally to execute the Villista prisoners if some one would lend him a pistol, a kindly offer which was, however, refused.

This terminated the fight at Ojos Azules, which though of small importance was nevertheless a very typical cavalry action on a small scale, characterized by a good deal of mounted work, and showing the mobility of the cavalry to the best advantage. The rapid deployment of the troops from column made a very pretty sight, and the first part of the action at least gave some idea of the effectiveness of the automatic pistol in mounted work.

Under the circumstances it was remarkable that there were no casualties on our side. Although the clothing of several of our men was hit, not a single man was wounded. We lost four horses. The official report showed that the Villistas lost 44 killed, while it was impossible to learn anything about the number wounded, though it must have been relatively large.

As First Sergeant Chicken of the Apache scouts said, when asked for his opinion, "Huli! Damn fine fight!"

Lieutenant Graham described this fight to the author a few days later. He told of leading his men through the ranch at top speed, jumping a gate which barred his way, overtaking the fleeing Mexicans, placing a pistol muzzle under a man's arm and literally blowing him out of the saddle. The horses of the American cavalry had made an all night march and for the last half mile had traveled at top speed, carrying heavy loads, so it is no wonder many of the Mexicans got away.

Later reports from native sources indicated that 61 Mexicans were killed in this fight. In justice to the Machine Gun Troop it should be explained that it was demonstrated very conclusively on this trip to Ojos Azules, and in fact during the entire course of this Expedition that mules assigned to the Machine Gun Troops were, almost without exception, unsuited for arduous cavalry service. Mules should be at least 15 hands high and weigh about 1,000 pounds. The ammunition mules, when loaded, carried a load of about 312 pounds, and the gun mules 292 pounds. To put these loads on mules standing 14 hands and weighing about 800 pounds simply means that the mules cannot keep up with cavalry in a hurry. The author, knowing the mules of the machine gun units were overloaded, took no machine guns with him on his drive to Parral. In the light of these experiences machine gun units of our army are now (1932) equipped with horses instead of mules, the pack saddles are lighter and better, and the loads not so heavy.

Major Howze remained in the vicinity of Ojos Azules until the 9th of May, scouting the country in a vain search for Villistas. He returned to San Antonio at 6:00 A. M. May 10th, having made an all night march from L'Alamo.

During the first week in May the regiments concerned in the order organizing districts had reached their designated localities, and the work of scouring the country and pursuing individual bands had begun. Meanwhile the relations between the two Governments became very tense and various Carranzista officials began to circulate rumors of war, and to announce that the Americans were to be driven out. On May 9th instructions were received from the Department Commander to withdraw the command to Dublan.

Although no information through local sources had reached General Pershing indicating any hostile movement at that time toward our line, the instructions received stated that the necessity for concentration was considered imperative. General Pershing having established his headquarters at Lake Itascate, about 34 miles north of San Antonio, informed the Department Commander that the situation did not seem to demand immediate withdrawal to Dublan, whereupon orders were received by General Pershing directing him to hold the troops where they were, and to make such tactical dispositions in the vicinity of Namiquipa as might seem desirable.

This change necessitated the abandonment of our advance stations, and left the command occupying the original line of communications with Namiquipa as the southern camp. Our cavalry troops covered the front, with supports at San Geronimo and Providencia. As our troops vacated territory, the de facto troops became more aggressive, patrols from both sides frequently meeting, and only by the exercise of great discretion and forbearance on the part of our officers were clashes avoided. In spite of the Carranzista interference our troops along the line were occupied in the pursuit of small bands of Villistas, and in running down reports of threatening movements of de facto troops.

Chapter XXXI

Behind the Scenes With the Politicians

The time has now come when I must take the reader behind the scenes and let him see how the politicians influenced General Pershing's campaign. It is well to remember that this was a presidential year, that the election was but a few months off, and that the war cry of the Democratic party was to be that their president had kept us out of war.

The following official letters have a bearing on this case:

The Adjutant General to Generals Scott and Funston.
(Telegram)
War Department,
Washington, April 26, 1916.

You will meet General Obregon and discuss with him the future military operation of our forces in Mexico on the following basis: The Government of the United States earnestly desires to avoid anything which has the appearance of intervention in the domestic affairs of the Republic of Mexico. It desires to cooperate with the de facto Government of that Republic, and its pursuit of the bandit Villa and his bands is for the sole purpose of removing a menace to the common security and the friendly relations of the two Republics. So long as he remains at large and is able to mislead numbers of his fellow citizens into attacks like that at Columbus, the danger exists of American public opinion being irritated to the point of requiring general intervention. For, of course, depredations on American soil and the loss of lives of American citizens cannot be tolerated, and one other such experience would make it difficult to restrain public opinion here. The Government of the United States realizes that the de facto Government of the Republic of Mexico is equally anxious to avoid occasions of conflict and misunderstanding. It likewise realizes that public opinion in the Republic of Mexico must be taken into consideration. It, therefore, has instructed its military commanders to observe the most considerate sense of all the proprieties, to recognize in every way the dignity of the Republic of Mexico and its de facto Government, and to proceed with its operations in harmonious cooperation with the military forces of Mexico towards an object which is, of course, of common concern and of even greater importance to the Government of Mexico than to that of the United States, since the major portion of the depredations and lawlessness committed by the bandit Villa is upon Mexican soil. Suggest to General Obregon that the presence of American troops in Mexico, if welcomed by Mexican authorities, can have no other appearance than that of friendly cooperation of two governments to suppress a cause of irritation to their common peace and their friendly relations. The American military commanders will respond instantly to all invitations for cooperation with forces of the Mexican Government. The Mexican Government has the means of locating more or less definitely the present whereabouts of Villa. Upon that fact being determined American military commanders will be glad to aid Mexican commanders in surrounding and capturing him and by such cordial cooperation the permanent friendly relations of the two Governments will be demonstrated to their respective peoples. If it be deemed better American

196

troops can be detained in the northern part of the State of Chihuahua while the forces of the Mexican Government drive Villa and his associates towards the north, in this way enabling the American troops to aid in his ultimate capture. The Government of the United States has no pride involved in who makes the capture, and its only interest is that it should be done expeditiously so that American troops can be withdrawn and the peace of the borders assured. If General Obregon shows a spirit of cooperation, it should be met fully and generously.

If, on the other hand, his attitude should be a peremptory command for the immediate withdrawal of the American troops across the border, General Scott and General Funston should say that that question is a diplomatic question and should be worked out through the agency of the respective Departments of Foreign Affairs of the two Republics. Generals Scott and Funston will, of course, treat with General Obregon on the basis of high military representatives of their respective Governments and emphasize the friendly attitude of the Government of the United States toward the Government and people of Mexico, but will insist that, so long as the possibility of further depredations by Villa exists, the withdrawal of American troops would increase the dangers and in any event be very difficult. It is possible that General Obregon will meet you with definitely stated objects on which alone he is authorized by the de facto Government to confer with you. If so, the limitations thus imposed on the conference may result in embarrassment in reaching a thoroughly satisfactory conclusion. It is therefore, desired that, without interfering with or delaying your conference with him, you advise the Secretary of War and the Secretary of State at once on the bases presented by General Obregon for negotiations. This will enable further instructions to be promptly communicated to you. Meanwhile, in your conference, you will proceed with full powers to discuss and agree upon all points raised by either of the conferees which relate purely to the military situation including questions of lines of supply and use of railways. All doubtful matters, and all matters which evidently concern the Department of State, will be referred by you to Washington for instructions. It is assumed that General Obregon may follow this course with his own Government in respect of matters on which he is not authorized to confer.

McCain.

Generals Scott and Funston to the Secretary of War.
(Telegram)
El Paso, Texas, April 30, 1916.

We received General Obregon and party on their official call this morning with every courtesy and arranged for conference this afternoon. Mexicans made quite a point of having conference in Juarez, which request was acceded to at once. We gave the views of the Department as laid down in instructions and endeavored to get full cooperation and use of railway. The conference was most amicable throughout but Mexicans contending always for immediate withdrawal of troops from Mexico, saying that Villa is dead, or, if alive, innocuous. Two hundred of his followers killed, remainder dispersed, and there is no one now to seek for. Obregon claims that continued presence of American troops in Mexico makes his task most difficult, as no satisfactory explanation can be made to Mexican people. He made no threats. He would not discuss cooperation as he several times put aside politely requests for cooperation and use of railway, declining to discuss anything but withdrawal of troops. Conference lasted two hours with deadlock imminent, when conference was amicably broken off, saying the Mexican position would be telegraphed our Government. Conference will be resumed on receipt of reply. General Funston and I think our approved proposition should be adhered to, viz: To hold our present position until our Government is satisfied that Villa is killed or captured, under no circumstances to retire north of Casas Grandes, Chihuahua, until this is accomplished. Very few Mexicans are in Santa Maria and Casas Grandes valleys and should be controllable if desire is sincere. We warned Obregon of collection of bandits near Victoria to invade lower Rio Grande river section of United States, which might bring on a condition in Tamaulipas similar to that now in Chihuahua. Obregon promised to investigate. Nothing has been given out to the press. Request early reply. Copy sent Secretary of State.

Scott
Funston.

This conference lasted until the 11th of May, when it was dissolved with no decision. The Mexicans would discuss nothing but withdrawal of American troops stating that Villa was dead, his forces dispersed and the American border safe from further Mexican violation. In the midst of these protestations on the part of Obregon that our border was safe, 75 armed Mexicans raided Glen Springs, Texas, killing three American soldiers of Troop "A," 14th Cavalry, and a boy nine years old; and later raided Boquillas, Texas, capturing and carrying off M. J. Deemer and L. Coy, American citizens. At the same time our secret service had positive information that Carranza and his generals were plotting to throw a large armed force between Pershing's command and the border, hoping to cut the American line of communications and destroy the entire American force. The Mexicans were encouraged in this by German and Austrian agents.

Under date of May 8th, Scott and Funston reported to Washington:

We feel that the whole proposition is redolent with bad faith, that Mexicans are convinced that they are not able to carry out agreement even if ratified and they desire to keep the United States troops quiet until Mexican troops are in position to drive them out of Mexico by force.

We expect many attacks along the whole border similar to latest attack in Big Ben Rio Grande (Glen Springs).

Our line is thin and weak everywhere and inadequate to protect border anywhere if attacked in force.

There are no adequate reserves. There are many calls for help on border which cannot be given, and we think the border should at once be supported by at least 150,000 additional troops.

We have struggled for a different result with all our intelligence, patience and courtesy, hoping against hope for a peaceful solution but are now convinced that such solution can no longer be hoped for.

In order to give additional protection to border points exposed to raids it is recommended that militia of Texas, New Mexico and Arizona be called out at once, final action as to that of other states to be deferred until receipt by us of Obregon's proposal.

As a result of this report organizations of the militia and National Guard of the States of Arizona, New Mexico and Texas were called into service of the United States on May 9, 1916, and directed to proceed from rendezvous direct to their border stations. This movement of troops gave the Mexicans cause for thought and tempered somewhat their enthusiasm for war with the United States, but not to any great extent, for early in June it was well known by our military and civil authorities that de la Rosa, well known leader of border raids, was recruiting in Monterey; that recruits were being concentrated near San Ignacio, 60 miles below Laredo; and that they openly asserted they were going to rob and burn border towns in Texas, and massacre Americans.

This Luis de la Rosa not only recruited his men under sanction of the de facto Government, but was furnished with a special car on which to leave Monterey. The Austrian consul at Monterey, Robert Bremer, openly advocated this anti-American demonstration in Monterey, and posted large notices in his windows inviting all good Mexicans to join in demonstrations.

This was the condition along our border early in June, when on the 19th of June occurred the outrage at Mazatlan mentioned in the early pages of this book. Why did not Mexico fulfill her threats to crush The Mexican Punitive Expedition, invade the United States and not stop "Until they watered their horses in the Potomac?" The answer is simple. Our War Department ordered about 150,000 National Guard troops into the service of the United States for duty along the Mexican border, and when Mexico saw this mass of soldiery, well armed and equipped, ready and eager for war, she had a change of heart and decided to defer the invasion, etc.

During these months of May and June the United States would have been fully justified in declaring war on Mexico. That we failed to do so was a fatal error, for our continued acceptance of Mexican abuse not only warranted Mexican contempt but weakened our prestige abroad, and above all we lost the excuse for organizing an army of half a million men with which to bring Mexico to her senses and at the same time impress upon Germany the danger of her underseas campaign against our commerce, for with such a force trained in war, Germany would have seen the futility of forcing us into the war on the side of the allies, and we should have been spared all that war has cost us up to date and for the generations to come.

(The reader is referred to Chapter **XXXV**, which describes the mobilization of the National Guard for Border Service)

Chapter XXXII

The Killing of Cardenas and Cervantes

While the Obregon-Scott-Funston conferences were going on at El Paso and Juarez, the de facto Government of Mexico was secretly conspiring to destroy Pershing's command. The Mexicans knew the American soldier's orders forbade him to do anything which the Mexicans could, by any stretch of the imagination, construe as an overt act, thus enabling them to concentrate troops at tactically and strategically advantageous points, to choose their own time and to strike at a moment most advantageous to them. Of course if attacked Pershing was to defend himself. But the best way for an army to defend itself is to attack first. However, General Pershing was not frightened by these unfair conditions his President insisted upon. He continued to comb the country for Villistas, occasionally getting one of their prominent leaders. The following is a stirring account of the death of Colonel, sometimes called General, Cardenas, an important member of Villa's staff.

Early in May several troops of cavalry were sent out in an effort to locate and capture Julio Cardenas, who was called a General and was Captain of the Doradoes or bodyguard of Villa.

Lieutenant G. S. Patton, Jr., 10th Cavalry, acting Aide de Camp to General Pershing, was attached to one of these troops, Troop "H," 11th Cavalry, Captain Eben Swift, commanding. This troop marched from Lake Itascate, east toward Rubio, and then north to a small ranch called San Miguelito where Cardenas' wife and mother were said to live. Just before reaching this place, the troop met a detachment of the 16th Infantry which had come up from San Antonio, Mexico, on a similar errand, but instituted solely on the authority of the regimental commander. They told the troop commander that in the early morning they had surrounded the house at San Miguelito, but before the envelopment was completed several armed Mexicans galloped from the house and escaped to the hills to the west.

Troop "H" continued its march and surrounded the house, but as was expected found nothing. The command camped there, and shortly after midnight marched west, combing the hills but finding nothing.

During the hours spent at the ranch Lieutenant Patton familiarized himself with the lay of the land, and the location of the gates in the corrals surrounding the house.

About a week later, on May 14th, the shortage of corn became acute, so General Pershing directed Lieutenant Patton to take three Dodge cars, one corporal and 6 privates of the 16th Infantry, and an interpreter, Mr. W. Lunt, and buy corn from some haciendas lying to the east of Lake Itascate. The start was made from the camp at the lake. The first ranch visited was called Las Cayotes and the second Rubio. At each of these some corn was contracted for, but not as much as was needed, so the party went on to a village called by the ubiquitous name of Las Cienegas. Lieutenant Patton knew that an uncle of Cardenas lived at this village, so decided to surround it and combine business with pleasure, so to speak. This was done, but only corn was secured.

San Miguelito was some six or eight miles farther north, but something in the confusion of the uncle led Lieutenant Patton to suspect Cardenas might be home, so he decided to investigate. In doing this a certain amount of caution seemed advisable, as a recent report had credited Cardenas with having a band of some 20 men.

A hill about a mile from the house defiladed the road to that point, so before topping the rise the cars halted and the following plan was explained by Patton. The house, which was fairly large, with a battle-mented roof, was to the east side of the road. It was built around a court with its single large door facing east. This was the only place from which a horseman could emerge, but there were some windows high on the west wall from which a man could drop.

In view of the fact that quite a number of the enemy might be encountered, it seemed wise to hold a majority of the party in a unit as a rallying point in case of necessity. It was therefore ordered that the leading car with Patton, Lunt, one soldier and the driver should pass the house and stop at the northwest corner. The soldier and the driver were to remain at the car and cover the west and north sides, while Patton and Lunt went around the north side to the front.

The second and third cars were to stop at the southwest corner, where six men were to remain covering the west and south sides, while two went around the south side to meet Patton in front of the east face.

The corporal was left with the group at the cars and all were to assemble there if a serious fight became necessary.

Due to his familiarity with the corrals and outbuildings gained in his former visit, Patton outstripped both Lunt and the soldiers and came to the east face well ahead of them. When he got there, he saw an old man and a boy skinning a steer in front of the gate. A moment later three horsemen emerged, armed with rifles and pistols and, on seeing Patton, wheeled and dashed toward the southeast corner, but on reaching it turned north again having seen the soldiers coming along the south face of the hacienda.

As orders in the Mexican Punitive Expedition prohibited firing until hostile identification was assured, Patton held his fire. When the Mexicans turned north they opened fire on Patton and Lunt who had joined him. Patton returned the fire with his pistol and knocked down one man, who then crawled in through the gate. It may be well to state here that at the time of this action Patton was one of the crack pistol shots of the cavalry service.

Both sides stopped to reload. At this moment the soldiers rounded the southeast corner and opened fire along the east face of the house. As Patton and Lunt were in the line of fire, they stepped around the northeast corner where Patton reloaded his revolver. As he completed doing this, the two remaining Mexicans galloped by at a range of ten paces firing at Lunt and Patton, missing both, a sad exhibition of marksmanship. Patton returned the fire killing the horse of the nearest Mexican, which fell on the man. Impelled by notions of chivalry, Patton did not fire on the Mexican until he had freed himself of the horse and rose to fire, then Patton killed him with a shot under the left arm.

When the second Mexican fell, the third swerved to his right and galloped to the east. Patton then opened fire on him and was joined in it by the two soldiers. Mr. Lunt, though he stayed beside the Lieutenant, was unarmed, so he could not fire. The third Mexican was killed. At this moment shooting was heard at the southwest corner where the corporal and three men were posted, and a man was seen running along the wall to the south. All fired at him and he, dropping behind the wall, returned the fire. Then he stopped shooting. Upon being approached he held up his left hand in apparent token of surrender, but when the soldiers were within five or six yards he suddenly drew his pistol with his right hand and fired one shot, then he died. On examination this man proved to have been hit but once, through the left forearm and chest with the 45 pistol carried by Patton. He was the first shot off his horse and was later identified as Cardenas.

The second man, also killed by Patton, was identified as Juan Gaza, a private. The third killed by the combined efforts of the Lieutenant and the two soldiers was said to be a captain.

During all of this fighting and flying bullets the old man and the boy kept skinning the steer. It speaks well for the discipline of the soldiers that these two workers were not fired on.

Now that all external enemies were accounted for Patton decided to climb to the roof of the building as he was uncertain as to whether or not there were more enemies within. It would have been the height of folly for the young commander to have ignored the possibility of a hostile fire coming from the fortified roof. A dead tree was placed against the wall and Patton was the first to mount. As he stepped on the dirt roof, he went through to his arm pits but managed to wriggle out before he could lose a leg from a machete blow. Two soldiers were now placed on the roof so as to command the court. Mr. Lunt having selected a rifle from one of the dead Mexicans accompanied Patton to the front of the house. Placing the old man and the boy in front of them, they forced the gate open and entered the court. To their great relief nobody was found in the hacienda but women and children.

As it was necessary to identify the dead Mexicans, they were lashed to the hoods of the three cars and the party started back. The road led through the town of Rubio, known to be filled with Villa sympathizers, so the telephone line from San Miguelito to Rubio was cut. The passage through Rubio was made without a fight, though the inhabitants were much excited by the sight of the dead. Camp was reached without further incident.

About this time, Candelario Cervantes, with 25 Villistas, boldly returned to the vicinity of Namiquipa and began to prey upon the peaceful inhabitants. Detachments were kept constantly in the field in his pursuit, following up all reports that sounded credible.

On May 25th a detachment under Lance Corporal Davis Marksbury consisting of 8 men of the Machine Gun Platoon, 17th Infantry, two men of the Corps of Engineers and one man of the Quartermaster Corps from Cruces, happened to be about six miles south of there, sketching roads and hunting cattle, when they were attacked by a party of 9 Villistas. Corporal Marksbury was killed and three men wounded. The Villistas lost two killed who, upon proper identification, turned out to be "Colonel" Candelario Cervantes and Jose Bencome. General Pershing stated: "Especial credit is due Private George D. Huelett, 17th Infantry, for success in this small skirmish, who killed both these bandits as they rode by firing at him. The killing of Candelario Cervantes was particularly fortunate as, next to Villa himself, he was the most able and the most desperate of Villa's band."

This man Cervantes was in the Columbus raid so here was "another scalp for Custer."

Word of this action was received by the commanding officer, 11th Cavalry, camped at Cruces, and within five minutes Captain Guy Cushman with Troop "F," 11th Cavalry, 40 men of the 13th Cavalry, under Lieutenant B. T. Merchant of that regiment, Captain Charles G. Lawrence, 17th Infantry, with a detachment of the Machine Gun Company, were in the saddle headed for the mouth of Alamia Canyon where they arrived at 11 A. M., just one hour out of camp. Here Cushman found the little squad of infantrymen retiring down the canyon in good order. Cushman advanced up the canyon about a mile when the trail forked, one branch turning to the right in a southeasterly direction and the left hand trail in a northeasterly direction. Lieutenant S. M. Williams, 11th Cavalry, took the trail to the right with the advance guard, while Lieutenant Merchant with the detachment of the 13th Cavalry turned left. Lieutenant Merchant's command was almost immediately fired upon, and had three horses and one mule wounded. This action took place in a narrow canyon, and at no time was the enemy seen. The fire came from the high and palisaded bluff about one thousand feet above the trail. Cushman pursued the bandits about three miles. The enemy scattered in all directions making it impossible to follow their trail, so the command returned to Cruces at five P. M.

Other detachments were sent out from Cruces by the commanding officer of the 11th Cavalry in the hope of rounding up this band, but as they had scattered and assumed the role of peaceful peons the results were a blank, except in the case of Major John M. Jenkins who ran into the bandits just about sundown on the 26th, at a place called Ortega, and in an exchange of shots knocked down two of the bandits. Darkness prevented giving chase, and the next day there was no trail to follow.

The following account is given by Major Alexander P. Withers, who at the time of the event was a Sergeant, Hospital Corps.

On May 25th (1916) I was on duty at Cruces. A few days prior to this date some men of the 17th Infantry had discovered a deserted ranch in the mountains with hogs in a semi-wild state nearby.

On this morning a hunting party composed of about 12 men, mostly from the Machine Gun Platoon 17th Infantry, left Cruces with the intention of shooting some of these hogs. Most of the party rode in an escort wagon driven by a machine gun soldier nicknamed "Barney Oldfield." Some of the party were mounted.

It was sometime before noon on the 25th when a Signal Corps sergeant, who had been a member of the hunting party, galloped into camp at Cruces with the news that the hunting party had been ambushed in the mountains at Alamia Canyon and would be killed unless help was immediately sent. The sergeant had in some manner slipped through the Mexicans who had the hunting party completely surrounded.

I was standing near Lieutenant Roderick Dew, who was acting as Intelligence Officer, when the Signal Corps sergeant rushed into camp. The Lieutenant and I saddled and started for the mountains immediately. As we left the 17th Infantrymen present were being hastily turned out as a mounted detachment by Captain Lawrence. Soon after we reached the mountains (at least 5 miles from camp) we heard firing. We had difficulty in determining the proper direction to take. When we finally arrived on the scene of the ambush near Alamia Canyon the Mexicans were withdrawing—no doubt they had observed the approach of the mounted infantry or the 11th and 13th Cavalrymen who had also hurried to the rescue. Lieutenant Dew and I had barely an opportunity to take some long shots at the fleeing enemy.

I remained with Lieutenant Dew while he searched the dead Mexicans for papers. The wounded and dead of the hunting party we carried to the mouth of the canyon and placed in an escort wagon which had been brought from camp.

Lieutenant Dew and I rode slowly beside the wagon of "Barney Oldfield" who had left his wagon and mules at the ranch house at the mouth of Alamia Canyon. The ambush had occurred approximately one mile farther into the mountains reached by a trail impassable by wagon.

At this time, as I recall, all the hunting party as well as the rescue party were in advance of us, headed for Cruces. The three of us were alone. We had barely left the ranch house when Lieutenant Dew signalled for us to stop. He had been busily studying the papers taken from the dead Mexicans, and when he halted us I sensed what was to follow. Lieutenant Dew turned to me: "We must have the bodies of those dead Mexicans for identification—one of them is Cervantes—you go get them."

With no little apprehension I proceeded along the rough mountain trail on my assigned mission. I considered my job far from pleasant. I was one mounted man directed to go back into mountains that had a most unfriendly look, by a difficult trail and get two bodies. The enemy had scattered when the relieving force from Cruces had been sighted. However our troops had now withdrawn and one lone American in a mountain defile encumbered with two dead bodies would make easy pickings for some concealed bandit.

Finally I arrived at the scene of the ambush. The two dead Mexicans with their two dead horses lay where they had fallen. I hurriedly dismounted and grabbed one of the bandits by a leg and pulled him over to a position opposite the other body. I secured a buckskin thong from one of the Mexican saddles and securely tied one leg of each bandit together as if for a three legged race. I then uncoiled a braided lariat from the other Mexican saddle and fastened it to the united legs of the two bandits and then ran the lariat to the front of my saddle and around the breast of my horse.

I mounted and started dragging the bodies down the rough trail toward the place where I had left Lieutenant Dew and Barney. I could easily imagine a hidden Mexican behind every bush and rock. At any moment I expected to hear a shot. My progress was slow in spite of my hurry. At one point the descent was so steep that my two dead companions rolled ahead of me down the slope.

Suddenly I made out a denim clad figure in the distance ahead. Hastily spurring my horse off the path I rode him to a bush and tied him. Taking my rifle from the saddle I ran with all speed to a thick clump of bushes 100 yards away, where I proposed to conceal myself and make my last stand. I crouched down among the bushes in a position offering a maximum steadiness in firing position and waited developments.

The man who had caused me to take up this position reappeared, much closer now. He was carrying a rifle. I withheld my fire intending to let him approach close enough so that there would be no danger of a miss. When I felt certain of a bull's-eye I lined up my sights and took up my trigger slack. At this instant my sixth sense told me there was something familiar about the walk of the approaching figure. I let up on the trigger and looked again, recognizing Barney Oldfield.

Lieutenant Dew being worried because of the time I had been absent had sent Barney up the trail on foot to see what had happened to me.

Together we dragged the bodies the remainder of the way to where Lieutenant Dew was waiting with the wagon. Loading the bodies into the wagon we proceeded to Cruces.

The bodies were so bruised from the trip over the mountain trail behind my horse that it was decided to bury them at Cruces after Lieutenant Dew had made what he regarded as positive identifications.

The papers Lieutenant Dew had taken, with a report, were sent to Expedition Headquarters at Colonia Dublan. Upon receipt of these papers and report headquarters telegraphed for the body to be sent immediately to Dublan via truck for identification there. It appears that Expedition Headquarters were certain from intelligence information in their possession that Cervantes was many miles from Cruces. The Expedition Intelligence Officer evidently felt certain that Lieutenant Dew had made an error in identification.

When the body reached Dublan a telegram very promptly reached Cruces demanding an explanation for the bruised condition of Cervantes body.

Norman Jay Boots, 2nd Lieutenant, 10th Cavalry, writes as follows:

General Gutierrez was believed by some of us to have been second in command to General Villa when the Mexicans raided Columbus, New Mexico.[*]

On their retirement South, following that raid, it seems that General Gutierrez picked up a Mexican's wife and baby and carried them to a small village on the Santa Maria River, about thirty miles northwest of Namiquipa. The husband subsequently located them and came in one day to General Pershing to advise him that General Gutierrez was secluded in this village, which I understood was the town where Pancho Villa was born. I was detailed to take my platoon and, with the husband as guide, attempt to capture General Gutierrez and bring him back to General Pershing. This happened sometime in April, 1916. We rode all day and arrived late in the afternoon on top of a mountain overlooking the village, which was stretched out for a mile along the north bank of the Santa Maria River.

From the mountain top, the husband indicated the next to the last house as the abode of General Gutierrez. I couldn't persuade the husband to go further with me as he stated that the General had a couple of rifles and was very clever in their use. I left the platoon on top of the mountain, and taking my orderly with me, descended the mountain side and inquired of various houses for edibles which I knew they did not have. Finally, I arrived at the house indicated to me. When I dismounted and pushed open the door, I found an old man and woman, apparently the permanent residents, together with a rather attractive young Mexican woman and an infant about two years old, but no signs of the General.

There was a corn field and the river behind the house, and I figured possibly the General might be out in the corn field. I therefore went around to the rear of the house overlooking the corn field, when a man sprang up and started to run through the corn to the river. I ran after him. We both crossed the river which was breast deep. As we proceeded, I took an occasional shot at him. My platoon, meanwhile, had seen or heard the excitement, and came galloping in and started to do a little shooting of their own.

---

[*] Author's Note: Pershing never considered Gutierrez as Villa's second in command. As to his being a Carranzista at one time, that is probably so, as these Mexican generals changed their politics and their flag with the ease and frequency of a Chinese war lord.

About this time both General Gutierrez and I were on the other side of the river and unhappily I was between the fire of my troops and the General. However, finally one of the bullets grazed the General's head and I ran up and jumped on him. His two rifles were cached about fifty feet from where he had fallen, and we also found two or three pairs of shoes and a couple of bolts of silk that he had taken from one of the stores in Columbus, N. M. I presumed this was the evidence which later convicted him. In any case, I turned him over to General Pershing and was informed later he had been sentenced to life imprisonment at Deming, N. M.

If he is still in prison I think he has been there long enough, possibly too long. Couldn't we get him out? He was a tall, well built man, and seemed to have plenty of courage. The husband was undersized, and certainly lacking in courage.

The last I saw of the husband was on my return to the house after calling on the general. I had a view of him leading a horse about a mile from us proceeding north with his wife and baby mounted up. I almost turned the General loose again.

Chapter XXXIII

The Fight at Carrizal

Accompanied by his chief of staff and one aide, General Pershing left Namiquipa for a conference at Dublan with General Gabriel Gavira, commanding the de facto troops at Juarez. These two generals met on June 1, 1916, in an effort to iron out the irritations which for the past month had been seriously threatening the peace between the two countries.

An agreement was finally reached which limited the number of de facto troops to be stationed along the lines of railroads, and specified that no de facto troops should occupy towns along our line of communications. This agreement was tentative and was, of course, subject to the approval of the respective Governments. It is presumed that the Mexican Government did not approve, as General Pershing heard nothing further from it.

The relations between the United States and Mexico had now become very tense, and the Mexican people were much aroused, in the belief that war was inevitable.

Mexican troops were being assembled at points on the railroads to the east and west of us, threatening our line of communications. The commanding general of the Mexican forces in the district of Ahumada had issued instructions for his troops to hold themselves in readiness to operate against the Americans. A force of 10,000 men was reported in the vicinity of Ahumada, and a large number of troops had moved from the south to the city of Chihuahua. It was understood among the Mexican people that these troops, instead of being sent to pursue bandits, were actually for the purpose of driving the Americans out of Mexico.

The commanding officer at Ahumada was in constant communication with the local commander at Casas Grandes, situated on General Pershing's line of communications, and was advised that the troops at Ahumada were preparing to attack the American lines and directed to cooperate.

The Mexican population held themselves entirely aloof from us, and the people who had been friendly became decidedly unfriendly. It was impossible to obtain the assistance of men who hitherto had been in our service as secret agents. The white population were alarmed and afraid to venture beyond our protection.

Our small fleet of airplanes had been wrecked in the early days of the campaign, and not one was available at this critical period. It therefore became necessary to rely upon the resources within the command to obtain information of the location and probable intention of Mexican troops. Frequent reconnaissances in all directions became imperative in order to keep informed of any hostile movements of de facto troops, and to be prepared to concentrate at any threatened point.

General Trevino, in command at Chihuahua, sent General Pershing a telegram to the effect that if the American troops were moved south, east or west, they would be attacked, further showing the intense feeling existing at this time among all classes. This telegram follows, with General Pershing's reply:

Chihuahua Headquarters, June 16, 1916.

General Pershing
Casas Grandes.

I have orders from my Government to prevent, by the use of arms, new invasions of my country by American forces and also to prevent the American forces that are in this State from moving to the south, east or west of the places they now occupy. I communicate this to you for your knowledge for the reason that your forces will be attacked by the Mexican forces if these indications are not heeded.

Courteously,
J. B. Trevino, The General in Chief.

Field Headquarters, American Expedition,
Casas Grandes, Mexico, June 16, 1916.

General J. B. Trevino
Chihuahua, Mexico.

I am in receipt of your telegram advising me that your Government had directed you to prevent any movement to the south, east or west of the American forces now in Mexico, and that should such movement take place the American force will be attacked by Mexican forces. In reply you are informed that my Government has placed no such restrictions upon the movements of American forces. I shall therefore use my own judgment as to when and in what direction I shall move my forces in pursuit of bandits or in seeking information regarding bandits. If under these circumstances the Mexican forces attack any of my columns the responsibility for the consequences will lie with the Mexican Government.

Respectfully yours,
John J. Pershing,
Commanding American Forces.

This same date, June 16th, the Mexican commander at Casas Grandes gave to General Pershing a verbal message in effect:

"That General Carranza had ordered that the American troops should not move in any direction except north."

In reply General Pershing asked him to telegraph his superiors that he, General Pershing, declined to respect such instructions, saying: "I do not take orders except from my own Government."

Because of these threats, it became more important than ever to keep informed of the movements of Mexican troops, so the American cavalry was kept constantly scouting in all directions and became in fact "the eyes and ears" of the command.

Among these reconnoitering detachments, Captain Charles T. Boyd, 10th Cavalry, commanding Troop "C," was sent eastward in the direction of Ahumada to scout the country thoroughly and to obtain information of Mexican troops and their movements. He was told that he could probably learn the facts at Santa Domingo Ranch or in that vicinity, and was cautioned not to bring on a fight. Captain Lewis S. Morey, commanding Troop "K," 10th Cavalry, was sent from Ojo Federico upon the same mission and with practically the same caution.

Adobe Buildings of Field Hospital at Colonia Dublan

Camp of Co. K. 17th Infantry, at San Joaquin

Captain Boyd and Captain Morey met at the Santa Domingo Ranch, about 60 miles east of Dublan, on the evening of June 20th. They obtained from the American foreman in charge, who had recently visited Ahumada, much reliable information concerning their mission without going to points garrisoned by de facto troops. Captain Boyd, however, considered his orders required him to go to Ahumada via Carrizal, so with his command strengthened by Captain Morey and Troop "K," he left Santa Domingo at about 4:00 A. M. June 21st for Carrizal, about seven miles away. This movement resulted in what is known as the Carrizal fight.

General Pershing, in his report of this action, states in part as follows:

Arriving in the vicinity of Carrizal on the morning of the 21st, he (Boyd) was met by the commanding general and other officers at the outskirts of the town, and told that their orders would not permit him to go farther to the east. Superior numbers of Mexican troops were in battle formation, both mounted and dismounted, at the edge of the town, and all their preparations indicated that they would carry out their instructions and oppose Captain Boyd's progress by force. After some further discussion Captain Boyd rode up within short range of the Mexican position and dismounted his troops preparatory to entering the town. At the moment of dismounting he received a heavy fire from all parts of the Mexican lines.

Captain Boyd's own men pushed forward with a dash and carried the Mexican position, Lieutenant Adair leading.

The memory of the splendid bravery of these two officers, who lost their lives, and of the men who personally followed them is cherished by this entire command.

The reader will please note that "Captain Boyd's own men pushed forward with a dash and carried the Mexican position." Troop "K," which was ordered to guide on Troop "C," instead of pushing forward laid down in the shelter of a slight depression, lost contact with Troop "C," and finally quit cold. The author has always firmly believed that had Troop "K" displayed the same dash as Troop "C," the Mexicans would have been driven from the field. As it was, the Mexicans were so severely punished that they failed to follow up their advantage, and allowed many men of both troops to wander around the country on foot for several days until picked up by rescuing troops sent out by General Pershing.

Boyd and Adair were killed about the time they drove the Mexicans from their first position, and as Troop "K" had quit, the command was now without leaders, of which fact the Mexicans finally became aware.

These were small troops. I believe Troop "K" had less than 30 men on the firing line, while Troop "C" could have had but few more. There were probably less than 70 rifles in all on the firing line, opposed by several hundred Mexicans. The American casualties were:

Troop "C": 2 officers and 6 enlisted men killed, 4 enlisted men wounded and 8 enlisted men prisoners.

Troop "K": 4 enlisted men killed, 1 officer and 6 enlisted men wounded and 15 enlisted men prisoners.

The Mexican casualties according to their own statement were:

12 officers, including General Gomez, and 33 enlisted men killed, and 53 enlisted men wounded.

Major Robert L. Howze, 11th Cavalry, had been sent out by General

Pershing to search for the survivors of this fight. The night of June 24-25 his command camped at San Luis Ranch, about midway between Dublan and Carrizal. About midnight a wagon containing Captain Morey, Mr. W. P. McCabe, foreman of the Santa Domingo Ranch, a Chinaman and four soldiers of the 10th Cavalry, ran into the outpost, and were taken to Major Howze. Captain Morey made a statement to Major Howze part of which I quote from a record made at the time:

Captain Morey, with Troop "K" 10th Cavalry, reached the Santa Domingo Ranch early in the afternoon of June 20th, and found Captain Boyd with Troop "C", 10th Cavalry, already there. That night the officers discussed at length the situation and the meaning of their orders. Captain Morey gave it as his judgment that in view of the superiority of the Mexicans in Carrizal that the American troops should not force their way through that village, and so construed his orders, but nevertheless placed himself under Captain Boyd's orders and expressed his willingness to go first or alone. He turned over his valuables such as money, etc. to Mr. McCabe, with instructions as to their disposition in case he failed to return from Carrizal. The two troops left the Santa Domingo Ranch at about 4:00 A. M. June 21st, and reached a point about 1¼ miles from Carrizal where a halt was made.

Quite soon thereafter a group of Carranza soldiers with a flag, advanced toward the American troops. Boyd and the guide (Spillsbury) met them about half way, parleyed a few minutes, returned and announced that "it looked good" and that he was going through the town. After a few minutes the troops moved forward over a flat plain about 2000 yards wide in the direction in which they were advancing, and between two irrigating ditches, the one nearest the town being 150 or 200 yards therefrom, and partly fringed with green timber. Troop "K" moved to the right side of the road leading to the town and Troop "C" to the left of it. Boyd said he would attack the southeast corner of the town and have Morey take care of the right flank and Adair the left. When the troops had advanced half way across the plain, another flag approached. Boyd met it and received a note from the Carranza General saying he could enter for a conference; but Boyd stated he thought it was a trap laid for us and that he was going to prepare for the emergency, and he formed the troops in line of foragers.

We advanced, one platoon of Troop "K" echeloned and refused to protect the right, and Adair's platoon similarly disposed on the left. When we got within four or five hundred yards of this village another flag came out and with it the general, whose name, I believe, was Gomez. Boyd and the guide met it and parleyed and returned. Boyd immediately formed the troops into line of platoon columns, and gave column right, and we were ordered to fight on foot, action left. We formed into skirmish line immediately and advanced about 15 yards, when we received a severe fire; Troop "K" the fire of one of the two machine guns. Troop "K" men laid down in a road of very slight depression, which entered the main road at an oblique angle and bent around to the right of Troop "K", thus naturally refusing the flank of the troop. Troop "C" advanced toward the ditch near the town and was then about 250 or 300 yards away.

Thus, at the very beginning, Troop "K" lost contact with the guide troop, failed to support Troop "C," and very probably caused the American defeat and humiliation.

This same night June 24-25, Mr. W. P. McCabe, foreman of the Santa Domingo Ranch, made a statement to 1st Lieutenant S. M. Williams, 11th Cavalry, as follows:

On the afternoon of June 20th four Mexican soldiers came from Carrizal to the Santa Domingo Ranch. They talked to Captain Boyd, Captain Morey, Lieut. Adair and Mr. Spillsbury. I do not know the subject of their conversation as I was not close enough to hear and no one told me. The Mexicans told me they had come after some beef which they had obtained and returned with.

After supper that evening Captain Boyd, Captain Morey, Lieut. Adair and Mr. Spillsbury held a conference about their plans for the next day. Captain Boyd sent for me and asked me to give him a description of the town, which I did.

He said that his orders required him to go *through* Carrizal to Villa Ahumada, and that he was going *through* the town. Mr. Spillsbury and I told Captain Boyd that he should send a message to the town that he was coming there. Captain Boyd said that he was not going to send a message at that time, but later in the night he decided to send in word that he was going through. I was present and heard Captain Boyd and Captain Morey talking over the situation. I told Captain Boyd that the main part of Carrizal was a nasty trap to go through, and I told Captain Boyd that he could go to the east of the town, where there were few buildings and the ground was clear and that he would still be going through Carrizal, that is that he could consider that he had gone through the town.

He said no, that he was going through Carrizal. The two Captains did not agree upon the interpretation of the orders. Captain Morey told Captain Boyd that it was his judgment not to try to force his way through the town, but that he was absolutely under Captain Boyd's orders, and would go into the town first or would go in alone if Captain Boyd ordered him to. Captain Boyd then made some remark to Captain Morey about "making history" which I did not catch the rest of.

Captain Boyd, 10th Cavalry, in command of Troops "C" and "K" 10th Cavalry, camped at Santa Domingo Ranch on the night of June 20th, and left about 4:00 A. M. June 21st. Captain Boyd told me he intended to go to Villa Ahumada via Carrizal and return to Santa Domingo that night. The troops left their picket lines, forage and surplus equipment at the ranch but left no men there. It is about 9 miles from the ranch to Carrizal. I remained at the ranch. About 8 or 9 o'clock on the morning of June 21st, five men rode into the ranch at a gallop and told me the Mexicans had fired on the troops and massacred the bunch. There were two loose horses with these men. The pack train came right behind these men and two or three more men came in. All of these men had rifles and ammunition. Most of these men were very much exicited and said they wanted a guide, and they were going for help.

"I told them they were doing a mighty poor thing to run off and leave their comrades and tried to get them to stop and remain there. I told them they all had arms and ammunition and that they should not run away. They replied that there were more of their men coming toward the ranch and that they were going for reinforcements. They insisted on going, and I gave them a guide and I have not seen them since. They left the ranch in the general direction of Galeana, riding fast.

The pack train was left there. A few minutes after these men left, a man named Corporal Green and two or three other men came into the ranch. (I think this man's name was Green, and that he was in Captain Boyd's troop, but I am not absolutely certain). Green told me he had been sent for reinforcements. I told him I had just sent a bunch with a guide for reinforcements, and he finally decided to stay. He took the ammunition off the pack mules, hid it in the corral and told me where he put it. Green told me he was going to stay there and stick it out. At this time a packer named Brown and four or five other men came in, riding fast, and said they were going for reinforcements. I told them one bunch had already gone with a guide. He said they didn't need any guide and they left. The pack mules got away between these two bunches.

This left Green and myself at the ranch, and we were there 15 or 20 minutes by ourselves. Then a few men came straggling in, some leading horses and some not, but all were mounted. I cannot say positively whether all the stragglers were armed or not as I did not see them all.

During this time I was at the house a while, the barn a while, and was trying to get a line on the situation. Stragglers had been passing the ranch while I was doing this. Then I noticed a bunch of them coming back to the ranch walking their horses, so I went down the lane to meet them. There I saw a second packer, I don't know his name, and asked him if he was bringing them back and he said yes. I think there were between 15 or 20 men in this bunch and a good many horses. The packer and I went into the yard, and this bunch of men came in, tied their horses on the line and fed them. One of the picket lines was pretty nearly full of horses and there were some on the other line. Most of these men were armed and I thought they were going to make a stand there. I believe that most of the horses of both troops were in the yard at this time.

While I was at the house, I saw two men riding toward Carrizal, and I asked this packer where these men were going. He said they were going out to reconnoiter. Those men went probably a mile and a half toward Carrizal. When I came back from the house about 15 minutes later I saw these men coming through the gate very fast, and a stirring around on the picket lines. I went down there and asked what they were going to do, and they said they were going to get out; that they were greatly outnumbered, and there were 1500 Mexicans coming. The whole bunch left immediately, riding at the trot. This left me, three or four Mexicans who worked on the place, and two Chinamen, the only people on the ranch.

The Corporal Green referred to, left with this last crowd. I saw no rifles left there at all. I then left the ranch, taking a few things with me, and hid some distance from the house, but where I could see the ranch all the time. I did not see a single Mexican soldier or any sign of any that day or night. I remained in hiding until four or five o'clock in the afternoon, and seeing no sign of any one around the house I returned to the house, had supper, and spent the night about a quarter of a mile from the house.

The last of the soldiers had left the ranch before noon. The next morning early, I went back to the house, ordered breakfast, and went down to the barn. There I found four colored soldiers inside of a locked inclosure. They said they came in afoot during the night. Two of these men were slightly wounded. I gave them breakfast, left them at the ranch, and went to the bushes. At sundown, June 22nd I went back to the ranch, found the place deserted and partially sacked. Everything left there by our soldiers had been hauled away.

I spent the night at the ranch with the two Chinamen who had been with me, and on the morning of June 23rd early, the Chinamen told me there were two men at the barn. I searched the place but was unable to find any-one. About 9:00 A. M. I saw 15 or 20 mounted Mexicans approaching the ranch from the direction of Carrizal, and I left immediately, with one of the Chinamen, both of us mounted. We rode off a couple of miles and watched the ranch. The Mexicans entered the ranch and the last I saw they were still there.

I left the ranch with the intention of going to Galeana. About 12 miles west of Santa Domingo I struck the Suterano Windmill where I found Captain Morey, 10th Cavalry, and four men of the regiment. Captain Morey was wounded and very much worn out when I found him.

I know nothing further about the situation.

W. P. McCabe.

Sworn to and subscribed in my presence this 25th day of June, 1916.

Robert L. Howze,
Major 11th Cavalry,
Summary Court.

Chapter XXXIV

The Evacuation of Mexico. An Inglorious Ending

When the fight at Carrizal was reported to General Pershing, orders were prepared and immediate steps taken to assume the aggressive with all available troops of his command. Instructions from higher authority indicated such action, and the situation certainly demanded it.

Further concentration for prompt movement became imperative if we were to be ready to meet without delay what appeared to be a crisis. Without going into details, the troops south of El Valle were ordered north by telegraph, truck trains were assembled for such use as might be required of them, and the command as a whole was at once placed and held in position for quick action.

Our State Department sent a peremptory note to the Mexican Government demanding the immediate return to the United States of all prisoners and Government property taken in the Carrizal fight. As a large force of our National Guard had assembled at strategic points along our border, Mexico made immediate compliance with this demand, and the prisoners were delivered to the American authorities at El Paso within ten days of their capture.

This was followed by an exchange of notes proposing that each Government name three commissioners who would hold conferences at some place to be mutually agreed upon and decide forthwith the question relating to the evacuation of the American forces in Mexico, and to draw up and conclude a protocol or agreement regarding the reciprocal crossing of the frontier by the forces of both countries, also to determine the origin of the incursions made, in order to fix the responsibility therefor, and to settle the difficulties pending or those which might arise between the two countries on account of the same or a similar reason, and to consider such other matters the friendly agreement of which would tend to improve the relations of the two countries, it being understood that such recommendations as the Commission might make would not be binding upon the respective Governments until formally accepted by them.

This Commission met at New London, Conn., September 6th, holding numerous sessions extending into 1917. In the meantime General Pershing had assembled his command at Dublan, where they went through a course of intensive training.

By the end of May most of General Pershing's army had arrived at Dublan and were assigned camp sites. This camp soon assumed the air of a concentration camp with the four regiments of cavalry, the 6th Infantry, the two batteries of field artillery, the engineers, the quartermaster corps, the large truck trains, wagon trains, pack trains, etc.

The camp was most uncomfortable, due to the high winds, frequent dust storms, tropical heat of summer, freezing cold of winter, deep mud in the tropical downpours, and swarms of flies. The soldiers had no tents or other shelter except the shelter half each man carried with him. The men soon set to work to build adobe walls on which they placed their shelter halves as roofs. Considerable ingenuity was shown in making cots of poles, and other "furniture" for camp comfort.

The regiments soon received their wagons, field desks, bedding rolls, cooking outfits, and other impedimenta cast aside when the drive to the south started. All of this added to the comfort of the command. Each troop, company and battery built its own kitchen of adobe bricks, thus enabling the men to eat under shelter from the dust or rain. Being much nearer the border, and there being no demand on the truck trains to serve the "flying columns," mail and supplies were received regularly, so the troops were once more well fed and clothed.

There were no amusements except what the men furnished for themselves. The training occupied a large part of the day, and furnished splendid physical exercise, but at night there was no place to go except to the huts built by the men. There was no chance to get away from each other and indulge in social relaxation away from the command, so necessary in a soldier's life. These men were uncomfortable all of the time. In spite of their best efforts, they could not escape the dirt of the dust storms and the swarms of flies.

Under these conditions the discipline should have suffered, but quite to the contrary the men were cheerful, well behaved, and ready at all times to respond to any demand their General might make upon them. During their entire time in Mexico no one of the command was guilty of anything that could bring discredit upon the Expedition.

Elaborate plans had been made, especially by the 10th Cavalry, to celebrate Christmas day properly. The 25th of December was ushered in by a cold norther and the Christmas dinner with its accompanying festivities, which had been long planned, was entirely spoiled by the tremendous wind storm that will long be remembered by every one who was in Mexico at that time. Whole steers that were being barbecued were so covered with the clouds of dust that they were unfit for food, and the troops had to seek what shelter they could. Very few men ate at all for twenty-four hours.

But this was the last of the many major discomforts our soldiers had born with fortitude. The slogan "Villa, dead or alive," was heard no more in Mexico; for in January, 1917, word at last came that the troops were to withdraw from Mexico. The homeward march began January 30th and the "line" was crossed at Columbus, February 5th, while the Commission at New London continued their "conversations."

If one has the gift of humor, many a laugh may be had from a reading of the diplomatic correspondence between the two countries during Mr. Wilson's first term as President of the United States. Just to illustrate: When Carranza notified our government that he intended to resist by force any movement of the Punitive Expedition except in a northerly direction, our Department of State replied that any act of force would bring the "gravest consequences," but Carranza had received so many

of these innocuous threats that he ignored the warning and his orders
stood. Then came the fight at Carrizal, a most practical demonstration
of Carranza's earnestness, and the "gravest consequences" consisted in
our State Department on July 7th, 16 days after Carrizal, addressing a
note to the Mexican Government dwelling upon the spirit of friendship
and solicitude which animates the American Government for the *con-
tinuation of cordial relations* between the two governments!!!

Villa, instead of being dead as General Obregon had insisted to Generals Scott and Funston in May, was very much alive. While the conferees at New London were trying to make it possible for the United
States to withdraw the troops from Mexico without the appearance of
having been kicked out, General Pershing was held at Colonia Dublan
impotent under orders to prosecute his campaign against Villa and his
band.

Villa, now completely resurrected, took advantage of this respite from
pursuit by American soldiers to leave his mountain refuge, come boldly
out into the open and begin organizing once more an "army."

General Pershing kept in touch with the Mexican situation as well as
his limited powers would permit, and reported from time to time to his
immediate chief, General Funston, stationed at San Antonio, Texas, who
relayed the messages to the War Department. Here are a few samples:

(Telegram)
Fort Sam Houston, August 15, 1916
Following received from General Pershing:
Through information received from Mexican prisoners who participated
in Columbus, N. M. raid, names of 60 Villa bandits from the vicinity of
Namiquipa, Cruces, San Geronimo and Bachineva, who accompanied Villa to
Columbus, N. M., have been obtained. These include 14 previously surren-
dered to civil authorities at Madera whose surrender was demanded of General Gaviroat during my conference with him. The list includes eight officers. The proof against all of them would be conclusive before any court in
the United States. Since the arrival of the Carranza garrison at Namiquipa,
Colonel Diaz, the commander, has granted amnesty to all these outlaws and
they have returned to their homes. This action can only be regarded as a
direct approval by the de facto Government of their offenses, and in defiance
of efforts of this Expedition. It is recommended that a strong representation
be made in this matter, accompanied by a demand for the capture and surrender to the American forces of these men, as a preliminary to negotiations
between the two Governments. A large proportion of these outlaws would
have been captured by our troops but for the open opposition of both civil
and military de facto officials.

Funston.

Of course, nothing came of this recommendation made by General
Pershing. Had our State Department made any such rude demand as
suggested by the General, there would have been no meeting of Commissioners at New London. The Mexicans were consenting to these
conferences for the purpose of making demands, not concessions. While
the Commissioners talked, Villa was gaining strength in the State of
Chihuahua.

General Funston to the Secretary of War
(Telegram)
Fort Sam Houston, September 20, 1916.
Following received from General Bell:
Evidence increases to show that Villa was completely successful in his

attack Saturday upon Chihuahua and accomplished all and more than he said he would do. There is diversity of opinion and statements as to the number of men with which he entered Chihuahua, some accounts state he only had about 500 while others give him 1700, but all agree that he was able to secure possession of the penitentiary, the Governor's palace and the federal buildings, and held them for several hours, and all this with a Carranza garrison at Chihuahua which no one places at less than 6,000. He liberated over 200 prisoners, secured and carried away more than 16 automobile loads of arms and ammunition, and actually took out artillery under an escort of deserting Carranza troops. He left Chihuahua with from 1000 to 1500 more men than he entered with. Villa retired leisurely and practically without molestation. The firing by Trevino's artillery occurred after Villa troops had withdrawn. On September 14 Trevino received a letter from Villa stating that he, Villa, would be in Chihuahua to shake hands with Trevino on the 16th, and he hoped he would have a suitable reception for him, that he might be hungry and would like to have something to eat. On the 15th of September it is reported that Villa personally entered Chihuahua, was seen by many of his friends there and reconnoitered the city. Of course he was in disguise. On the night of the 15-16 Villa approached Chihuahua from a camp which he had maintained for two days within 22 miles of the city. After Villa columns had secured possession of the penitentiary, the Governor's palace and the federal buildings, Villa himself entered the Governor's palace, went to the main balcony, displayed his face and made a short speech which in substance was as follows: "Viva Mexico! You do not have your liberty; I will give you your liberty for I am your brother. I am going to return in a few days." It appears that there had been a banquet attended by most of Trevino's officers and that about two o'clock this banquet was finished and most of the officers of the Carranza garrison were asleep. As soon as Trevino heard of the trouble he started towards the Governor's palace, but his personal escort deserted him and went over to Villa. The party that attacked the federal building rode into the building on horseback and the guard there deserted to them. It is reported that many of the Carranza troops who were killed were killed by other Carranza troops probably as a result of artillery firing from Santa Rosa Hill. Copy to Pershing.

Funston.

Fort Sam Houston, September 25, 1916.
Following received from General Bell:

The following report was obtained from an American ranchman who arrived from Chihuahua today. He is reliable and a man of standing, as is shown by the fact that he was able to obtain an interview with Trevino. He says that Villa personally entered Chihuahua and directed his men and that they simultaneously attacked the federal buildings and all the military caurtels, that they were in Chihuahua from 2:30 A. M. until 10:00 A. M., and fighting all the time. That most of the prisoners and many of the townspeople went out with him when he left, and that they took large quantities of ammunition, that there were about 100 Villistas and 300 Carranzistas killed, that after leaving Chihuahua Villa and his men went to San Andres and killed the Commanding General and some of his men there, and that the balance of the men joined him, that General Cavazos returned with only four men, as Villa had killed two captains and the remainder of the force. General Ramos left Chihuahua yesterday with 600 men over the Northwestern to fight Villa. Villa blew up the large steel bridge over the San Andres River. Villa is accredited with having over 1500 men, and others from the whole mountain country are flocking to him and he is getting stronger every day while the majority of the people in Chihuahua are pro-Villistas. General Trevino told him yesterday that conditions are very serious, also talked with General Cavazos and thinks it only a matter of days when Villa will attack Chihuahua again. He says that General Salazar and Colonel Selvestri Devedo and Tino and all the important prisoners went with Villa.

Funston.

General Pershing to General Funston.

Headquarters Punitive Expedition, U. S. Army,

In the Field, Mexico, November 2, 1916.

1. Referring to my letter of October 21st, information that comes in from many sources, several brief reports of which have been forwarded by telegraph from time to time, seems to confirm the opinion that the Carranza Government, as at present conducted, is wholly unable to put down banditry in the State of Chihuahua. Villa's prestige continues to grow, and his numbers are increasing. It is known that he is coercing natives to follow him, but men so impressed would probably not remain with him if there were any other alternative. When Villa recently resumed activities, the people in towns along the Northwestern Railroad, including Madera, Guerrero and other towns in that section, sent word through their leaders to the de facto Government that they would gladly take up arms and help the Government against him if supported, but no notice was taken of this offer. The rural people of Chihuahua naturally wonder why the Carranzista Government does not send some of their ablest officers north to command and clean up things. It is almost the general opinion among the people that if this were done Villa would not last long. To an observer here on the ground, it is inconceivable that the de facto authorities should not know the inefficiency, if not disloyalty, of their commanding officers in Chihuahua and apply the remedy.

2. One of Villa's generals has recently issued a manifesto, copy inclosed, which explains itself. It was found on Garcia, now a prisoner of the Carranzistas. This would seem to confirm the view that he is receiving support from the Legalista party. Villa is working south with approximately 1000 men, presumably with Jimenez as objective. He is said to have been in command at the Carmargo fight. His command is not well mounted, and has very little ammunition. He gathered up many horses both north and south of the railroad and has taken quantities of supplies from the people in that section. The territory included in the Guerrero valley through which he has been operating, is reported to have good crops, corn and beans being plentiful.

3. The local Carranzista commanders are doing little or nothing to save their country from the ravages of this bandit. The fact that these northern commanders, including Trevino at Chihuahua, Gonzales at Juarez, Diaz at El Valle and Cortina at Madera, do not appear to want peace established. They undoubtedly form a clique to run things in Chihuahua themselves. They collect the taxes and dispose of the products of the mines and ranches for their own benefit. They make only a flimsy pretense of hunting bandits, as numerous incidents prove. In fact, there are many rumors that the commanding officer at Juarez and the troops under him are only awaiting an opportunity to turn over to the Legalistas.

4. The de facto troops in Chihuahua are variously estimated at from 3000 to 9000, the former number probably being more nearly correct. It is safe to say that of these but a small proportion would remain loyal to the Carranzista Government, as they are poorly paid and are short of provisions and clothing. An intercepted radio message sent by Trevino to Obregon stated that the troops were suffering for want of blankets, 10,000 blankets were asked for, but Obregon answered that the contractor had been unable to furnish them.

5. In view of the conditions it certainly does not appear probable that the Carranzistas can restore anything like order. If further operations on our part should be contemplated, the occupation of the city of Chihuahua by the larger part of this command would be very advantageous, as it would bring us much nearer the theater of operations. It would probably not be difficult now to occupy Chihuahua city, as there would be little opposition on the part of de facto troops, while the population would doubtless welcome us.

John J. Pershing.

General Funston to the Secretary of War.
(Telegram)
Fort Sam Houston, December 9, 1916.
Following received from General Pershing:

"Villistas gathering cattle, horses, Santa Clara Valley. Entire district said now to be for Villa. Small parties Villistas reported operating between Lake Guzman and Ahumada. Number Villistas detrained San Antonio and marched north to San Diego del Monte on the 4th instant. Local guards various towns previously reported, said to be concentrating at Providencia. Generally rumored that Villa intends to go south. In view of Villa's daring, and comparative inefficiency Carranzista forces Villa's power almost certain to increase. Reports regarded as authentic place his forces at 6,000. Four train loads of supplies captured at Chihuahua arrived San Ysidro 5th instant. A swift blow delivered by this command should be made at once against this pretender. Our own prestige in Mexico should receive consideration at this time. In the light of Villa's operations during the past two weeks, further inactivity of this command does not seem desirable, and there is no longer doubt as to the facts. As stated in previous communications aggressive action would probably meet no resistance by Carranzistas, and should meet their approval. Civilian element would welcome us, as they now wonder at our inactivity."

I approve of the foregoing recommendation. Villa's successes are rapidly placing him in control of a large part of the State of Chihuahua. Carranzistas opposed to him have not been successful; on the contrary they have been seriously and decisively defeated several times during the last month. I can see no reason for believing that they will be more successful in months to come, as Villa is constantly gaining in strength, influence and power, and is extending area over which he has complete control. Secret service reports show that there is strong Villa sympathy in Coahuila and Nuevo Leon and I believe if he is allowed to continue his career unchecked that in the course of a few months he will control all of northern Mexico. A quick decisive blow directed against him now by John J. Pershing's command would check this rising power and if allowed to continue until Villa is captured would put an end to the whole movement, thereby greatly benefitting de facto Government. John J. Pershing states that he believes that such action would meet with no resistance by Carranzistas. It would certainly seem that it should meet not only with their approval but with their cooperation. This would involve the use of the Mexico Central or Mexico Northwestern Railroad from Juarez, as John J. Pershing must have one of these railroads for his line of communications. There could be no assurance of success in pursuing Villa without provisions being made for following him into Durango, Distrito Federal.   Funston.

These recommendations, I might say pleas, of Generals Pershing and Funston were not in accord with President Wilson's Mexican policy, so the American troops remained inactive at Dublan, Villa grew in power, the Carranzista Government continued to flout the United States and the Commissioners talked at New London, except when they were being entertained on the President's yacht.

General Pershing's mission was very clearly stated in a telegram from the War Department dated March 13th, 1916, as follows:

The President desires that your attention be especially and earnestly called to his determination that the expedition into Mexico is limited to the purposes originally stated, namely the pursuit and dispersion of the band or bands that attacked Columbus, N. M.

The reader has seen how thoroughly General Pershing accomplished his mission up to the time President Wilson called off the chase. Our first contact of any importance with the enemy was at Guerrero, where

Dodd administered to them a crushing defeat, killed General Hernandez, and caused the band to disperse into smaller units seeking safety in flight, and again at Tomochic on April 22nd he administered another dose of American justice. Then Howze at Ojo Azules practically wiped out the band of Julio Acosta, Cruz Dominguez and Antonio Agua; and Brown at Aguas Calientes scattered Beltran's forces; while the different flying cavalry columns kept the Villistas constantly on the jump running away from American retribution.

So the bands were dispersed, and a number of Villa's principal lieutenants were killed, viz: General Hernandez at Guerrero; Pablo Lopez wounded at Columbus, captured by Carranzistas, and executed in April; Captain Silva killed by Howze at La Joya April 10th; Lieutenant Beltran killed by Howze at Santa Cruz de Herrera April 11th; Cervantes, Villa's chief lieutenant in the Columbus fight, killed May 25th by an infantry scouting party; Colonel Cardenas killed May 14th by Lieutenant Patton.

This was a very worthy accomplishment, and it would have been a finished job had not Carranza ordered President Wilson to call off the chase, an order that was meekly obeyed. In all of Mr. Wilson's dealings with Carranza the "First Chief" dominated the situation. To quote a few examples: When Mr. Wilson asked Carranza to attend the Conference of Niagara Falls, the latter refused, with which our President conformed. When Wilson opposed the demand of Carranza for the unconditional surrender of Carvajal, Wilson finally yielded. When Carranza was invited by Wilson to celebrate peace with the Villa faction, Carranza answered that it was not the business of Wilson to meddle in the contests of Mexicans, to which Mr. Wilson had nothing to reply. When the American Government associated with six complacent Latin-American Governments, invited the warring factions to a conference of peace, Carranza was the only one who rejected the invitation, demanding, in exchange, that he be recognized, which was quickly done. Although President Wilson had announced himself as "the champion of constitutional government on this continent" and declared that he would not have as a government in Mexico one which should not be regulated by the constitution of the country, he nevertheless recognized the dictator Carranza. When the Punitive Expedition took place, Carranza prohibited the American forces from using the Mexican railroads and from entering the towns and villages, to all of which Mr. Wilson acceeded with meekness. When Carranza forbade the troops of General Pershing to move in any direction but north, Mr. Wilson obeyed. And finally, when Mr. Wilson had menaced with "The gravest consequences" any act of violence against the Punitive Expedition, Carranza troops destroyed an American column at Carrizal, and the "gravest consequences" of this act were the invitation to the conferences at New London. When Villa learned that the American President had hobbled the American army he came out of hiding, called his scattered forces together, marched at will and unopposed through the State of Chihuahua, even capturing the capital city, and grew stronger than he was at the time of his attack on Columbus, all because Carranza said the American army must do no more.

In spite of the obstacles placed in their path by President Wilson and

General Carranza, the troops of the Expedition earned the following tribute from their commander:

The splendid services that the regular troops comprising this Expedition have performed under most adverse conditions, again proves that for natural ability, physical endurance, unflinching persistence, general efficiency, and unquestioned loyalty and devotion to duty, the well trained officers and men of the regular army are unexcelled by the troops of any other nation.

Lieutenant-Colonel James D. Glennan, Medical Corps, Chief Surgeon of the Expedition, said:

The Punitive Expedition lived nearer to the earth and learned to get along with less than any command in our experience. It was hardened by active service, and profitably interested and occupied by professional work and training. It has been cheerful and has maintained the good health and sanitation that goes with good discipline. The country has never had a more thoroughly trained and fit command.

CHAPTER XXXV

The National Guard on the Mexican Border

By Brig. General Henry J. Reilly, O.R.C.[1]

The National Guard Service on the Mexican Border was a mile-post in the history of this country.

It was the beginning of a new era in our national defense. It profoundly affected the combat value of the National Guard on French battlefields in 1918 and therefore the value of the American Expeditionary Force.

It was the beginning of a new era in our national defense because for the first time in our history state units passed into Federal service without a complete metamorphosis. It was the opening of a new chapter in the war-time use of our civilian soldiery in which, instead of waiting until war comes to organize him as part of the Army of the United States, he is already so organized in time of peace. The National Defense Act of 1916 began this transformation [2] in that it provided for the entry of the National Guard into Federal service, once an oath to the Federal Government has been taken. This just as the units stand in their state organizations. The last act which has completed this transformation into an integral part of the Army of the United States is that passed in the 73d Congress published in W. D. Bulletin No. 12, Wash. D. C., July 3, 1933. By it the units, when the Federal Government no longer needs them, pass back into the service of their state without disruption.

Thus the days of the Militia roundly cursed in the days of George Washington and the War of 1812-15 have gone forever. Equally have disappeared the hastily organized, wasteful and, for the first period of their service, inefficient volunteers of the Mexican and Civil Wars. Also, the days of 1898, when National Guard regiments were reorganized into volunteers and in some cases were so made over as to be practically new green regiments, are a thing of the past.

Many of the National Guardsmen who went to the border in 1916 remembered the raising of our war army in 1898 and thus welcomed the National Defense Act of 1916. This because it was a long step away from the confusion, waste, inefficiency and unnecessary loss of life through sickness which characterized the 1898 mobilization.[3]

However, while the mobilization of 1916 and subsequent concentration on the Mexican Border were a considerable improvement of 1898, they were far behind that of 1917. That with its reorganizations was equally behind any mobilization which would take place today.

The only step missing today is the lack of any trained Reserve to bring National Guard units to war strength. Both in our Regular Army and National Guard today the consequent necessity to either send units to the front at peace strength or else fill them to war strength with green recruits is the greatest present deficiency.

---

[1] Brig. General Henry J. Reilly, O. R. C. went to the border as Captain Battery E, 1st Ill. F. A., which he had helped organize in Chicago the preceding winter. After several months he was detailed in the Military Information Division, in which he had previously served in the Regular Army. He was sent along the Border from Brownsville, Texas, to Columbus, New Mexico, and thence to General Pershing's Expeditionary Force in Chihuahua.

[2] June 6, 1900 Congress appropriated $1,000,000 of Federal funds for supplies for the Militia. Thus began Federal interest in the force. Subsequent laws increased this. However, the 1916 Act was the real beginning.

[3] In 1898 General Reilly ran away and enlisted in the 22d Kansas Infantry serving through the state mobilization period at Topeka, Kansas.

Madero's overthrow of President Diaz, in 1911, began the period of disorder in Mexico which led to raids across our border. These culminated in Pancho Villa's raid on Columbus, New Mexico, in March 1916 and General Pershing's pursuit into old Mexico. However, the event which directly caused the calling out of the National Guard was the refusal of President Carranza to ratify the Obregon agreement.

The last of April and first part of May 1916 General Hugh L. Scott, Chief of Staff of the Army, and General Frederick Funston in command of the Southern Department held a series of conferences with the Mexican commander General Obregon at El Juarez on the Mexican side of the Border and at El Paso on our side.

In these General Scott impressed upon General Obregon that whenever the Mexicans could preserve order on their side of the border thereby stopping Mexican raids on American territory, then the withdrawal of General Pershing's expeditionary force from Chihuahua would be considered.

A tentative agreement was reached with General Obregon. This Carranza refused to sign. His refusal showed clearly that the hostile attitude of the Federal (Carranzista) troops in contact with General Pershing's force was not merely a reflection of the viewpoint of the local commanders, but was the Mexican governmental one.

In other words, General Pershing might be attacked at any time by all the forces the Mexican Government could bring against him.

General Scott says: "The entire Regular Army stationed in the United States, with the exception of a regiment of Cavalry and some of the Coast Artillery, was either distributed along the border or with General Pershing's expeditionary force." [1]

General Pershing's position was a dangerous one in case of a simultaneous, concerted attack by all available Mexican troops. Deep in Chihuahua with a long line of communications maintained by motor trucks plowing through the desert sand at a slow rate of speed and a secondary railway not entirely in his hands, his position invited attack.

The Mexicans held the main railways from the border south. These with their east and west connections gave them interior lines. Thus they could switch their troops from the lower Rio Grande to attack Pershing more quickly than the American troops from that same region could be sent to reinforce Pershing.

Furthermore sending these troops would leave that part of the border unprotected unless more troops could be gotten from the rest of the United States to take their place.

Also, if left unprotected, the Mexicans instead of concentrating against Pershing could cross the lower Rio Grande and invade Texas in force.

General Funston had information which he considered reliable that such an invasion with San Antonio as the objective was being planned.

Therefore he asked that several divisions of National Guard troops be called out preferably from those States having complete divisions and brigades.[2] This in addition to the Texas, New Mexico and Arizona Guard called out prior to the main call.

The call for these three States was telegraphed by the Secretary of War Mr. Newton D. Baker to their governors May 9, 1916.

The second call similarly telegraphed by the Secretary of War to all Governors of States was made on June 18th.

Each began with the words: "Having in view the possibility of further aggression upon the territory of the United States from Mexico and the necessity for the proper protection of the frontier the President has thought proper to exercise the authority vested in him by the Constitution and laws and call out the Organized Militia * * *."

The second call came as the result of a cabinet meeting.

Undoubtedly it resulted from General Funston's fear of an attempted invasion of Texas from the lower Rio Grande towards San Antonio and General Scott's report on the Obregon negotiations.

[1] Annual Report for 1916. Vol. I, page 189.
[2] Told Captain Reilly by General Funston at San Antonio, Texas, when he reported personally for duty in the M. I. D.

General Scott says: "The Mexican leaders became insistent upon the withdrawal of General Pershing's expeditionary force and threatened to attack any of our detachments in Mexico marching in any direction other than towards the Mexican border. Conditions became such that an immediate increase in the border troops was necessary * * *." [1]

Besides what is quoted above, the second call had in its first sentence immediately after the words, "Organized Militia," the phrase: "and National Guard."

This was due to the National Defense Act of 1916, approved June 3, a short two weeks before the second call and almost a month after the first.

This act completely reorganized both the Regular Army and the Organized Militia as the National Guard was then known. The consequence was that the Guard was in the process of being converted from its Organized Militia status to the National Guard one provided for. The main feature of this transformation was the taking by each officer and enlisted man of the Federal oath laid down by the Act.

To include all organized National Guard units desired for the mobilization, whether still organized militia or converted into federalized National Guard, the second call was made for both categories.

Everyone who took part in the mobilization will remember the discussions as to whether or not the Federal oath was constitutional, whether or not to take it, and the alibi for not going to the border which it conveniently furnished in the cases of some individuals.

For a number of years the Division of Militia Affairs in the War Department and leading National Guard officers in various States had been working on a scheme to organize the Guard into divisions.

As a result of this and the approval of a number of Governors of States to whom the scheme had been submitted, the Bureau of Militia Affairs issued Circular No. 8 in August 1913. In August 1914 the Bureau of Militia Affairs issued Circular No. 19, which provided for 12 National Guard divisions.

They were numbered from 5 to 16, inclusive. The 5th was made up of the Guard of the New England States, the 16th of the Pacific Coast States, and Montana, Utah, Idaho and Nevada. Only two states had complete divisions, New York the 6th and Pennsylvania the 7th. The 11th and 12th embraced two states each: Michigan and Ohio, and Illinois and Indiana, respectively. The 8th was composed of the Atlantic States from New Jersey to Virginia, inclusive, and West Virginia and the District of Columbia. The 9th had the balance of the Atlantic States from North Carolina to Florida, inclusive. The 10th was Alabama, Mississippi, Tennessee and Kentucky. The 15th included the Mexican border states and Oklahoma, Arkansas and Louisiana. The 13th had North and South Dakota, Iowa, Wisconsin and Minnesota. The 14th stretched from the Mississippi to the Rockies including Missouri, Kansas, Nebraska, Colorado and Wyoming.

For three reasons the Guard did not serve in these divisions upon the border. First, this organization was not complete when the call came. Second, the need for troops to reinforce the border was so great that in most cases regiments were sent as soon as ready to whatever part of the border then most in need of such reinforcement. Thus units of the same division were widely scattered. Third, in many cases regiments were held in their state mobilization camps for a number of months, until sent to the border to relieve other regiments of the same division ordered home for muster out.

However, this paper divisional organization is interesting because it was the basis of the sixteen National Guard divisions resulting from the N. D. Act of 1916 which with the addition of the Rainbow made up the 17 National Guard divisions of the A. E. F.

The fifth and 26th, sixth and 27th, seventh and 28th were the same. The eighth and 29th, the sixteenth and 41st were almost the same. The ninth furnished the nucleus for the 30th and 31st. Illinois, which furnished the greater part of the 12th, became the 33d. The 13th furnished the nucleus for the 34th, and the 15th furnished the nucleus for 36th and 40th. The 10th furnished the greater part of the 39th. Ohio, which made up the greater part of the 11th, became the 37th. The 14th became the nucleus for the 35th. The 32d came equally from the 11th and 13th, the 38th from the eighth, tenth, and twelfth and the 42d from the majority of these original national guard divisions. Thus only the last three are unable to claim direct if only paper descent from these federally organized National Guard divisions, the first to appear in the history of our country.

The result of the impossibility of sending these divisions as such to the border was that General Funston was ordered by the War Department on August 4, 1916 to organize the National Guard in Federal Service into 10 provisional divisions and 6 separate brigades. However, even this organization was not physically completed on the border. This because some of the units included in it when organized were at state mobilization camps. When they finally went to the border units there returned home to be mustered out.

Though all available Field Artillery, Cavalry and auxiliary units were included in the two calls and the troops not called were all Infantry, the lack of the first and the excess of Infantry made a complete divisional organization impossible.

On June 30, 1916, the National Guard troops in Federal service from a divisional organization viewpoint had 17 too many Infantry regiments and lacked 52 troops of Cavalry, 58 batteries of Field Artillery, 49 machine gun companies, 8½ battalions of Engineers, 26 field hospitals, 17 ambulance companies, 17 sanitary detachments and 12 medical supply depots.

The situation was analagous to that which Lord Haldane describes as true of the British Regular Army prior to his reorganization of its home forces into the Expeditionary Force which distinguished itself in 1914.[1] "....it lived in peace formations only, in small and detached units which would have to be refashioned into quite different formations before they could be ready to be sent to fight. This state of things involved much delay in mobilization. A careful inquiry made in 1906 disclosed that in order to put even 80,000 men on the Continent, a period which might be well over two months was the minimum required."

Approximately this number were landed in France in six days (August 12 to 17), in 1914, as the result of the war divisional organization introduced while Lord Haldane was the British Minister of War.

In 1911, the disorder on the Mexican border with the consequent necessity to concentrate troops there demonstrated a similar inefficiency because of the lack of divisional organization by our Regulars.

In March of that year the concentration of a manoeuver division of 3 brigades of Infantry, one of Field Artillery and one of Cavalry with the proper proportion of auxiliary troops and services was ordered at San Antonio and of a temporary Brigade of 36 companies of Coast Artillery provisionally organized into 3 regiments, at Galveston.

The troops not only were assembled from all over the country, but also the commanding generals and the individual officers of their staffs.

This division and brigade never reached their prescribed strength in personnel. Aside from the delay in ordering their many constituent parts from all parts of the country was that due to our lack of strategic railways and of preparation of our railroad companies for a rapid war concentration, upon our borders. The last regiment arrived only after several months' delay.

Despite the lessons drawn from this by General Leonard Wood, then Chief of Staff, and his recommendations, the situation in 1916 was just as bad.

The Secretary of War, Mr. Newton D. Baker, wrote in 1916: [2] "The railroads of the United States were built in response to commercial and industrial needs.... It is probably just to say, however, that very little thought has been given in our railroads' development to their possible use for military purposes. We have built no strategic railways. Our frontiers have been neglected as possible scenes of military operations and there has accordingly been little or no railroad building which has as its object a possible call upon the railroads of the country rapidly to transport large

[1] BEFORE THE WAR, by Viscount Haldane, page 186.
[2] Annual Report Secretary of War for 1916. Vol. I, page 17.

The Expedition Returns to Columbus

bodies of men and to maintain a continuous stream of military supplies for their support."

In other words, despite the lessons of 1911 nothing had been done to better matters by 1916, five years later. This regardless of the fact that not only within Mexico but on our own side of the border American property and lives were continuously endangered and frequently destroyed. Furthermore prior to the outbreak of the European War in 1914 signs were not wanting that unless we protected the lives and property of Europeans in Mexico various European nations would. When the war was well under way and our disputes with Germany had reached the point where our entry against her was becoming a certainty, her agents did what they could to use Mexico as a means of keeping our small military forces too busy to be used to organize, train and lead an army large enough seriously to intervene on the Western front.

Since Japan first began early in the present century to build up friendly relations with the Latin American countries she has cultivated Mexico.

A glance at the map shows plainly that the Mexican network of railways in 1916 was ideal for the invasion of this country. The north and south lines cross our border almost at regular intervals. They are connected by east and west lines, the terminals of which are on either the Pacific Ocean or the Gulf of Mexico, or both. Together they make a perfect transportation system for the movement of troops and supplies for the invasion of the United States.

Every European and Asiatic General Staff which has studied a possible war with this country recognizes the great advantages which would accrue from an alliance with Mexico.

Since 1916 the Mexican railway situation has been bettered. On our side of the border we are practically no better off than we were in 1916.

The difficulties experienced in transporting the Guard to the border led to so many complaints from officers and men that the House passed a resolution [1] which the Secretary of War answered by a letter dated July 21, 1916. The charges which he answered were: that troops had been moved in day coaches, that cars were furnished without lights, that trains were sidetracked or delayed, that insufficient rations were furnished and that many cars lacked the essentials to health and safety en route.

Investigation showed the majority of complaints to be properly classified, under the heading: "Unprepared to meet war conditions."

How some of the men who complained about traveling in American day coaches must have longed for them when they later rode around in the famous "40 and 8" French freight cars!

The Pullman Company answered: "It was found necessary to fill rush orders received for equipment for the transportation of troops to press into service numbers of extra sleeping cars lighted by electricity from which axle generators and batteries were removed when cars were placed in storage.... When the demand was suddenly sprung upon us for all our extra equipment....there was only one thing to do and that was to equip emergency cars for lighting by candles."

"Trains were not sidetracked or delayed beyond what should be reasonably expected due to the great number of special trains employed, most of them manned, no doubt, by extra train crews." [2]

The lack of food where it did exist was shown to be due to ignorance of the way to handle and make sufficient for the time issued, the travel ration and coffee money.

And so on, the answer to each complaint proved no preparation for such an emergency. The reason was the lack of a General Staff of sufficient size and power in Washington, to foresee, plan and complete the necessary arrangements, to move a hastily mobilized force, not organized for war, to a distant border much of which was inaccessible!

The first organization to reach the border of those mobilized under the

[1] 64th Congress. 1st Session Resolution No. 292.
[2] Secretary of War letter of July 21, 1916.

National Guard Organizations Called for Service on the Mexican Border, 1916

States, or District	Regiments of Infantry	Cavalry	Field Artillery	Engineers	Signal Corps	Sanitary Troops	Field Troops	Strength Peace	Strength War
Alabama	1st, 2d, 4th	1st Regiment	Batteries A, B		1st Company	Ambulance Co.	Field Hospital	4,410	7,646
Arizona	1st							990	1,915
Arkansas	1st, 2d							1,980	3,830
California	1st, 5th, 7th	1st Squadron						3,956	7,125
Colorado	1st,[1] 2d[1]							1,558	2,621
Connecticut	1st, 2d	Troops A, B		Company A, B		1st Ambulance Co.	1st Field Hospital	3,222	6,043
Delaware	1st,[1] 2d[1]	10th Regiment		Cos. A, B	1st Company	1st Ambulance Co.	1st Field Hospital	551	1,168
Dist. of Columbia	1st,[1] 3d				1st Company	1st Ambulance Co.	1st Field Hospital	1,731	3,104
Florida	2d	Troop A	1st Battalion		Company A	Ambulance Co.	1st Field Hospital	1,028	1,963
Georgia	1st, 2d, 5th	2d Sq., Tr. A	1st Battalion	Company A	Company A	Ambulance Cos. 1, 2	Field Hospitals 1, 2	3,823	7,043
Idaho	2d		1st Regiment		Company A	Ambulance Co.	Field Hospital	990	1,915
Illinois	1st, 2d, 3d, 4th, 7th, 8th	1st Regiment	1st Regiment	Company A	Company A	Ambulance Cos. 1, 2	Field Hospitals 1, 2	8,108	14,395
Indiana	1st, 2d, 3d	1st Squadron	1st Battalion	— do —	— do —	Ambulance Cos. 1, 2	Field Hospitals 1, 2	3,656	6,691
Iowa	1st, 2d, 3d	Troop A	Battery A	Company A	— do —	Ambulance Co.	Field Hospital 1	3,874	7,043
Kansas	1st, 2d	Troop A		Company A	— do —	Ambulance Co.	Field Hospital 1	2,268	4,191
Kentucky	1st, 2d, 3d					1st Ambulance Co.	Field Hospital 1	3,143	5,998
Louisiana	1st	2d Separate Tr.	Bat. Washington Arty.		— do —	1st Ambulance Co.	— do —	1,528	2,641
Maine	2d	Troop A	Battery A			Ambulance Co. 1	Field Hospital 1	990	1,915
Maryland	1st, 4th, 5th	1st Squadron	1st Regiment		Company A	Ambulance Co. 1	Field Hospital 1	3,267	6,185
Massachusetts	2d, 6th, 8th, 9th	1st Squadron	Batteries A, B; 1st Regiment	1st Battalion	1st Battalion	Ambulance Cos. 1, 2	Field Hospitals 1, 2	5,561	9,762
Michigan	31st, 32d, 33d	Troops A, B	1st Regiment	Company A	Company A	— do —	— do —	3,674	6,801
Minnesota	1st, 2d, 3d	1st Regiment	1st Regiment			1st Ambulance Co.	— do —	3,906	7,066
Mississippi	1st				Company A	— do —	— do —	990	1,915
Missouri	1st, 2d, 3d, 4th	Troop B	1st Battalion	Company A	Company A	Ambulance Co. 1	Field Hospital 1	4,633	8,556
Montana	2d	Troop A			Company A	Ambulance Co.	Field Hospital 1	1,068	2,018
Nebraska	4th, 5th	Troop A		Company A	— do —	Ambulance Co.	Field Hospital 1	2,100	3,985
New Hampshire	1st	Troop A	Battery A		— do —	Ambulance Co.	Field Hospital 1	2,018	2,349
New Jersey	1st, 4th, 5th	Troop A	Battery A / Battalion	1st Battalion	— do —	— do —	— do —	3,885	6,954
New Mexico	1st	1st Squadron			Company A	1st Ambulance Co.	1st Field Hospital	1,316	2,091
New York	2d, 3d, 7th, 12th, 14th, 23d, 69th, 71st, 74th	1st Regiment, Squadron A, M-G Troops	Battery A, Battalion, 1st, 2d, 3d Regts.	22d regt. (6 cos.); 2 separate cos.	1st Battalion Aero Company.	1st, 2d, 3d, 4th Ambulance Co.	1st, 2d, 3d, 4th Field Hospital	12,820	22,665
North Carolina	1st, 2d, 3d	Troops A, B		Company A, B	1st Company	Ambulance Co. 1	1st Field Hospital	3,885	6,454
North Dakota	1st	1st Squadron		1st Bat. & Co. D	1st Battalion	1st, 2d Ambulance Companies.	1st, 2d, 3d Field Hospitals.	1,128	2,091
Ohio	2d, 3d, 4th, 5th, 6th, 8th	1st Squadron	1st Battalion	1st Battalion	1st Battalion	1st, 2d Ambulance Companies.	1st, 2d, 3d Field Hospitals.	8,339	13,727
Oklahoma	1st	Troops A, B		Co. D	Company A	Ambulance Co. 1	Field Hospital 1	1,283	2,449
Oregon	3d	Troop A, B	Battery A	Cos. A, B	Company A	Ambulance Co. 1	Field Hospital 1	1,196	2,194
Pennsylvania	1st, 3d, 4th, 6th, 8th, 10th, 13th, 16th, 18th	1st Regiment	Battery A; 1st, 2d, 3d Regts.	Cos. A, B, C	1st Battalion	Ambulance Cos. 1, 2	Field Hospitals 1, 2	13,304	23,148

State									
Rhode Island	Troops A, B, C, M	Battery A	—	—	—	Ambulance Co. 1	—	496	676
South Carolina	1st, 2d	Troop A	—	Company A	—	—	1st Field Hospital	2,157	4,177
South Dakota	4th	—	—	—	—	—	—	990	1,915
Tennessee	1st, 3d	Trs. B, C, D	Battery A	—	—	—	Field Hospital 1	2,270	4,296
Texas	2d, 3d, 4th	1st Squadron	Cos. A, B	—	—	—	1st Field Hospital	3,608	6,756
Utah	1st	1st & 2nd Sqs.	1st Battery	—	—	—	— do —	796	1,081
Vermont	1st	—	—	—	—	—	—	990	1,915
Virginia	1st, 2d	1st Squadron	1st Bn., Btry. C	Company A	—	—	Field Hospital 1	3,061	5,298
Washington	2d	Troop B	—	—	do	—	—	1,140	2,100
West Virginia	2d	—	—	—	—	—	—	990	1,915
Wisconsin	1st, 2d, 3d	Troops A, B	Battery A	—	—	—	Field Hospital 1	3,287	6,204
Wyoming	1st,¹ 2d¹	—	—	—	—	—	—	564	1,153
								140,016	254,814

¹ Battalion.

second call was the First Illinois Infantry, which arrived at San Antonio, Texas, the evening and night of June 30th.

By midnight July 4, 27,160 troops had reached the border. This equivalent of an A. E. F. infantry division which reached the border on the 16th day from that of the call, came from 14 states. Their homes were as far apart as the limits of our country permits. They included units from California to Maine.

By midnight July 31, 1916, there were 110,957 officers and enlisted men of the Guard on the border. There were 40,139 in state mobilization camps. The total in Federal service was thus 151,096.

The maximum number to be in Federal service was 158,664. By November 30, 1916, the total was 100,628 when 96,447 were on the border and 4,181 were at home stations waiting to be mustered out. Of the number who served approximately 57 per cent had previous service in the National Guard, while 43 per cent were recruits.

The maximum number on the border was 111,954. This was at the end of August.

They were stationed along the whole border in moderate size detachments and in four large camps at Brownsville, Texas; San Antonio, Texas; El Paso, Texas; and Douglas, Arizona.

The total of the units not called into Federal service was 18,176.

The war strength of the units called was 267,925. The difference between this and the 158,664 furnished is 108,361.

The National Defense Act of 1916 provided for a National Guard Reserve. As a consequence the Chief of the Militia Bureau held that members of the National Guard whose three-year enlistment expired on the border could be held as reservists called to active duty. However, the Judge Advocate General of the Army decided to the contrary.

In an endeavor to make good some of this deficiency in war strength the regular army recruiting service in June began recruiting for the National Guard in Federal service. By the end of October 1916 they had recruited 15,107 men.

Besides the lack of a reserve to bring units to war strength was the necessity to recruit to make good losses due to men failing to report when units were called out, men found physically unfit when examined for muster into Federal service and discharge for a variety of reasons during the border service.

To meet the situation caused by dependent families without other support, the fathers of such families were at first ordered discharged. However, this was stopped when Congress appropriated $2,000,000 to take care of such cases.

Two National Guard Major Generals and 24 Brigadier Generals were mustered into Federal service. The Major Generals were O'Ryan in command of the New York division stationed along the lower Rio Grande, and Clement in command of the Pennsylvania division at El Paso, Texas.

The service on the border will never be forgotten by those who took part in it. There was no danger. In France there was. However, in many cases the service on the border meant greater physical discomfort. The sand, the heat, the animal pests were worse than the wind and cold of France. Also the border service became extremely monotonous, while service in France was never that; perhaps sometimes there was too much excitement!

There were some events of interest. The then Colonel Bandholtz of the Regulars, later Provost Marshal of the A. E. F. and therefore responsible for all the MPs, was Chief of Staff of the New York Division. He had formerly been Chief of the Philippine Constabulary. As a consequence he both spoke Spanish well and knew intimately the reactions of people of Spanish descent.

He proposed and General O'Ryan carried out a review of the New York Division in honor of the Mexican Commanding General across the border. The Mexican officers were treated with every courtesy. They obviously both enjoyed their visit and returned to their side of the Rio Grande impressed with the military appearance and strength of the Division.

The Pennsylvania division in carrying out its training made a march of a number of days. They began by marching from their camp north of El Paso down into that town which is separated from Mexican soil only by the Rio Grande. The galloping around and other movements soon to be seen on the Mexican side of the border showed that the Mexicans believed the American invasion of Mexico was beginning. The fact that the Division did not head for the international bridge but marched west through El Paso along the north bank of the Rio Grande did not lessen the excitement. It continued day and night until the Division headed north, turning its back on Mexico.

As time went on the officers and men who had gladly gone to the border expecting war service became restless to return to their families and normal occupations.

Many of them were making real sacrifices. Letters from home told them of family and business troubles. Many firms did not live up to their promises with respect to paying salaries and holding open positions. They heard of promotions in their civilian firms which they knew would have been theirs had they remained at home. Many wives continually urged them to come home. Some insisted it was their duty to do so.

All this helped emphasize the fact that a relatively small number of citizens were making a real sacrifice to serve their country while the majority made none.

The month after month of what practically became a peacetime garrison duty job showed that such service was of a type which should be done by Regular soldiers, men whose lives and interests are in the Army and not far away in a civilian community.

In other words the border service emphasized the facts that the country should maintain a Regular Army large enough to handle situations short of general insurrection or war and that the National Guard should not be counted on for continuous duty except in these two cases.

It also showed that to raise a war army to an effective strength and keep it there, some form of selective service is the only method which is both efficient from a military point of view and fair from the point of view of equality of sacrifice on the part of the civilian.

While those who served first on the border and then in the A. E. F. appreciate what the border service did in speeding the subsequent Great War mobilization and concentration in France, the public at large does not.

First both the National Guard and the Regulars learned to transport, train, supply and in all other ways handle bodies of troops in the field, in numbers far beyond that to which they had been previously accustomed.

There can be no doubt that the subsequent, on the whole, excellent staff work in France was largely due to the discovery by the National Guard of their great deficiencies in this respect and by the Regulars of the difference between working out problems on paper at Leavenworth and the War College and practically, above all, with a hastily raised army.

General Pershing's expedition into Mexico and the border mobilization laid the foundation for the large scale use of motor transportation by the Army from 1917 on.

Nearly 600 trucks were purchased during the fiscal year 1916. They were used not only for supply purposes, but also to increase the efficiency of the border patrols.

In other words the Mexican Border Service taught the National Guard and the Regulars what the large scale maneuvers of Continental European Armies teach them in time of peace.

Without such maneuvers the rapid and efficient mobilizations and concentrations of the French and German Armies in 1914 could never have taken place.

Without the Mexican Border Service it is extremely doubtful if General Pershing would have had the 300,000 with which he intervened in the Second Battle of the Marne; the 500,000 with which he smashed the Saint Mihiel salient and prepared the way for Foch's intended November 14th attack to open the Moselle Valley Route into Germany and the 1,200,000 used in the Argonne to first push back and then break the pivot of the German line in France.

General Pershing's evacution of Mexican soil having been determined upon, General Funston was authorized January 17, 1917, to designate 25,000 of the Guard then on the border to return home for muster out.

The movement was begun February 2d, General Funston reported it would be complete February 20th.

At 3 P.M. on February 5th the last of General Pershing's expeditionary force crossed the border between old and New Mexico just south of Columbus, the scene of Villa's raid in March of the previous year.

On February 16th, General Funston was ordered to send home all the Guard then on the border.

However, before this movement could be completed, President Wilson, afraid of interference by German agents with "the postal, commercial and military channels and instrumentalities of the United States and lacking enough Regulars," called into service or directed the retention in service of a large part of the National Guard.

The Mexican Border duty of the National Guard, in which none had been killed or wounded at an enemy's hand, thus gave place to their Great War service in which it furnished 17 of the 43 divisions which made up the A. E. F.

Appendix A

SOME CAVALRY LESSONS OF THE MEXICAN PUNITIVE EXPEDITION

In this appendix I shall touch lightly on the lessons learned by my column in this campaign. To the young cavalry soldier these lessons will be of great value in the event of another such campaign.

Troops "M" & "K" 13th Cavalry, Major Frank Tompkins Commanding, From Dublan to Parral and return to San Antonio March 21st, 1916 to May 1st, 1916.

Methods of Conducting March

In moving south we passed mostly through a mountainous country devoid of trails, obliging us to move in column of troopers, keeping a small point in front and a few men in rear. This formation was made necessary by the nature of the country, and while we were in danger of being ambushed many times each day, nevertheless should the attack come from a flank we would be always deployed, and should the attack come from the head or rear but a few men would be under fire at a time.

Wherever the country was sufficiently level we moved at a slow trot of about seven miles per hour regardless of time, trotting wherever the country would permit. This was easier on the horse than the constant walk, and covered the ground with no strain on the animals' heart, lungs, or feet, and it enabled us to constantly cut down the lead of Villa and his band. In the very hilly regions and rough parts of the trail each officer and man dismounted and lead his horse. We halted every two hours. More frequent halts were not necessary as the animals had shrunk and were worked down to hard condition, making it easy for the saddle and equipment to stay in place without constant adjustment. These two hour halts averaged about ten minutes each. At noon we always halted in some sheltered place for one hour, allowing the horses to drink and graze. We tried to hit camp about an hour before sun down, when we would water the animals, unsaddle and turn them loose to graze under a suitable guard. The horses were too tired and too hungry to run away. At the same time we all cooked our evening meal, and the officers sized up the situation with reference to defensive measures in case of attack during the night. At dark the horses were tied on a picket line where the grazing was good and fed grain.

Character of Country Covered

Going south mostly mountainous, very rough, but well watered and timbered until we reach Conchos. From Conchos to Parral was a rolling open country with but little water and practically no grass. In moving north we were in an open country. Moving on the main highway of this region, an excellent road most of the way, and well watered, with plenty of grass north of Conchos, except at Satevo, where the grass was practically nil.

Spirit of the Men

The spirit of the officers and men composing my command could not have been better. They joked about the freezing nights, the hot sun of mid day, their semi-naked condition, their constant hunger, and the hard marches. Their sole idea was to bring to a successful conclusion their dangerous mission. The hardships were simply an incident of the march, and were accepted as a part of the day's work.

Work Accomplished

This expedition showed beyond a shadow of a doubt that the Carranza military forces were hostile to our purpose, and would do all in their power

231

to oppose us. We had the satisfaction of chasing "The Lion of the North" some five hundred miles south of the northern boundary of Mexico with two troops of United States Cavalry much inferior in numbers to the Villista forces. At all times the enemy were in a country friendly to them, but in spite of the great advantage in numbers, information and position enjoyed by Villa and his command, we could not tempt them into a fight. The fact that Villa was chased so far south by this small command and other like commands undoubtedly caused him to lose much of the military and political prestige he enjoyed previous to the Columbus Raid. In addition to the foregoing our troops learned a great deal of Mexico and Mexicans. We now know that we can enter that country with small commands, cut loose from the base and exist off the country for an indefinite period. We also taught the Pacificos that the American soldier does not make war on women and children, that he pays for what he gets, that he respects persons and property, and that wherever he goes those who treat him honestly are benefitted by his presence.

Experienced Gained

My experience in Mexico operating in any enemy country far from the base, making it necessary to live off the country, has convinced me of the following:

The Soldiers Mount:

This service showed that the compactly built horse stood the campaign much better than the tall, leggy type. Our horses never even got half feed and it was a constant effort to keep the big ones on the job. The little fellows also did better in the mountains and the rough places. The cavalry horse should be an animal low on his legs, of full form, one that when in low flesh does not show it—a horse whose bone, muscular development, energy and reserve power are denoted by a certain balance not often seen in horses over 15 hands 2 inches. The height of the cavalry horse should range between 14-2 and 15-2.

I cannot leave this subject of cavalry mounts without a tribute to my little horse Kingfisher. At the time of this campaign he was four years old, 14 hands three inches high and when in hard flesh weighed a little under 800 pounds. He was an Arab stallion with some of the best Arab blood in his veins. His breeding was a matter of record and is beyond dispute.

This little horse crossed the international boundary line into Mexico March 15, 1916 in pursuit of Villa and his outlaw band.

From March 15th to March 26th he was ridden 219 miles, and from March 31st to April 12th 362 miles, across the deserts, over the mountains, and through the waterless wastes of Northern Chihuahua, carrying his rider, food for man and horse, in addition to the usual pack an officer must take when operating in a hostile country far from the base or line of communications; a load well over 200 pounds.

After marching 219 miles in eleven days on less than half forage, on March 31st he led a small band of horsemen in a dash after Villa which ended in the fight at Parral on April 12th, covering a distance of 362 miles in 13 days. In this drive he had but little grain, and that corn which he had never before eaten, no hay, and what dead grass he could get during the night while tethered to a short chain. He negotiated the snows of the mountain passes, he sweated through the noon-day heat of the lower levels, and he shivered at night from the icy winds of these high altitudes.

He never showed any signs of fatigue, never lost courage, and was a constant inspiration to his rider. He lost but little flesh, always moved with a quick springy step with head and tail alertly raised, animated and watchful. In battle he was fearless, being quite content to keep on the firing line without fuss or objection.

From April 22nd to June 9th he was ridden 300 miles but under better conditions than he experienced previous to April 12th. He went lame but once due to a thorn in the frog, but he did his work just the same. He was never sick and he was always ready.

Fully aware that the success of our mission depended in a large measure on the fitness of our horses, officers and men bent every energy to the care of their mounts. We did not, however, sacrifice mobility in order to save animals as a reference to our itinerary will show (From Dublan to Parral and back to San Antonio we marched about 667 miles); and also that we arrived at San Borja three days in advance of the next American column and at Parral two days ahead of any other American column. Our horses were ready at all times for a last and supreme effort in the event of encountering Villa and his men.

It is of interest to note that in troop "K" three horses were abandoned on the trail from exhaustion, and that of these one horse had been pronounced unfit for service before we left the United States, one had been just received from another regiment, and one was a young remount not yet hardened to service. In Troop "M" four horses were abandoned on the trail from exhaustion, and that of these one had been pronounced unfit for service before we left the United States, and three horses were just received from another regiment. The horses sent from the other regiment were probably the least desirable in the regiment.

The Bridle:

The bridle should be strong and of simple construction with but few buckles, and admit of the use of the bit and bridoon. In the field the curb bit should be left at home as a horse can drink easily and quickly with the snaffle bit in his mouth when he cannot drink with two bits; and for the same reason he can graze with one bit when he cannot with two; it being often dangerous or through lack of time impracticable to remove the bits from the animal's mouth.

Each bridle should be equipped with the link strap. This strap should be attached to the off snaffle ring, pass under the chin, through the near snaffle ring and snap in the bridle on the near side of the horse's head. In linking unsnap and snap into halter ring of horse on left. This is not only quicker than tying horses together by reins, but it is certain, and there is no chance for bungling in moments of excitement.

The Halter:

Should be made strong. The nose band should run through a ring attached to the throat latch by a short strap, the tie chain strapped into a ring in the nose band, thus any strain on the chain simply conveys the pull to the animal's nose with but little strain on the throat latch. The present halter is constantly breaking at the throat latch. The tieing device should be a chain with a snap and swivel at each end. In the field away from salt, horses soon chew up leather, webbing and rope shanks, thus getting loose at night, and in some instances wandering off and not returning. The chain is durable, will not break, and cannot be eaten, and when passed around the animal's neck on the march is soundless.

The Saddle:

I believe the McClellan saddle a better military saddle than the hinged saddle. The McClellan, however, should be changed in certain minor points: the pommel arch should be higher and wider, more like the stock saddle. All of our saddles are modeled to fit the backs of horses in full flesh, while as a matter of fact horses in campaign are always thin. Why not have a saddle made to fit a horse when he is thin? The stirrups should be hung about two inches farther to the *rear*, and should have the same tread as now with the leather *hood*. The knife edge metal tread is hard on the foot and offers no protection from sun rain or snow. In emergencies the hoods can be used to sole the troopers' shoes. This campaign has shown that both officers and men must carry on their saddles, in addition to the usual pack, food and grain in quantities never before thought possible, and to do this the saddles must admit of being packed with as little injury to the horse as possible. In this entire campaign there were no emergency rations issued; had there been such issues the problem of supplying food to the flying columns would, to a certain extent, have been solved. There had been on hand at Fort Huachuca (Hdqrs. 10th Cav.) over 800 Armour emergency rations which had been inspected by an Army Inspector, condemned and ordered sold; this over the protest of Col. W. C. Brown, who had tested several and found them to be perfectly good.

After the expedition had started Brown by telegraph had these bid in on his personal account and ordered shipped to the command with the intention of dividing them among the advance troops. These rations never arrived, and Brown even lost the $25 which he had paid for them.

I believe the McClellan saddle can be better and more easily packed than any other saddle in our service. The rifle should be carried on the saddle, under the trooper's leg, on near side of horse. When carried with the butt in a bucket, or on the trooper's back, the barrel sloping upward with the muzzle above the soldier's shoulder is very apt to catch in branches while passing under trees, resulting in a heavy and dangerous fall for the man. This accident has happened several times with men equipped with the new equipment.

The Blanket:
No change.

Bandoleers:
The cotton bandoleer was never intended to be carried day after day over the soldier's shoulder. This, however, was done in this campaign. We soon found out that the friction wore holes in this bandoleer and much ammunition was lost. Each trooper, in addition to his belt, should be issued two web bandoleers. These web bandoleers could be made to take the place of the cartridge belt suspenders.

The Lariat:
Should be retained. A light but strong rope similar to the kind used by cow men. The picket pin might well be dispensed with. Hobbles should be issued as they would be a great aid in herding horses, and many times grass is the only food a horse can get. The use of hobbles would make a stampede impossible.

Pistol:
I believe the 45 cal. Colt revolver is a better weapon than the automatic pistol. The automatic sometimes jams when the pistol is dirty, and then it is dependent absolutely on the magazine. Damage or lose your magazine and the weapon is useless. It is an arm of two parts while the revolver is all in one piece.

Sword:
The present saber or sword is too heavy. I believe in a straight short blade with a cutting edge, something like a machete. This weapon would not only be dangerous to an enemy, but it would find many uses in camp. A trooper equipped with such a tool could cut a bundle of grass for his horse in short order.

Breeches:
They should be reinforced at the knee so as to cover the knee above, below and to the outer seam. There should also be a reinforcement covering the seat. The breeches first give way at the knees and then at the seat.

Leggins:
The leather leggin worn on this campaign was a failure in that it soon wore out, was uncomfortable, and in some cases damaged the soldier's foot just above the heel. When this campaign was over I recommended the adoption of the canvas legging used in 1898 with the spat effect over the instep and the strap under the instep. This leggin for cavalry and field artillery should be reinforced with leather on inner side of calf and so placed as to take up wear of stirrup leathers.

Shoes:
Unlined, flesh side out, double soles, hob nailed, leather laces.

Hat:
As at present.

O. D. Shirt:

Present issue with longer tails. The long tail acts as an abdominal band, is a protection to the stomach, and can be used as a suspensory.

Canteen:

Issue of 1898 carried on saddle and not in saddle pockets. Old model quart tin cup is the best. Aluminum mess kit soon melts under daily service in individual cooking. Old tin issue the best.

Rifle:

The present rifle is too long and too heavy for the cavalry. I suggest a carbine about the size of the old Krag carbine chambered to shoot same ammunition as the infantry rifle.

Pack Train:

Each troop for every fifty men should have, a pack train of 12 mules, with packers, assigned as follows:

1 mule carry cooking outfit, one day's rations, three days' emergency rations.

1 mule carry horseshoer's outfit and extra shoes.

1 mule carry picket line and extra shoes.

9 mules carry rations and forage.

Individual cooking is a mistake. Better to dismount a man and use his horse to carry cooking outfit. When each man does his own cooking there is a waste of rations, sickness, and the horse suffers a certain amount of neglect that would not be the case when cooking is central. It also takes time that could be spent in resting, cleaning arms, overhauling equipment etc.

Horseshoes:

With the McClellan saddle the extra shoes should be wired to the under side of the stirrup tread, the front shoe on under side of right stirrup and the hind shoe on the left stirrup, or in specially constructed pockets on outside of saddle bags. We experienced great difficulty in keeping our horses shod, as the native shoes were entirely too small, and the stony nature of the soil was such as to wear away the shoes quickly, and in addition the large horses were constantly stubbing their toes on the rocks of the narrow trails, causing many shoes to be cast. Whenever we passed a dead horse, if he had any shoes on, we pulled them off for future use. We also tried changing a half worn right shoe to the left foot, and a half worn left shoe to the right foot, thus bringing the wear on a new place and lengthening the life of the shoe from seven to ten days, before it would break.

Appendix B

REPORT OF THE OPERATIONS OF THE FIRST AERO SQUADRON, SIGNAL CORPS, WITH THE MEXICAN PUNITIVE EXPEDITION, FOR PERIOD MARCH 15 TO AUGUST 15, 1916.

By Capt. Benjamin D. Foulois, *Signal Corps, U. S. Army*[1]

By virtue of its participation as a combat unit with the Punitive Expedition into Mexico, the 1st Aero Squadron was the first organization of its kind that was ever used in active field service in the history of the United States Army. The Squadron took the field with airplanes of very low military efficiency, and with less than fifty percent of its authorized allowance of truck transportation.

Receiving orders on March 12, 1916, to join the Punitive Expedition into Mexico, the 1st Aero Squadron proceeded to Columbus, New Mexico, and immediately began to assemble the aeronautical equipment shipped from Fort Sam Houston, Texas. This equipment consisted of eight airplanes. The Squadron personnel numbered 11 officers, pilots; 84 enlisted men, including two from the Hospital Corps; and one civilian mechanician. The piloting personnel were Captains Benjamin D. Foulois, T. F. Dodd, Lieuts. C. G. Chapman, J. E. Carberry, Herbert A. Dargue, Thomas S. Bowen, R. H. Willis, Walter G. Kilner, Edgar S. Gorell, Arthur R. Christie and Ira A. Rader. Upon its arrival at El Paso, Texas, the Squadron was joined by 1st Lieut. S. S. Warren, Medical Reserve Corps, and one enlisted man.

With ten trucks and one automobile and two additional trucks, later received from the Depot Quartermaster at El Paso, Texas, the Squadron had about fifty percent of its necessary motor transportation. This transportation, on March 16-17, 1916, was turned over to the Quartermaster of the Punitive Expedition for hauling supplies to troops on the march into Mexico.

In addition to performing its regular functions, the Squadron assisted the Quartermaster Corps in assembling its motor transportation. On March 18th, 27 Jeffrey truck chassis with escort wagon bodies (knocked down) arrived at Columbus. The Quartermaster Corps having no men or material to install these escort wagon bodies, the Engineer Section of the Squadron, with its portable machine shop, took charge of this work and remained at Columbus until it was completed. Approximately one half of the enlisted strength of the Squadron was also left at Columbus until such time as transportation became available.

The first reconnaissance flight into Mexico was made on March 16th, Captain Dodd piloting Airplane #44, with Captain Foulois as observer.

Telegraphic orders being received from the Division Commander at Nueva Casas Grandes, Mexico, for the Squadron to proceed at once to that point for immediate service, all of the eight airplanes of the Squadron were started in flight from Columbus at 5:10 P. M., on March 19th. Due to motor trouble, one of the airplanes was compelled to return to Columbus. Darkness overtook the seven other planes before they reached their destination, four of them being landed at Ascencion, Mexico, and the three remaining ones which became separated in the darkness landed at as many different points, one at Ojo Caliente, one at Janos, and the third was wrecked in landing near Pearson. Three days later, a detachment was sent to salvage such parts of airplane No. 41, wrecked at Pearson, as were serviceable. This detachment returned and reported that it had been fired upon by Mexicans in the vicinity of Pearson. A detachment was again sent the

---

[1] Now Major General, Chief of Air Service, U. S. A.

following day, March 23rd, to Pearson, and returned to Dublan with such parts of the wrecked airplane as could be considered serviceable.

On March 20th the four pilots who landed at Ascencion proceeded south to Casas Grandes and reported for duty. The pilot who was compelled to return to Columbus, and the one who had landed at Janos, arrived at Casas Grandes at approximately the same hour. The pilot who had landed at Ojo Caliente arrived at Casas Grandes several days later, having incurred slight damage to his plane which had to be repaired. The airplane which crashed near Pearson was so badly damaged that the pilot abandoned it and made his way to Casas Grandes on foot.

Upon reporting to the Division Commander, instructions were received to make an aerial reconnaissance south toward Cumbre Pass, in the heart of the Sierra Madre Mountains, for the purpose of locating troops moving south toward Lake Babicora.

At noon on March 20th, Captain T. F. Dodd, pilot, with Captain B. D. Foulois, observer, in Airplane #44, proceeded south from Casas Grandes, but only traversed a distance of about 25 miles, being unable to rise over the foothills of the Sierra Madre Mountains. Whirlwinds and terrific vertical currents of air were constantly encountered, and insufficient engine power effectually prevented the airplane rising to an altitude sufficiently high to enable it to cross the mountains which at this particular locality rise to a height of over 10,000 feet above sea level.

Misfortune overtook Lieut. T. S. Bowen, pilot, who on this same date, while attempting to land Airplane #44, was caught in a whirlwind. The plane was completely wrecked, but Lieut. Bowen escaped with a broken nose and minor injuries.

The mission assigned the Squadron on March 21st was to ascertain the whereabouts of the troops under Colonel Erwin in the Galeana Valley. Captain T. F. Dodd, pilot, flying Airplane #44, with Captain B. D. Foulois, observer, took off from Dublan, located these troops at Galera Lopena, landed, reported to Colonel Erwin, received a report from him and returned to Dublan. As a result of this reconnaissance and report from Colonel Erwin, six trucks of the Squadron, loaded with supplies, were sent to Colonel Erwin's column.

Of the two missions assigned the Squadron on March 22nd, the one which was successful was the locating of Colonel G. A. Dodd's command in the Galeana Valley. It was flown by Lieut. W. G. Kilner, pilot, and Lieut. Ira A. Rader, observer, in Airplane #42, and by Lieut. J. E. Carberry, pilot, in Airplane #45. Reaching the Galeana Valley and locating the troops, the pilots landed, reported to Colonel Dodd, and then returned to Dublan with reports from him to the Division Commander. The mission which was participated in by Captain T. F. Dodd, piloting Airplane #44, with Lieut. A. R. Christie as observer, and Lieut. C. G. Chapman, piloting Airplane #53, resulted in failure, due to unsuitable flying equipment. Flying south in an endeavor to locate the troops moving south on the Mexican Northwestern Railroad, the airplanes were driven into the heart of the Sierra Madre Mountains as far as the northern end of the Cumbre Pass tunnel. Due, however, to the terrific vertical air currents and whirlwinds, which at times drove the airplanes within 20 feet of the tree tops the pilots were unable to cross these mountains and were compelled to return to Dublan.

As a result of the failure of the airmen to accomplish the reconnaissance directed, the Squadron Commander submitted a memorandum to the Division Commander recommending the purchase of new equipment, since experience had shown that the airplanes with which the Squadron was equipped were not capable of meeting military service conditions. The new equipment which he requested be immediately purchased is enumerated below, as follows:

Two Martin airplanes, Model S, with army standard landing gear, Hall-Scott 125 h.p. 6-cylinder motors.

Two Curtiss airplanes, Model R2, Curtiss 160 h.p. steel cylinder motors.

Two Sturtevant airplanes, 140 h.p. Sturtevant motors.

Two Thomas airplanes, 135 h.p. Thomas motors.

Two Sloane airplanes, 125 h.p. Hall-Scott 6-cylinder motors.

All of the airplanes above to be completely equipped and ready for immediate use.

The manufacturer to furnish one spare motor for each two machines purchased and, in addition, the following airplane and motor spares:

Two spare propellers.

One set lower wings, complete, with fittings and wires.

One landing gear complete.

One set tail control surfaces complete with fittings and wires.

Three spare radiators.

Three spare magnetos.

Receiving orders on March 23rd to communicate with Colonel G. A. Dodd's troops in the Galeana Valley, Lieuts. Christie, Carberry and Chapman, piloting Airplanes #44, #45 and #53, respectively, flew to El Valle, landed, and reported to Colonel Dodd. The pilots were unable to return to Dublan until March 25th, due to high winds, dust and snow storms.

On March 30th, the Squadron Commander, Captain B. D. Foulois, submitted the following plans to the Division Commander which contemplated the establishment of airplane and fuel bases in advance of Division Headquarters:

PLAN I.

OBJECT: To maintain aero communication between Columbus, N. M., Casas Grandes, El Valle and Namiquipa.

(a) Two airplanes with sufficient commissioned and enlisted personnel and supplies to take station at El Valle. One airplane to fly from El Valle to Namiquipa every morning, returning the following morning to El Valle.

(b) Two airplanes to be assigned to maintain aerial communication between Casas Grandes and Columbus, as follows: One airplane to leave Casas Grandes every morning, flying to Columbus without stop, returning the following morning without stop.

(c) Two airplanes to be assigned to maintain aerial communication between Casas Grandes and Namiquipa, as follows: One airplane to leave Casas Grandes every morning, flying to Namiquipa without stop, returning the following morning without stop.

The foregoing plan contemplates the maximum use of all aviators and all airplanes for maintaining aerial communication between Columbus—Casas Grandes—El Valle and Namiquipa only, and does not contemplate the use of airplanes for communication south, east or west of Namiquipa.

PLAN II.

OBJECT: To maintain aerial communication between Casas Grandes—El Valle—Namiquipa—and points south of Namiquipa, communication between Casas Grandes to be maintained by radio-telegraph, motorcycles and road transportation.

(a) Transfer entire squadron of six airplanes to Namiquipa, maintaining fuel bases only, at Casas Grandes, El Valle, and an advanced fuel base south of Namiquipa, location to be determined later.

(b) Upon transfer of Squadron to Namiquipa, the following assignment of airplanes to be made:

(1) Two airplanes to maintain daily communication between Namiquipa and Casas Grandes.

(2) Two airplanes to maintain daily aerial communication between Namiquipa and El Valle.

(3) Two airplanes to maintain daily aerial communication between Namiquipa and points south, within effective radius of airplanes.

PLAN III.

(a) Upon the establishment of effective radio-telegraph communication between Namiquipa and Casas Grandes, the following is recommended:

1. Discontinue the use of airplanes between Namiquipa and Casas Grandes except in emergencies.

2. Continue the airplane communication between Namiquipa and El Valle, if radio-telegraph, motorcycles, or other means fail.

3. Concentrate all available airplanes at Namiquipa for daily communication between Namiquipa and advanced troops.

4. If communication between Namiquipa and El Valle is of secondary importance only and can be maintained by radio-telegraph, motorcycles, or other means of communication, the use of airplanes between these two points should also be discontinued, and every available airplane concentrated at Namiquipa for the purpose of maintaining communication south of Namiquipa.

PLAN IV.

(a) In the event that contact is gained with the enemy, it is recommended that every available airplane be concentrated at the front for observation and reconnaissance of the enemy, as far as practicable.

In connection with the foregoing plans for the effective use of the airplanes of the 1st Aero Squadron, the Squadron Commander stated that the six airplanes in use were for nearly ten months subjected to severe weather conditions in Oklahoma and Texas, being exposed to rain, high winds and severe cold weather. As a result of the wear and tear on these planes during these months of field service, and with the present extreme field service conditions, every machine is liable at any day to be placed out of commission as unfit and too dangerous for further field service.

The Squadron Commander further stated that these airplanes are not capable of meeting the present military needs incident to the expedition, their low power motors and limited climbing ability with the necessary military load making it impossible to operate them safely in the vicinity of the mountains which cover the present theater of operations. These same limitations as to power, climbing ability, and weight-carrying ability limit these planes to safe operations for a few hours each day, chiefly on account of the altitude and extremely severe atmospheric conditions encountered every day in the present theater of operations.

In conclusion, the Squadron Commander urged that the organization be supplied at the earliest possible moment with at least ten of the highest powered, highest climbing and best weight carrying airplanes that could be found and purchased in the United States, stating that with this new equipment the present commissioned and enlisted personnel of the organization will be able, under the present service conditions, to increase its effectiveness to the expedition at least five hundred percent. So far as concerned the present equipment of the Squadron, even the united efforts of the entire technical ability of the command cannot make the planes suitable to meet the present military needs, although the entire commissioned and enlisted personnel are exerting every effort to maintain all airplanes in the best possible condition for further field service.

Plan No. III was approved and ordered placed in effect on April 1st.

Between the dates of March 26th and April 4th, inclusive, the piloting personnel of the 1st Aero Squadron made a total of 79 flights, most of them for the purpose of carrying mail and dispatches. During this period the planes traveled between Columbus, New Mexico, and such points in Mexico as Dublan, Espindoleno, Galera Lopena, El Valle, Cruces, Namiquipa, San Geronimo, Santa Ana, and Bachineva. Starting on March 26th with 9 flights, a total of 7 was made on March 27th, 2 on the 28th, 6 on the 29th, 3 on the 30th, 9 on the 31st, 19 on April 1st, 14 on the 2nd, 6 on the 3rd, and 4 on the 4th.

On March 28th, Airplane #53, piloted by Lieut. Chapman, was flown east and south from El Valle for a distance of 110 miles and back. On March 30th, that portion of the Squadron personnel left at Columbus, N. M., to assemble truck bodies, reported at Dublan. These men, after the departure of the Squadron from Columbus, had assembled and installed 54 truck bodies on two Quartermaster truck trains in four days and nights.

During the nine flights by four airplanes on March 31st between Dublan, El Valle, Namiquipa and San Geronimo, carrying mail and dispatches, severe rain, hail and snow storms were encountered, necessitating several forced landings away from the base at Dublan until the storms had passed. Similar weather conditions on the following day caused more forced landings.

The Squadron, on April 5th, changed its headquarters to San Geronimo. On this date seven flights were made by four airplanes, between Dublan, El Valle, Namiquipa and San Geronimo, carrying mail and dispatches. Orders were received to locate Colonel W. C. Brown's column, which was reported in the vicinity of San Antonio. With Captain Foulois as observer, Lieut. H. A. Dargue, piloting Airplane #43, left San Geronimo on this reconnaissance, flew to San Antonio and located a pack train of Colonel Brown's column returning towards San Geronimo. Landing and receiving information that troops were proceeding toward Cusihuirachic, Lieut. Dargue flew towards the canyon of that name, located the troops entering it, landed and reported to Colonel Brown. He then flew back to San Geronimo with a report from Colonel Brown to the Division Commander.

During one of the four flights made by three airplanes on April 6th, carrying mail and dispatches to troops between Namiquipa, San Geronimo and Cusihuirachic, Airplane #44, was so badly damaged on landing at San Geronimo that all serviceable parts were salvaged and the remainder of the plane condemned and destroyed.

Perhaps the most dramatic incident experienced by the American airmen during their service with the Punitive Expedition occurred on April 7th at Chihuahua City, Mexico. Airplanes #43 and #45 were flown from San Geronimo to Chihuahua City by Lieut. Dargue, with Captain Foulois as observer, and by Lieut. Carberry with Captain Dodd as observer, the object of the mission being to deliver dispatches to Mr. Marion Letcher, the American Consul at that point. Lieut. Dargue carried the original dispatches and Lieut. Carberry duplicates thereof. Both airplanes arrived at Chihuahua City at the same time, causing considerable excitement.

Through previous arrangement, Lieut. Dargue landed on the south side of the city and Lieut. Carberry on the north side. After Captain Foulois left the plane, Lieut. Dargue was directed to fly his plane to the north side of the town in order to join Airplane #45. As he started off, four mounted rurales opened fire on him at a distance of about one-half mile. Captain Foulois, having started into town, heard the firing, proceeded in the direction of the rurales and stopped their firing. He was then arrested by the rurales and taken to the city jail, followed by a mob of several hundred men and boys. Enroute to the jail, Captain Foulois succeeded in getting word to an American bystander, requesting that he notify the American Consul of his arrival in that city and that the Consul take the necessary steps for the protection of all aviators and machines that had arrived in the city. Upon his arrival at the city jail and after considerable delay, Captain Foulois succeeded in getting in touch with Colonel Miranda, Chief of Staff to General Gutierrez, Military Governor of Chihuahua. Colonel Miranda then took Captain Foulois to see General Gutierrez, who soon ordered Captain Foulois' release. The latter then requested that a guard be placed over the two airplanes, which was granted. In company with Colonel Miranda, Captain Foulois then proceeded to the north side of the city to locate the other three aviators and airplanes. Arriving at the landing place, only Lieut. Dargue, with Airplane #43, was found, and he reported that after landing alongside of Airplane #45, Captain Dodd proceeded into Chihuahua City to locate the American Consul and deliver his duplicate dispatches; that after Captain Dodd had left, a large crowd of natives, Carranzista soldiers, and officers, had collected and proceeded to crowd around the machine, making insulting remarks; that several natives burned holes with cigarettes in the wings of Airplane #43; that others had slashed the cloth with knives in several places and extracted bolts and nuts from both machines.

Feeling that the mob would ultimately wreck the planes, Lieuts. Dargue and Carberry decided to fly them to the smelters of the American Smelting and Refining Company, located about six miles from Chihuahua City. Lieut. Carberry got away safely without encountering any further difficulties.

The Old and the New. Four Line Teams Passing a Mired Truck

Aircraft Used on the Border

Lieut. Dargue took off in the midst of a shower of stones, thrown at him by the mob. He had only flown a short distance when the top section of the fuselage flew off and damaged the stabilizer, causing him to make an immediate landing, which he accomplished safely. He then stood off the crowd without further damage to the airplane or to himself until the arrival of the guard. Captains Foulois and Dodd spent the remainder of the day with the American Consul in arranging for supplies to be sent to the advance troops by railroad. Lieuts. Dargue and Carberry spent the remainder of the day repairing the damage done by the mob on the two airplanes.

On the following day the pilots and observers took off from Chihuahua City to San Geronimo with dispatches from the American Consul to the Division Commander. Orders were received to move the Squadron base to San Antonio, Mexico.

Five airplanes participated in ten flights between Namiquipa, San Geronimo and San Antonio on April 9th.

Orders being received on April 10th to locate troops in the vicinity of San Borja, Mexico, Lieut. Dargue, piloting Airplane #43, with Captain Foulois as observer, and Lieut. J. E. Carberry, piloting Airplane #45, with Captain Dodd as observer, reconnoitered the area from San Antonio to Ojo Azules—Ojo Caliente—San Borja—Santa Maris—Tres Hermanos—Satevo—San Lucas—Santa Cruz—Manula—Carretas—Santa Ysabel and return to San Antonio. No troops were discovered in this area. The Squadron base was moved to Satevo, in compliance with orders.

Squadron activities on April 11th were featured by a 315 mile flight by Lieut. H. A. Dargue with Lieut. Gorrell, as observer, from San Antonio, Mexico, to Columbus, New Mexico, with one stop at Dublan. Ten flights, by five airplanes, were made between Satevo, Santa Rosalia, San Lucas, San Antonio, Namiquipa, Dublan and Columbus, N. M. Flying Airplane #53 on a reconnaissance trip to Santa Rosalia, south of Chihuahua City, on Mexican Central Railway, Lieut. Chapman, upon landing at Santa Rosalia, was taken by Carranza troops to the Commanding Officer of the Carranza garrison. During his absence from the plane, his field glasses, goggles and considerable ammunition were stolen by the Carranza soldiers. The squadron truck train, which arrived at Satevo at 11:00 P. M., was fired upon by a Villista band in passing the village of Cienagas, about 15 miles north of Satevo. No casualties occurred, however.

Among the six flights made by three airplanes on April 12th between Satevo, San Geronimo, Namiquipa and south towards Parral, was a reconnaissance mission by Lieut. Chapman in Airplane #53, for the purpose of locating troops moving in the direction of Parral.

Another reconnaissance flight south towards Parral was made the following day by Lieut. Ira A. Rader, piloting Airplane #42, for the purpose of locating troops. None were located, however. Four flights were made in three planes between Satevo, Chihuahua City and San Andreas. Flying Airplane #45 to Chihuahua City with dispatches for the American Consul, Lieut. Carberry, pilot, and Captain Foulois observer, received first information regarding the fight at Parral.

A non-stop flight of 315 miles, the record up to that time for distance with two men in the plane, featured the activities of the Squadron on April 14th. This flight, was made by Lieut. H. A. Dargue, with Lieut. Gorrell as observer, using Airplane #43, was for the purpose of making a reconnaissance from Columbus, N. M., to Boca Grande, Pulpit Pass, Oxaca Pass, Carretas, Janos, Ascencion and return to Columbus, in order to locate a large Carranzista force reported to be moving east towards the American line of communications. No hostile troops were located within the area covered.

In a reconnaissance flight south from Satevo towards Parral, Lieut. Rader, piloting Airplane #52, located Major Robert L. Howze's command in the vicinity of Ojito, near Duranga State line. The pilot was compelled to land on very rough ground and damaged the airplane. Being in a hostile country, 100 miles from the nearest base, and unable to make the necessary repairs, Lieut. Rader abandoned the plane and proceeded to Major Howze's column.

In a flight in Airplane #45 from Chihuahua City to Satevo, Lieut. Carberry, pilot, with Captain Foulois, observer, carried dispatches from Mr. Marion H. Letcher, the American Consul, and from General Gutierrez, the Military Governor of Chihuahua. Later in the day, Captain Foulois and 14 enlisted men of the Squadron proceeded from Satevo to Chihuahua City in automobile and truck with dispatches for the American Consul and General Gutierrez. Due to the intense feeling in Chihuahua City over the clash between the American troops and troops at Parral, the detachment of enlisted men was placed in concealment in the outskirts of the city. Captain Foulois, accompanied by Corporal Arthur Westermark (chauffeur) proceeded to the American Consulate, delivered the dispatches for the American Consul and the Military Governor, left the city without difficulty and returned to Division Headquarters at Satevo.

Lieut. Dargue, on April 15th, exceeded all previous long distance flights in accomplishing a reconnaissance mission from Columbus, N. M., to Boca Grande, Pulpit Pass, Dublan, Namiquipa and Satevo. This flight totalled a distance of 415 miles, with stops at Dublan and Namiquipa. Three other flights were made between Satevo, San Antonio and Namiquipa, carrying mail and dispatches. Airplane #42 was dismantled, condemned and destroyed. Its lower wings, however, were placed on Airplane #45 to replace those damaged in the flight to Chihuahua City.

From April 16th to April 18th, two flights were made each day between Satevo, San Antonio and Namiquipa, carrying mail and dispatches. On April 17th the Squadron headquarters was moved to Namiquipa.

Airplane #43, which carried Lieut. Dargue on several notable flights during the flight operations of the Squadron with the Punitive Expedition made its last flight on April 19th. It was piloted by Lieut. Dargue on a reconnaissance mission from San Antonio to Chihuahua City, with Captain R. E. Willis as observer. All roads in the vicinity of Chihuahua City were reconnoitered and several photographs taken. While reconnoitering roads in the hills west of Chihuahua City, motor failure necessitated a forced landing in the hills, completely wrecking the plane. Lieut. Dargue escaped without injury, but Captain Willis, who was pinned under the wreckage, sustained a severe scalp wound and was considerably bruised about the legs and ankles. Wrecked beyond all hope of repair, the airplane was burnt on the spot, and the two aviators with their personal equipment started to walk to San Antonio, their nearest base, a distance of about 65 miles. Two days later, after constantly suffering hardships due to lack of food and water, they reached San Antonio, where they remained until April 23rd and then proceeded by automobile to Namiquipa and reported the results of their reconnaissance to the Division Commander.

With only two airplanes left, and these in unserviceable condition, the Squadron received orders on April 20th to return to Columbus, N. M., to secure new airplanes, and arrived there on April 22nd. Awaiting them were four airplanes which had been purchased from the Curtiss Aeroplane Company. The period from April 23rd to 29th was utilized by the Squadron in testing these four new airplanes. In practical flight tests, however, it was found that they were unsuitable for Mexican field service.

Two Curtiss R-2 type, 160 h.p. planes were received on May 1, 1916, and by the 25th of that month twelve planes of this type had arrived. During the months of May, June and July, constant troubles and difficulties were encountered with defective propellers, motor parts and defects in construction. The propeller question was the most vital. Propellers were received from manufacturers all over the United States and sent to Columbus to be tested. To perform this work properly, the Squadron constructed a motor and propeller testing stand for testing all motors and propellers received. On account of the lack of field facilities for accurate work, testing operations progressed very slowly but sufficiently satisfactory to determine the suitability of all propellers received for test.

Since practically all types of propellers received proved unserviceable, chiefly due to climatic conditions, steps were taken to build propellers at

Columbus, and three civilian employees of the Curtiss Aeroplane Company arrived on June 29th and commenced the work of building propellers.

In addition to the problems encountered in connection with the mechanical defects of airplanes, motors and propellers, the Squadron carried on extensive experiments with an automatic camera, considered to be one of the most valuable adjuncts in existence for use in aero-reconnaissance. The Squadron Commander stated that this camera takes a continuous string of pictures, of a limited section of terrain over which an airplane may be passing. These pictures, when developed and fitted together, are equivalent to a road map of the section traversed, and superior to the road map in the detail that is represented.

A total of 21 new Jeffrey (Quad) trucks were received and assigned to the Squadron on April 12th, all of the old trucks then in use being then transferred to the Quartermaster Corps. In the following three months a large amount of work was required in making alterations and repairs to all new trucks, it being found that, while the new trucks were of the same type as the old trucks used by the Squadron in Mexico, they were very much inferior in workmanship. Many of the troubles encountered with the new trucks were eliminated, but they were still behind in efficiency as compared to the old trucks of the same type. Comparative tests were carried on by the Squadron, in cooperation with the Jeffrey Company, with the object of developing improvements in motors and chassis.

In addition to the foregoing duties, the Squadron drew up a complete Unit Equipment for an Aero Squadron which was submitted to the Chief Signal Officer for approval.

Due to the lack of airplanes with greater carrying capacity, flying officers were continually called upon to take extraordinary risks in every reconnaissance flight made while on duty in Mexico. All officers thoroughly appreciated the fact that motor failure while flying through mountainous canyons and over rugged mountains would invariably result in death. They also realized that, in the event of a forced landing, even if safely made, there was every possible risk of being taken prisoner by an enemy whose ideas of the laws of war might not be on a par with those of our own country.

All officer pilots on duty with Squadron during its active service in Mexico were constantly exposed to personal risk and physical suffering. Due to the inadequate weight-carrying capacity of the airplanes, it was impossible to carry even sufficient food, water or clothing on many of the reconnaissance flights. During their flights the pilots were frequently caught in snow, rain and hail storms which because of their inadequate clothing, invariably caused excessive suffering.

In several instances, the pilots were compelled to make forced landings in desert and hostile country, 50 to 70 miles from the nearest troops. In every case, the airplanes were abandoned or destroyed and the pilots, after experiencing all possible suffering due to the lack of food and water, would finally work their way on foot, through alkali deserts and mountains, to friendly troops, usually arriving thoroughly exhausted as a result of these hardships.

During the operations of the 1st Aero Squadron with the Punitive Expedition, from March 15 to August 15, 1916, 540 flights were made for a total flying time of 345 hours and 43 minutes. The distance flown during this period totalled 19,553 miles.

It is interesting to note that during the first month's operations of the Squadron, March 19th to April 20th, five of the eight airplanes taken into Mexico were wrecked and one, which was damaged in a forced landing at a point too distant from any repair facilities, was abandoned, so that on April 20th only two airplanes, Nos. 45 and 53 remained, and these were in such condition as to be unsafe for further field service. They were forthwith flown back to Columbus, N. M., and ultimately condemned and destroyed.

In concluding his report of the operations of the 1st Aero Squadron with the Punitive Expedition from March 15 to August 15, 1916, the Squadron Commander, Captain B. D. Foulois, made the following recommendations:

(a) As a result of actual experience in the field, one or more aero squadrons, operating in the field should have a base, conveniently located, from which all supplies, material and personnel should be drawn. This base should be independent of the field aero squadrons as regards its personnel and equipment. It should be fully equipped to receive, assemble, and test all new airplanes and motors intended for field service, and to make repairs and alterations on same whenever necessary.

(b) The organization of an aero squadron, consisting of 12 machines, should have a minimum enlisted strength of 149 men. The present tables of organization provide for 129 men only.

(c) There should be a minimum of 25 trucks with each aero squadron of 12 airplanes.

(d) A field aero squadron should confine its duties to the military application of the airplane for use in active service, and all airplanes consigned to a field squadron should be ready for such service when received. On account of the numerous problems which have been encountered during the past three months, a great amount of repair and alteration work has been done at this station which normally should have been done by the manufacturers before the airplanes, motors and propellers were shipped from the factories. In other words, an airplane consigned to a field aero squadron should, upon receipt and assembly, be ready for field service without wasting a lot of time in overhauling and altering motors and airplanes.

(e) Heretofore all airplanes received by the Government have been tested at or near sea level altitudes and generally under most favorable conditions. Tests under such conditions are not service tests. Airplanes intended to be used in field service should be tested under as severe conditions of service as possible. Such tests should include flying in localities where great variations of temperature and low percentage of humidity are found. They should be tested where the starting altitude is approximately 5,000 feet above sea level and where sand and rain storms are frequently encountered. These are the exact conditions under which the 1st Aero Squadron performed its flying work in Mexico and New Mexico, and it is believed that these are the maximum service conditions to which an aero squadron will be subjected in any field service that may be encountered in North America.

It is, therefore, recommended that no airplane be accepted for field service with a mobile army unless it has been tested under service conditions as stated herein, and that, whenever alterations are necessary to place an airplane in fit condition for field service, such alterations shall be made by the manufacturer.

(f) With reference to conducting service tests of all airplanes intended for service in the mobile army, it is recommended that the Government establish an airplane testing station at Fort Bliss, El Paso, Texas, or some other military station on the Mexican Border where the altitude above sea level and the average climatic conditions throughout the year are more closely related to maximum service conditions.

Asserting that the earnest and willing spirit shown by every officer in the command in performing this new and perilous service, with inadequate equipment and under very severe conditions, is deserving of the highest commendation, and that foreign governments have decorated their flying officers for far less perilous flying, Captain Foulois stated that the officers of the Squadron considered their hardships and their service with the Punitive Expedition as part of the day's work and simply in line of duty.

Captain Foulois also commended the spirit and efficiency of the enlisted personnel of the Squadron, stating that without their willing and efficient cooperation the flying service of the Punitive Expedition would have ended at Columbus, New Mexico. On many occasions they worked day and night to keep airplanes in fit condition for service. Their technical skill was in demand time after time in the repair of automobiles and trucks of the Quartermaster Corps, especially in the earlier days of the Expedition, and later as the Expedition advanced into Mexico.

The enlisted truck drivers of the Squadron performed especially hard service throughout the entire period the Squadron was in Mexico. Due to lack of sufficient motor transportation in the Squadron, they were constantly called upon to perform double duty, not only in connection with aviation work but frequently in connection with the needs of the entire Expedition regarding transportation of supplies to advance troops.

At the time of submitting this report, as of August 28, 1916, Captain Foulois stated that the Squadron was maintaining two airplane sections with the necessary personnel and equipment at Division Headquarters in Mexico; that the entire Squadron, less two sections, was being held at Columbus, N. M., for the purpose of assembling and testing 18 new airplanes under order for shipment to this station. The Squadron received 12 Lewis Machine Guns and 100 bombs; that instruction has commenced in the use of these weapons and also in the use of the Brock Automatic Camera for service in aerial photography.

Captain Foulois and his officers were of the firm belief, after their service in the field, that aviation was indispensable to military operations, and that airplane design should tend to greater speed, dependability and weight carrying capacity.

In conclusion, Captain Foulois stated that the experience gained by the commissioned and enlisted personnel of the Squadron while on active duty with the Punitive Expedition was of the greatest value, and he expressed his belief that the knowledge gained by all concerned should result in more rapid and efficient development of the aviation service in the United States Army.

MOTOR TRANSPORT EXPERIENCES WITH THE MEXICAN PUNITIVE
EXPEDITION

By CAPT. FRANCIS H. POPE, *Quartermaster Corps, U. S. Army* [1]

The Mexican Punitive Expedition was the first opportunity given the United States Army to handle motor transportation on a reasonably large scale, and the experience so gained, although confined to comparatively few officers, was of inestimable value in our subsequent operations in the World War.

As in most pioneering ventures, there are practically no written data on these motor transport experiences, and any record thereof must be drawn from the recollections of those who were participants therein.

Therefore, these reminiscences may verge on the personal, instead of the impersonal, but they are set forth in the hope of bringing back memories of the many other interesting incidents of this unique campaign of the American Army.

When the Expedition was first organized, during the early part of March, 1916, two truck companies were made up from vehicles that had been in use in Texas City and along the border, and one company of White 1½ ton trucks, mounted with escort wagon bodies. These first two trains were commanded by Captain H. A. Hegeman and Captain J. W. Furlow.

About March 15, 1916, the writer, who was at that time a Captain of Cavalry detailed in the Quartermaster Corps, arrived at El Paso from San Francisco and ran into Captain C. B. Drake, who had just arrived from Philadelphia, each of us with a War Department assignment as commanders of truck companies to be organized at El Paso for duty with the Punitive Expedition.

At about the same hour, there arrived by express shipment twenty-seven White 1½-ton chassis, and twenty-seven Jeffery Quad chassis, together with their civilian crews, organized by the factories themselves.

Captain Furlow had come up from Columbus, and had found a small wagon shop, in which to mount on these chassis escort wagon bodies secured from the El Paso Depot, then under the command of Major William Elliott, Q.M.C.

During the two days necessary to complete this work, the civilian personnel for these trains were outfitted with personal equipment, including rifles and pistols, and the necessary company equipment secured. At the last minute, authorization was obtained to equip each company with a Dodge touring car. This latter piece of equipment proved a godsend to the subsequent operations of the company commanders.

Truck Co. No. 3, composed of White trucks, having received its body equipment, was the first to leave El Paso for Columbus. This was followed later in the day by Truck Co. No. 4, composed of Jeffery Quads, a four-wheel-drive type, the later was to become so well known in the A.E.F. as the Nash Quad.

The road from El Paso to Columbus passed through Deming, some 80 miles away, with an additional 25 miles from that place to Columbus. In the innocence of our hearts, we figured that driving a truck company consisted in getting in front of the column, mounted in the Dodge car, and saying "Follow on and don't spare the gas."

---

[1] Later Brigadier General and Assistant Quartermaster General, U. S. A.

It was figured that the run to Deming would take about six hours, bringing us there about 10:00 P. M. in a brilliant desert moonlight.

However, before the swelter in the western outskirts of El Paso was reached, this brilliant dream was dispelled, and the fact was borne in upon us that running a truck company was no white collar job.

In fact, Deming was reached at 11:00 A. M. the next day, after being up all night, and experiencing all the trials and tribulations that fall to the lot of truck drivers. Looking back on this experience, with the knowledge gained during the ensuing years, I marvel that we got there at all, considering our ignorance of trucking matters, and the lack of discipline, knowledge, and capacity of the civilian personnel with the truck train.

However, we rolled into the thriving village of Columbus, New Mexico, late that afternoon, and reported for duty.

At that time, Columbus had all the appearance of a typical boom town. Railway sidings were being extended, buildings erected, and tents pitched, with apparently no relation to any definite expansion scheme. There was a large mess running for the civilian employees, many of whom were arriving in Columbus in what are euphemistically termed "side door Pullmans."

For some days, no check was kept on the men reporting to the mess for meals, so that during the first couple of weeks Columbus must have been a hoboes' paradise. This condition, however, was corrected.

The day after reporting at Columbus, orders were received sending trucks with their drivers in small detachments to various points on the trail to Colonia Dublan, so that, within twenty four hours, all of the elements of Truck Co. No. 4 were scattered up and down the trail, leaving the company commander practically alone in Columbus with his Dodge car. However, he was busily engaged in holding down the car, to keep it from being taken away, and figuring on how he was to account for all the Ordnance and Quartermaster property that had disappeared down the trail with the trucks, which latter were about the most expensive items of equipment for which he had ever given a memorandum receipt.

However, he was informed that another train load of trucks was due in by express in a few days, and given instructions to get hold of personnel to form another company, as it would be ordered down the trail immediately after arrival.

Mindful of the sad experience on the road from El Paso, a very fine exhibition of rustling was given for the next few days, so that when the trucks did arrive, fortunately this time equipped with bodies, a personnel had been lined up, half soldier and half civilian, but with a good first sergeant and, more important, a good field cook, who had been lured from a pack train by promises of hiking in an automobile instead of on the hurricane deck of a mule.

So after loading with commissaries, including a fair proportion of cigarettes, tobacco and candy, items vociferously demanded by the troops at the front, the train pulled out of Columbus one fine afternoon, down the trail into Mexico, that it was to travel without cessation for the next four months.

Every truck company commander went through practically the same experience in organizing his train, though possibly few had the pleasure of organizing two under such conditions.

The dispersion of the train brought over from El Paso, and the organization of the second one at Columbus are mentioned as this later gave rise to a rather unique incident.

On my arrival back at Columbus after the first two weeks' trip down the trail, there were received from El Paso complete invoices of the Ordnance and Quartermaster property issued to the truck train organized there. For the next three months every effort was made to locate this property.

It was an almost impossible job. Many of the trucks had been abandoned on the trail, and all identifying marks obliterated.

Many of the personnel had returned to Columbus singly or by groups and had been discharged without any check of the property issued to them.

During all this time, the responsible and accountable officer was working up and down the trail, with the second truck company, and had no means of even knowing of such happenings.

Before leaving Columbus (some four months later) he submitted survey reports covering all this property that could not be located. Among the items were rifles, pistols, equipment, and even motor trucks. After many vicissitudes, and horrified remarks from certain administrative officers as to the enormity of the procedure, he finally succeeded in dropping on survey reports practically the entire equipment of a truck train, including both Ordnance and Quartermaster property. It is believed that this constitutes almost a record in survey procedure *in peace time.* (If indeed this *was* peace time, Ed.).

Before taking up the experiences on the Mexican trail, it may be of interest to note an amusing angle relative to the extremely large volume of express shipments coming into Columbus. These express shipments included trainloads of supplies, and carloads of equipment such as motor vehicles, tractors, and every conceivable article, from points as distant as San Francisco and New York.

During one of the visits to the railway station, I asked the station agent, who was passenger, freight and express agent, all in one, why he did not wire the express company for help, as he told, me he had hired several men out of his own pocket to assist him.

He told me that the last thing he wanted was for the express company to hear about it. He said he handled the express on a commission basis and he was now getting more in an hour than he used to get in a year. However, much to his sorrow, the express company changed this method of business at the tank town of Columbus about a week later.

During the first month of the expedition's activities, the trail went due west from Columbus to Gibson's Ranch, some fourteen miles, when it turned south, entering Mexico, and continued through Boca Grande, Espia, Ascencion, Corralitos, to Colonia Dublan. From there south, the trail led to Galeana, El Valle, Las Cruces, and Namiquipa, and then on to San Geronimo, and San Antonio. The main line of communications, as far as major truck operations were concerned, did not go beyond Namiquipa.

In April, the original trail via Gibson's Ranch was discontinued for the shorter route via Palomas, Vado de Fusiles, and Ascencion. From there to Dublan was an alternative route through Ojo Federico. Similarly, during May, there was an alternate route from Dublan to El Valle, by way of San Joaquin.

During the early part of the operations, this trail was indicated merely by wagon ruts across the country, or by the Signal Corps telegraph line. The first vehicles down had a comparatively easy time, as the ground was hard, and the going rather good. However, it was not long before the trails got cut up into deep ruts and deeper chuck holes, and so became almost impassable.

In places where it was not hemmed in by high banks or rocks, the trail gradually widened, until in some places the truck tracks extended over a width of half a mile.

The worst condition encountered was mud, when the rainy season started. In the mud the trains practically came to a halt and operations could not be resumed until the ground had dried.

Ruts and chuck holes were another incident of the roadway, that were not conducive to good humor. Many were the breakages in springs, and even steel disc wheels, caused thereby. In the Dodge car, with its comparatively low clearance, it was necessary to straddle the ruts for miles, and on one stretch of near sixty miles, the car had to be run in low gear, changing only occasionally into second speed.

During the first four months, the efforts of the Engineers to improve the roadway were only partially successful, as the job was entirely too great for the means available.

It was during the latter months of the Expedition's activities that good headway was made, and that the Lincoln Junior Highway was worthy of its name.

The first trip down the trail took the Truck Company through Colonia Dublan, and on to Namiquipa. Arriving at the latter place, it was ordered to proceed immediately to San Geronimo, which was General Pershing's advanced headquarters. Although there were very strict orders to run without lights, it would have been impossible to get anywhere in the dark, so with a volley of rumbling and a blaze of light, we rolled into San Geronimo about midnight, but fortunately without awakening anyone in authority.

We left the next day and returned directly to Columbus, where we arrived after an absence of about two weeks. These two weeks, however, had taught us an invaluable lesson in motor trucking, of which we were prompt to take advantage.

In the first place, there was a welcome weeding out of inefficient personnel, and a revamping of articles of equipment. Each truck was equipped with a ten gallon milk can to carry water. This made the train independent of water holes for camping places or other halts.

Two fireless cookers were fixed up from similar milk cans. In this way, a hot meal could be served at each noon hour, no matter what the location of the train. In addition, each man could be served with a big cup of hot black coffee, which kept him awake and on the job during the long afternoon grind.

Similar cans were used to carry subsistence like corn meal and oat meal, as it was desirable to give each truck driver a good filling breakfast for the hard day's work ahead, and as the kitchen wagon was a two ton truck, there was no lack of carrying space.

Having a cook who knew his business, the field range was left behind at Columbus, only the utensils being taken. All cooking was done over a narrow trench, using a radiator guard on which to put the pans. In this way, it was an easy matter to have sufficient wood on the truck at all times for the kitchen fire, and the morning start was not delayed by waiting for a stove to cool off.

All of these expedients were of very great help in our subsequent operations up and down the trail.

While each man in the truck company was armed either with a rifle or pistol, though probably many of them did not know how to use them, it was the policy to detail a noncommissioned officer and squad from a line organization as a train guard.

However useful or useless they might have been in case of attack, they came in very handy for guard work during the night halts of the train.

Driving a truck from early morn to dewy eve over those Mexican roads was extremely heavy work, and the truck drivers were generally all in when the night halt arrived. Also, many were almost invariably called on to make repairs on the trucks which took several hours after the train halted for the day. Therefore, the guard detachments were invaluable for the night outpost work.

During the early weeks of the Expedition, it was customary to camp at one of the various stations along the trail. However, as conditions became stablized, the commanding officers of these various places got into the habit of issuing standing orders as to just what the train commander would do, where he would camp, how many outposts he would put out, to whom he would report, and many similar restrictions. In addition, such camping places became rather undesirable, after being used by various over-night campers.

Therefore, it became the practise, in the particular train with which the writer was connected, to avoid camping at any station other than Colonia Dublan, which was one of the truck train bases, and at other times, to camp at some selected place along the trail, where the train commander would be responsible to no one but himself. This was easily practicable, as the water supply was taken care of by our milk cans, and there was always sufficient wood in the kitchen truck.

The only exception was in the case of Las Cruces, which boasted of an excellent water hole, on a fine stream. This was our bathing and recreation beach, and an effort was always made to reach this spot early in the afternoon as a sort of rest camp.

During a portion of the time this camp was not occupied by troops, so that the truck train had it practically to itself. On the last trip north, after stopping at Las Cruces, two regiments of cavalry came along and halted there for the night. Thereupon, the truck company pulled up stakes and went about ten miles farther north, where there was a small but excellent spring called Agua Sorca. We were westerners, with the urge for the wide open spaces and plenty of elbow room. Also, we thought of road conditions, with trucks and animals trying to get through a canyon at the same time.

When camping for the night, it was customary to put out two double sentinel posts. Whether or not this would have been ample protection was never tested out, as no Mexicans, other than lone horsemen, were ever encountered except in the little villages along the trail. One afternoon, on leaving Namiquipa for the north, there was a rumor that the camp was to be attacked by a large force of bandits. On camping that night, some ten miles north, the trucks were parked in corral or hollow square formation, like the wagon trains in old Frontier days. Nothing happened, and that is the only time any such formation was taken up.

It used rather to amuse us to go through the variously fortified stations on the trail, with the mined roads as at Ascencion, or the Verdun Junior fortress at Ojo Frederico, hearing stories of the dangers from bandits, and then go bumping along by ourselves well into the night and halt in our lonely camp under the stars. We knew that we had to roll along any way, and got to be fatalists as to what would happen if bandits were actually encountered. Even if such should happen, we always felt that we could give a very good account of ourselves.

In fact, the personnel had been instructed as to what to do in case of alarm, and such drill had been gone through several times. But candor forces the statement that we got quite careless along the road.

There was great competition among the line troops for the detail as truck train guard. We had for two months the same detachment, a sergeant and from six to eight men from the 24th Infantry. They got to be very handy, especially as kitchen police.

About half of them would ride on the kitchen truck, which was always at the head of the train, and the remainder on a truck near the end. They got so expert that they could shoot craps while the trucks were bumping down the trail.

In addition to this desire of the soldiers for detail as guards, were the constant applications of troops along the trail for detail as truck drivers. The sight of a man pounding up and down the trail on a motor vehicle aroused the envy of the foot hiker and even of the trooper. They did not realize that such service was fully as hard as any other kind of soldiering, even if the rate of march was very much greater.

Another factor, undoubtedly, was the monotony of camp life along the trail, especially at some of the way stations that had little to recommend them. We always had a certain number of soldiers along going through a try-out for drivers, and many thus obtained, became very valuable motor transport men.

This entire personnel question was very difficult, especially in the earlier period of the operations. Practically all of the regular Quartermaster Corps soldiers were sergeant-chauffeurs. As noncommissioned officers, they objected to doing work such as kitchen police and the like. This condition was not corrected until several years later when the specialist ratings were established to take care of such situations. Another drawback was that these sergeants had gotten their grades through competitive written examinations.

One old sergeant in particular is recalled, as he knew nothing about driving a truck. When asked how he got to be a sergeant chauffeur, he stated that he had taken a correspondence course in automobile mechanics, and had passed the examination, though he had never driven a motor vehicle. He was detailed in charge of our camp at Columbus, and we saw him or the camp only about once a month.

The civilian personnel sent with the trucks from the factory were for the most part a bunch of amateur drivers who knew absolutely nothing of such open air life as encountered on the border. While a good many became pretty good truck men, most of them went by the board in the early days.

Their presence brought up several nice problems in military law. They, of course, were camp followers, but the application of military law to them, especially at Columbus, was debatable. On many occasions down the trail, especially at Colonia Dublan, some were thrown in the guard house, and otherwised punished, yet we got away with it more on account of the actual conditions, than from a purely legal standpoint.

Now while road conditions and the personnel question made these truck train operations anything but a sinecure, the most difficult problem was that of repair and maintenance, or in other words, keeping the trucks running. This is an angle of motor transport operation that, even today, is not appreciated by the average Army officer.

It is not realized that, with mechanized equipment, efficient operation is impossible unless supplemented by efficient maintenance.

Due to the inexperience of the entire personnel, motor vehicle breakage was much greater, during the first few months than it should have been. However, this condition was encountered, on a much vaster scale, in our operations during the World War.

In the personnel of each truck company were supposed to be at least two experienced motor mechanics, to handle such repairs as could be made with the tools at hand.

At Columbus, there was organized a rather ambitious repair shop, to which all trucks were sent for inspection or overhaul each time a train returned to Columbus. During the early months of the Expedition, the output from this shop was rather meager, as was to be expected. Considering the conditions, it functioned remarkably well.

However, that was the only shop or supply point in the theater of operations. Therefore, each truck company had to carry an exceptionally large assortment of repair parts, as frequently it would not get nearer to Columbus than Colonia Dublan for weeks at a time.

Then some of the types of trucks were unduly liable to breakage on account of poor quality of material. There was an especially high rate of breakage in springs, due to the exceedingly rough roads.

It is needless to expatiate on the various methods and devices that were resorted to in keeping this equipment rolling, as such would be of interest only to professional truck men. However, this experience was of inestimable value in our motor transport operations later on.

Naturally, there were many interesting features in connection with this maintenance work, but the interesting side was lost, at the time, in the grief that it caused. When a presumably solid steel disc wheel would break in the middle of the desert, there was nothing to do but leave the truck, re-assigning its load, as far as possible, to the other vehicles. But as it was customary to load the trucks to the guards, when they had any load at all, this rearrangement was accompanied by difficulties.

The worst feature in this connection was that trucks would go out of commission singly, and not several at the same time.

There might be a break in a gas line, a carbureter might choke up with dirt, or some minor part might be broken. Any one of these would cause a delay of some fifteen or twenty minutes. A broken spring might take half an hour to repair.

This would mean a delay of the entire train for that period, for under the circumstances in which we were operating, the train had to be kept closed up. Very early in the game, the company commander learned that he could best conduct the march by riding in rear of the column.

Now while the breakdown of one truck might delay the march from fifteen to thirty minutes, ordinary breakdowns to be expected daily in a column of over twenty trucks would run such road delays up to a period of many hours.

One well remembered incident was the breakage of a spring on a gasoline tank truck that had been issued to the train at the last minute. This truck was of a different make than the other vehicles in the train, and moreover there were no spare parts for this make of truck in Columbus.

One fine day, in the middle of the desert, a spring broke. The mechanic, who happened to be extremely capable, fashioned a new spring from various spring leaves that we always carried in the repair truck. The operation, however, took over five hours.

We could not leave the truck as it contained half of our gasoline supply. But that taught us one very valuable principle, namely, that all vehicle equipment in a company should be standard, so that, if one breaks down, its load, no matter what the character, can be immediately transferred to another vehicle. I always wanted to carry the gasoline in drums, on a regular cargo truck, and to assign tank trucks to regular gasoline supply trains.

Another feature, which afterward was so prevalent during the World War, was the robbing of trucks left along the roadside. Knowing this condition, great care was taken with one truck left behind at El Valle on account of some broken part, to turn it over to the Commanding Officer with the earnest request to prevent anything being taken off. He was informed that the particular part in question could be obtained at Dublan, and that this truck would be put in shape on the next trip down, about a week thence. On our return the next week, however, our truck looked like one of the gaunt skeletons of the cattle so often seen on the desert. Nothing was left but the frame and the headlight, which latter had been installed on the roof of the adobe guard house.

On another occasion, some time and much effort were taken to dismantle an engine from one of these abandoned trucks, and this engine was turned in to the storehouse at Dublan with the remark that some truck company would probably be glad to get parts from it. A week or so later, we had occasion to need nearly a complete engine, but on calling for it at this storehouse, we were calmly met with the remark: "Oh, we sent that junk back to Columbus last week."

These are but a mention of the incidents that show forth our inexperience in motor transport matters during the first few months of the Expedition.

The adventures that transpired with our operating activities were legion. In the first place, either due to the exigencies and changing conditions of the military situation or for other reasons, the truck trains were always hurriedly dispatched up and down the trail. It was not unusual to load and reload several times before leaving Dublan, which was in reality the advanced base.

Then it was also a matter of frequent occurrence for two trains to pass each other on the road, one going north and one south, both trains loaded or both trains empty.

Whenever we passed a group of hiking foot soldiers, we would always stop and take the footsore or weary on the trucks, as many as could be accommodated. At that time, the principle of carrying combat troops on motor vehicles had not been accepted by our Army, and many organization commanders thought it would be a reflection on the discipline and training of his command to sneak a ride, so to speak.

However, he did not feel that such would apply to any sick or footsore, who ordinarily would ride in the ambulance. It was quite amusing sometimes to run alongside such a marching group, and see how many were limping along. One organization commander used to line up the men and tell the disabled to go over to the trucks and climb on. Generally, there would be a foot-race, in which case, all who forgot to limp had to rejoin the company and continue on foot.

Of the various cargoes, however, that it fell to my lot to carry, the most interesting were two truck loads of sharpened sabers turned in by certain cavalry regiments, in the interior of Mexico. These were hauled up in my train during the first week in April.

This incident was of particular interest to me personally, as during several years previously, as a captain of cavalry, I was one of those upon whom efforts were being made to graft a resuscitated cavalry idea, that the saber should be the sole weapon of the horse soldier. In fact for several years, my regiment had been put through its paces in various tentative drill regulations, designed to relegate all fire arms to an extremely minor role.

I had never seen the logic of reverting from our well-founded cavalry principles to those of by-gone times, even though tradition still kept extant such antiquated practises in some European armies, in spite of the efforts of forward looking officers in these latter forces. In fact, it looked as if we were trying to adopt the European tradition, while in exchange, they were trying to take over our modern cavalry system, developed during the Civil War and later on our western plains.

So it was with a peculiar feeling of satisfaction that these sabers were hauled away from cavalry regiments in which certain of the field officers had been outstanding protagonists of the "Arme Blanche."

One of the interesting features of the Mexican trail was the contrast between the Mormon settlements, called "Colonias," and the Mexican villages. One of these former settlements, Colonia Diaz, stands out in particular.

Situated in the midst of the desert, some fifty miles from the border, and although abandoned for some years, it was a veritable oasis. Houses in good repair stretched along streets lined with magnificent shade trees. The houses were surrounded by green fields and flowers in profusion. It certainly presented a picture of what that region might become under other conditions.

Another interesting feature was the rapidity with which Chinese stores and restaurants would appear on the fringes of all the little stations along the trail. How these Chinamen packed in the food and drink they offered for sale was always a mystery. However, it was not many weeks before many of these thriving installations were in full blast along the trail.

To the truck trains, pounding up and down the trail, one of the standbys was the long wagon train, commanded by Captain Bryson, that, day in and out, toiled along the road, as regular in its schedule as a railroad train, carrying forage for the mounted outfits which formed the backbone of the Expedition. Many a mile did this magnificent and highly efficient mule column make during its many months of operation.

If the old order were giving away to the new, in that dawn of the mechanical age in our Service, it may be truly said that our well-tried friend, the mule was going out in a blaze of glory.

While this motor truck service was extremely difficult, and entailed more hard work than any other expedition I had ever been on, it was replete with interest, involving as it did an entirely new and coming type of field transportation. There was also a relief from the monotony that must have been the lot of many organizations who were located more or less permanently in the many camps along the line of communications. A truck company being constantly on the move, at least enjoyed a continual change of scenery.

That the hours of march were long and hard, no one realizes better than one who has ever travelled with a truck train.

Leaving camp in the chill dawn, the train plugged along the trails, until after darkness had fallen. All during the day, in addition to maneuvering the vehicles over difficult country, there were the constant breaking down of trucks, and the incidental road repair.

Also, mechanics often worked far into the night after camp had been made. Well known were the difficult features of the various portions of the route, such as the long dusty and sandy stretches to Ascension, where there was no water hole for nearly fifty miles, the swamp and quicksands near

Ojo Frederico, the gullies north of Namiquipa, and the long and tortuous canyons near Las Cruces, with their steep grades.

While there are many more incidents of an interesting character that a careful search of memory could bring to light, it is believed that those already set forth will give a general picture of our pioneering motor transport work in this expedition, that seemed made especially for our training in the great events that were to come. These reminiscences cover, however, only the first four months of the activities of the expedition, as due to promotion and assignment to duties elsewhere, the writer's immediate connection therewith terminated in the middle of July, 1916.

However, during that period, he covered with his trucks, over four thousand miles of Mexican trails, and reached a point some 300 miles south of the border.

However, I feel that all of us whose lot was cast by the fortunes of war, in this motor transport experiment, realized that a great opportunity had been offered, and, for one, I shall always look back with interest and pleasure to my service with the Mexican Punitive Expedition.

Appendix D

The following rosters of commissioned officers carried on the rolls of units which were attached to the Punitive Expedition were taken from the official consolidated returns which were prepared at Headquarters of the Expedition. Names of officers who did not join their units or who did not enter Mexico are indicated by an asterisk (*).

Due to the nature of the service and attendant administrative difficulties, such as wide scattering of units and separation from field desks for long periods, these rosters probably contain errors and omissions.

Appendix D

COMMISSIONED PERSONNEL OF THE U. S. ARMY WHO SERVED WITH THE PUNITIVE EXPEDITION

HEADQUARTERS, PUNITIVE EXPEDITION

Brigadier General John J. Pershing, *Commanding Expedition.*
First Lieutenant James L. Collins, *11th Cavalry, A. D. C.*
First Lieutenant Martin C. Shallenberger, *16th Infantry, A. D. C.*
Lieutenant Colonel DeRosey C. Cabell, *10th Cavalry, Chief of Staff.*
Captain Wilson B. Burtt, *20th Infantry, Assistant to Chief of Staff.*
Major John L. Hines, *A. G. D., Adjutant.*
Captain Allen J. Greer, *16th Infantry, Judge Advocate.*
Major John F. Madden, *Q. M. C., Quartermaster.*
First Lieutenant Nicholas W. Campanole, *6th Infantry, On Special Service with Expedition.*
First Lieutenant George S. Patton, Jr., *8th Cavalry, On Special Service with Expedition.*
Major Jere B. Clayton, *M. C., Surgeon.*
Colonel Lucien G. Berry, *4th Field Artillery, Inspector.*
Major James A. Ryan, *13th Cavalry, Intelligence Officer.*
Captain Everett S. Hughes, *O. D., Acting Ordnance Officer.*
Captain William O. Reed, *6th Cavalry, On Special Service with Expedition.*
Second Lieutenant Walter F. Winton, *5th Field Artillery, On Special Service with Expedition.*
Lieutenant Colonel Henry T. Allen, *11th Cavalry, Inspector.*
Lieutenant Colonel Daniel L. Tate, *5th Cavalry, Assistant Inspector.*
Major Thomas S. Bratton, *M. C., Sanitary Officer.*
Captain Hugh S. Johnson, *J. A. D., Assistant to Judge Advocate.*
Captain Leon B. Kromer, *11th Cavalry, Assistant to Division Quartermaster.*
Captain William E. W. MacKinlay, *11th Cavalry, On Special Service with Expedition.*
Lieutenant Colonel George O. Cress, *I. G. D., Acting Inspector.*
Lieutenant Colonel James D. Glennan, *M. C., Division Surgeon.*
Captain Walter M. Whitman, *Q. M. C., Division Quartermaster.*
Major James L. Bevans, *M. C., Assistant to Division Sanitary Inspector.*
Major Edward S. Walton, *17th Infantry, Acting Adjutant General.*
Major John H. Parker, *24th Infantry, Judge Advocate.*
Major Joseph H. Ford, *M. C., Assistant to Division Surgeon.*
Major Jacob M. Coffin, *M. D., Director of Ambulance Companies.*

HEADQUARTERS, SECOND CAVALRY BRIGADE

Brigadier General George F. Dodd, *Commanding 2nd Cavalry Brigade (until retirement).*
Brigadier General Eben Swift, *Commanding 2nd Cavalry Brigade from November 25, 1916.*
First Lieutenant Carl F. McKinney, *36th Infantry, A. D. C.*
First Lieutenant Albert J. Myer, Jr., *7th Cavalry, A. D. C.*
Captain Rush S. Wells, *7th Cavalry, Acting Quartermaster.*

FIFTH CAVALRY

Colonels
Wilbur E. Wilder
Daniel L. Tate

Majors
Nathaniel F. McClure
Lawrence J. Fleming
William J. Glasgow
August C. Nissen
Edward R. Schreiner, M. C.

Captains
Lewis Foerster
Charles S. Haight
Thomas M. Knox
Wallace B. Scales
Theodore B. Taylor
George J. Oden
Harry C. Williard
William M. Connell
Robert R. Wallach
Robert M. Barton
William D. Forsyth
David H. Scott
John G. Winter
Duncan Elliott*
Oscar A. McGee
Edward P. Orton*
Frank R. Tompkins
William A. Wickline, M. C.
James I. Robinson, M. C.
Alloyne von Schrader, M. R. C.
Theodore B. Taylor, 4th Cav.

First Lieutenants
Frank E. Davis
Philip H. Sheridan
Victor M. Whitside
Joseph H. Barnard
E. R. Warner McCabe
Alexander M. Milton

Thomas L. Sherburne
Eugene J. Ely
Thomas H. Cunningham
Herbert E. Mann
Henry T. Bull
Homer M. Groninger
Francis C. V. Crowley
Daniel D. Gregory
Andrew S. Robinson, M. R. C.
George B. Jones, M. R. C.

Second Lieutenants
William H. W. Youngs
Paul D. Carlisle
Harry D. Chamberlin
Harold Thompson
Frederic W. Boye
John P. Wheeler
Edward J. Miller, Jr.
Joseph W. Byron
Clifford B. King
Joseph B. Treat
John McD. Thompson
Frederick R. Lafferty*
Robert L. Beall*
Leo G. Heffernan*
John Millikin*
William T. Haldman*
Victor W. B. Wales
Oliver I. Holman
Winchell I. Raser*
Edwin D. Morgan, Jr.*
Arthur D. Connor*
Donald S. Perry*

Chaplain
Timothy P. O'Keefe

Veterinarians
Burton A. Seeley
Robert vans Agnew*
Joseph R. Jeffries

SEVENTH CAVALRY

Colonels
James B. Erwin
Selah R. H. Tompkins

Majors
Edward B. Winans
Alexander L. Dade
Edmond M. Leary
George P. White
William R. Eastman, M. C.
Arthur W. Morse, M. C.

Captains
Theodore B. Schultz
William B. Cowin
Charles H. Boice

Samuel F. Dallem
James E. Fechet
Rush S. Wells
Alvan C. Gillem
William J. Kendrick
William P. Moffet
William C. F. Nicholson
Peter J. Hennessey
Walter H. Smith
Henry E. Mitchell
Robert M. Campbell
Emil Engle
Charles E. Stodter*
Henry Gibbins
Leonard L. Deitrick*
Herman A. Sievert

SEVENTH CAVALRY (Continued)

Captains (Continued)

Andrew W. Smith
C. Emery Hathaway
Dorsey R. Rodney
Edward C. Register
Ernest G. Bingham, M. C.
Archibald F. Comiskey
Samuel B. Pearson*

First Lieutenants

Joseph C. King
Horace M. Hickam
Albert C. Wimberly
Pearson Menoher
Robert E. Carmody
Edwin B. Lyon
Albert J. Myer, Jr.
Thoburn K. Brown
Frank K. Chapin
Arthur W. Holderness*
William W. Erwin
Stanley C. Drake
William C. Ryan
George E. Lovell, Jr.*
Orlando Ward
Paul C. Reborg*
George E. A. Reinburg*
Sidney V. Bingham
Waldemar A. Christensen, M. R. C.
Harry C. Blair, M. R. C.*

John Kennard
Howell Brewer, M. R. C.
Olney Place
Frank K. Ross
Spencer A. Townsend
Arthur W. Jones
Frederick T. Dickman
William A. Quinn, M. R. C.
Percy J. Carroll, M. R. C.
Verne R. Bell*

Second Lieutenants

Otto Wagner
Sylvester D. Downs, Jr.
John J. Bohn
John C. Garrett
Harry B. Flounders*
James R. Finley*
Leslie C. B. Jones*
Gordon J. F. Heron*
Donald O. Miller*
George M. Herringshaw*

Chaplain

John M. Moose

Veterinarians

Samuel Glasson, Jr.*
Daniel B. Leininger

TENTH CAVALRY

Colonels

William C. Brown
Ellwood W. Evans
Jacob G. Galbraith*

Lieutenant Colonel

Charles Young

Majors

S. McP. Rutherford
George B. Pritchard
Robert J. Fleming
William L. Lowe
Henry C. Whitehead
Chandler P. Robbins, M. C.

Captains

William C. Gardenhire
Alfred E. Kennington
William S. Valentine
George B. Rodney
William L. Luhn
Albert E. Phillips
Lewis S. Morey
Emmett Addis
Orlando C. Troxel
Albert B. Dockery
John C. Pegram

Willard H. McCornack
Charles T. Boyd
Harry La T. Cavenaugh*
James S. Greene*
Selwyn D. Smith
Ralph S. Porter, M. C.
John R. Barber, M. C.
Charles C. Demmer, M. C.
Oliver P. M. Hazzard
Warren W. Whitside*
Chalmers G. Hall*

First Lieutenants

Henry R. Adair
Reynold F. Migdalski
Henry A. Myer, Jr.
Eustis L. Hubbard
Norman J. Boots
Henry Abbey, Jr.
Joseph F. Richmond
Ray W. Barker
John E. Lewis
Albert H. Muller*
Lewis A. O'Donnell*
Albert L. Grisell*
Frank K. Ross*
Jerome W. Howe
William B. Peebles

TENTH CAVALRY (Continued)

First Lieutenants (Continued)

Arthur B. Conard*
Robert Blaine
John C. F. Tillson*
Harold L. Gardiner
Leo A. Walton
William L. Sharp, M. R. C.

Second Lieutenants

Benjamin F. Hoge
Andrew L. Walton
Thorne Deuel, Jr.
John B. Brooks*
Fay B. Prickett

DeRosey C. Cabell, Jr.
W. H. Cureton
John C. Mullenix*
Willard S. Wadleton*
Richard D. Gile*

Chaplains

George W. Prioleau*
Oscar J. W. Scott

Veterinarians

Charles D. McMurdo
William C. van Allstyne

ELEVENTH CAVALRY

Colonels

James Lockett
Henry T. Allen
George H. Sands
William J. Nicholson

Lieutenant Colonels

Robert L. Howze
John M. Jenkins

Majors

Melvin W. Rowell
Charles A. Hedekin*
Robert M. Thornburgh, M. C.
Julian R. Lindsey

Captains

James F. McKinley
William B. Renziehausen
Guy Cushman
Eben Swift, Jr.
John E. Hemphill
Joseph E. Cusack
Julien Gaujot
Douglas McCaskey
James A. Shannon
Gordon Johnston*
Frank Parker*
Alexander M. Miller*
Verne La S. Rockwell*
George B. Lake
John R. Bosley
Patrick W. Guiney*
Morton C. Mumma
Albert S. Bowen, M. C.

First Lieutenants

Alden M. Graham
Edwin L. Cox
Charles McH. Eby
John A. Pearson
Emil P. Laurson
Summer M. Williams
Carl H. Muller
Seth W. Cook

William D. Geary
Wade S. Westmoreland
Wilfrid M. Blunt
Irvin L. Hunsaker*
Edward M. Zell
Charles S. Hoyt
Carlton L. Vanderboget
Peter M. Keating, M. C.

Second Lieutenants

Joseph E. Viner
Burton Y. Read
Kenneth P. Lord
Harding Polk
Stafford LeR. Irwin
John F. Crutcher
Henry J. F. Miller
Cuyler L. Clark
John P. Kaye*
John M. Jenkins
Allen G. Thurman
Warren P. Jernigan
Victor B. Taylor
John C. McDonnell*
William A. Robertson*
Frederick G. Rosenburg
Meade Frierson, Jr.*
Thomas A. Bobyne*
John W. Rafferty
William Spence
Hale S. Cook*
Hugh D. Blanchard*
James G. Monihan*
Robert W. Crow*

Surgeon

Edward F. Gedding

Chaplain

George J. Waring*

Veterinarians

Lester E. Willyoung
Alexander MacDonald

THIRTEENTH CAVALRY

Colonel
Herbert J. Slocum

Lieutenant Colonels
Tyree R. Rivers
Samuel G. Jones

Majors
Elmer Lindsley
Frank Tompkins
James A. Ryan
George H. R. Gosman, M. C.
Mortimer O. Bigelow*
William G. Sills

Captains
George Williams
Hamilton Bowie
Alexander H. Davidson
William F. Herringshaw
John H. Lewis
Jens E. Stedje
Rudolph E. Smyser
Aubrey Lippincott
Otto W. Rethorst
Walter C. Babcock*
Thomas F. Ryan
Edward Davis*
Harry N. Cootes*
Guy V. Henry
Wallace M. Craigie*
Frederick G. Turner
Osmun Latrobe, Jr.
Nathan K. Averill*
Sebring C. Megill
Sherrard Coleman
Alexander T. Cooper, M. C.
Samuel Van Leer*

First Lieutenants
Claude de Busse Hunt
George H. Baird
Levi G. Brown
James T. Castleman
George B. Hunter

William A. McCain
William W. West, Jr.
Clarence Lininger
John G. Quekemeyer*
Robert S. Donaldson
Walter H. Neill
Bekerley T. Merchant
George F. Patten*
Arthur E. Wilbourn
James P. Yaney
Claude W. Cummings, M. R. C.
William L. Sharp, M. R. C.
Robert C. Rodgers
Innis P. Swift
John C. Rogers*
John A. Robenson

Second Lieutenants
John P. Lucas
Harvey B. S. Burwell
Ralph Hospital
John C. Prince
Elkin L. Franklin
Philip J. Kieffer
Horace Stringfellow, Jr.
Earl H. Coyle
Albert D. Chipman*
Clarence C. Benson
Lindsey D. Beach
James R. Hill
Joseph W. Allison, Jr.
Harry B. Flounders
Edmun M. Berman*
Dwight K. Shurtleff
Lucien S. S. Berry
Rexford E. Willoughby*
Cyrus J. Wilder*

Chaplains
Simon L. Lutz
Walter K. Lloyd

Veterinarians
Joseph R. Jefferies
Walter Fraser

SIXTH CAVALRY

Colonel
Joseph A. Gaston

Majors
Matthew C. Butler
James J. Hornbrook
Edward D. Anderson*

Captains
Walter J. Scott
James E. Abbott
Alexander E. Williams
Frank T. McNarney
George T. Bowman

George E. Mitchell
Alvord Van P. Anderson
William O. Reed*
Stuart Heintzelman*
Elvin R. Heiberg*
Hu B. Myers*
Roger S. Fitch*
Joseph R. McAndrews*
Francis W. Glover*
Alvin S. Perkins*
John P. Hasson
Robert M. Blanchard, M. C.
Edward M. Talbott, M. C.

SIXTH CAVALRY (Continued)

First Lieutenants

Edwin A. Keyes
William M. Cooley
Orlando G. Palmer
Stanley Koch
Thurman H. Bane
George Dillman
Frederick D. Griffith, Jr.
Thomas F. Van Natta
James A. Mars*
Frank Keller*
Kenyon A. Joyce*
George V. Strong*
John T. Kennedy*
Frank P. Lahm
Albert J. Hoskins, M. R. C.

Geoffrey Keyes
Ralph P. Cousins
William S. T. Holcomb
Hugh P. Avent
Frank D. McGee
Carlyle H. Wash
John A. Considine
Stephen M. Walmsley
Mack Garr
Earl H. Gorman
Herbert E. Taylor
Philip Caldwell*
Joseph P. Aleshire*

Chaplain

Charles W. Freeland

Second Lieutenants

Edwin O'Connor
John F. Steven

Veterinarians

Jules H. Uri
George A. Hanvey, Jr.

TWELFTH CAVALRY

Captains

John A. Degen
Ben H. Dorey
Roy B. Harper
Richard W. Walker

First Lieutenants

John T. Sayles
Ronald D. Johnson
Arthur E. Wilbourn
Harry L. King

Second Lieutenant

Walter B. Wynne

HEADQUARTERS AND BATTERIES "A," "B" AND "C," 4TH FIELD ARTILLERY

Colonel

Lucien G. Berry

Majors

Thomas E. Merrill
Richard H. McMaster
Williard F. Truby, M. C.
Fred W. Palmer, M. C.

Captains

Roger O. Mason
George M. Apple
Henry L. Newbold
Laurin L. Lawson
Daniel F. Craig
Lesley J. McNair
Taylor E. Darby M. C.
Donald C. Cubbison

First Lieutenants

Charles W. Harlow
Charles M. Busbee
Francis J. Dunigan
Clinton W. Howard
Everett S. Hughes*
Leo P. Quinn*
Joseph W. Rumbough

Richard C. Scott
Albert W. Waldron
Cortlandt Parker
Thomas J. Smith
Allen C. McBride
Harold H. Bateman
Hamilton E. Maguire
Henry C. Jones
George A. Pollin*
Stanley S. Warren, M. R. C.
George B. Jones, M. R. C.
Arthur E. Midgley, M. R. C.

Second Lieutenants

Norman P. Morrow
Joseph M. Swing
Harvey M. Hobbs*
Richard E. Anderson
Harold H. Ristine*
Robert H. Ennis*
David E. Finkbiner*
Clifford H. Tate*

Veterinarians

Daniel Le May
William A. Sproule*
Herbert S. Williams

BATTERIES "B" AND "C," 6TH FIELD ARTILLERY

Majors

Charles C. Pulis
George F. Juenemann, M. C.

William H. Dodds, Jr.
Telesphor G. Gottschalk
Harold E. Miner
Alfred K. King

Captain

Edgar H. Yule

Second Lieutenants

Frank A. Turner
Raymond Marsh
Ernest J. Dawley
Oliver L. Haines*
Yarrow D. Yesely*

First Lieutenants

Charles P. George, Jr.
Herbert S. Clarkson
William C. Houghton

COMPANIES "E," "G" AND "H," 2ND BATTALION OF ENGINEERS

Colonel

George A. Zinn

Lt. Colonel

Meriwether L. Walker

Majors

Lytle Brown
W. Goff Caples

Captains

U. S. Grant, 3d
Ernest Graves
Glen E. Edgerton*
Charles L. Hall
James A. O'Connor
Henry A. Finch
Ernest G. Bingham, M. C.
Robert W. Kerr, M. C.

First Lieutenants

William C. Sherman
Bradford G. Chynoweth
Milo P. Fox
George F. Lewis
John F. Conklin
Oscar O. Kuentz
George J. Richards

John S. Smylie
Dwight F. Johns
Arthur P. von Deesten
Lehman W. Miller
Edward N. Whitney
Earl E. Gesler
Harrison Brand, Jr.
Brehon B. Somervell
George Mayo
Paul T. Bock
Charles O. Boynton
Gordon R. Young
Henry F. Lincoln, M. C.
Albert H. Eber, M. C.
Wilhelm D. Styer
Ernest F. Miller
Layson E. Atkins
Ralph G. Barrows
Thomas B. Larkin
William F. Tompkins
Edward C. Smith
William A. Snow
Bernard A. Miller
Frederick S. Skinner
John H. Carruth

Chaplain

John A. Randolph

SIXTH INFANTRY

Colonels

John H. Beacom
Robert H. Noble
Erneste V. Smith

Lt. Colonel

Edson A. Lewis

Majors

Frank A. Wilcox
Matthias Crowley
Louis H. Bash
Lambert W. Jordan, Jr.
Harold D. Buck, M. C.

Captains

Ernest H. Agnew

Leon L. Roach
Richmond Smith
Walter H. Johnson
Henry C. Bonnycastle
Arthur R. Kerwin
Charles R. W. Morison
Leonard H. Cook
Pearl M. Shaffer
Philip J. Lauber
Henry D. Mitchell*
Eleutheros H. Cooke
Frederick E. Wilson
Wyley T. Conway
Edward L. Napier, M. C.
Frederick R. De Funiak
John R. Bosley, M. C.
Gordon R. Catts

SIXTH INFANTRY (Continued)

Captains (Continued)

George R. Guild*
Richard Wetherill
Ralph H. Leavitt

First Lieutenants

Thomas N. Gimperling
Keith S. Gregory
Robert H. Fletcher, Jr.
William F. L. Simpson
Jesse D. Elliott
Lewis K. Underhill
Courtney H. Hodges
Albert S. Peake
Thomas H. Monroe
William H. Simpson
Dennis P. McCunniff
John E. Rossell
Leon M. Logan
Thomas S. Bridges
Norman W. Peek
John T. Rhett
John W. Leonard
Nicholas W. Campanole

Alfred A. Hickox*
Matthew H. Thomlinson*
DeWitt C. T. Grubbs
William H. Lloyd, M. R. C.
Thomas W. Maloney, M. R. C.
Raymond P. Campbell
Felix R. McLean
Norman F. Ramsey*

Second Lieutenants

Thomas G. Hearn
Michael F. Davis
James B. Ord*
Fred Stall*
Claud E. Stadtman*
Charles P. Stivers*
Paul W. Mapes*
John D. Townsend*
Oscar F. Carlson*
Athael B. Ellis*
Kirk A. Metzerott*

Chaplain

John A. Randolph

SIXTEENTH INFANTRY

Colonel

William H. Allaire

Lt. Colonels

Charles S. Farnsworth
Frank L. Winn

Majors

James T. Moore
George H. McMaster
Clyde S. Ford, M. C.*
Joseph H. Ford, M. C.
Edward C. Carey

Captains

Allen J. Greer
Frank S. Bowen
Frank W. Rowell
William G. Ball
Frank C. Burnett
Elliot Caziarc
Martin L. Crimmins
William F. Creary
James N. Pickering*
George W. Wallace*
Charles M. Bundel
Alfred W. Bjornstadt
Charles E. Morton*
Douglas Potts*
Edgar Ridenour
George F. Juenemann, M. C.
Addison D. Davis, M. C.
Clemmens W. McMillan, M. C.
Roy C. Heflebower, M. C.

John C. McArthur*
D. W. Wallace
Charles M. Gordon*
Arthur M. Shipp

First Lieutenants

David A. Henkes
Alva Lee
Lowe A. McClure
David P. Wood
Lawrence E. Hohl
John H. Hester
Harrison C. Brown
Robert J. West*
Otho E. Michaelis*
Walter C. Short
Charles F. Thompson*
Edward H. Pearce*
Bloxham Ward*
Herbert C. Fooks
Richard R. Pickering
Charles K. Nulsen
Hugh J. Duffy, M. R. C.
John P. Bubb
Edward G. McCleave
George C. Marshall, Jr.*
Frank T. Hogeland, M. R. C.
Fred P. Weltner, M. R. C.

Second Lieutenants

Oliver S. Wood
Ziba L. Drollinger
Clifford J. Matthews
Whitten J. East

SIXTEENTH INFANTRY (Continued)

Second Lieutenants (Continued)

Frederick C. Rogers
Jesse B. Hunt
Thomas F. Taylor
Sydney C. Graves
William R. Orton
Carroll A. Bagby
George A. Sanford
Francis M. Brannan
John E. Martin

William R. Wilson
Frederick Schoenfeld*
Stuart G. Wilder*
Allen F. Kingman*
Seeley B. Fahey*
Leonard R. Boyd*
William McK. Spann*

Chaplain

James W. Hillman

SEVENTEENTH INFANTRY

Colonel

Charles R. Noyes

Lt. Colonels

Robert Alexander
George B. Duncan*
John B. Bennet*

Majors

George C. Saffarrans
Benjamin F. Hardaway

Captains

John W. Wright
Percy C. Cochran
Charles C. Lawrence
Henry S. Wagner
Robert C. Humber
Alexander M. Wetherill
Frederick S. L. Price
James G. Taylor
Bryan Conrad
Frederick Goedecke
Edward S. Walton
William B. Gracie
James S. Young, Jr.
Merrill E. Spalding
Ebenezer G. Beuret
Forrest E. Overholser
Gerret van S. Quackenbush*
Arthur L. Bump
William K. Bartlett, M. C.
John R. Bosley, M. C.
Alexander T. Cooper, M. C.
James M. Kimbrough, Jr.
Philip G. Wrightson

First Lieutenants

Benjamin F. Miller
Charles A. Thuis

Jesse Gaston
Thorne Strayer
Roderick Dew
Thomas C. Musgrave
Fred L. Walker
Ralph S. Kimball
Howard Donnelly
Frank B. Clay
Floyd D. Carlock
Gilbert S. Brownell
Robert L. Williams
Whitmon R. Conolly
J. Warren Weissheimer
James A. Sarratt
Vernon E. Pritchard
Leland S. Devore
Thomas W. Brown*
Charles F. Severson*
Frederick W. Boschen
Hornsby Evans*
Jasper A. Davies
Thomas L. Martin
Emil W. Leard*

Second Lieutenants

George P. Nickerson
Hugh B. Keen
Paul B. Parker
Earl J. Dodge*
Edward A. Allen*
Joseph N. Dalton*
Henry C. Long, Jr.*
Orville M. Moore*
Joseph J. McConville*
Alfred D. Hayden*
Melville W. Fuller*
Robert W. Brown*

Chaplain

John L. Maddox

TWENTY-FOURTH INFANTRY

Colonels

Charles W. Penrose
Frank L. Winn

Lt. Colonels

Charles C. Ballou
Mark L. Hersey

TWENTY-FOURTH INFANTRY (Continued)

Majors

Frederick W. Lewis
Girard Sturtevant
John McA. Palmer*
John H. Parker
William Newman
William E. Vose, M. C.

Captains

Rinaldo R. Wood
Laurence Halstead
Daniel H. Berry
Clement A. Trott
William E. Gillmore
Ralph B. Parrott
Joseph L. Topham, Jr.
Arthur J. Davis
James W. H. Reisinger, Jr.
John M. True
Homer N. Preston
Henry A. Wiegenstein*
George J. Holden
Henry M. Fales
Harry S. Grier
Martin C. Wise*
George M. Holley
Charles F. Andrews
Richard J. Herman
Joseph E. Barzynski
Andrew J. Dougherty*
John S. Battle*
Edward J. Moran
Taylor E. Darby, M. C.
John J. Reddy
Ralph McCoy
Calvin P. Titus
Kneeland S. Snow*

First Lieutenants

Joseph C. Hattie
Arthur J. Hanlon
Edward L. Hoffman
Merl C. Schillerstrom
Charles S. Little
John P. Edgerly
Sydney H. Foster
William A. Reed
Alfred S. Balsam
Lindsey McD. Silvester
George T. Everett*
Walter M. Robertson
Xavier F. Blauvelt
Alexander W. Chilton
Eugene W. Fales
Manton G. Mitchell
Haig Shekerjian
Tom Fox
Jesse A. Ladd
Harold H. Taintor*
Clarence S. Brown, M. R. C.
Philip B. Peyton*
Ursa M. Diller*

Second Lieutenants

Joseph H. Grant
Bartlett James
Alexander P. Withers
Frederick W. Huntington*
James K. Bolton*
Harry I. T. Creswell*
William E. Lucas*
William F. McCutcheon*
Arthur Hoffman

FIRST AERO SQUADRON, SIGNAL CORPS

Major

Benjamin D. Foulois

Captains

Townsend F. Dodd
Robert H. Willis, Jr.
Samuel B. Pearson, Cav.
Stanley S. Warren, M. R. C.
John F. Perry

First Lieutenants

Carleton G. Chapman
Herbert A. Dargue
Joseph E. Carberry
Walter G. Kilner
Arthur R. Christy
Edgar S. Correll
Ira A. Rader
Thomas S. Bowen*
Byron Q. Jones*
Henry W. Harms*

Harry Gantz*
James L. Dunsworth*
Joseph C. Morrow
John D. von Holtzendorff*
Ralph Royce*
Roy S. Brown*
Carl Spatz*
Bert M. Atkinson*
Harold S. Martin
John B. Brooks*
John W. Butts, 3d Cav.*
Sheldon H. Wheeler, 25 Inf.*
Millard F. Harmon, 27 Inf.*
Paul L. Ferron, C. A.*

Second Lieutenants

Clinton W. Russell, 8 Inf.*
Howard C. Davidson, 27 Inf.*
Davenport Johnson, 19 Inf.*
Maxwell Kirby, 3 Cav.*

TWENTIETH INFANTRY

Major

William R. Sample

Captains

Charles C. Smith
George H. Estes
Wilson B. Burtt

First Lieutenants

Austin M. Pardee
Otto M. Brunzell

Allen W. Gullion
Hugo D. Selton
Arthur R. Underwood

Second Lieutenants

Clarence H. Danielson
Tolbert F. Hardin
John L. Parkinson
Harley D. Parkinson
John N. Robinson

DETACHMENT, QUARTERMASTER CORPS

Lt. Colonel

Thomas H. Slavens

Major

John F. Madden

Captains

Francis H. Pope
James W. Furlow
Samuel B. Pearson
Linwood E. Hanson
Harry A. Hageman
Lorenzo D. Gasser
Alvin K. Baskette
Walter M. Whitman
Ward Dabney
James H. Bryson

Wilson G. Heaton
Joel R. Lee
Frederick S. Young
Frederick L. Buck
William F. Jones
Manuel L. Garrett
Henry E. Mitchell

First Lieutenant

Jesse W. Boyd, 11 Inf.

Second Lieutenants

Joseph I. McMullen
Vernon G. Olsmith, 23 Inf.
Frank F. Scowden, 11 Inf.
Frank T. Neely
Edward T. Comegys

DETACHMENT, SIGNAL CORPS

Captains

Charles D. F. Chandler
Hanson B. Black
Charles E. Swartz
Alvin C. Voris, 22 Inf.
John Scott

First Lieutenants

David H. Bower

Roy S. Brown
Bert M. Atkinson
Walter L. Clark
Richard E. Anderson
Octave De Carre
Walter Smith
Victor V. Taylor
Walter E. Prosser

ORDNANCE DEPARTMENT

Captain

James L. Walsh

First Lieutenant

Dwight K. Shurtleff

FIELD HOSPITAL NO. 7

Majors

Jere B. Clayton
William R. Eastman

Captains

William L. Hart
Wibb E. Cooper
John S. Coulter
Thomas H. Scott
Taylor E. Darby

First Lieutenants

Harold D. Cochrane
Arthur E. Midgley

Dental Surgeons

Dale E. Repp
Bruce H. Roberts

AMBULANCE COMPANY NO. 7

Captains
Harold W. Jones
Joseph E. Bastion
Daniel F. Maguire
Jacob M. Coffin
Louis H. Hanson

First Lieutenants
David D. Hogan
Edward Bailey

FIELD HOSPITAL NO. 3

Major
Frank C. Baker

Captains
Albert S. Bowen
George H. Scott
Robert W. Kerr
Craig R. Snyder
Henry L. Brown
Ray W. Bryan
Ray W. Brown
Thomas E. Harwood, Jr.
Thomas E. Scott

First Lieutenants
Nathan Winslow
Wilbur M. Phelps
Harold D. Scott
Benjamin O. Thrasher
Charles Dew Deyton

Dental Surgeon
Raymond W. Pearson

AMBULANCE COMPANY NO. 3

Captains
Louis H. Hanson
Jacob M. Coffin
Daniel F. Maguire
Joseph E. Bastion
Duncan MacCalman

First Lieutenant
Raymond C. Bull

CANTONMENT HOSPITAL

Lt. Colonels
Euclid B. Frick
Edward R. Schreiner

Major
George M. Ekwurzel

Captains
Glenn I. Jones
Larry B. McAfee
Craig I. Snyder
James S. Fox
Theodore M. Lamson
Charles G. Sinclair
Robert C. Loving
William A. Wickline
William H. Thearle
Lucius L. Hopwood
Alloyne von Schrader

First Lieutenants
Allen C. Wood
Basil A. Warren
Dale R. Rhett
Bruce H. Roberts
Charles D. W. Dayton
R. W. Bell
Harvard C. Moore
Maurice L. Puffer
Frederick J. Smith
Benjamin H. Frayser
William S. Rice

Dental Surgeon
Wilfurth Hellman

TRUCK TRAIN COMPANIES

Captains
Harry La T. Cavenaugh, 10 Cav.
Roy B. Harper, 12 Cav.
Ralph A. Lister, Q. M. C.

Milosh R. Hilgard, Q. M. C.
Philip H. Sheridan, 5 Cav.
Charles S. Hoyt, Cav.
John M. True, Inf.

TRUCK TRAIN COMPANIES (Continued)

Captains (Continued)

Ben H. Dorcy, 12 Cav.
Richard W. Walker, 12 Cav.
James G. Taylor, 17 Inf.

First Lieutenants

Leland S. Devore, 25 Inf.
Robert M. Campbell, 7 Cav.
Oliver P. M. Hazzard, 10 Cav.
D. M. Garrison, 10 PING
Dorsey R. Rodney, 7 Cav.
C. D. Shaw, Jr., 2d PING
Frank P. Scowden, Cav.

R. H. Anderson, 2d MING
Walter Ettinger, 6 PING
R. H. Fletcher, Jr., 6 Inf.
Ronald D. Johnson, 12 Cav.
D. S. Gressang, 2d PING
Charles S. Chambers, 8 PING
J. M. Rose, 3d PING
Arthur G. Brown, 2d MING
Archie F. Murray, 2d MING
Hayes B. McLaughlin, 8th PING
Frank E. Smith, 4 PING
Byron B. Brogden, 2 Ark. Inf.
Arthur W. Brock, 4 PING

While attached to the Expedition on the American side of the border, no National Guard units entered Mexico.

FIRST NEW MEXICO INFANTRY, NATIONAL GUARD

Colonel

Edmund C. Abbott*

Lt. Colonel

William C. Porterfield*

Majors

Charles B. Ruppe*
Arthur Bail*
Norman L. King*
Harry B. Kauffman*

Captains

Fitzwarren W. Thompson*
Phillip E. Dossauer*
William W. Dean*
Jefferson D. Atwood*
Gerald H. Totten*
James Baca*
Joseph H. Toulouse*
Thomas J. Molinari*
Clyde E. Ely*
Perry Keown*
Arthur W. Brock*
Edward L. Safford*
William A. Tenney*
Henry A. Ingalls*

First Lieutenants

Joshus D. Powers*
Eugene A. Roberts*
King C. Windsor*
Fred W. West*
Frank Newkirk*
Jans A. Isaacks*
J. E. Gorman*

Harry M. Peck*
Cyrian W. McSherry*
John C. Watson*
Hubert R. Miller*
James C. Compton*
John M. Gorman*
James C. Tompkins*
James H. McHughes*
Walter R. Ames*
Samuel D. Swope*
Harry M. Baker*
Frank W. West*

Second Lieutenants

John J. McMillan*
Archer W. Bedell*
Antonia Lune*
Curley P. Duson*
Richard Daugherty*
Edwin L. Holt*
Michael Gorman*
Marshall E. DeBord*
Melvin R. Chapin*
Clyde E. Ely*
John C. Linkart*
T. W. Noe*
John B. Lassator*
Herman E. Bechtel*
Charles R. Guinn*
Miguel A. Otero, Jr.*
Howard B. Blackmar*
Hazael La F. Keeley*
Earl B. Wilson*

Chaplain

Zachary T. Vincent*

SECOND MASSACHUSETTS INFANTRY, NATIONAL GUARD

Colonel

William C. Hayes*

Lt. Colonel

Edward R. Gray*

Majors

Albert C. Beckam*
Alfred F. Foote*
Herbert H. Warren*
Ernest A. Gates, M. C.*

Captains

Paul J. Norton*
Ernest R. Burger*
Herbert F. Hartwell*
Frederick H. Lucke*
James L. Loomis*
William Stevenson*
Edmund L. Slate*
Harry L. Deane*
Ambrose Clougher*
Benson G. Munyon*
Eugene F. Burr*
Thomas J. Hammond*
George A. Roberts*
Herbert N. Kelly*
James T. Potter*
Albert L. Woodworth*
Walton S. Danker*
Harry C. Martin, M. C.*
Thomas F. Brown, 8 Mass.*

First Lieutenants

Alexander MacDonald*

Walter E. Warren*
Howard W. Robbins*
Charles E. Dunn*
Robert H. Anderson*
Arthur C. Brown*
Wallace A. Choquette*
Archie F. Murray*
George W. Hasmer*
William H. Barr*
Herbert L. Searles*
Burton A. Adams*
Frank J. Reardon*
Arthur L. Curran, M. C.*
Clyde C. Johnson, M. C.*
Charles H. Ingram*

Second Lieutenants

Francis L. Cody*
Edward S. Bird*
Albert S. Christensen*
James Kerr*
Henry R. Hoyle*
Jacob Bechtold*
Burdett E. Madison*
James A. MacKenzie*
John A. Jones*
Henry R. Knight*
Donald B. Logan*
Ralph R. Safford*
Edgar A. Stromwell*
Charles I. Goodhue*
Harry Adamson*
Harry A. Hoyle*
James G. Rivers*

Brigadier General John J. "Black Jack" Pershing, Mexico 1916

HIGH-LONESOME BOOKS

"Published in the Greatest Country Out-of-Doors"

At HIGH-LONESOME BOOKS we have a great variety of titles for enthusiasts of the Southwest and the great Outdoors -- new, used, and rare books of the following:

Southwest History

Wilderness Adventure

Natural History

Hunting

Sporting Dogs

Mountain Men

Fishing

Country Living

Environment

Our catalog is FREE for the asking. Write or call.

HIGH-LONESOME BOOKS
P. O. Box 878
Silver City, New Mexico
88062
505-388-3763

Also, come visit our new bookshop in the country
at High-Lonesome Road near Silver City